D1171030

VENGEANCE
OF THE
SWALLOWS

VENGEANCE OF THE SWALLOWS

Memoir of a Polish Family's Ordeal Under Soviet Aggression, Ukrainian Ethnic Cleansing and Nazi Enslavement, and Their Emigration to America

by TADEUSZ PIOTROWSKI

McFarland & Company, Inc., Publishers
Jefferson, North Carolina, and London

British Library Cataloguing-in-Publication data are available

Library of Congress Cataloguing-in-Publication Data

Piotrowski, Thaddeus M.
Vengeance of the swallows : memoir of a Polish family's ordeal under Soviet aggression, Ukrainian ethnic cleansing and Nazi enslavement, and their emigration to America / by Tadeusz Piotrowski.
p. cm.
Includes index.
ISBN 0-7864-0001-3 (lib. bdg. : 50# and 70# alk. paper) ∞
1. Polish Americans—Biography. 2. Piotrowski, Thaddeus M.—Family. 3. Piotrowski family. 4. Poland—Biography. 5. World War, 1939–1945—Refugees. I. Title.
E184.P7P56 1995
940.53'159'0922438—dc20
[B] 94-24862
CIP

Manufactured in the United States of America

McFarland & Company, Inc., Publishers
Box 611, Jefferson, North Carolina 28640

To my family
and all the other
displaced persons
of the world

Acknowledgments

In researching such a work as this, one is called upon to pry into the private lives and thoughts of old people who have suffered a great deal, to stir up old memories that are painful to recall, to inflame old wounds which will never heal. Such research requires the ability to sit quietly through long moments of silence and the common decency to temper one's academic zeal and curiosity with compassion, to turn away one's gaze while wrinkled faces with watery eyes struggle in vain to regain their initial composure, their initial deceiving youthful look of confidence, hope and optimism. Words cannot express, therefore, my gratitude to all those who on my account relived and shared their tragic East European history with me, especially Stanisława Plaza, Ewa Kujański, Stanisław Domalewski, Jan Miszkiewicz, and Helena Piotrowiak.

I am also indebted to my brother-in-law, Ryszard Pedowski, for his excellent firsthand knowledge of partisan warfare in the province of Wołyń; to Henryk Kołodyński, President of Chicago's Koło Ziemi Wołyńskiej, for his references to works about Wołyń's obliterated villages and the resistance movement; to my two Warsaw correspondents, Janusz Macichowski, Director of the Ośrodek Naukowej Informacji of the Wojskowy Instytut Historyczny (WIH), and Stanisław Rudnicki of the Komitet Organizacyjny Środowiska b. Żołnierzy Istriebitielnego Batalionu z Różyszcz na Wołyniu, as well as my Canadian correspondent, Richard Tyndorf, vice-president of the Adam Mickiewicz Foundation in Canada, for their invaluable assistance.

Many thanks to the Joseph Regenstein Library of the University of Chicago, where upon finding a detailed map of pre–World War II Wołyń and my own small village of Ryświanka, I cried out "Eureka!"—thus drawing the attention of all quiet researchers to my discovery—for its permission to use the map "Ryświanka and vicinity"; the University of Chicago Library Photo Duplicating Department for photographing this map; the University of New Hampshire Instructional Services for technical assistance in preparing my family photographs and documents for this publication; the University of Toronto Press for its kind permission to quote extensively from its published translation of *The Poetical Works of Taras Shevchenko: The Kobzar;* Staatsarchiv Bremen for my family documents; Antoni B. Szcześniak for his permission to use the three photographs of the Ukrainian Nationalists from *Droga do nikąd*; and Stanisław Żerański of WIH, Pracownia Dokumentacji Naukowej for his expert cartography as well as other research-related services.

I am grateful to the University of New Hampshire both at Durham and Manchester, Henry W. & Sophie P. Berounsky, and the Stella Pinska Keene Trust for financial assistance; to the UNH–M library staff for all their efforts in my behalf; to Caroline Skillin, Denise Gray, and especially Rose Grenon for their secretarial assistance; and to my wife, Teresa, for her computer wizardry which saved this work several times from oblivion.

Finally and above all, I am greatly indebted to my brothers and sisters, both in the United States and Poland, who at my request searched the far corners of their memory in order to help me reconstruct our happy childhood in Ryświanka, our painful five-and-a-half-year history in the course of the Second World War under the Soviets, the Ukrainian Nationalists, and the Nazis, as well as our five-year sojourn through the various displaced persons camps in West Germany under the American occupation. I only regret that I was not able to interview my parents about all these matters and that now it is too late. Many of their memories, however, have been preserved by us, their children, and incorporated into this account.

Table of Contents

List of Abbreviations

A.A.F. Allied Air Force
AK (*Armia Krajowa*). Home Army
a.k.a. also known as
AWIH (*Archiwum Wojskowego Instytutu Historycznego*). Archive of the Military Historical Institute
BBH (*Bergbauernhilfe*). Mountain-Peasants' Help
B.V.M. Blessed Virgin Mary
CBS Columbia Broadcasting System
DDT D(ichloro)d(iphenyl)t(richloroethane)—a deadly insecticide
DGFP *Documents on German Foreign Policy 1918–45*. Files of the German Foreign Office
d.o.b. date of birth
DP Displaced person
DUN (*Druzhyny Ukrainskykh Natsionalistiv*). Brotherhoods of Ukrainian Nationalists
GESTAPO (*Geheime Staatspolizei*). Secret State Police
GI Government Issue. Also, any member of the United States armed forces, especially an enlisted soldier
IGC Inter-governmental Committee on Refugees
IRO International Refugee Organization
ITS International Tracing Service
KGB (*Komitet Gosudarstvennoi Bezopasnosti*). Committee for State Security
KONR (*Komitet Osvobozhdeniia Narodov Rossii*). Committee for the Liberation of the Peoples of Russia
M.G. Military Government
MP Military Police
NCA *Nazi Conspiracy and Aggression*. Part of the Nuremberg documents
NCWC National Catholic Welfare Conference
N.D. Nuremberg document
NKVD (*Narodnyi Komissariat Vnutrennikh Del*). The People's Commissariat for Internal Affairs
NOW (*Narodowa Organizacja Wojskowa*). National Military Organization
NSZ (*Narodowe Siły Zbrojne*). National Armed Forces
OST (*Ostarbeiter*). Eastern workers
OUN (*Orhanizatsiia Ukrainskykh Natsionalistiv*). Organization of Ukrainian Nationalists
OUN-B The OUN faction led by Stepan Bandera
OUN-M The OUN faction led by Andrii Melnyk

PC-IRO Preparatory Commission for the International Refugee Organization
POW Prisoner of war
R.A.F. Royal Air Force
ROA (*Russkaia Osvoboditelnaia Armiia*). Russian Liberation Army
SB *United States Strategic Bombing Survey*
SD (*Sicherheitsdienst*). Security Service of the SS
SEP Surrendered enemy personnel (camp)
SP (*Sicherheitspolizei*). Security Police
SS (*Schutzstaffel*). Hitler's elite guard or Blackshirts
SSR Soviet Socialist Republic
SSSR (Soyuz Sovietskikh Sotsialisticheskikh Respublik). Union of Soviet Socialist Republics: six Moslem nations—Azerbidzhan, Kazakhstan, Kirghizistan, Tadzhikistan, Turkmenistan, Uzbekistan; three Baltic—Estonia, Latvia, Lithuania; three Slavic—Byelorussia, Russia, Ukraine; three Christian, non-Slavic—Armenia, Georgia, Moldavia. In English: USSR. In Polish ZSRR (Związek Socjalistycznych Republik Radzieckich)
TMWC *Trial of the Major War Criminals Before the International Military Tribunal.*
TWC *Trials of War Criminals Before the Nuremberg Military Tribunals*
UACC Ukrainian American Coordinating Council
UCC Ukrainian Canadian Committee
UCCA Ukrainian Congress Committee of America
UHVR (*Ukrainska Holovna Vyzvolna Rada*). Ukrainian Supreme Liberation Council
UK United Kingdom
UN United Nations
UNA (*Ukrainska Natsionalna Armiia*). Ukrainian National Army
UNK (*Ukrainskyi Natsionalnyi Komitet*). Ukrainian National Committee
UNO *United Nations Organization*
UNRA (*Ukrainska Narodna Revoliutsiina Armiia*). Ukrainian National Revolutionary Army
UNRRA United Nations Relief and Rehabilitation Administration
UPA (*Ukrainska Povstanska Armiia*). Ukrainian Insurgent Army
URSR (Ukrainian: Ukrainska Radyanska Sotsialistychna Respublika. Russian: USSR [*sic*]—Ukrainskaya Sovietskaya Sotsialisticheskaya Respublika). Ukrainian Soviet Socialist Republic
US United States
USA United States of America
USAT United States Army Transport
USFET United States Forces, European Theater (American headquarters for occupation of Germany)
USSR English: Union of Soviet Socialist Republics. Russian: See URSR above
UVO (*Ukrainska Viiskova Orhanizatsiia*). Ukrainian Military Organization
UVV (*Ukrainske Vyzvolne Viisko*). Ukrainian Liberation Army

VVN (*Viiskovi Viddily Natsionalistiv*). Nationalist Military Detachments (of the OUN)

WCFU *World Congress of Free Ukrainians*

WIH (*Wojskowy Instytut Historyczny*). Military Historical Institute

WiN (*Wolność i Niezawisłość*). Freedom and Independence

Preface

Dark was the face of Europe in the first half of the twentieth century. After the horrors of the First World War, the peace Treaty of Versailles ushered in a time of territorial disputes, political conflicts, international tensions, revolutions, and civil wars. Everywhere, it seemed, and for the first time on the European continent, some version of fascism reared its ugly head: in Flanders, Finland, and France; in Norway and the Netherlands; in Rumania, Hungary, Great Britain, and Spain where it was called the Falange. Many of these fascist movements were of little consequence. Those of Austria, Germany, and Italy, however, were not and these fascist regimes with their dreams of world domination, their brazen slogans and misshapen emblems, their public spectacles and private conspiracies, their scapegoats, and their arsenals of mass destruction, paved the way for another, more brutal world war.

What did all these movements have in common? They were fiercely nationalistic and intolerant of all ideologies which differed from their own. They were racist; not only anti-Semitic, but generally ill-disposed toward all not of their own kind. They gloried in the past achievements of their countries and of their national leaders, bloody though they often were. Although undemocratic through and through, they courted and—if that failed—coerced all citizens high and low to support their dubious causes. And finally, they were led by immoral, aggressive and violent men of war whose only triumph was to produce, in the words of Hermann Rauschning, a "revolution of nihilism."

In addition to these fascist regimes, the Soviet Union, under its own brand of totalitarianism, Communism, was blatantly pursuing its own imperialistic agenda of nihilism by subjugating or annihilating millions in the Ukraine and, after 1939, by imposing its reign of terror on the independent nations to its west, including eastern Poland.

Into such a troubled world, then, was I born: a world ruled by ruthless dictators who, for their own ambitions and personal glory, plunged entire continents into the twilight zone of such macabre realities as can only be associated with the inhumanity of war. And what a war that was; a war such as the earth has never seen either before or since, a war which was eventually to claim the lives of 50 million people and transform the lives of millions more.

When my father was born in 1885, thrice-partitioned Poland did not exist on any map of Europe. When I was born 55 years later, it had just lost its regained independence once more. Thus, we were both born in a country occupied by a foreign power. Poland is now independent once again, but the eastern part in which both my father and I were born and which was home to my family is no longer a part of Poland. If I were not a citizen of the United States, I would consider myself a man without a country.

Germany attacked Poland on September 1, 1939. The Soviet Union attacked her on September 17 of that same year. Thus began the fourth partition of Poland, sealed by the secret protocol of the Soviet-Nazi Non-Aggression Pact signed that August. The political, social and economic consequences of that partition for those of us who lived in the eastern territories (*Kresy Wschodnie*) were most devastating. More terrible still were the summary executions and the mass deportations to Siberia, the first of which began on the day I was born, February 10, 1940—in temperatures thirty to forty degrees below zero.

Needless to say, the full extent of the Soviet atrocities against the Polish citizens of the eastern territories is still unknown. Only now, more than fifty years later, has it become possible to research, speak and write of these things in Poland. Perhaps with the help of Russian archives, we will eventually know as much about these atrocities as we do about the atrocities that were perpetrated at the same time in the western part of Poland.

With the invasion of the Soviet Union by Germany in 1941, the Nazi reign of terror embraced us as well. About this calamity much is also known. What is unknown and perhaps will never be known fully, is the reign of terror foisted upon the civilian population of Poland's eastern territories by the Ukrainian Nationalists who had close ties with the Nazis for the greater part of the war. This is another area of research that was forbidden in Poland by the former Communist regime, an area which is only now being investigated. It was fear of the Ukrainian Nationalists that preoccupied my family the most during World War II.

After my family was split up and deported to various forced-labor camps of Nazi Germany, our very existence continued to be threatened by hard labor, malnutrition, various epidemics, and the tons of Allied bombs which fell continually all around us. The city of Essen, for example, was 75 percent destroyed. Indeed, a bomb landed on the very building in which we were first enslaved. This was but one of the many times that death knocked on our door, then turned away.

That we survived when so many around us perished had absolutely nothing to do with what we or they did or failed to do. It was all simply a matter of phenomenal luck or, if you will, divine providence. In either case, my entire family, although fragmented and displaced, somehow managed to survive the greatest Holocaust in the history of our species. After the war, three of my sisters were repatriated and the rest of us, having spent five more years in the

Displaced Persons camps of West Germany, emigrated to America. Once here, my family pursued the American Dream while I, having completed the requirements of grammar school, entered the Franciscan Order (which I subsequently left) to pursue a life of poverty, chastity and obedience, and to pray for world peace.

Presently, I live in New Hampshire with my wife (Teresa) and children (Renia, Ala, Andrzej). Two of my sisters are still in Poland. The rest—except for my parents who are now deceased—reside in the Chicago area.

Over the years I have learned that such extreme suffering and adversity as we and others have had to endure can either destroy or ennoble. I have known people in both categories. Speaking for myself, I sometimes draw great strength from my troubled past. "Having survived all of that," I say to myself, "I have nothing left to fear and life is good." But if the truth be told, at the very core of my being where no one ever looks, I tremble, I continually tremble. In that intimate inner sanctum, I am still that three-year-old child, crying in a potato field, hiding in my mother's skirts, and in great fear of that fire which is still engulfing my home in far, far away Ryświanka. Do not show me a picture of an African, Bosnian, Palestinian, Israeli, British, Irish, Iraqi or any other child of war... unless you want to see a grown man cry.

So what have we learned from the terrible lessons of World War II? True, we have managed to avoid another global conflict and end that mutually dangerous and economically destructive cold war between the West and the former Soviet Union. Yet, as we all know so well, the central lesson has not been learned at all and naked aggression, violence, ethnic cleansing and war continue to plague us still. Change but the name, time and place, and you can read all about the history of my family in any contemporary newspaper and witness the horror of it all on your local evening news.

When will it all end? Must this century's anti-utopian motto: "The greatest misery for the greatest number of people?" continue into the next? Will there be that dreaded thermonuclear war to end all wars? Oh, what a dismal race we have turned out to be and if there is a God, what must He think of His proud creation? And if there is no God, then surely, we are becoming Satan and the earth a living hell.

Why did I write this book? Although I have reflected on my family history throughout my life, it was not until the mid–1980s that I first began putting down my thoughts on paper. By that time, I had come to believe what I always tell my sociology and anthropology students at the University of New Hampshire at Manchester: "Write, for when a person dies, a whole library is lost." Since I was not getting any younger, I did not want that fate to befall me or my children. I did not want my children to know as little about me as I knew about my nineteenth-century parents who never wrote because they were almost completely illiterate.

And so I began. At first to leave something of value to posterity and then, when I realized that the history of my family during the Second World War was also a history shared by so many other people now scattered throughout the world and by the victims of current ethnic cleansing and wars, I began to address them and their children as well. They became the imaginary readers which every author needs. In telling our story, I was hoping to tell theirs as well. And, if I failed in this, I at least hoped to inspire them or their children to take up their pens and tell their own version of these tragic historical events before it is too late. The swallows must sing, and their song will become their vengeance, and perhaps the salvation of the human race. Otherwise, war, death, and destruction will become a way of life for us all. For some of us it may be already too late. But, surely, our children deserve a better fate!

I also wrote the book so that I could re-read it from time to time, have a good cry, and remind myself both of my past and my responsibility to the future.

The composition of this historical memoir followed an unconventional pattern. After interviewing my brothers and sisters and drawing on my own memory, I first wrote and then did the research. As it turned out, the research—which included interviews in the United States, European published oral histories, United Nations proceedings, Nuremberg testimonies, Polish, English and, to a lesser extent, translated Ukrainian, German, and Russian sources, informal discussions and recent correspondence from Warsaw—not only confirmed my family's recollections but also provided the larger historical contexts and the explanations for what happened to us during and after the war. This blend of personal biography and documented factual information is history in the truest sense of the word: the remembered past consisting of both fact and interpretation. Ultimately, all history is personal. In addition, the photographs, maps and documents which appear in this book speak eloquently for themselves.

I hope my work will stand as a testament to those who shared our experiences during the Second World War. I hope it will serve as an inspiration to others to begin or to continue their own memoirs. I hope it will shed some light on the fate of the non-Semitic population of Europe during World War II, thus complementing the many documentaries, histories, and memoirs dealing with the Jewish Holocaust. I hope that, given the contemporary democratic bent of the world system of societies, it will also serve as an indirect criticism of current self-serving nationalistic interests and their dire consequences for the global community, especially when they assume the specter of ethnic cleansing. And most of all, I hope that in some small way it will move nations in the direction of peace by helping to discredit aggression, violence, and war.

Tadeusz Piotrowski
Manchester, 1994

While Vishnu slept, Shiva laid waste the world. I was uprooted and banished to the vast and boundless constellations of the zodiac. Brahma will never find me. I am aphelion bound.

Once, I sought in earnest for the path of my deliverance. Each time I wrenched my ice-bound spirit from one forbidding orbit, my homeward trek led but to a different star, another orbit, and renewed bondage. Now, I have become immune both unto my destiny and to what might have been. I am, and will remain, a child of contradictions—my freedom and my chains left forever hanging in the balance of the ancient goddess with chameleon eyes.

My childhood lost amid the ravages of war, my youth surrendered to medieval promises of peace, I age in the waning twilight of new, nameless gods.

BOOK I

POLAND

1

Ryświanka

I have not always been a displaced person. Once I was well placed, as well as anyone could be in Eastern Europe, near the 1921 Polish-Soviet border, in the province of Wołyń, the county of Równe, the township of Tuczyn, on a proprietary colony of a rustic village called Ryświanka.

Even now, when I hear that long forgotten name, my thoughts take wing like a startled watch of nightingales launched skyward by the sudden peal of thunder. Rainbow colors flood my imagination. Images of long, winding, country roads, of wooden structures with stucco walls, of thatched roofs, of verdant fields heavy with their bounty, of roaming livestock, harnessed brood mares, and domestic fowl surface in my consciousness. Perhaps this romantic reconstruction is nothing more than a cloud-woven version of some preposterous reality which I have never known. But if that is so, then what am I to make of those dark, somber shadows which I also perceive, although less distinctly, diffusing silently over all this pastoral splendor, commingling with it, and becoming one with my own reflections on what might have been? Surely, they must also belong to that imagined past, these shrouded ghosts of my once-upon-a-time Ryświanka, these restless spirits of those whose memory has long since been all but erased, not only by the mists of time and distance, but also by the senseless ravages of man's ultimate folly.

My story, then, begins at a time when all the ethereal beings of my imagination were real warm-blooded inhabitants of the Wołynian landscape such as it really was in the early part of the twentieth century.

Call us provincial, but to us all the province of Wołyń—with its still enchanted, predominantly forested and marshy terrain, its numerous Ukrainian and Polish villages, and its far-flung but, by erstwhile standards, prosperous towns—was the whole world . . . although tales abounded of the East—of Moscow, the Ural Mountains, and the great Siberian wastelands; and of the West—of Germany's forbidding Black Forest and of the vast civilized world beyond. Except for the veterans of foreign wars, few people from our village, at least in living memory, had actually ventured forth into those great beyonds. Except for the roving Gypsies—forever trafficking in relics of the true cross, feathers from the wings of the Archangel Gabriel, and vials of salty tears from the eyes of the Blessed Virgin Mary—few had ever come to us therefrom. On the local level, however, there was a great deal of wandering, especially after Poland's hard won independence and its annexation of the Russian and Ukrainian territories, including the western part of Wołyń, which once belonged to its vast medieval empire.

My parents (Józef, born on August 15, 1885, in the village of Kalinówka, the county of Włodzimierz, the province of Wołyń, and Maria Górska, born on December 30, 1891, in Lublin, in the county and province by the same name) wed on the eve of World War I (January 25, 1914) in the town of Tuczyn, and settled in a village called Cecylówka. Here, my oldest sister, Janina, was born on December 1, 1914. Responding to the call of duty, Józef left his young wife with child to defend his country. Upon his safe return, he fathered two more children, Kazimierz (d.o.b. unknown) and Aniela (July 20, 1921), and then moved to Natalja, where he begot Stanisława (March 10, 1923). After this, my father moved to Anował, where my youngest sister, Anna (January 2, 1925), was born. Subsequently, he resettled his expanding family again, this time in Leonówka, to live with his brother and sister-in-law, Stanisław and Marynia. Here my two surviving brothers, Franciszek (January 5, 1931) and Jan (March 2, 1933), were born. After about six years, my father built a house and barn in Amelin, near his own parents and brother Franciszek, and moved his family there. In 1935, he bought a small farm from a Ukrainian, a stone's throw from the village of Ryświanka, where I was born. All these many places of our residence lay within a twelve-kilometer radius of this village.

Ryświanka was located just northeast of the Równe-Kostopol-Tuczyn triangle. Równe, a predominately Jewish settlement, lay twenty-eight kilometers to our southwest. This thirteenth-century trading center, with its ruins of a medieval palace, is located on the Ustye River (a branch of the Goryn—or as we used to call it, Horyń—River) and was, in the 1930s, a prosperous manufacturing center with a population of about 41,000. Kostopol, fourteen kilometers to our northwest (1931 population: 6,523), is located thirty kilometers north-northeast of Równe, and was a predominantly sawmilling, iron smelting, and flour milling town. Tuczyn, eight kilometers to our south (1931 population: 2,940), is located on the Goryn River, twenty-four kilometers northeast of Równe. Here we went to church and milled our grain.[1] To the south of this triangle, Równe forms another triangle with Ostróg on the east and Dubno on the west—both about forty kilometers away.

These were the largest towns in our area, an area which in the eleventh and twelfth centuries together with the rest of Wołyń belonged to a much larger Russian principality by that same name. In the thirteenth century this area was raided by the Mongols. In the fourteenth century it passed to Lithuania; in 1569 from the Grand Duchy of Lithuania to Poland; from Poland to Russia in 1793 (Poland's second partition); from Russia to Poland in 1921; and back again to the USSR in 1945. Meanwhile, between 1939 and 1941 it was occupied by the Soviet Union and between 1941 and 1944 by Germany. Because of this thousand-year history, eventually the predominantly Ukrainian population of Wołyń became ethnically diverse and included Poles, Germans, Russians, White Russians, Czechoslovakians, and Lithuanians, as well as Jews and other minorities.

All of the residents of Ryświanka were Ukrainians, except for a forester and a Jewish shopkeeper, both of whom were Polish. We, along with several other Polish families, lived in precarious harmony with our many neighboring Ukrainians on the outskirts of the village. While that harmony prevailed, we spoke each other's languages and shared mutually cherished traditions. We served reciprocally as godparents to each other's children, who often played together, became friends, and sometimes even married.

Our family wealth consisted of a house and barn, a variety of two- and four-legged animals, the children, and two and a half hectares (about six acres) of the planet earth. Ours was not the best of soils—a mixture of silty clay which in the early spring turned to quicksand, and in the summer's heat to fine, powdery dust. Yet, somehow, we managed to eke out a meager existence as an independent family unit. In leaner times, my sisters would take on outside employment—usually as domestic servants on one or another of the many large and prosperous country estates owned by the Polish veterans of war. Anna recalls:

> Because we were poor, father used to hire us out for domestic service. Janina was hardly ever at home. She always lived among strangers. Stasia, because she was still small, used to pasture geese and cows. Not having proper clothing or boots, she often froze in the winter. The marks from frostbite are still visible on her feet today. I was also sent into service.

Our two-room house, replete with porch and pantry, was nestled on a gentle knoll flanked by two small pools of water. It was said that someone had drowned in one of them, but who it was and under what circumstances will forever remain hidden from my eyes. Perhaps it was only a story, one of the many told to children to keep them safe from harm. Perhaps it was not.

To the south lay our flower garden and the first pond, surrounded by weeping willows and birches. Beyond the pond was a patch of cultivated blackberries which grew well in our silty soil. A dirt road separated our field from a small forest called *Ochrona*, on the other side of which stretched a ribbon of sand hemmed by several Ukrainian households. This country road was intersected by a major artery which ran northward toward Kostopol and southward toward Ryświanka. The main street of our village lay perpendicular to this road. Both the store kept by the Jew and the forester's home were located at the juncture of these two roads, that is to say, at the west entrance to the village. The main road continued through another forest called

Las Ryświanecki, on the other side of which was Amelin and beyond that, Tuczyn.

To the west stood our barn and our pine grove, beyond which lay our main field, flanked by another country road leading to a larger forest called *Kaziony*. It was in this national forest preserve that my family hunted for berries, nuts, and mushrooms to supplement our diet. A winding path led to the homes of our two Ukrainian neighbors, Pivarchuk and Omel'ko, and just beyond them was the Polish household of Gruntkowski.

To the north stood a young orchard flanked by another field, and in the distance, a one-room schoolhouse where sporadic lessons were given to those interested by Mr. Dzikoński. Between the school and our property lived several Polish families, including the Domalewskis, whose son, Felek, showed an obvious interest in our Stasia, and whose brother, Antek, courted our Janina.

To the east was our yard, with a well and an outdoor cooking stove. Beyond that was the second pond, another field, and a path leading to our Polish neighbor Filip. Across the main road lived several more Ukrainian families, including those of Mykyta, Voronka, and Pasichnyk. Such were our immediate, pre–World War II environs.

Kocik was our cat; *Krówka*, our cow; *Koza*, our goat; *Owca*, our sheep; and if we had owned a horse, a sure sign of prosperity, he would have been called *Konik.* Peasant children were often wont to call farm animals by their generic names, there being so many. Only *Burek* lived with us under the same roof. As man's best friend, he merited special consideration. *Bociek*, on the other hand, nested safely on the household roof. *Bociek* was a stork.[2]

Supposedly, poor *Bociek* was abandoned as a chick by his cruel stork mother. The children found him near one of the ponds, brought him home and successfully—in spite of *Burek*—fed and nursed him through one of those cold and bitter winters of Poland. In the spring he was let go, but much to everyone's surprise, he chose to build his sturdy nest on the top of our thatched roof.

All summer long *Bociek* remained perched upon our house. People came from miles around to marvel at and learn from this humanitarianism reimbursed. Neighboring children envied our good luck, expected many babies to be born. No one entered or departed from our house without an upward glance and stork-like salutation. By summer's end, our roof was littered with the strangest gifts in various stages of decay.

That fall, some ancient urge seemed to distress poor *Bociek*. He became restless. He would not eat. He took to brooding and to flying skyward higher than he had ever done before. We all knew the source of his dilemma and commiserated with the choice he was being called upon to make: to spend another winter with his trusted friends or journey southward with the departing flocks of his own kind.

When the ancient urge prevailed, when nature's stern voice finally reclaimed her own, when friendship gave way to the call of duty, we watched with watery eyes and bade a fond farewell to our feathery friend as he soared toward and mingled with what probably was the last troop of migrating storks. (*Little did we suspect that all too soon we, too, would be called upon to engage in our own migration from which we were never to return.*)

Judge then of our surprise when, in the course of the following spring, *Bociek* remembered us and, having the whole wide world at his disposal, chose to return to our humble housetop. For years thereafter he nested on us all out of sheer gratitude, and perhaps good sense as well. We loved him so!

Swallows, too, abounded in our countryside. I remember a story which is worth recounting for its sheer improbability if nothing else. Once, so the story goes, as the industrious swallows were building their muddy nests high in the eaves of our barn, a lazy, pretentious sparrow came to inspect the work. Finding it quite in order, she flew into the nest nearest completion and proceeded to occupy it with no thought of leaving.

The swallows had a fit! The next day, after a restless night no doubt, they launched forth with reinforcements and finished building the nest without the slightest regard for the uninvited occupant within. There was one slight modification in their engineering design, however: the failure to leave the usual opening for the entrance. They simply walled her in! On the third day, when the nest was knocked down to check on the condition of the captive bird, it came as no surprise that the sparrow was quite dead. (*Prophetically, our nest, too, would soon be invaded and occupied by hordes of pretentious armies. Perhaps they should have been forewarned of the vengeance of the swallows!*)

Black forests surrounded our small settlement, and in those forests lived man-eating wolves. Once, they almost ate my mother as she was making her way home on foot in the dead of winter, after a somewhat prolonged visit to the local folk practitioner in the adjoining village. She suffered from some painful malady of the eyes. The treatment consisted of a rather strange diagnosis, a stranger prescription, and the strangest cure.

The old *babusieńka* made my mother lie down, dangled a magic amulet over her eyes, burnt some flax, and wafted the billowing smoke toward her face. If the smoke stayed low, she was told, it would be a bad omen and the situation would be quite hopeless. If, on of the other hand, it rose—as smoke usually does—then the condition was amenable to treatment. The smoke rose, an appropriate "physic of the field" was prescribed, and the patient was discharged.

It was in the course of her homeward trek on that desolate wintry eve that a pack of hungry wolves began to stalk my mother as their prey. And, as if the burning eyes and the wolves were not enough, a blinding snowstorm swept through the forests and blanketed the country roads that day, making her safe return to Ryświanka all but impossible.

Thanks to the vigilance of my father, who like any decent husband first began to wonder what in the world was taking her so long and then decided to set out after her with a team of borrowed horses, her life was saved. (*In the ensuing years this misadventure became a sign to her that she was among those to be spared by the dogs of war as well.*)

All in all, it must not have been a very harsh winter as Polish winters go, for otherwise both she and my father would have most certainly perished. The hyperborean snowstorms killed without mercy, and starving wolves were seldom deterred by even the most stalwart of men with fire, arms, and horses at their disposal. *Wywołać wilka z lasu* (to call the wolf out of the forest) is a Polish proverb with no uncertain meaning.

It was probably also at this time that my mother formulated that ultimate matrimonial expression of fidelity, which I heard her utter only once to my father—some twenty years later: "Kill me if you must, but I will never leave you." The herbal remedy worked, too!

Life's tempo in our village was governed by the turning of the seasons. The seasons, on the other hand, were governed by the ancient liturgical calendars of the Ukrainian Autocephalous Orthodox Church, the Ukrainian Byzantine Catholic Church, the Roman Catholic Church, and Judaism—with a full measure of still more ancient paganism added for sheer relief. Nearly a thousand years of the Judeo-Christian tradition failed to purge the Slavic faith of its preoccupation with the dark, chthonian demons of its ancestors and the tellurian deities of the nether world. This unique syncretism produced a melancholy people inclined both to fatalistic thoughts and messianic destinies.

In the nineteenth century, each Slavic nation considered itself to be the suffering savior of mankind—suffering usually at each other's hands. Many, such as thrice-partitioned Poland, were already said to be in the third day of their entombment, anxiously awaiting their resurrection and their rightful reinstatement at the head of the European community. All were disappointed! Nazi Germany, with its "Thousand-Year Reich," was to be the chosen nation; Adolf Hitler, its messiah; the swastika, a broken cross, its party emblem and symbol of anti-Semitism.

Since our parish church was located some distance from our house, we rarely attended any of the obligatory Roman Catholic services. Instead, my parents spent much time praying at home. On Sunday afternoons, my father would take out a rather large prayer book and solemnly recite various prayers *viva voce* without the slightest concern as to their liturgical propriety. While father prayed, mother kept herself busy by preparing his dinner, and we were allowed to do as we pleased so long as we kept quiet.

After dinner, mother would sit down by the kitchen stove, take out the same prayer book that my father used, and quietly recite her prayers by the hours. (She told us later that this is how she was attempting to learn to read as well.) While mother was engrossed in her prayers (and her studies), the girls could not resist gathering around her to comb and to arrange the beautiful raven-black hair, cascading over her shoulders like a shawl, into various currently fashionable coiffeurs before finally braiding and pinning it up on top of her head in the traditional bun.

Besides private devotions, we also held many public services in each other's homes on a rotating basis—such as the Stations of the Cross, *Gorzkie Żale, Zielone Świątki*, and the Marian feasts of May. Every family in our neighborhood had a makeshift altar which would be beautifully decorated for these occasions, with flowers and greenery adding freshness and fragrance to our humble homes. (*It was under such altars that, in 1942-44, tunnels were dug leading to shelters in the gardens, orchards, or woods.*) When it was our turn to host the ceremonies, one of my older sisters would often assume the role of the "priest" by intoning the hymns and leading the "congregation" in prayer.

In Wołyń, as throughout much of Europe, the season between the vernal equinox and the summer solstice officially began with the celebration of Easter, originally a pagan vernal festival. Although my mother baked bread every week, her art reached perfection in quantity, artistry, and comestible delight on Holy Saturday. All the baking was done in our large kitchen wood stove. After the ashes were removed and the coals were evenly raked, my mother would place the kneaded dough inside the oven and arrange her various creations by means of a long-handled wooden spatula. While the breads rose and baked to perfection, the children crowded around the stove and waited most impatiently for the first golden-brown loaves to appear. Before each new loaf was cut, it was reverently blessed. If a piece happened to fall on the floor, it was immediately picked up and kissed before it was consumed because, as my mother used to say: "It was holy."

Holy Saturday also brought us the annual visitation of the parish priest for the traditional blessing of the house and all therein:

> PRIEST: God's peace be in this home.
>
> ALL: And in all who live here....
>
> PRIEST: Let us pray. Hear us, holy Lord and Father, almighty everlasting God; and as you guarded the homes of the Israelites from the avenging angel on their flight from Egypt, if their homes were signed with the blood of a lamb—therein prefiguring our Easter sacrifice in which Christ is the victim—so likewise in your goodness send your holy angel to watch over and protect all who live in this home, to be with them and give them comfort and encouragement; through Christ our Lord.
>
> ALL: Amen.[3]

(Despite this blessing, neither the blood of lambs nor Christ's supreme sacrifice would save our home when the accursed angel of 1939 was set loose upon the face of the earth.)

The *Benedictio domorum* was then followed by the traditional blessings of the lamb (*Benedictio agni paschalis*), sheep (*Benedictio ovorum*), new produce (*Benedictio novorum fructuum*), bread (*Benedictio panis*), pancakes (*Benedictio placentarum*), beer (*Benedictio cerevisiae*—at least I think it was beer), cheese and butter (*Benedictio casei et butyri*), and the *Benedictio quodcumque comestible* (whatever is edible), which included the eggs.[4]

In the Middle Ages, the consumption of meat, dairy products, and eggs was strictly prohibited throughout the great Lenten fast and abstinence. When the feast of Easter brought this rigorous period of mortification to an end and these foods were again allowed to grace the table, the faithful showed their joy and gratitude by first having the food blessed. Moreover, they hoped that the Church's blessing would remedy whatever harmful effects the body might have sustained from the long period of self-denial. There was even a special blessing for (anyone's) medicine: *Benedictio cujuscumque medicinae*.

Ancient rituals advised the clergy to dispense these blessings in moderation, to refrain from over-patronizing the nobility at the expense of the commoners, to encourage the faithful to bring their produce to the parish churches instead of making house calls (thus minimizing clerical absenteeism), and to conduct themselves soberly on these occasions: " . . . *et saepe bene poti, vix redeunt ad levandum de sepulchro Christum Dominum, imo ad missae sacrificium in die illo festivo inepti, cum ingenti scandalo et Cleri approbrio.*"[5]

Of course, an Easter house blessing demanded the presence of the priest on the premises, and while he was there, sober or not, we had him bless our fields, our orchard, our well, our animals, and all our *quodcumque comestible*, including our beautifully colored Easter eggs. Not being aware of the Holy Synod's admonition that the parish priest should not tarry too long at any one household, we took no chances, had everything sprinkled and crossed, and were edified by the fact that he never seemed to run out of either holy water or blessings.[6]

We called our Easter eggs *pisanki* and *kraszanki*. The Ukrainians called them *pysanky* and *krashanky*. Legends abounded as to why all Christendom went to all that trouble splashing colors on lowly chicken eggs. The earliest references to this ancient custom are to be found in the works of Juvenal, Ovid, and Pliny. However, leaving these three pagans content in their unmarked graves, the Greco-Christian rendition, handwritten in a script reminiscent of the tenth century, seems to approximate the "original" Polish version most remarkably.

According to this legend, an angel of the Lord was said to have appeared to poor Mary Magdalene—the reformed sinner—sorrowing by the tomb of Jesus and to have said: "Do not weep, Mary, for Christ is risen!" Uplifted by the good news, she ran home to find all the eggs in her house colored red. Later that day, she met some of the apostles, and, giving them each an egg, she informed them of the miracle and of the Resurrection. Responding to the touch of the apostles, the red eggs miraculously metamorphosed into doves—as a sign that from Christ's death sprang hope eternal for bloodstained mankind.

Elsewhere it is written that the stones that killed the first Christian martyr, Saint Stephen, turned into a riot of colored eggs.

One final legend, and the one to which I am most partial, has to do with Jesus' final journey to His place of execution. As Christ was being led about the streets of Jerusalem, a kind passer-by—that is, a total stranger—who just happened to be carrying a basketful of eggs to the local marketplace, took pity on the Man and, leaving behind his basket, helped Him bear His heavy cross. When the man returned to reclaim his eggs, he found them all transformed into *kraszanki* and *pisanki*. And because it is my favorite legend, I do not apologize for taking liberties to revise this grand tradition to say what it should say: It was the man himself who was transformed; who gives a tinker's damn about his woven rushes and his paltry eggs!

I ja tam z gośćmi byłem, miód i wino piłem
A com widział i słyszał, w piśmie umieściłem.[7]

Of course in my poor village we did not have supermarketed, polychromatic, comestible egg-coloring sets; but there were herbs (as good for coloring eggs as for healing sore eyes), and other means of pigmentation. Prior to the days of synthetic dyes, all egg colors came from trees, plants, and vegetables. For a golden-yellow color, eggs were cooked either in onion skins, or in the bark of wild crab apple trees, or in the blossoms of marigolds. Violet was obtained by using the petals of the tall hollyhock flower as the base for the dye. Green came from the pistils of alum, the leaves of mistletoe, or freshly cut sprouts of young rye. The crocus flowers produced orange. The bark of an alder tree, or the new leaves of a maple, yielded a black dye. Finally, dipping the eggs in a "broth" made from the so-called "June Bugs" would color them bright red. All artistic designs were drawn on the eggs with a pin-stylus dipped in melted beeswax.

Both Polish and Ukrainian Easter baskets brimmed with these finely decorated *pisanki* and *krashanky*, with homemade breads and freshly churned butter, with smoked hams and bursting sausages, with spices, herbs, and salt.[8] Children waited anxiously until the magic holy water blessed the woven baskets and, right after the traditional first offering of home-brewed spirits and choice food to the usually famished parish priest, dove for their favorite Easter eggs.

Then began the ancient ritual (without supportive legends) of the children depriving one another of their precious caches. One would hold his egg with an end upturned while the other would strike it with his own. After a careful mutual inspection of the damage, the proprietor of the broken egg would woefully surrender it to the one whose egg withstood the blow. Clever children used practically indestructible duck eggs; cunning ones used foolproof, cleverly disguised eggs made of solid hickory wood.

Easter Monday was *Śmigus-Dyngus* day, the daylong licensed sloshing of poor village girls with water by the all-too-willing boys. On that day many an unwary female found herself thrown bodily into the nearest river, pond, or stream. The hills resounded with the chase. The unconvincing protests of the maidens, the sinister glee of sporting lads in hot pursuit, the envious wagging of old silvery heads—all gave one the notion that this most certainly was not a Christian sort of sport. My sister, Stasia, recalls one such occasion:

> I remember that near our house was a hill (*Góra po Tartaku*) and two small ponds wherein frogs habitually conducted their evening concerts for our listening pleasure. It so happened that one *Śmigus-Dyngus* day, Felek's brother, Antek, took me by the hand and, swinging me around and around on that hill, released me so that I had no choice but to land in the middle of one of these ponds, my wide skirt opening up like an umbrella in the shallow water. All day long I tried to get even with him by carrying a bottle of water in my pockets and splashing him unsuspectingly whenever the opportunity presented itself.

She tells of another interesting "custom," at least as it pertained to the Piotrowski household, full of eligible young ladies:

> We never locked our door at night because there were no thieves in our area. However, on Easter Eve, late at night, after we were fast asleep, some prankish boys would secure our front door from the outside with ropes. Father would always become enraged at this since it was he who would leave the house first in the morning.

On the feast of St. John the Baptist, in the evening, young maidens gathered on the river banks throughout our district. Each girl would cast two hand-braided flower wreaths upon the water and hold her breath. It was said that if her two wreaths kissed before disappearing out of sight, she was sure to marry within that same year. Already married people had more important things to do on the evening of St. John the Baptist Day!

Spring, then, was the season of rejoicing, of eternal hope, of regeneration from the dark womb of winter. Christ resurrected was the sign of life or, rather, the reprieve from death. It was the end of the forty days of fasting, suffering, and of sacrificing—of Lent, that wise design to sanctify the inescapable lot of poor, downtrodden folk, of making sure provisions lasted till the bitter end.

Spring marked the rekindling of old neighborly ties, of long deliberations on the topic of the land, of holy baptisms, of proposals, and of love. Boys became men. Girls reached maidenhood. People married. Babies were conceived.

The sounds of amorous bulls, of newborn bleating lambs, of purring pussy willows, of rustling meadows, of mountain melodies, of straining snowdrops, of bursting buds, of babbling brooks, of fluttering butterflies, of meadowlarks, of bees, of storks upon the wind—these were our sounds of spring.

The fragrant scent of apple blossoms, of wildwood flowers, of falling rain, of flowing sap and nectar, yes, even rotting cow manure upon the open fields—these were our smells of spring.

Spring was the season for the plowing of the land into long black furrows. Men with stout horses pulling hand-forged plows dotted each horizon. And although every draft horse was followed by ten dancing crows and every plowman scrutinized by a thousand watchful eyes, somehow, Mother Earth got planted. She too would conceive.

It was also the time to discover who survived the winter and who froze to death within their empty home. If we received the latter news with mixed emotions, even inner joy, it was because we were not among the dead.

(*Little did we know how often this familiar thought would continue to sustain us in the deathlike years ahead!*)

Of summer's pleasures little need be said. Our summers were so short, so sweet, so energetic. Summers were for prolonged visitations with old friends, for lengthy trips to neighboring villages, for endless conversations late into the night. For children, they were the time for being out of doors, for staying out till dark, for carefree frolicking in the flowery meadows.

In summertime, church attendance usually tripled. This was due, in part, to the improved condition of the weather; but also, no doubt, to the desire on the part of the faithful to hear about the avoidance of temptations, the favorite topic of all lusty souls. How many scandals were uncovered after church! How many more invented in the uneventful years! Gossip was the spice of life, and all availed themselves of it profusely.

Much time was spent in honest labor too: in tending home and garden; in pasturing sheep and cattle; in going to the marketplace; in haggling over some commodity; in trading of hand goods; in buying and selling of livestock and of labor; and in both well-advised and ill-advised ventures aimed at procuring a modest fortune.

(*Little did we know how these familiar skills would continue to sustain us in the hopeless years ahead!*)

Fall, with its chilling airs, signaled the time for the harvest to begin. Except for the youngest toddlers, who were often left alone at home to fend for themselves as best they could, every able-bodied soul worked the fields.

On the morning of the appointed day, just before the mists of dawn ascended along the pathways of the sun, reapers appeared upon the land and filled the air with their deft stoning of dulled scythes and sickles. Weathered whetstones blazed in metronomic precision along curved lengths of cold, hand-forged steel combining into an eerie symphony of twanging sounds and moods. Mowers marched boldly across prolific landscapes, swinging rhythmically their razor-edged instruments of death, leaving in their wake neat, alternating, parallel rows of swathes and stubble. Ancient songs of reapers commingled with the still more ancient muffled moans of Mother Earth despairing for her tender progeny. In this grim endeavor no quarter was asked for and none was given. How awesome was this systematic mowing, mowing, mowing of proud wheat and barley, oats and rye, and hay! How sad it was in afterthought!

After the mowing came the gathering, and the thrashing, and the grinding of the harvest grains in the windmills of the townships. Hay was stacked up in great heaping mounds, and when the barns were filled, the rest was left to weather in the open fields. When all was in its proper place, when it was finally over, we gave thanks to Mother Earth, ate, drank, rested, and were merry.

Besides the normal round of harvest celebrations involving one and all, the youth conducted their own social, called *Andrzejki*, on November 30. This last youthful gathering before the Advent season would begin with the boys chatting and the girls chatting, baking, and cooking. After the orchestra arrived (paid for by the young men), there would be singing and dancing. Finally, while the boys watched with great interest, the girls would engage in fortune telling with respect to their own marital prospects.

To find out who among them would be the first to marry, each girl would place a piece of bread on the dance floor. Then, the family dog was brought in, and the order in which he ate the bread was said to indicate the sequence of the girls' weddings. To find out whether the husband-to-be would be a bachelor or a widower, a section of the fence surrounding the house was chosen, and beginning arbitrarily with either "bachelor" or "widower" the words were alternated with each slat until the last. The designation corresponding to that slat would be the girl's lot.[9] Finally, to learn the characteristics of the future husband, melted wax was poured into a pan of water and the shape it took was said somehow to reveal his personality.

(*Little did we know how these familiar memories would continue to sustain us in the empty years ahead!*)

Winter, oh black winter, how charming are your first overtures to frail mankind: Christmas, New Year, and Epiphany; larders bursting with provisions, smoked meats of every kind, full potato cellars, salted fish, dried fruit, mountains of freshly cut wood, warm hearths, and the glorious transformation of the earth by that first of many gently falling snows.[10]

Needless to say, Christmastime in Poland was especially rich in customs and traditions. Christmas Eve itself deserves a special mention. Without exception, every village displayed a festive mood that day as its inhabitants prepared for the celebration of the *wigilia* (vigil) on that most holy night. The table was set out in advance upon a billowy bed of hay and oats spread profusely beneath a white linen cloth: hay in honor of the manger; oats to assure a plentiful harvest in the coming year. An extra plate was set as a sign of welcome to any passing guests, be they spirits or mortal men. *Gość w domu, Bóg w domu.*[11] A chain was placed around the table to represent family solidarity. The freshly felled Christmas tree was decorated with wooden ornaments, paper angels and chains, straw baskets, clip-on candles, red apples from the root cellar, countless homemade cookies, and specially purchased candy in rainbow-colored wrappers. Often the children were allowed to sleep under all this splendor, their parents knowing full well that by the early morning hours all the cookies and candy would vanish without a trace.

With the appearance of the first evening star, the father brought in a small sheaf of grain and, placing it near the table, said:

Niosę plon w Boży dom,
Żeby to zboże plonowało,
Dziesięć korcy z kopy dało.[12]

The mother would then bring in a handful of hay, saying:

A ja niosę siano,
Panu Jezusowi pod głowę i kolano.[13]

After these rhymes, the entire family would gather around the table and engage in the traditional breaking of the *opłatek*.[14] The ceremony began with the head of the household breaking and sharing his bread-wafer with his wife, while wishing her health and happiness in the coming year and asking her forgiveness for his many past transgressions. This he would do with everyone, his wife following suit, and then the elders, guests and, finally, the children.

After the *opłatek*, the candles on the Christmas tree were lit and all sat down to a meatless, but hearty, twelve-course meal consisting of various soups, fish, noodles, fried fruits, mushrooms, and *pierogi* stuffed with potatoes, cheese, or *kapusta* (sauerkraut).

Carols were generally sung immediately after supper, but on occasion, Gypsies came a-caroling too. The oldest of the troupe would hail the family with his own version of the Polish language and the usual ending rhyme:

Niek będzie pofalony Jezus Krystus. Winszujem wom na to Boże Narodzenie żebyście się dockali drugiego Bożego Narodzenia we scęściu, we zdrowiu, przy Boskim pożegnaniu. Żeby wom się chowały bycki jak w lesie jedlicki, żebyście mieli domowego ptactwa jak w lecie robactwa.[15]

This quaint salutation was followed by a series of violin-accompanied Polish Christmas carols which spoke of peace on earth and good will to men. After that, the singers would be well endowed with baked goods and cheeses.

It may be added that the roving Gypsies held a special fascination for the children of the household. After all, stories abounded of how angry parents handed over wicked children into their keeping; of how cruel Gypsies stole bad children without bidding; and worse, of how they broke the children's bones to make them double-jointed, and thus suitable for acrobatics in their wandering circuses and freak shows. After a while, it was even difficult to discern the real Gypsy children from those abducted. For instance, which of these caroling children were which? It was impossible to tell! No wonder the little ones clung to their own mothers during the performance like metallic shavings to a magnet! No wonder they felt much relieved when the dark carolers vanished into the black night whence they came!

Saint Nicholas? Why, yes, we knew of him—but he looked like a bishop and came much earlier, on December 6. He brought us our much-needed clothes, our *trepy* (clogs), our toys, and Christmas cookies—all handcrafted to perfection with love. Bad children, we were told, received bunches of twigs which were to be handed over to their parents in times of need. But there were never any of those bad children in our house!

Among the more interesting yuletide customs and traditions in our area were the following:

—The injunction against women visiting each other's households on Christmas Eve. Supposedly, to do so would be to bring bad luck and ill health to those visited. The men always did what they pleased.

—After the *wigilia*, the farm animals were supposedly given the gift of speech. It was usually the father who went out to hear and to report what they had to say about the family.[16]

—After the *wigilia*, water drawn from the nearest well was said to turn into wine.

—After the *wigilia*, young girls would go outdoors and listen for the direction from which their future husbands would come, as indicated by any barking dog.

—On St. Stephen's Day (December 26) the father would feed the farm animals with bread and the *opłatek* so as to insure their health in the coming year.

—If folks went to church on St. Stephen's Day, they came prepared with oats—to throw at the priest after the *Asperges me*.[17] This was symbolic of the stoning of St. Stephen and also served as a gentle reminder to the parish priest.

—During the Christmas season, weather permitting, the priest would visit the homes of the parishioners, collect his due, and impart still another blessing on the house:

> Lord God almighty, bless this home, and under its shelter let there be health, chastity, self-conquest, humility, goodness, mildness, obedience to your commandments, and thanksgiving to God the Father, Son, and Holy Spirit. May your blessing remain always in this home and on those who live here.[18]

(*After 1939, none of these words would have any meaning to us for a long, long time.*)

Besides Nativity, New Year's, too, was festive as well as Epiphany. On New Year's Day, a Polish tradition counsels all to place their foot on the cold steel of an axe before getting out of bed—for good luck in the ensuing year.

One anecdote from the early chronicles of Polish history tells of clever Old King Zygmunt, who, upon receiving only two kings in a game of cards on Epiphany, proclaimed that he had *three*. After his hand was called, the other players asked: "And where is the third king, your majesty?"

Supposedly, he replied: "Why, here I am!"—and won the match.

But while kings played cards, the peasants were already thinking about next year's crops. Among us, it was said that whoever would be the first to bring a sheaf of grain into his barn on January 6 would also be the first to gather in his harvest in the fall.

Alas, both the social and the economic abundance of Christmastide gave way, all too soon, to Lent, which began on Ash Wednesday with the sobering words: "Remember man, that you are dust and into dust you will return."

Somber moods prevailed throughout the land in keeping with the season. Mournful songs, in keys with many flats, were intoned by the clergy in the parish churches and continued by the laity in the homes by makeshift altars: *Gorzkie Żale* (Bitter Lamentations); *Suplikacje* (Supplications); *Ludu, Mój Ludu* (People, My People); *Dies Irae* (Day of Wrath). Only the last belonged to official Christendom. All spoke of suffering, death, and judgment. All begged God's forgiveness, mercy, and protection. The *Suplikacje* began:

> *Święty Boże! Święty Mocny! Święty i nieśmiertelny!*
> *Zmiłuj się nad nami. (3x)*
>
> *Od powietrza, głodu, ognia i wojny*
> *Wybaw nas Panie. (3x)*
>
> *Od nagłej i niespodzianej śmierci*
> *Zachowaj nas Panie (3x)*
>
> *My grześni Ciebie Boże prosimy,*
> *Wysłuchaj nas Panie. (3x)*[19]

Yet, it was not these heart-rending melodies that echoed through the countryside when people died. At such times, entire villages would gather in procession behind plain, black coffins and weep and wail, and wring their hands in anguish, and chant melancholy dirges the entire length of those somber one-way journeys to the grave.

> *Ciężko ci jest na świat iść, ciężko i odchodzić.*
> *Miałby człowiek wolę chcieć, chciałby się nie rodzić,*
> *Chciałby minąć wojnę tę, co się żywot mieni,*
> *Chciałby sobie cicho spać u matuchny ziemi. . . .*[20]

The winter months were often unpredictable. If the season was too long, poorer folks ran out of provisions and starved to death; if it was too cold, they froze to death; if it was too wet, they became ill and died; if it was too gloomy, they developed strange diseases of the mind; if it was too harsh, they stole, killed, and were killed in turn—all crimes against humanity. That is why we had large families: twelve children on my mother's side, eight of whom survived (Paweł, Wojtek, Stanisław, Franciszek, Antoni, Wacław, Bronisława); a remnant of eight on my father's side (Andrzej, Franciszek, Stanisław, Władysław, Edward, Mania, Pawlina); and eight in their own family of procreation—minus one.

Yet, even in these terrible months, when children often disappeared out of sight in waist-high honeycombs of snow, there was sociability. Winter was a time for friendly evening get-togethers called *wieczorki*; to talk, to make shoes, to spin flax, to knit and embroider, to make down pillows and *pierzyny* (quilts). Our Ukrainian neighbors, Pivarchuk and Omel'ko, often hosted these *wieczorki*. My sisters have many fond memories of these bygone days:

> Sometimes, the women and their daughters would gather in a given household to pluck chickens and geese, to sing, and to gossip. Often, the boys would come over uninvited to cause trouble by blowing on the piles of downy feathers and setting them airborne throughout the house. Then, the girls in half-pretend fashion would chase them off in the midst of mischievous laughter and good-natured merriment. After our work was done, the company would partake of some refreshments (which never included liquor) before retiring to their own homes.

> In the long winter evenings, by the flickering light of a kerosene lamp, my mother would sit by a large spinning wheel and draw miles of linen thread out of ordinary flax while singing softly to herself. From this, cloth would be woven for table linen, sheets, dresses and shirts. These were often embroidered with multicolored threads. My mother spun so fine that people from the surrounding area would often bring her work. They would then take the spun fibers and weave them into cloth in their own domestic workshops.

The long wintry evenings were also conducive to story-telling, our favorite pastime in the days before electricity, radios, and televisions. While the adults spun their ancient tales, the children crouched near the fireplace or lounged on top of the kitchen stove, still warm from the day's cooking, and listened intently to the stories they would someday repeat.

Za górami, za lasami, za siedmioma rzekami, żył sobie. . .[21] they would begin, in verse or in prose, ranging just as far and wide as the imagination of the narrator and the listener would permit. Like the legends of every nation, these also dealt with universal themes, clothed in the idiom of the day and the imagery of the remembered past.

Ours were the stories of enchanted nobility and disenchanted peasantry, of evil witches and innocent maidens, of ungrateful children and wicked step-parents (usually stepmothers), of saints and of sinners, of intimate but unrecorded details in the lives of Jesus, Mary, and Joseph, of Polish Bethlehems and Polish Golgothas, of golden fishes and fleeces, of dragons who breathed fire and ate flesh (usually the flesh of children)—dragons who dwelt beneath cavernous castle walls and were eventually conquered by some clever folk hero.

Yet there were local stories too—stories of fantastic beings who were said to inhabit Wołyń's many forests, like the shy, beautiful, harmless little-people, *Krasnoludki*; and *Genowefa,* who was forever raising her little feral child alone amid the terror of the wolves; and sinister *Baba Jaga*.

And there were stories of *Janko Muzykant*, who could have very well been one of Ryświanka's many gifted children; of *Koza Dereza*, which could have been anybody's goat; of *Kwiat Paproci Świętojański*, which probably grew in our *Ochrona, Las Kaziony,* or *Las Ryświanecki*, blossoming each Christmas Eve at midnight, just waiting to endow some lucky passer-by with a lifetime of happiness and prosperity; and *Złota Rybka*, which was said to live in the mighty sea, but perchance also in one of our twin pools of water . . . if we could only catch her! . . . and many, many more.

Whether native or imported, these stories were passed down from generation to generation by word of mouth, ever changing, ever more embellished by still another version of the same old plot. It was usually said to be done for the sake of the children, but it was really done for the sake of human solidarity and cohesion.

(*Little did we know how all these familiar traditions would continue to sustain us in the desolate years ahead, or how much they would change in just one generation!*)

It was in the course of one such winter that my five-year-old brother, Kazimierz, died of scarlet fever many years before I was conceived. It was in the course of another such winter that I was born.

The details of my incarnation escape me now. I know, however, that I was conceived about one month after Hitler issued his directive for "Operation

White"—the invasion of Poland. For that very reason, mine must have been a most uneasy pregnancy for my almost-half-century-old mother. How could she not sense the gathering storm? How could she not feel the incipient winds of war? Yet, in spite of her foreboding, she bore me full term, and with the help of a village midwife, on a cold and blustery February morning, I was delivered from one world of darkness into another. Heinrich Himmler once described that terrible winter of 1939-40 in an address to the *SS Leibstandarte*:

> [It] happened in Poland in weather forty degrees below zero, where we had to haul away thousands, tens of thousands, hundreds of thousands; where we had to have the toughness—you should hear this, but also forget it immediately—to shoot thousands of leading Poles. ... Gentlemen, it is much easier in many cases to go into combat with a company than to suppress an obstructive population of low cultural level, or to carry out executions or to haul away people or to evict crying and hysterical women.[22]

The details of my birthing escape me as well. I only know that on that day, out I came just as I was, naked and afraid—a condition in which I was to remain for the next ten years of my life. Hitler raped Poland on September 1, 1939. On September 17, Stalin sodomized her from the east. I was born about five months after these events.

Traditional astrologists would place my birth under the eleventh sign of the zodiac. But being in Wołyń at the time, my real sign has always been the large S-shaped constellation near the celestial equator with the steel hammer lying across each of its bloody crescents, which in the year following my birth twisted into a broken cross flanked on each side by a fearsome trident.[23]

On February 10, 1940, as Maria Piotrowski was straining every muscle in her body to squeeze me out into this wicked world, the first of many Soviet transports with their involuntary human cargo were just beginning their desolate journeys along hard, steel rails toward the forbidding wastelands of Siberia. The Polish children of Wołyń remember my birth day very well:

> In the year 1940 on February 10 at two o'clock at night four NKVD men burst into our apartment....[24]

> On 2.10.1940 at 4 o'clock in the morning they surrounded our house and ordered us to get ready to leave....[25]

> On February 10, 1940 at six in the morning three Russian soldiers came to us and tell us that we should pack because in two hours we are leaving.[26]

> On February 10 [1940] the Soviets came into the room where we were all asleep....[27]

> . . . February 10, '40, in the morning we were still sleeping, suddenly we heard a knocking. Daddy got up, opened the door and I saw NKVD.[28]

> They arrested us Feb. 10, 1940.[29]

> On February 10, 1940, they took us and brought us under Soviet guard to a station at Ozenin. . . .[30]

> On February 10 [1940] they deported the military colonists and foresters with their households to the depths of Russia to work.[31]

> On February 10, 1940, an unusually frosty day [the winter of 1939-40 was extremely severe], the first groups of Poles were exiled into the depths of Russia. This was brutally conducted, with children freezing to death in train cars.[32]

> . . . on February 10 [1940] at night the Ukrainians came with the "Moskale" [a derogatory word for Russians] and deported our entire settlement and even the neighboring settlements to Russia. . . .[33]

> . . . on 2.10.1940 . . . they started evicting us from our native settlements. This is a day which I shall remember for as long as I live. We were exiled to Soviet Russia.[34]

> On February 10, 1939 [the correct year is 1940], the Soviets exiled us they took us away in tightly sealed freight cars they would not even allow us out to get water.[35]

> Feb. 10, 1939 [1940], I was deported with my parents to the land of Siberia.[36]

> On 2/10 of 1940 we were exiled to the Ural.[37]

> After the first mass deportations to Russia in February 1940, when with 30° C below zero the military colonists and their families were deported in unheated freight cars, all the Poles expected the same thing sooner or later.[38]

On February 21, 1940, Richard Gluecks, head of the Concentration Camp Inspectorate, informed Himmler that he had found a suitable site for a new "quarantine camp" at Auschwitz. In that same month, Stepan Bandera, the son of a Ukrainian Catholic priest, radicalized the OUN (*Orhanizatsiia Ukrainskykh Natsionalistiv* — Organization of Ukrainian Nationalists), the progenitor of the dreaded UPA (*Ukrainska Povstanska Armiia* — Ukrainian Insurgent Army). And in that first year of my life on earth, Wołyń's native son, Taras Borovets, known as "Taras Bulba," sold his black soul to the devil.[39]

Of this I am certain: had my poor mother known of these historical events, she would not have sung the usual Polish lullaby over the cradle of her newborn son; rather, she would have hummed the traditional funeral dirge of Polish peasantry.

Ciężko ci jest na świat iść, ciężko i odchodzić.
Miałby człowiek woļ chcieć, chciałby się nie rodzić,
Chciałby minąć wojnę tę, co się żywot mieni,
Chciałby sobie cicho spać u matuchny ziemi. . . .

Winszowana dobra śmierć i letkie skonanie,
Winszowany cichy grób, co mi się dostanie,
Terazże się powróćcie, kędy wasza droga,
A ja będę cicho spał, na łonie u Boga. . . .[40]

2

Dies Irae

And now, my friends, a difficult task confronts me: to tell in human words of inhuman deeds, of the APOCALYPSE, of many grim riders upon many a pale horse, of countless seventh seals, of war and of destruction, of man's sheer inhumanity to man.

I do not speak only of Stalin's Communist Russia or Hitler's Nazi Germany. I speak of long forged friendships gone awry, of common neighbors killing . . . no, not killing; murdering . . . no, not murdering; *executing* one another; of the reaping and grinding of entire generations in the mills of ancient hatreds, of the steeping of our own fields with our own blood, of red poppies where once only white ones grew, of times when bloodstained mankind again merited salvation, of mass hysteria and sheer insanity under the guise of war.

All this surely must have been a sign of what was to follow, but for my own family, the rest, though on a much grander scale and much worse, was not as tragic as what transpired there in the vicinity of our own Ryświanka. The rest was done to us by strangers in strange lands. All I can say is that no matter how improbable my tale, how nightmarish, how fantastic, it is not even dimly as improbable, as nightmarish, as fantastic, as the plain realities of those apocalyptic years.

I know these are strong words. I know I will rekindle old hatreds. I know I sow the seeds of old contentions in new fields. I do not wish to speak. "Why stir up the past?" But if the truth must be told, let those concerned defend themselves as best they can. Let those who share my grief be still awhile. Speak, brother Ukrainians. I accuse your people—namely, those in the province of Wołyń and all of Poland's eastern territories who in the 1940s called themselves "nationalists" and their collaborators—of unspeakable atrocities and racially motivated genocide![1]

Even so, I do not hate you now. Perhaps I never did. Then, unlike my family and relations past the age of reason, I was too young. Today, as I reflect sorrowfully on the enormity of the evil which surrounded us, I still cannot bring myself to partake of that bitter cup, and I beg forgiveness for that deeply ingrained feeling that I fear to feel, and for my recounting of this episode to the countless generations which will follow.

This, then, is the story of our paradise lost and our consequent displacement.

> April 3, 1939—Hitler issues a directive to his commanding generals for "Operation White": war with Poland, the first country with which he signed a Pact of Non-Aggression.
>
> August 24, 1939—Germany and Russia sign a Non-Aggression Pact, part of which is a secret protocol for the reorganization of Central Europe. In effect, the Pact is nothing more than a clever bribe aimed at having Russia look the other way in exchange for its share of the spoils of war. For the fourth time, Poland is to be partitioned.
>
> September 1, 1939—Hitler's hungry war machine attacks Poland at dawn. The guns of September will not be silenced for another five and a half years.
>
> September 17, 1939—In violation of the Polish-Soviet Non-Aggression Pact, Russia also invades Poland.
>
> September 18, 1939—Soviet and German armies meet at Brest Litovsk. Ancient Poland is no more.

The rapid fall of Poland took the whole world by surprise. It was its first experience with *Blitzkrieg*. The swift fighter planes, the deadly bombers, the screaming Stukas, the rumbling tanks, the self-propelled, rapid-firing heavy artillery . . . the motorized army of a million and a half warriors left utter ruin and devastation in its passing. The hastily mobilized thirty-five divisions of ill-equipped Polish soldiers, the Polish Air Force (most of which never even left the ground), and the foolhardy, but valiant, Polish cavalry (*Pomorska Brygada*), which was cut down by German tanks in the Corridor, were no match for the Nazi forces.

Meanwhile, Poland's Western Allies, France and Britain, stood idly by. Earlier that year (March 31), after his rude awakening over Czechoslovakia, Neville Chamberlain told the House of Commons:

> In the event of any action which clearly threatened Polish independence and which the Polish Government accordingly considered it vital to resist with their national forces, His Majesty's Government would feel themselves bound at once to lend the Polish Government all support in their power. They have given the Polish Government an assurance of this effect. I may add that the French Government have authorized me to make it plain that they stand in the same position in this matter.[2]

Furthermore, on August 21 (one day before the first scheduled attack on Poland), England and Poland signed a Mutual-Assistance Pact.

France's commitment was specified in the Franco-Polish Military Convention of May 19, 1937. The French had agreed to "launch . . . offensive operations against limited objectives toward the third day after General Mobilization Day"—which was September 1, 1939. It was also agreed that "as soon as the principal German effort develops against Poland, France will launch an offensive action against Germany with the bulk of her forces, starting on the fifteenth day after the first day of the general French mobilization."[3]

If these promises had been carried out, the Second World War would have perhaps been averted. According to General Halder:

> The success against Poland was only possible by almost completely baring our Western border. If the French had seen the logic of the situation and had used the engagement of the German forces in Poland, they would have been able to cross the Rhine without our being able to prevent it and would have threatened the Ruhr area, which was the most decisive factor of the German conduct of the war.[4]

General Jodl was of the same opinion:

> If we did not collapse in 1939 that was due only to the fact that during the Polish campaign the approximately 110 French and British divisions in the West were held completely inactive against the 23 German divisions.[5]

And so was General Keitel:

> We soldiers had always expected an attack by France during the Polish campaign, and were very surprised that nothing happened. . . . A French attack would have encountered only a German military screen, not a real defense.[6]

A little more than two weeks after Hitler crossed our western border to occupy Poland and part of Lithuania, shortly before the day of Poland's final, heroic collapse, Russian armies crossed our border to the east in a frenzied effort to occupy the territories allotted to them by the August Agreement, which included Estonia, Latvia, Lithuania, Bessarabia, all the eastern provinces of Poland (Wilno, Nowogród, Polesie, Wołyń), three of its four southern provinces (Lwów, Stanisławów, Tarnopol), and its central province of Białystok. With them marched the Unholy Trinity: Death, Anguish, and Terror.

Stalin's justification for his failure to honor the Polish-Soviet Non-Aggression Pact and for his invasion of Poland was finalized on September 16-17:

> The Polish State has disintegrated and no longer existed; therefore, all agreements concluded with Poland were void . . . the Soviet Government

> considered itself obligated to intervene to protect its Ukrainian and White Russian brothers and make it possible for these unfortunate people to work in peace.[7]

The Polish ambassador in Moscow was then informed that Russia intended to maintain strict neutrality in the Polish conflict! German military records clearly indicate that this neutrality consisted of supplying Germany (from the summer of 1939 till June of 1941) with English zinc and rubber, 1,000,000 tons of grain, 500,000 tons of wheat, 900,000 tons of oil derivatives, 100,000 tons of cotton, 500,000 tons of phosphates, 10,000 tons of flax, 80 million *Reichsmarks'* worth of lumber, and an unspecified amount of manganese and platinum.[8]

According to Stalin, the joint aim of Germany and Russia was "to restore peace and order in Poland, which had been destroyed by the disintegration of the Polish State, and to help the Polish people to establish new conditions for its political life."[9] The September 29 "German-Soviet Boundary and Friendship Treaty" announced the new boundary of the "respective national interests" of Germany and Russia in "the former Polish State" and maintained that both Germany and Russia would reestablish "peace and order" and "assure the people living there a peaceful life in keeping with their national character."[10] But in a secret protocol, Hitler and Stalin agreed to subject Poland to a reign of terror in order to suppress its political and sociocultural life forever.

When the Russians first came to Ryświanka, they proceeded to build an airport in the sandy field near the village and to court my sisters. According to Aniela, after the project was completed:

> I, Stasia, and several of our neighbors' daughters went to work there and were befriended by Russian air force lieutenants. (Everyone there was some kind of an officer!) After work, in the evening, they would escort us home through the forest. The first time this happened, Father, upon hearing the commotion outside, looked out the window and frantically informed Mother that there were Russian soldiers in our yard with their daughters! Mother came running out and said, "Aniela, Stasia, come into the house this minute!"
>
> But one of the lieutenants said to her, "*Daragaya matushka, nye boysya. Pozvol'te dyevochkam yeshcho nemnozhko pozostat', sey chas paydut.*"[11]
>
> So poor Mother had to go back in. The soldiers remained for another hour talking, singing loudly in Polish, Ukrainian, and Russian, and trying to kiss us. After they departed, we also came into the house. No sooner did we cross the threshold than Father started to shout and scream: "Never bring those Russian soldiers here again! Let this be the last time!"
>
> And on he went until finally Mother calmed him down.

The next night, the Russians held a party to which we were all invited. After the party, the gentlemanly officers walked us home again but this time they stopped by the barn so as not to upset my parents. However, when *Burek* began barking viciously, they let us go home. Father, who was asleep, woke up and said to my mother, "From the way *Burek* was barking, I think the Russians must have been here again."

This went on every night for quite some time, and although our parents did not approve of our socializing with the soldiers, they did not forbid us to work at the airport either, because we were poor and needed the money.

Besides supplying their reluctantly and otherwise repatriated proletariat with new opportunities for work, leisure, and wages, the Russians also provided an annual subsidy of 2,000 rubles to all families with seven or more children, the youngest of whom was no older than five. Because of a rumor to the effect that the money came with a membership card to the Communist Party, not all eligible families signed up for this generous allotment. My father, however, had no such scruples, or if he did, the poverty of his household was more convincing than the rumor, which subsequently proved to be false anyway. With our 2,000 rubles we bought clothes. (The price of an ordinary coat at that time was 300 rubles.)

Thus, for us at least, the Russian invasion began innocently enough. Perhaps Nikolai Aseyev's poem in the September 18 edition of *Pravda* spoke the truth:

> The landlords' [*panski*] flag has been trampled underfoot,
> But you, Polish people, have not been humiliated...
> You toilers of Poland, do not believe the tale
> That we have stepped forward
> Just to add to your sorrows.
> If we have crossed the frontier,
> It is not to make you afraid;
> We do not want you to cringe to us;
> Proudly you can hold up your heads.[12]

We tried. But soon we noticed that from the fall of 1939 until we left Poland, no provisions of any kind were available in any of the stores in our area. We lived on what we grew and squirreled away. Some maintained that the Jews hoarded all the provisions. A more likely explanation is that they were confiscated first by the Russians and then by the Germans. Soldiers often took whatever they needed, whenever they needed it, from whomever happened to have it.

In this respect, the Soviets were more guilty than the Nazis—first, because by 1941 there was not much left to confiscate except for raw materials; and second, because by comparison, although much poorer than Germany, Poland's eastern territories were much better off in material goods, culture, and civil liberties than Russia. The destitute Russian invaders, whose life was characterized by poverty and deprivation of human rights, were simply amazed that the downtrodden masses they came to rescue were better off in every respect than they themselves. So, in truly Communistic fashion, they simply helped themselves to everything we had: food, animals, all the material products of our civilization and even the factories which produced those products—which they disassembled and shipped piecemeal to the heart of Russia. In other words, as so often happens, our "liberators" contributed immeasurably to our misery.

Just after my birth, in the spring of 1940, several armed Russian soldiers came to our house in evil tempers, swearing profusely at the quagmire which used to be our road and which, evidently, had just swallowed several of their army trucks. They "requested" the use of our chains and promised to leave us two sacks of sugar for our "generosity." We have often wondered where those two sacks of sugar were to have come from. If we had received them, perhaps I would now have at least an anecdotal answer to the question of what happened to all of Wołyń's provisions. As it was, we never got the sugar, and the "dirty Commies" kept our chains.

So, for a time at least, it was no worse living under this army than it had been under the other six which had occupied Wołyń on a rotating basis since the Bolshevik Revolution and the First World War: the German Army and Skoropads'kyi's[13] marionette government; the Russian Army in one part of Wołyń and that of Petliura[14] in another; the Polish Army; the Red Army in July of 1920; the Polish Army that August; and now the Russian Army again.[15]

But this time it really *was* different. To begin with, the NKVD massacred twenty-two thousand Polish officers and state officials in places like Kharkov, Mednoye, and Katyn.[16] Then, they deported to Germany all those even remotely connected with the Third Reich by virtue of their heredity. Next followed the execution of the Polish intelligentsia and the mass deportations of February, April, and June 1940, and July 1941. Among those deported were politicians, merchants, industrialists, civil servants, artisans, teachers, doctors, judges, lawyers, retired officers, landowners, political activists, foresters, and even the clergy. (This is what happened to all the families who employed my sisters as domestic servants. Ryświanka's Polish forester, Mr. Pinkowski, was given only two hours in which to pack his belongings.) The grand finale consisted of the systematic sweeping of the stage of all remaining indigenous civilians, not for the anticipated resettlement by Russian citizens, but as it turned out, for the theater of war.[17]

Often, there were no warnings, no accusations, no trials; no semblance of justice. People were simply rounded up like cattle, packed into cattle cars, and shipped off to Siberian exile or Kazakhstan. Over 150,000 people (Poles,

Ukrainians, and others) were deported from Wołyń alone. In all, over one and a half million people were forcefully displaced from Poland's eastern territories by the Soviets in their short, but brutal, reign.

> The population of Soviet-occupied Poland was unprepared for the cruelty that characterized the deportations. People were usually awakened in the early morning hours by squads of soldiers and local militiamen, given little time to pack, and quickly driven to the nearest railway station. There, freight trains awaited them. They froze in unheated cattle cars in February and suffocated in the June heat four months later. They were locked in for weeks with only meager rations of food and water, with a hole in the car's floor for all facilities. Men, women, and children of all ages were mixed together. Because even the sick and aged, as well as newborn infants, were put on the trains—there were no exemptions from the deportation order—many died, and the corpses traveled with the living before being discarded at some railway stop. . . . Although ethnic Poles constituted an absolute majority among the deportees, no social category or ethnic group from the area was spared. Almost one-third of the forcibly deported population was Jewish (52 percent Poles, 30 percent Jews, and 18 percent Ukrainians and Belorussians). A similar fraction of the deported, almost one-third of the total, consisted of peasants and workers.[18]

The residents of these territories were also cruelly tortured, mutilated, and murdered. Surprised by the rapid advance of the German armies into Western Ukraine, the NKVD began to slaughter the prisoners whom they did not have time to "evacuate." During the week of June 22, 1941:

> Major massacres occurred in the following places: in Lviv (about 1,500 victims), in Sambir (about 1,200), in Stanyslaviv (about 2,500), in Zolochiv (about 800), in Chortkiv (about 800), and Dobromyl (about 500). These figures do not include the many small towns and villages where dozens of prisoners died. Thus, an estimated 10,000 prisoners were killed in Galicia. In neighbouring Volhynia, particularly in the towns of Rivne and Lutske, about 5,000 more were executed.
>
> It was not only the numbers of the executed but the manner in which they died that shocked the populace. When the families of the arrested rushed to the prisons after the Soviet evacuation, they were aghast to find bodies so badly mutilated that many could not be identified. It was evident that many of the prisoners had been tortured before death; others were killed en masse. In Sambir on 26 June 1941 the NKVD dynamited two large cells crammed with female prisoners. In Stanyslaviv three huge cells were stacked to the ceiling with corpses that were so badly decomposed that no attempt was made to bury them. The townspeople simply cemented up the cells. In Zolochiv the people found cells full of mutilated

> bodies next to the torture chambers strewn with tongues, ears, eyes, and tufts of hair.[19]

All of this—with the exception of the grand finale, which was a long-range plan—was accomplished in twenty-one short months! Although not his grandest achievement, this purge will stand as an eternal testament to Stalin's unbending will and the power and the efficacy of his hammer and sickle, forged in the crucible of Ukrainian blood in the decade preceding 1939.

Were it not for these atrocities, we would have accepted the Russians for what they styled themselves to be: our liberators, or as they put it in the tons of propaganda leaflets which they dropped on our heads, our "allies"—passing through our territory on their way to fight the Germans. The August Agreement did not come to light until after the war.

> May 10, 1940—Hitler, elated by his speedy conquest of Poland, encouraged by the passivity of the French and British, secure on the east by his Pact of Non-Aggression, attacks the West.
>
> December 18, 1940—Hitler signs Directive 21: the invasion of Russia ("Operation Barbarossa").
>
> June 22, 1941—"The world [holds] its breath" as Hitler invades the Soviet Union at dawn.
>
> September, 1941—Hitler abandons his offensive against Moscow to secure the agricultural and industrial resources in the Ukraine.
>
> July 16, 1942—Hitler moves his headquarters to Vinnitsa in the Ukraine.

So it was that, just as we were about to be liberated to the frozen wastelands of Siberia by the Soviets, a new war broke out, this time all around us. Three million German soldiers, supported by 3,300 tanks, 600,000 other vehicles, over 7,000 pieces of artillery, 2,770 aircraft, and 625,000 horses,[20] swept through our land, accompanied by the same Unholy Trinity that had previously marched with the Russians.

The Nazis had a master plan similar to that of the Russians, but eminently more grandiose and at the same time more pragmatic. The Jewish and the Gypsy populations were to be killed outright. (This is what happened to the Jewish shopkeeper, Mr. Romanowski, and his family in Ryświanka.) Jews and Gypsies were considered vermin, unfit for work or slavery. This "final solution," this wholesale genocide systematically planned and reserved for them alone, was mainly carried out in the more than thirty principal extermination camps located within the German-occupied territories. (Exceptions were made, however; for instance, they could be worked to death, or used as guinea pigs in extermination camp experiments.)

All the rest, once their remaining intelligentsia were murdered, were either to be conscripted into the service of the German militia and police, as was the case with many cooperative Ukrainian Nationalists, or else to be deported to Germany to work in forced-labor camps, on farms and in private German households, as was the case with the Ukrainian, Polish, Russian, and other Slavic people. Once in Germany, however, they too could be worked to death, killed, or allowed to starve without remorse, since all non–Germans were considered to be *Untermenschen* (subhumans). In the New Order there was to be only one master race.

Heinrich Himmler and Reinhard Heydrich were assigned the task of liquidating the Jews. Hans Frank was to eliminate the intelligentsia, clergy, and nobility. Fritz Sauckel was put in charge of the slave program. This division of labor, however, was only nominal. The following testimony from the Nuremberg trial gives us a glimpse of the nature and the scope of this gruesome endeavor.

ON THE JEWISH QUESTION: THE "FINAL SOLUTION"

> I herewith commission you [Göring instructed Heydrich] to carry out all preparations with regard to . . . a *total solution* of the Jewish question in those territories of Europe which are under German influence. . . . [21]

> The *Einsatz* unit would enter a village or town and order the prominent Jewish citizens to call together all Jews for the purpose of "resettlement." They were requested to hand over their valuables and shortly before execution to surrender their outer clothing. They were transported to the place of executions, usually an antitank ditch, in trucks—always only as many as could be executed immediately. In this way it was attempted to keep the span of time from the moment in which the victims knew what was about to happen to them until the time of their actual execution as short as possible.
>
> Then they were shot, kneeling or standing, by firing squads in a military manner and the corpses thrown into the ditch. I never permitted the shooting of individuals, but ordered that several of the men should shoot at the same time in order to avoid direct personal responsibility. Other group leaders demanded that the victims lie down flat on the ground to be shot through the nape of the neck.[22]

> The actual purpose of these vans [gas vans for the execution of women and children] could not be seen from the outside. They looked liked closed trucks and were so constructed that at the start of the motor the gas [exhaust] was conducted into the van causing death in ten to fifteen minutes.[23]

> My foreman and I went directly to the pits. I heard rifle shots in quick succession from behind one of the earth mounds. The people who

had got off the trucks—men, women and children of all ages—had to undress upon the order of an S.S. man, who carried a riding or dog whip. They had to put down their clothes in fixed places, sorted according to shoes, top clothing and underclothing. I saw a heap of shoes of about 800 to 1,000 pairs, great piles of under-linen and clothing.

Without screaming or weeping these people undressed, stood around in family groups, kissed each other, said farewells and waited for a sign from another S.S. man, who stood near the pit, also with a whip in his hand. During the fifteen minutes that I stood near the pit I heard no complaint or plea for mercy. . . .

An old woman with snow-white hair was holding a one-year-old child in her arms and singing to it and tickling it. The child was cooing with delight. The parents were looking on with tears in their eyes. The father was holding the hand of a boy about 10 years old and speaking to him softly; the boy was fighting his tears. The father pointed to the sky, stroked his head and seemed to explain something to him.

At that moment, the S.S. man at the pit shouted something to his comrade. The latter counted off about twenty persons and instructed them to go behind the earth mound. . . . I well remember a girl, slim and with black hair, who, as she passed close to me, pointed to herself and said: "twenty-three years old."

I walked around the mound and found myself confronted by a tremendous grave. People were closely wedged together and lying on top of each other so that only their heads were visible. Nearly all had blood running over their shoulders from their heads. Some of the people were still moving. Some were lifting their arms and turning their heads to show that they were still alive. The pit was already two-thirds full. I estimated that it contained about a thousand people. I looked for the man who did the shooting. He was an S.S. man, who sat at the edge of the narrow end of the pit, his feet dangling into the pit. He had a tommy gun on his knees and was smoking a cigarette.

The people, completely naked, went down some steps and clambered over the heads of the people lying there to the place to which the S.S. man directed them. They lay down in front of the dead or wounded people; some caressed those who were still alive and spoke to them in a low voice. Then I heard a series of shots. I looked into the pit and saw that the bodies were twitching or the heads lying already motionless on the top of the bodies that lay beneath them. Blood was running from their necks.

The next batch was approaching already. They went down into the pit, lined themselves up against the previous victims and were shot.

[The next morning] I saw about thirty naked people lying near the pit. Some of them were still alive. . . . Later the Jews still alive were ordered to throw the corpses into the pit. Then they themselves had to lie down in this to be shot in the neck. . . . I swear before God that this is the absolute truth.[24]

The "Final Solution" of the Jewish question meant the complete exter-

> mination of all Jews in Europe. I was ordered to establish extermination facilities at Auschwitz in June 1941. At that time there were already in the General Government of Poland three other extermination camps: Belzec, Treblinka and Wolzek....
>
> I visited Treblinka to find out how they carried out their extermination. The camp commandant at Treblinka told me that he had liquidated 80,000 in the course of half a year. He was principally concerned with liquidating all the Jews from the Warsaw ghetto.
>
> He used monoxide gas and I did not think that his methods were very efficient. So when I set up the extermination building at Auschwitz, I used Zyklon B, which was a crystallized prussic acid which we dropped into the death chamber from a small opening. It took from three to fifteen minutes to kill the people in the death chamber, depending upon climatic conditions.
>
> We knew when the people were dead because their screaming stopped. We usually waited about a half hour before we opened the doors and removed the bodies. After the bodies were removed our special commandos took off the rings and extracted the gold from the teeth of the corpses.
>
> Another improvement we made over Treblinka was that we built our gas chambers to accommodate 2,000 people at one time, whereas at Treblinka their ten gas chambers only accommodated 200 people each.
>
> We had two S.S. doctors on duty at Auschwitz to examine the incoming transports of prisoners. These would be marched by one of the doctors, who would make spot decisions as they walked by. Those who were fit to work were sent into the camp. Others were sent immediately to the extermination plants. Children of tender years were invariably exterminated since by reason of their youth they were unable to work.
>
> Still another improvement we made over Treblinka was that at Treblinka the victims almost always knew that they were to be exterminated, while at Auschwitz we endeavored to fool the victims into thinking that they were to go through a delousing process. Of course, frequently they realized our true intentions and we sometimes had riots and difficulties. Very frequently women would hide their children under the clothes but of course when we found them we would send the children in to be exterminated.[25]

In all, of the ten million Jews living in the territories occupied by Hitler, about six million succumbed to the "final solution." Of this total, about half perished on Polish soil. (The presence of the large Jewish population in prewar Poland has but one reasonable explanation: relative tolerance. That is why 75 percent of all the Jews in the world today can trace their ancestry back to Poland. Poland's total war losses, representing about 23 percent of its 1939 population, were—proportionately speaking—the largest of any nation and included about 3.5 million non-Jews as well.) In addition, an estimated quarter of a million Gypsies perished throughout Europe between 1939 and 1945. Volhynia's toll was 4,000.[26]

ON THE SLAVIC QUESTION: ENSLAVEMENT

As for the ridiculous hundred million Slavs, we will mold the best of them to the shape that suits us, and we will isolate the rest of them in their own pigsties; and anyone who talks about cherishing the local inhabitant and civilizing him, goes straight off to a concentration camp![27]

The Slavs are to work for us. In so far as we don't need them, they may die. Therefore compulsory vaccination and German health services are superfluous. The fertility of the Slavs is undesirable. They may use contraceptives or practice abortion—the more the better. Education is dangerous. It is enough if they can count up to 100.... Every educated person is a future enemy. Religion we leave to them as a means of diversion. As for food they won't get any more than is absolutely necessary. We are the masters. We come first.[28]

We are the Master Race and must govern hard but just.... I will draw the very last out of this country. I did not come to spread bliss.... The population must work, work, and work again.... We definitely did not come here to give out manna. We have come here to create the basis for victory.

We are a master race, which must remember that the lowliest German worker is racially and biologically a thousand times more valuable than the population here.[29]

It is indispensable to bear in mind that the Polish gentry must cease to exist; however cruel this may sound, they must be exterminated wherever they are....

There should be one master only for the Poles, the German. Two masters, side by side, cannot and must not exist. Therefore, all representatives of the Polish intelligentsia are to be exterminated. This sounds cruel, but such is the law of life.[30]

The men capable of leadership in Poland must be liquidated. Those following them ... must be eliminated in their turn. There is no need to burden the Reich with this ... no need to send these elements to Reich concentration camps.[31]

Poland can only be administered by utilizing the country through means of ruthless exploitation, deportation of all supplies, raw materials, machines, factory installations, etc., which are important for the German war economy, availability of all workers for work within Germany, reduction of the entire Polish economy to absolute minimum necessary for bare existence of the population, closing of all educational institutions, especially technical schools and colleges in order to prevent the growth of the new Polish intelligentsia. Poland shall be treated as a colony. The Poles shall be the slaves of the Greater German Reich.[32]

> Army Group Center intends to apprehend forty to fifty thousand youths from the age of 10 to 14 . . . and transport them to the Reich. The measure was originally proposed by the Ninth Army. . . . It is intended to allot these juveniles primarily to the German trades as apprentices. . . . This action is being greatly welcomed by the German trade since it represents a decisive measure for the alleviation of the shortage of apprentices.
>
> This action is not only aimed at preventing a direct reinforcement of the enemy's strength but also as a reduction of his biological potentialities.[33]

> In the usual limitless mistreatment of Slavic peoples there were applied the "enlistment methods" which recall the darkest pages of the slave trade. There started a regular man hunt, and without regard to health, condition, or age, the people were deported to Germany.[34]

> The wild and ruthless man hunt, as exercised everywhere in towns and country, in streets, squares, stations, even in churches, at night in homes, has badly shaken the feeling of security of the inhabitants. Everybody is exposed to the danger of being seized anywhere and at any time by the police, suddenly and unexpectedly, and of being sent to an assembly camp. None of his relatives knows what has happened to him.[35]

The code name for the massive kidnapping operation was "Hay Action." In the larger towns people were simply abducted off the streets as they came out of churches and theaters. Sometimes a section of town was sealed off and all able-bodied men and women were nabbed. Villages were surrounded, searched and raped. When resistance was encountered the villages were burned to the ground and their inhabitants carried off. In rural communities, lists were drawn up (there were always lists and meticulous record keeping) and names were selected of who from which family was to report for deportation. Those who resisted or failed to show up at the appointed time and place were simply executed on the very spot where they were caught. All had to carry identification papers to facilitate the process. German transports waited patiently in all designated cities, towns, and villages. When enough people arrived, they were loaded and carted off to Germany in freight-train boxcars for slave labor. All in all, about 2.8 million *Ostarbeiter* (eastern workers) were deported to Germany as slaves of the Third Reich. Of these, about 2.3 million were from the Ukraine.[36]

At the beginning of it all, totally oblivious of what was transpiring in the castles of the high and mighty—of the secret courtships and the mutual treacheries, of the cloaked ambitions and the endless memorandums—we, the chesspawns of the masters of war, could offer no explanation for our rapidly deteriorating condition save that of human folly or divine judgment on sinful mankind. It was as if some mighty warlock had cast an evil spell upon the world, enveloping it in an impenetrable shroud of darkness and iniquity.

How shallow was our understanding! How narrow our perspective! How provincial our *Weltanschauung!* How dim our vision of the horsemen in the Seventh Heaven and of the Grand Design!

Who among us could know of the macabre Master Plan? Who could possibly imagine such unearthly things? What ancient prophecies could have possibly described in human words this kind of Armageddon?

We, simple people of the earth, simply reaped the bitter harvest of each unfolding scroll. We simply suffered one day at a time.

Life in our village under both the Russian and the German occupations was a nightmare. All the stores were empty, all provisions confiscated, all necessities begrudgingly rationed. At the end of 1939 we were already splitting wooden matches into four and waiting two days in relief lines for half a gallon of kerosene. To keep from starving, we hid farm produce in the fields and woods. Life as we knew it simply ceased to exist. God only knows how we managed to survive there until August of 1943.

Yet it was neither the brutal policies of the Russians and the Germans, nor our relentless quest for life's necessities that constituted our greatest cross. Our greatest cross was our fear of the roving bands of Ukrainian Nationalists who, after the German invasion of the Soviet Union, in the immoral climate created by the Gestapo, began a systematic execution of the Russians in 1941, of the Jews in 1942, and of the Poles in 1943.[37] With them, too, marched the Unholy Three. More death. More anguish. More terror.

> As soon as the German armies entered our territory, they began to murder the Jews and the Russians. The Ukrainians helped them in this endeavor. Many of them signed up for the German Army and police. Then, in the fall of 1942, the Ukrainians began to slaughter Polish people and to burn their homes and villages. They operated primarily in the form of bands consisting, at times, of up to 200 men or more. At first the attacks were carried out at night, then, both night and day, every night and day.[38]

> The Ukrainians murdered many Polish people and burnt our homes and villages.[39]

The reasons for this wholesale fratricide lie in the post–World War I history of Wołyń and the German political ideology, carefully worked out in the 1930s and implemented in 1941, relative to the *Reichskommissariat Ukrainen* which included the *General Bezirk Wolhynien und Podolien*.[40]

The acquisition of the province of Wołyń after the First World War (Treaty of Riga, 1921) increased Poland's territorial holdings by 9.1 percent. It also gave Poland its number one producer and exporter of wheat—a rather surprising fact, since only one-half of Wołyń is dry land and only a half of that is suitable for farming. Thus, 75 percent of the acquired terrain consisted predominantly of forests, but also of wind-swept deserts, marshes, bogs, swamps and quagmires. This provincial landscape, together with its 416,000 horses (in 1938), was to play an important role in the subsequent formation of both terrorist and partisan movements.

Demographically speaking, in 1939, Wołyń's eleven counties contained just over two million inhabitants, or 6.4 percent of all the residents within Polish boundaries. In terms of density, there were approximately 58 people per each square kilometer of land (residing primarily in rural areas), but they were not of similar ethnic background. The distribution of these people by mother tongue and place of residence was as follows:

PERCENT OF POPULATION ACCORDING TO MOTHER TONGUE

	Total	*Polish*	*Ukrainian*	*Russian*	*German*	*Yiddish/ Hebrew*	*Other*
Wołyń	100	16.6	68.0	1.6	2.3	9.9	1.6
Towns	100	27.5	16.1	5.6	1.1	48.6	1.1
Villages	100	15.1	75.2	1.1	2.4	4.5	1.7

Thus, it is clear that the Polish people constituted a minority especially in the villages. A curious paradox emerges, however, when we look at Wołyń's agricultural patterns:

OWNERSHIP OF FARMS (PER 1,000) RELATIVE TO THEIR SIZE

Size of Farms (in hectares)	*Polish*	*Ukrainian*
0–1	84	107
1–2	130	173
2–5	337	405
5–7	144	146
7–10	120	103
10–15	116	47
15–20	39	12
20–30	22	5
30–50	8	2
Total	1,000	1,000

As the table shows, the differences become quite significant in the 10–50 hectares range, in disfavor of the Ukrainians. That is to say, for every 66 Ukrainian farmsteads of 10 hectares or more, there were 185 Polish ones (per 1,000 farms).

There is little doubt that this inequitable distribution was the direct consequence of the Polish government's land-grant policy throughout its newly acquired territories. By means of that policy, the Piłsudski administration sought to create an efficient and productive strata of Polish *Grossbaueren* (large farm owners) such as those existing in Germany.

Moreover, although many Polish people had already lived in this area for countless generations, the Polish government wished to resettle many more of its loyal citizens there, about six million more, in order to assure itself of Western Ukraine's and Western Byelorussia's allegiance to their "fatherland," to have the necessary votes in referendums favorable to itself, and to secure the Polish eastern border against Soviet aggression. Such a grandiose plan would inevitably necessitate the assimilation, the resettlement, or the extermination of the indigenous Ukrainian and White-Russian populations.

This pattern in itself was nothing new for Europe. It was the standard procedure whenever one or another boundary of its many feuding nations got rearranged. What was new, however, was that the land had been given predominantly (but not exclusively) to deserving veterans of war without any regard to their agricultural experience or qualifications. This unfortunate lack of selectivity proved to be disastrous. Instead of a cradle of prolific farmsteads, Poland's eastern territories soon became a nest of small Polish fiefdoms with field hands, servants and maids drawn generally, but not solely, from the Ukrainian peasantry and with little concern for the productive potential of the land. Instead of allegiance, there was now a great deal of resentment, not only on the part of the Ukrainians but also on the part of the resident Polish peasantry, toward the Piłsudski administration and its landed gentry—the *szlachta* or the *polskie pany,* as they were called. As A. Zalewski once put it, there came a time when "the masses looked upon our government and our armies with both curiosity and suspicion. What do they bring with them this time? Lordship, slavery, hetmanship, anarchy? Or peace, order, and equality under the law for all? The masses, nourished over the course of centuries on suspicion and hatred toward all that is Polish, equated the Polish rule with the rule of the aristocracy."[41] The land-grant program was discontinued, at least in principle, in 1924. Nevertheless, statistics indicate that in 1939, there were 7,800 of such settlers in Wołyń with parcels of land in excess of 10 hectares.

Although a veteran of the First World War in good standing, Józef Piotrowski was not one of the fortunate land-grant recipients. It was just as well, because my mother always said that he was not a very good farmer. However, this did not prevent my father from harboring a certain resentment toward the Piłsudski administration for overlooking his generous contribution to his country during World War I. For that reason alone, he could not be counted among the true Polish loyalists. But then again, neither did he side with the Soviets, and less so the Germans. Like so many others in Wołyń, he was first and foremost a Wołynian.

Be that as it may, my father became much less resentful of his bureaucratic anonymity and unacknowledged merit after 1939, for in the long run, that anonymity proved to be our salvation. By mid-1941, most of the land-grant recipients in all of the Polish eastern provinces were either dead or in Siberian exile.

The Polish government's policy in respect to politics, education, and religion in the annexed territories also contributed to the problem of a smooth transition.

By 1939, the governance structure of Wołyń was dominated by the Polish minority. Out of 103 chief officers of a cluster of villages (*wójt*), 81 were Polish and 19 Ukrainian. At the administrative levels of village councils (*gmina*), 69 percent of the offices were in the hands of the Polish people and 26 percent in the hands of the Ukrainians. On the county level (*powiat*), the proportion was 75 percent to 16 percent, again in favor of the Poles. The situation was even worse in the towns and cities.

It was the same story in respect to public education. In 1936, there were 1,732 public schools, of which only 11 were Ukrainian. Whereas 96 percent of the Polish children attended classes, only 69 percent of the Ukrainian children did so—often having to go to Polish schools. Is it any wonder, then, that the illiteracy rate within the Ukrainian population was significantly higher than that within the Polish? It may be added, however, that the overall illiteracy rate in Wołyń, especially in the villages, was also quite high.[42]

Finally, although Eastern Orthodoxy was the prevalent religion in Wołyń (69.8 percent in 1939), Roman Catholicism (16.2 percent) was the religion of the Polish people, the privileged people, the people with political power and education.[43] Catholicism was synonymous with the Polish rule and the Polish rule, as we have seen, with the rule of the aristocracy. Many Ukrainians, therefore, converted to Catholicism in order to improve their own social standing—to become eligible for public office, for farmland, for employment. In 1923, there were a total of 82 Catholic parishes in Wołyń with 193,481 members. By 1937, the number of parishes increased to 133 and the number of parishioners to 311,133. In 1935, the Roman curia in Łuck reported the annual number of converts to be 3,400.[44]

Meanwhile, shortly after gaining military control over Western Ukraine in 1919, and in violation of the Versaille treaty on the treatment of minorities, the Polish government began to take a series of retaliatory measures against the Ukrainians who had fought against them in the recent Polish-Ukrainian (1918–19) war. Among these measures was the arrest and deportation of several thousand Ukrainians, as well as the promulgation of policies antithetic to Ukrainian sociopolitical life.[45] This in turn prompted Ukrainian strikes, boycotts, demonstrations, and "isolated acts of terror, assassinations, bombings, and sabotage directed by the UVO [*Ukrainska Viiskova Orhanizatsiia*—Ukrainian Military Organization] during the 1920's against Polish authority."[46]

This, in turn, prompted a "pacification" action by Polish authorities which "took the form of beatings and arrests leveled against Ukrainians especially in villages, and the sacking and closing of Ukrainian reading rooms, cultural centers, newspaper offices, and cooperatives."[47] The newly created militant organization, OUN, responded to these repressive measures with increasing acts of violence in the 1930s, with the result that its leaders were put in jail—and not just any jail, but Bereza Kartuska.[48] Thus by 1939, the seismometer readings on Western Ukraine's frozen volcano of anger and bitter resentment, which spanned the four Polish provinces of Wołyń, Lwów, Tarnopol and Stanisłlawów, were already off the charts. Approximately 2.85 million Poles and 5 million Ukrainians inhabited these regions.

In all of this, it is clear that the policies of the Polish government in these territories during the interwar years, whether cunningly proactive or legitimately reactive, only served to fan the already hot embers of Ukrainian nationalism.[49] And then came September 1, 1939 . . . and six-plus years of living hell.

But would the subsequent "dictatorship of the proletariat" be any better? When the Russian armies swept through Wołyń in 1939, they were greeted throughout the countryside by people with homemade signs which read, "Welcome brothers, we have waited for you these twenty years to free us from the rule of the *polskie pany*!"[50] On November 1, on the basis of a "referendum" conducted by the Russian occupation authorities, Wołyń became incorporated into the western part of the Ukrainian Soviet Socialist Republic.

It should come as no surprise that the Soviet rule—as administered by the chief of the NKVD, Lavrenti Beria—was no bed of roses. Yet, even as the now-united but still-enslaved Ukraine suffered, another "liberator" was preparing to make his move.

> In the Soviet Union, we found on our arrival a population weary of Bolshevism, which waited longingly for new slogans holding out a prospect of a better future for them. . . . The population greeted us with joy as liberators and placed themselves at our disposal.[51]

In the Ukraine, the advancing German armies were greeted with bread and salt, the traditional welcome reserved for friends. *Generaloberst* Heinz Guderian, Commander of Panzer Group 2, recalled that "women came out from their villages on to the very battlefield bringing wooden platters of bread and butter and eggs and, in my case at least, refused to let me move on before I had eaten."[52] The Führer's guard unit, the *Leibstandarte-SS "Adolf Hitler,"* was met in the south by "laughing and cheering people."[53] According to Goebbels, "The inhabitants of Ukraine were more than inclined at the beginning to regard the Führer as the savior of Europe and to welcome the German Wehrmacht most cordially."[54]

To this day, the full extent of that miscalculated welcome has never been adequately documented. Yet, as one peruses the historical literature of the Second World War, here and there troubling footnotes appear. A Ukrainian "catechism" published in 1940 states that the Ukrainian people belong to the "Aryan" race.[55] Orthodox clergymen declare themselves subservient to the Teutonic legions. Periodic attempts are made to form an anti-Russian, pro-German Ukrainian Army. Large numbers of Ukrainians desert to the German Army. Many are conscripted into the Ukrainian militia and aid in the extermination of the Jews (as was the case in Dubno).[56] Many assist the military and SS detachments that destroy literally thousands of East European towns and villages together with their unarmed civilian populations. Many are sent to Trawniki, the SS training center for concentration camp guards. In Treblinka alone, over 100 Ukrainians assist the Nazis in their sadistic endeavors; in Belzec and Sobibor there were hundreds more.[57] My sister Anna recalls simply that "the Ukrainians collaborated with the Germans."

There were several reasons why the Ukrainians, perhaps more than anyone else in Eastern Europe, initially were anxious to collaborate with the Germans.

First (in Eastern Ukraine) was their hatred of the Soviet system (especially the collectives) and of Stalin's harsh rule. Between 1929 and 1934, during Stalin's unrelenting war against the Ukrainian peasantry, twenty million farms were collectivized and fifteen million people perished—half in Siberia, to which they had been deported, and half in the Ukraine. In 1932-33 alone, the years of the artificially induced Ukrainian famine, six million people starved to death. (Some estimate the number to have reached ten million!) It was indeed a "harvest of sorrow."[58] Moreover, the "Great Terror" of 1936-38, which struck both at the Ukrainian leadership and peasantry and which produced the mass graves at Vinnitsa, was not soon to be forgotten.

Second (in Western Ukraine) was their hatred of the Polish and the subsequent Soviet rule—the reasons for which have already been stated.[59]

Third (in all of Ukraine) was their hatred of the Jews. For both economic and religious reasons, the Ukraine has always been a hotbed of anti-Semitism. The first of the great European pogroms transpired on Ukrainian soil. On this point, although not all and not alone, they and the Nazis were of like mind but not quite of the same disposition.[60]

And fourth and foremost, especially in fiercely nationalistic Western Ukraine, was their hope—during the Second World War—of securing an "independent Ukrainian State . . . in . . . alliance with the German Reich" even as Alfred Rosenberg had promised in 1941.

Moreover, their relatively benign treatment at the hands of the German occupation forces during World War I bolstered their belief that Nazi Germany was the lesser of the twin great evils between which they had to chose. After the catastrophic events of the quarter century preceding 1941, little doubt remained that the primary foe of the Ukrainian people was the Soviet Union.

According to Otto Bräutigam, the Ukraine was God's gift to Nazi Germany.

> Our policy [was intended to make] the Ukraine a counterweight against mighty Russia, against Poland and the Balkans, and a bridge to the Caucasus.[61]

Rosenberg couldn't agree more. As early as 1927 he noted that the "natural hostility between Ukrainians and Poles" would serve German interests quite nicely:

> Once we have understood that the elimination of the Polish State is the first demand of Germany, *an alliance between Kiev and Berlin* and the creation of a common border become a necessity of people and state for a future German policy.[62]

Fourteen years later, Rosenberg got his "historic" opportunity for translating his dubious insight into a policy recommendation. On April 7, 1941, he hoped that

> . . . an independent Ukrainian State, with all its consequences, [would emerge] in close [and] indissoluble alliance with the German Reich.[63]

By May of that year, however, perhaps because he did not think Hitler would approve of his scheme, he drafted instructions to the future German ruler of the Ukraine which contained a two-stage approach. First, during the war the Ukraine was to provide Germany with food and raw materials; thereafter, "a free Ukrainian State in closest alliance with the Greater German Reich" would emerge. Meanwhile, he urged all "Ukrainian writers, scholars, and politicians" to "work for a revival of Ukrainian historical consciousness, so as to overcome what Bolshevik-Jewish pressure had destroyed in Ukrainian *Volkstum* in these years."[64]

Disregarding Rosenberg's May memorandum, the Ukrainian Nationalists issued a Ukrainian declaration of independence on June 30, 1941, in Lwów, just 175 kilometers southwest of Równe, the Ukrainian "capital" of *Reichskommissar* Erich Koch. On that day, the declaration was also promulgated over the radio by Iaroslav Stetsko in the hope that the German authorities would be more inclined to approve a *fait accompli*. "The newly created Ukrainian nation," reads the declaration, "will work closely with the national socialist Germans who, under the leadership of their leader, Adolf Hitler, are creating a new order in Europe and the world. . . ." The proclamation ended with the following words: "Long live free Ukraine! Long live the Great German Reich and its leader, Adolf Hitler!"[65]

During the ceremonies, the chaplain of the *Nachtigall* battalion, O. Hryniuk, in the name of Roman Shukhevych, offered his regards to the Reich. Congratulations were also sent to Stepan Bandera, the leader of the OUN-B (the Bandera contingent of the Organization of Ukrainian Nationalists), to the "Creator of Great Germany Adolf Hitler," to the "Famous German Army," and to the Metropolitan Sheptytsky. In attendance were several high officers of the German Army. Hans Koch, who spoke in their name, urged the Ukrainian Nationalists to "fruitful" activity as well as the closest collaboration with Hitler's army.[66]

Furthermore, a provisional government was established of which Iaroslav Stetsko was to be the "Prime Minister." Metropolitan Sheptytsky, a vigorous supporter of the Ukrainian Nationalist movement, blessed the endeavor by promulgating a pastoral letter in which he naively exhorted the Ukrainian people to be thankful to their "liberators" and to support the newly proclaimed government: "We greet the victorious German Army as deliverer from the enemy. We render our obedient homage to the government which has been erected. We recognize Mr. Iaroslav Stets'ko as Head of the State Administration of the Ukraine."[67] These are not the words of a poor illiterate peasant, but of a high-ranking church official!

Shortly thereafter (July 6, 1941), the Ukrainian Nationalist leaders (including Andrii Melnyk) addressed an appeal to Hitler through the *Abwehr*[68] which ended with the following words: "We request that we be allowed to march shoulder to shoulder with the legions of Europe and with our liberator, the German Wehrmacht, and therefore we ask to be permitted to create a Ukrainian military formation."[69]

At the same time a newspaper called *Nova Ukraïna* appeared preaching Ukrainian national consciousness. Leaflets were printed (probably in Germany) exalting the "German-Ukrainian Alliance." "Down with Bolshevism!" they shouted, showing a green-sleeved arm demolishing a red flag with the hammer and sickle. "Our alliance will give happiness to all the nations of Europe!" they proclaimed. "None will lay down his arms while our Ukraine is enslaved by the Bolsheviks!"[70]

In the end, however, those Ukrainians who, for whatever reason, sympathized and collaborated with the Nazis—together with all the others who sought to court Satan to their own advantage—wound up disillusioned. They, too, were considered to be *Untermenschen*. In keeping with the Nazi racial ideology and its "Extraordinary Pacification Action," Göring once advised Koch to "kill all the men in the Ukraine . . . and then to send in the SS stallions."[71] As we have already seen, by the time it was all over, nearly 2.8 million (some set the number at 4 million) people from the Soviet Union—mostly from the Ukraine—were shipped westward in boxcars to toil as *Ostarbeiter*. The Germans did not distinguish among Poles, Ukrainians, Russians, and the rest. Slavs, all Slavs, were considered subhuman.

> Basically it is important that we dismember this big cake in a handy way so that we can: 1) occupy it, 2) administer it, 3) exploit it.[72]

> Gentlemen: I am known as a brutal dog. Because of this reason I was appointed as Reichskommissar of the Ukraine. Our task is to suck from the Ukraine all the goods we can get hold of, without consideration of the feeling or the property of the Ukrainians.
>
> Gentlemen: I am expecting from you the utmost severity towards the native population.[73]

> With the inherent instinct of the Eastern peoples, the primitive man soon found out that for Germany the slogan "Liberation from Bolshevism" was only a pretext to enslave the Eastern peoples according to her own methods. . . . The worker and peasant soon perceived that Germany did not regard them as partners of equal rights but considered them only as the objective of her political and economic aims. . . . With unequaled presumption, we put aside all political knowledge and . . . treat the peoples of the occupied Eastern territories as "Second-Class Whites" to whom Providence has merely assigned the task of serving as slaves for Germany.[74]

> The forty million Ukrainians who greeted us enthusiastically as liberators, are today quite indifferent to us and gravitate to the enemy's camp.[75]

Although the German political ideology in regard to the *Reichskommissariat Ukrainen* sought to court the common man directly through its massive propaganda machine, its chief aim was always to exploit the existing inter–Slavic conflicts to its own advantage by organizing, training, and arming both military and para-military Ukrainian detachments which would serve the German war effort.

The natural candidates for this diversionary activity were the many Ukrainian Nationalist groups which were already living in and operating out of Germany. Their members were actively recruited not only from all of Western Ukraine but from a number of other European countries as well. In 1929, these various factions consolidated into the OUN,[76] whose slogan, *Samostiyna Ukraïna* (Independent Ukraine), found a sympathetic ear among some elements of the oppressed Ukrainian population, especially in Wołyń.[77]

The plan to incorporate the OUN into the German war effort was discussed by Hitler and Canaris on a train in Ilnau on September 12, 1939. According to Canaris, at that time Hitler was already contemplating the creation of a nominally "free" Galicia under German auspices. Canaris, who was in contact with and supported the leadership of the Ukrainian Nationalist movement, wrote in his journal that, in the event of a German advance on Western Ukraine:

> I would have to make appropriate preparations with the Ukrainians so that, should this alternative become real, the Mel'nyk Organization (OUN) can produce an uprising which would aim at the annihilation of the Jews and Poles.[78]

Thus, the Nazis intended to strike a deal with an already existing Ukrainian organization within Germany in return for a promise of a "free" Ukraine alongside the victorious Third Reich—a clever lie which they knew would appeal to the interests of the Ukrainian Nationalists and their sympathizers. Meanwhile, the German radio station in Vienna began (in the fall of 1938) to transmit a stream of propaganda to the Ukrainians in the Soviet Union portraying Germany as a champion of an independent Ukrainian state.[79] All this concerted effort on the part of the Third Reich bore abundant fruit.

In general, the pro-Nazi Ukrainian military and para-military formations which emerged during World War II can be divided into three broad categories: those established by the Ukrainians in cooperative agreement with the German authorities; those organized by the German authorities themselves; and the underground units which had their own agenda but were careful not to cross the German authorities.

The first category consisted of the Nationalist Military Detachments (VVN—organized in 1939 by the OUN), the Brotherhoods of Ukrainian Nationalists (DUN—created in 1941 before the invasion of Russia, consisting of the *Nachtigall* and the *Roland),* the Galician Division of the *Waffen-SS* (SS Volunteer Division "Galizien") organized in mid-1943, Ukrainian Units in the Russian Liberation Army (ROA), the Ukrainian Liberation Army (UVV—organized in 1944, consisting of the former Ukrainian units of the ROA), and the Ukrainian National Army (UNA—formed in early 1945 and consisting of the remnants of all the above-mentioned units).

To the second category belonged all the guard, labor, and police units such as the *Werkschuts* (factory police, plant guards), *Bahnschuts* (railway security police), *Baudienst* (compulsory labor service), *Hilfswillige* (volunteer auxiliaries in German armed forces), as well as the Ukrainian auxiliary police, the *Schutzmannschaften*.

The third category consisted of various underground units, the foremost of which was that headed by Borovets, variously named the UPA (in 1943 this designation embraced all the Ukrainian Nationalist groups), *Poliska Sich*, and the Ukrainian National Revolutionary Army (UNRA).[80]

The main purpose of the following section is not to "prove" that there was a conspiracy between the Nazis and the Ukrainian Nationalists. Rather, it is to make it abundantly clear that without the sanction of Nazi Germany, the mass murder of the civilian populations by the Ukrainian Nationalists, alluded to in this chapter and described in greater detail in the next, simply could not have occurred in Western Ukraine. Since it did occur, it is reasonable to assume, even without evidence, that the Nazis had something to gain in exchange for allowing the Ukrainian Nationalists to have a free hand, that some type of collusion must have existed between them—the opposite of "collusion," in this case, being "collision."

In point of fact, these same Ukrainian Nationalists were relatively quiescent under the interwar Polish regime, under the wartime regime of Russia, and under the postwar era of Communist domination. Why were they so "active" under the Nazi regime? Was Nazi Germany any weaker than either Poland or Russia in its dealings with the residents of these (same) occupied territories? Was it helpless in the face of the Ukrainian Nationalist organizations? Was it obliged to compromise its fascist ideology in order to accommodate their demands? Then, why did it look the other way? There can only be one reasonable answer to that pointed and barbed question: there was a conspiracy. No other explanation makes any sense.

Here, as elsewhere in this work, the words "conspiracy," "collaboration," "alliance," "collusion," and any other designation which links the Nazis with the Ukrainian Nationalists, must be properly understood. Irrespective of Rosenberg's grandiose plans backed by empty promises, I am not so naive as to suggest that the Nazis and the Ukrainian Nationalists had a similar objective in mind: the creation of a German-Ukrainian empire or some such idiotic notion. No, each side had its own politico-military agenda, and each side tried to use the other for its own ends. In the long run, these discordant melodies could never be harmonized. Or, as Dallin puts it: "Sooner or later, the marriage of convenience was bound to result in serious domestic discord."[81]

For the Germans, the objective was the conquest and subjugation of the whole of Russia. This demanded manpower, diversionary tactics, and the primordial element of all evil, chaos.

First of all, it was thought that the local Ukrainian organizations could be used to neutralize the partisan threat. As things stood, the Germans did not consider the factional partisans as a real danger to the almighty *Wehrmacht*. To be sure they would be a prick, an aggravating scruple in the high-stepping boots of the Nazis, a bothersome nuisance. However, the potential for a real military threat was always there. An armed, disciplined cadre of pro–Nazi Ukrainians, it was thought, would prevent the formation of a united partisan front in the East which could cause havoc on the heels of the Moscow-bound German Army, specifically in the communication and transportation networks.

Secondly, such a contingent could be used, in conjunction with the Gestapo, to create a reign of terror in Western Ukraine which would further weaken anti–German resistance. The Nazis knew full well that each time a village burned or a civil-defense center was attacked, the "soft-hearted" partisans would inevitably abandon their constant dogging of the German armies engaged in "Operation Barbarossa" in order to render assistance to the helpless civilians: old men, women of all ages, children. It was the old military strategy that never fails: placing civilians at risk, nay, at the front, in the line of fire.

And thirdly, the reign of terror would serve another sinister agenda as well: the creation of a pool of displaced persons for the slave-labor camps of the Third Reich.

The Ukrainian Nationalist agenda was simple enough: in return for their assistance both military and diversionary, they hoped to obtain a *Samostiyna Ukraïna*. This in turn, at least in their minds, necessitated a policy of ethnic cleansing. Then as now, for so many countries, the idea of a pluralistic society seemed absurd, a contradiction in terms.

Four distinct periods can be identified in conjunction with this German-Ukrainian Nationalist conspiracy.[82]

1. SEPTEMBER 1939–JUNE 1941. During this time, the Nazis supported all OUN activities; trained cadres of Ukrainian Nationalists for the army, the party, the military police and diversionary forces; and actively supported and protected all Ukrainian emigrants. At this time, there were over one-half million Ukrainians living within the newly created "General Government"—the Nazi occupied section of Poland.[83] According to Armstrong:

> As early as 1940 the Germans surreptitiously formed military training units for Ukrainians. Their enlistment was concealed by official statements that the units were *Volksdeutsche* (ethnic Germans) only, and the purpose of the units was disguised by designating the Reichsarbeitdienst (Reich Labor Service) to be the supervising agency in the Generalgouvernement. Under this camouflage large numbers of Ukrainians were trained for police duty. More advanced training was carried out in Germany under direction of the Wehrmacht. In a number of camps instructors for future Ukrainian police units and interpreters for liaison with the German army were prepared.[84]

According to Dallin,

> In 1939, as the prospects of war against Poland increased, the Ukrainian collaborators were brought into action. First they appeared in the short-lived Carpatho-Ukrainian government of March 1939. Then the Abwehr secretly organized a regiment of OUN members, known clandestinely as *Bergbauernhilfe* (BBH, literally Mountain-Peasants' Help). Holding open the possibility of a future "Ukrainian state," the Abwehr groomed the Ukrainian unit both for action as a legion and for a revolt behind enemy lines in case of a German attack on Poland.[85]

The problem of moving the German-trained personnel into the Soviet Union before the invasion was greatly facilitated by German-Soviet Boundary and Friendship Treaty signed in September 1939. In one of its protocols, this treaty provided for the return of ethnic Germans, Byelorussians, and Ukrainians to their respective homelands.

Moreover, in the spring of 1941 an agreement was reached between the directors of the OUN-B and certain *Wehrmacht* officers to allow the Bandera party to carry on political activities in the Ukrainian lands which would soon be occupied by Germany.[86]

After Germany's attack on Russia, regular Ukrainian military units arrived in the Ukraine together with the German Army. These units, specifically in the notorious *Nachtigall* and *Roland* death battalions organized by OUN-B in conjunction with *Abwehr*, belonged to the specially formed Brandenburg Division. Among the many bloody deeds of the *Nachtigall* (Nightingale), for example, was the murder of the professors at the University of Lwów on July 4, 1941, and the extermination of the Jewish and Polish populations in the larger towns and settlements, including those in the south of Wołyń.[87]

The *Pokhidni hrupy* (expeditionary groups), organized by the OUN in its Western European bases, also entered the Ukraine with the *Wehrmacht*. Their task was to spread nationalist propaganda and to help inaugurate a new Ukrainian administration.[88] Moreover, the Ukrainian *Schutzmann* Police—the *Black Police*—was put in charge of the towns and villages and was furthermore complemented by military guard units known as the *Ukrainische SS Wachmannschaft*.

II. JULY 1941–SEPTEMBER 1942. At the height of their military power, the Nazis dispensed with all pretenses, refused to honor any of their promises in respect to the creation of a *Samostiyna Ukraïna* and declared the whole of Ukraine, with its vast territory and its abundant agricultural resources, to be a part of the Third Reich—an ancient German land which was now to be colonized by the *Herrenvolk* in need of more *Lebensraum*.

Perhaps Rosenberg's *Ostministerium* was still sympathetic with the nationalistic ambitions of the Ukrainians, but it had little influence on the military authorities in the Ukraine and Berlin. Neither Hitler, nor Göring, nor Himmler, nor Erich Koch—who set up his headquarters in Równe and not Kiev—was interested in Ukraine's autonomy. The independence movement was simply regarded as being fundamentally irreconcilable with the German objectives in the Ukraine.

With these objectives in mind, the German high command welcomed Ukrainian assistance—but only on its terms. All independent political organizations were to be suppressed. All Ukrainian units, including both factions of the OUN, were forbidden independent action, and periodic attempts were made to disarm them. They were to subject themselves now to the organizational discipline of the German Army and assist the Gestapo in "Hay Action" and the "Extraordinary Pacification Action," which included the massive extermination of the Jewish people. Bandera himself was arrested and sent to Berlin, where he was interned until September 1944.[89]

Furthermore, the members of the newly created Ukrainian Provisional Government were arrested in Lwów shortly after their proclamation of *Samostiyna Ukraïna.* The OUN expeditionary groups were suppressed. The *Roland* and *Nachtigall* battalions were apprehended in Vinnitsa, reorganized into police units and sent north to fight the Soviet partisans in and around Wołyń.[90]

On December 12, 1941, German forces seized the newspaper *Ukraïnske Slovo* and arrested all its leading editors. Two days later, the *Nove Ukraïnske Slovo* appeared under the directorship of Constantine Shtepa, a bitter enemy of the Ukrainian Nationalist movement.[91] In March 1942, the Hetman's trident was struck from the front page of *Nova Ukraïna* and several of the organizers of the Ukrainian Propaganda Department were shot—just two months after the department began its operation.[92]

This unexpected turn of events alienated many members of the Ukrainian police and resulted in the formation of autonomous, armed contingents of men who began to operate primarily in the form of roving bands. (We called them *bandyty*—bandits.) The Germans planned to squelch this nascent, undisciplined threat, but before their effort got under way, the winds of war had shifted on the eastern front and the help of the Ukrainian Nationalists was needed once more.

III. OCTOBER 1942–JANUARY 1944. While the powerful German Army was being decimated in the heart of Russia, the partisan activity against German objectives in the Ukraine (specifically in the forested terrain of Wołyń) intensified to such a degree that German appeals were made to the Ukrainian Nationalists for a united front against the Bolshevik threat. The Bandera contingent (OUN-B) was to provide the counterweight to the partisan forces consisting of all anti-German factions, but generally called "Russian."[93]

When, on May 4, 1943, the formation of the *SS Galizien* (the Ukrainian Galician division of the *Waffen-SS*[94]) was officially announced by the *Wehrmacht*, Volodymyr Kubiiovych, the president of the Ukrainian Central Committee, welcomed the news with a supportive proclamation. Both the Ukrainian Autocephalous Orthodox Church and the Ukrainian Catholic Church also supported it; Bishop Josyf Slipyi, the soon-to-be successor of Metropolitan Sheptytsky, celebrated it with a church service at St. George Cathedral in Lwów; and the son of the vicarial Bishop of Kiev (Mstyslav) joined its ranks. Alarmed as he was over the massacre of the Jews by the notorious SP (*Sicherheitspolizei*—Security Police), and in particular by their use of the Ukrainian police in this gruesome endeavor, the bedridden Metropolitan Sheptytsky himself, just over a year before his own death, told Kubiiovych that "there is virtually no price which would not be paid for the creation of a Ukrainian army." Not only did he personally applaud the formation of the *SS Galizien*, he also designated one of his senior clergymen, Father Vasyl Laba, to serve as its chief chaplain. (It is interesting to note that, contrary to its normal practice, the SS allowed chaplains in several of the Ukrainian divisions.) Father Laba, in turn, preached a sermon which was duly filed and preserved by the Germans, calling on the Ukrainians to help "Hitler and the German people" destroy Bolshevism. Finally, the OUN-M leadership also expressed its unreserved support for the division, and although the OUN-B was against it initially, its opposition ceased when the two factions merged. Mindful of his valuable military experience in the Ukrainian police, Roman Shukhevych not only felt that service in the *SS Galizien* would prove to be an invaluable training experience for Ukrainian youth, but also ordered many of his followers to enter the division, where they were given prominent positions. Given this overwhelming support of the Ukrainian secular and clerical intelligentsia, it should come as no surprise that in twelve months' time the quota for the unit was surpassed several times over and that tens of thousands of eager volunteers had to be turned down.[95]

(Unfortunately for the *Waffen-SS* and the *SS Galizien* which fought by its side, on July 20, 1944, at the battle of Brody, a little town on the main highway between Równe and Lwów, the Soviet Army decisively defeated the combined German and Ukrainian forces, and the several thousand surviving Ukrainians—with all their military experience *and* arms—either retreated with the remnant of the German Army or stayed behind to join the UPA.[96])

The Ukrainian police at this time, under the command of Roman Shukhevych, numbered 12,000 men in Wołyń and Podole. In March 1943, when the UPA marched into the forest, from 4,000 to 5,000 members of this police force marched with it.[97] In September of that year, Shukhevych assumed the command of the UPA.[98] Thus, the UPA began, in part, as a German-organized and German-trained military police force turned guerrilla.

Besides the UPA, which functioned as an independent unit since the spring of 1943, a number of other more or less autonomous groups of Ukrainian Nationalists emerged throughout Wołyń. These groups, with their self-appointed, unscrupulous leaders, were primarily responsible for initiating the savage cruelty and repressive measures aimed at the Polish population. The largest and the most bestial of these terrorist groups was led by the infamous Taras Borovets, otherwise known as "Taras Bulba."[99]

Before the final consolidation of the UPA under the experienced Shukhevych (chief Ukrainian organizer of *Nachtigall*, chief of the Ukrainian police and, after his desertion in the spring of 1943, chief commander of all OUN-B "partisan" forces), the Ukrainian directorate called for a unification of the various nationalist factions, but to no avail. Consequently, the OUN-B was commanded to attack both Melnyk (in July) and Borovets (in August) and to compel their men to join the OUN-B which now called itself the UPA. Those who did not comply were executed. It seems that all the *Bulbowcy* (Bulbists) complied without bloodshed.[100]

As luck would have it, Borovets escaped the fraternal trap and intended to go personally to Warsaw in order to solicit German assistance for his return to power. But as luck would have it again, in the middle of a discussion with some *Wehrmacht* officials, he was suddenly arrested by the German police and incarcerated. On January 26, 1944, Melnyk himself met a similar fate on the suspicion of subversive propaganda.[101]

IV. FEBRUARY 1944–END OF THE WAR. As the once powerful *Wehrmacht* was being driven out of Western Ukraine by the Red Army, the Germans sought to bolster their crumbling defenses by utilizing the Ukrainian "reserves" still in their hands: the thousands of refugees, several hundred thousand prisoners of war, a quarter of a million auxiliary troops, and even the uncounted numbers of forced laborers (*Ostarbeiter*). The task of organizing these millions into productive political and military forces was given to General Vlasov.[102]

Meanwhile, efforts were made to contact and direct the various Ukrainian nationalist groups in and out of Western Ukraine. By October 1944, Melnyk, Bandera, Borovets and other nationalist leaders were released in order to help Germany in the war effort . . . but by that time all of Ukraine was already in the hands of the Red Army.

Securing the backing of a number of prominent Ukrainians predominantly from Kiev, Vlasov formed the Committee for the Liberation of the Peoples of Russia (KONR)—to the utter dismay of the Nationalists, who wanted no part of Vlasov or the peoples of Russia. Responding to a proclamation issued by Vlasov and the Committee (Manifesto of Prague, November 14, 1944), ten non–Russian nationalist groups addressed a "protest" (signed by Melnyk alone) to Hitler through Rosenberg. In this protest they reminded *der Führer* of Germany's great debt to the nationalists in the following words:

> It is therefore not astounding that these [non–Russian] peoples greeted the outbreak of the German-Russian war with the greatest joy. They placed themselves at the side of the German army from the first day on, helped where they could, welcomed the troops with open arms, and with cordial friendship. Standing shoulder to shoulder with the German soldiers in battle, they proved their loyalty to the national idea.[103]

The protest also made the following demands:

> 1. Forbid any claim of General Vlasov to the leadership of our peoples;
> 2. Recognize the right, to take effect immediately, of our peoples to independent states and to pronounce a definite recognition of our national representative bodies;
> 3. Organize our national military formations under unified command of their own leaders, subject to the German Wehrmacht in operative

> matters, for the fight against Bolshevism, and turn over the political leadership within these formations to our national representative bodies.[104]

But Hitler had other matters on his mind just then, and so the Germans made no choice for Vlasov's or Melnyk's group and let come what might.

Two armies emerged: Vlasov's pro-Nazi Russian Liberation Army (ROA) of some 300,000 men of whom 30 to 40 percent were Ukrainians, and General Shandruk's pro-Nazi Ukrainian Liberation Army (UVV) of some 75,000 men led by German officers. The ROA units wore the St. Andrew's cross, an old religious Russian symbol; the UVV units wore the trident, the symbol of their nationalist aspirations. (Borovets was to form a parachute detachment to be dropped behind the Soviet lines.[105])

Meanwhile, the Nazis continued to direct the activity of the Ukrainian Nationalists against the partisans and the Red Army and to equip them with military intelligence and weapons. In conjunction with the armaments brought in by the Ukrainian police, the *SS Galizien* survivors, and the raids on Soviet units, this last-minute arming of the Ukrainian Nationalists by Germany contributed significantly to the formation of an armed Ukrainian underground which became entrenched in the Carpathian mountains and continued to plague the Communist Galician lowlands of both Poland and the Soviet Union (including Wołyń) until 1950.[106]

In the last months of the war, the German leadership attempted to unify the various factions of the nationalists in the interest of defending the Third Reich. To this end, all the major Nationalist leaders were called to Berlin where, on March 12, 1945, the Ukrainian National Committee (UNK) was formed under the leadership of Pavlo Shandruk.[107]

Thus, the symbiotic relationship between Nazi Germany and the Ukrainian Nationalists lasted for the greater part of the war, waxing or waning depending on the course of the war itself. To be sure, at first the Ukrainian Nationalists supported the Third Reich in the hope of securing their own independence. But later, when that hope was dashed again and again, why did they continue to support the Nazis?

A partial answer to that question is that the leaders feared what would happen to the millions of *Ostarbeiter* and Ukrainian prisoners of war if they withdrew their support. (They needn't have worried. After the Jews and the Russians, who were treated in the worst possible way, all the *Ost* forced laborers and prisoners of war, as we shall see, were treated equally badly.)

Another explanation is that, anticipating the collapse of Germany and fearing the reprisals which would follow (it will become clearer in the next chapter why they would follow), their real aim was to build up a strong nationalistic military force which would survive the war. (Here, too, they were mistaken. The balance of power they had hoped for never materialized. The

Soviet victory was complete, and if the consequences of that victory were more ruthless than they needed to be, it was *because* of that German–Ukrainian Nationalist alliance.)

A psychological explanation is that they were attempting to prevent their own loss of power and lives. (In this respect, some of them at least did achieve a measure of success, for although their power was greatly diminished with the passing nightmare of the Third Reich, their organization lingered on for another five years after the end of World War II, as did their acts of terror.[108])

Melnyk's first appeal to *der Führer*, dated July 6, 1941, signed in his own hand ("retired colonel") and bearing the signatures of other nationalist leaders, pleaded: "We request that we be allowed to march shoulder to shoulder with the legions of Europe. . . ." His last appeal of November 1944, signed with his own name and again representing the sentiments of the nationalist leaders, uses a similar expression: "Standing shoulder to shoulder with German soldiers in battle. . . ."

In the final analysis, during the course of the Second World War, the Ukrainian Nationalist movement ended as it had begun, a sinister, misguided, useless German-Ukrainian conspiracy. It was, to use the title of Szcześniak's and Szota's study, *droga do nikąd* (a road to nowhere), or more aptly put, a one-way street to hell. At first they conspired because they wanted to; at last, because they had to. So it is when one courts the devil.

Various Ukrainian authors will, no doubt, disagree with the above sketch of the German–Ukrainian Nationalist conspiracy. They will point out that although initially, like many other ethnic groups in Western Ukraine, the Ukrainian Nationalists may have "toyed" with the idea of collaboration, later (in the second half of 1941 and subsequently) when the OUN roundups began and they realized that Nazi Germany had no intentions of honoring its promises, they not only refused to succumb to the discipline of the *Wehrmacht*, not only disavowed any allegiance to Germany, but also became anti–Nazi partisans.

Even if this assertion is true, since the UPA (consisting of the OUN-M, OUN-B, and after August 1943, of "Taras Bulba's" gang of cutthroats and sadists) was also anti–Soviet, anti–Polish, anti–Jewish, and anti-everyone who was not a Ukrainian Nationalist, it stands to reason that, in a significant way, it must have also *contributed* to the German war effort. The primary objective of the UPA was simple and straightforward: *Samostiyna Ukraïna*, and to hell with everyone else. Ihor Kamenetsky puts it much more nicely:

> The ultimate purpose of the Ukrainian Insurgent Army was an Independent Ukrainian state; their immediate task was the protection of the Ukrainian population against the more abusive forms of German colonial policy. Their strength was the popular support in Ukraine, due mainly to the fact that they declared war against both the German and

> Soviet regimes. Another strong point was the idea which they preached: "Liberty to men and freedom to the nations." This set them above the narrow nationalists. This call secured them not only the cooperation of all classes in Ukraine but also the cooperation and support of many nationals such as Slovaks, Jews, Georgians, and Tartars. Their weakness was their international position. None of the great powers, Germany, the Soviet Union, or the Western Allies, would or could sympathize with their ultimate goal.[109]

Here's what one of these "great powers" thought of the Ukrainian "partisans":

> Fight against the German helpers, the German–Ukrainian Nationalists. These various categories of Banderowcy, Melnykowcy and Bulbowcy are traitors to the Ukrainian people. Seeing the hatred of the Ukrainian people towards the German invaders, they are now trying to set up "partisan detachments" supposedly against the Germans, but in reality created to fight against the partisan groups helping the Red Army. . . . Do not give into the lies of these fascist lackeys [*faszystowskich sługusów*]. Destroy these traitors and wheeler-dealers [*zdrajców i szachrajów*] at every step. . . . They want to hand us over to eternal German slavery. They fight with and destroy the Polish people who together with us, fight in the partisan units.[110]

Here's another statement by another Ukrainian author:

> Thus, while the OUN was a factor in promoting collaboration among Ukrainians before the war and during the first phase of the Soviet-German war, it was also the first to oppose German policy actively, thereby negating the very idea of collaboration. The high point of the Ukrainian resistance to German domination was the organization of the UPA, which took up arms against the Nazi occupiers.[111]

But just how strong was the anti–Nazi sentiment of the UPA? After reviewing the evidence, Armstrong draws the following conclusion regarding the anti–Nazi activity of the Ukrainian Nationalists in 1942, the year of their greatest disenchantment with the *Wehrmacht*: Neither OUN-B nor OUN-M offered any resistance to the Nazis, and "consequently, the only Ukrainian nationalist organization which could *remotely be described as a partisan group* during the first year of the Reichskommissariat's administration of Volhynia was the Poliska Sich (Polessian stronghold) under Borovets'." He goes on to say, steering his arguments right down the middle of this slippery road:

> It is extremely difficult to ascertain just what activities the UPA carried out during 1942. That it fought sporadically with small groups of Red

partisans in the winter and spring appears certain. It is also certain that it existed illegally, in defiance of a German order for its dissolution, and that it gathered arms surreptitiously, and it is reasonably sure that some of its members from time to time had armed encounters with German security forces. *It is, however, by no means certain that the group carried out open attacks against the Germans, or that the latter were entirely dissatisfied with the state of affairs in which the illegal band kept a region of difficult terrain and low economic potential from serving as a Red base behind the German lines.*[112]

Finally, just to give both sides equal time, here is another assessment of the situation by the first secretary of the Communist Party of the Ukraine, Nikita Khrushchev, who, although a Communist and therefore a propagandist at heart, was at least closer to the action. I do not cite his words as "proof," but only as a counterweight to the exaggerated claims of some Ukrainian authors:

> If one asks the Ukrainian–German Nationalists how many of the German occupiers they destroyed, how many German formations they wiped out, how many bridges they blew up, in order to prevent the aggressors from transporting arms for subjugating and annihilating the Ukrainian people, they can make no reply.[113]

For proof, I will simply cite a proclamation issued by the Ukrainian Nationalists themselves in July 1943 which states the same thing in the *German* language:

> Our Organization is not turned against You. Do not allow yourself to be awakened into battle with us. Spare yourselves the useless loss of blood.
>
> We do not destroy German communications, we do not disturb German armed forces. Do not allow yourselves to be drawn into battle with a peaceful people lest the whole Ukrainian nation turn against You.
>
> Long live the understanding of nations against the Bolshevik threat....[114]

And finally, this from a Ukrainian Nationalist newspaper:

> Some local elements hate us for our cooperation with Germany. We are proud of this cooperation ... and are sure that the New Order created by Adolf Hitler shall reign supreme in Europe and throughout the world on the ruins of the degenerate ideologies.[115]

How strong were the anti–Nazi sentiments among the Ukrainian Nationalist "partisans," when in the eleventh hour of the war, when Germany was on the very edge of defeat, when resistance on its part was pointless, they still aided and abetted the *Wehrmacht* at every turn—as Melnyk's signed "protest" written in late November 1944 clearly states?

While it may be abundantly clear by now that there was indeed a German–Ukrainian Nationalist conspiracy, an understanding, an agreement, an alliance (the word does not matter, the reality and the consequences do!), it should be also pointed out that Ukrainian nationalism was neither a Nazi invention nor the *direct* result of Poland's "repressive" measures against the Ukrainians in its eastern territories during the interwar years. The dark roots of that movement run deep in the murky waters of early European history.[116] Neither is it true that the OUN/UPA was synonymous with the Ukrainian nation or its aspirations. These organizations, after all, were fascist in structure and in ideology, in spirit and in deed. Their version of *Samostiyna Ukraïna,* with Lwów as its capital, would have mirrored those of Hitler's Germany, Mussolini's Italy, and Stalin's Russia. Neither is it true (I will say it again) that the vast majority of the Ukrainian population espoused the cause of the OUN/UPA or was itself fanatically nationalistic. According to Szcześniak and Szota:

> It turns out that the Ukrainian people did not support the idea of a "free, independent, and sovereign" [*Wilnej, Samostijnej i Sobornej*] Ukraine, and that without popular support there was no way to bring it about. . . . Without German assistance, given the overall antagonism of the Ukrainian masses to the nationalistic idea, the OUN would have been completely powerless in these regions.[117]

Cybulski is of the same opinion,[118] and so is Dallin,[119] and so are Sobiesiak and Jegorow, who write that

> among the fugitives there were a great number of Ukrainians who, threatened by the UPA bands, had to go into hiding in the same way as the Polish people. The UPA treated their own brothers, who did not want to cooperate with the bands the same [as the Poles]. The upright Ukrainians numbered in the thousands. Often entire Ukrainian villages were forced to flee from their homes in dread of the UPA. Those caught were hanged, or burned at the stake. . . .[120]

Although Armstrong also draws the general conclusion that the "essential mass remained uncommitted" to Ukrainian nationalism, he qualifies the statement by stating earlier: "The widespread support given the various groups of nationalist partisans indicates, however, that nationalist feeling was strong in Volhynia."[121] In Wołyń, it was very, very strong.

Consider the following words of Iaroslav Halan, a well-known Ukrainian writer:

> For the second year in a row, Wołynian soil flows with streams of hot, human blood. For the second year in a row, such occurrences transpire there as would turn the hair of young maidens grey. Armed, from head to toe, bands of Ukrainian Hitlerites surround Polish villages, at dawn, burn homes, and axe [*rąbią*] the people fleeing from the burning huts. They do this carefully, solicitously so that not a single soul would survive the terrible slaughter.
>
> And not only Polish villages. At the hands of the yellow-blue Hitlerites already perished thousands of Ukrainian peasants, suspected of having sympathy for the partisans and the Red Army. In a single night, the Hitlerite Ukrainians butchered [*wyrznęli*] the entire population of a village near Różyszcze—800 people. . . .[122]

Consider also the words of an old Ukrainian Nationalist, a former member of the Petliura administration.

> Let us not take comfort in any esteem. Here, they refer to all the incoming Ukrainians that is, us, as fascists, spies, Hitler's partners. . . .[123]

Consider the ultimate heroism of numerous Ukrainians who risked their lives by bringing help to the Polish people, facilitating their escapes, or warning them of imminent danger from the Ukrainian Nationalists. All these activities were, after all, regarded by the UPA as treason punishable by death. Many Polish people owe their lives to those decent and brave human beings.[124]

Cases in point: In the village of Kraszynów near Lwów, Ukrainians resisted the UPA with arms and did not allow them to attack the Polish people; in the village of Skwarzowa in the region of Złotów, both Polish and Ukrainian residents confronted the *Banderowcy* (members of the Bandera contingent), bore the brunt of their attack, and emerged victorious. The same was true in the region of Dolina and elsewhere.[125]

Consider the following notice put out by the OUN in 1943:

> TO ALL UKRAINIANS, WHO LEFT THEIR
> LOCALITIES AND ARE WANDERING AT LARGE
>
> It has been ascertained that many Ukrainians who left the police and civil service have not joined the OUN and are sitting quietly at home or wandering about the territory not realizing the gravity of the moment.
>
> Therefore, the OUN decrees that:
>
> All Ukrainians, who left the police and civil service and are wandering about the territory, should immediately join the OUN and submit themselves to its orders.

After April 20, 1943, the OUN will catch and shoot as deserters all those who will be wandering about the territory.

5 IV 1943

Glory to the Ukraine
Glory to the Heroes

Jarosław Czornomorec
Okr. Dca OUN[126]

Consider the many failed attempts of the UPA to mobilize the general Ukrainian population under threat of death.[127]

Consider the *need* for the OUN/UPA to "pacify" its own people—individuals, families, entire villages; for instance, on August 28, 1943, in Szelpe, Wołyń, twelve Ukrainian youths were murdered by the UPA for refusing to join its ranks.[128]

Consider how the Ukrainian partisans supplied arms to the Polish ones and how they fought not only alongside one another but in each other's regiments as well.[129]

Consider, finally, the fact that even Rosenberg, a Ukrainian Nationalist at heart, had his doubts as to the actual strength of the Ukrainian national consciousness. "I believe," he said,

> that we can safely assume this consciousness to exist in the broad masses of the people in only a latent and apathetic [*dumpf*] form; but even if it should exist in a smaller degree than we believe likely . . . then especially we must make every effort finally to revive this Ukrainian national self-consciousness.[130]

On June 20, 1941, Rosenberg (not all of his ideas were rejected) outlined his vision of how the "New Order" for the occupied Soviet Union was to be achieved:

> Russia was never a one-nation state. She was always a state of many nations. . . . The task of our policy seems to be the exploiting of the desire for liberty of all peoples (within the Soviet Union) and the crystallization of these strivings in a determined state form.[131]

The "state form" would be determined, naturally, by the political and military might of Nazi Germany. Be that as it may, Rosenberg's assessment of the situation, at least in Wołyń, was absolutely correct—and quite self-evident. The Poles wanted it, the Russians wanted it, the Ukrainians wanted it, and of course, the Germans wanted it and got it. Their attitude toward their competitors can be best summarized by a wishful statement made by Governor

General Hans Frank on January 4, 1944, but it could have been made by *Reichskommissar* Erich Koch as well:

> Once we have won the war, then for all I care, mincemeat can be made of Poles and the Ukrainians and all the others who run around here.[132]

In that same year, the October issue of *Bolshevik* (renamed *Kommunist* after the war), the principal ideological journal of the Communist Party, commented on the Rosenberg plan as it was being implemented in Byelorussia:

> Ideological and political education is of exceptional importance in the newly-liberated areas. . . . The enemy has spread the poison of racialist theories in these areas, inciting Ukrainians against Russians, Byelorussians against Lithuanians, Estonians against Russians, etc. . . . The Nazi invaders have also inflamed private-property instincts among these peoples. They liquidated the "kolkhozes," distributed the land among German colonists, destroyed the intelligentsia, encouraged trading and profiteering, and played off workers and peasants against each other. . . .[133]

The same article, in its own inimitable way, goes on to summarize the German-Ukrainian alliance in this last year of the war:

> White emigrants, Ukrainian Nationalists, Bandera, Bulba and Melnikov bands are being extensively used by the Germans in the Ukraine. . . . These contemptible flunkeys of Hitler placed their nationalist slogans at the service of German imperialism, and also actively participated in the massacres organised by the Germans. The Party organisations must intensify their work, especially in the rural areas of the Ukraine. They must remember that until this German-Ukrainian nationalism is completely weeded out, the restoration of the Ukrainian economy and national culture is impossible.[134]

Alexander Werth, who quotes these passages in his book *Russia at War*, placed an asterisk by the word "massacres" and added in the footnote: "The massacres *obviously* refer to the massacres of Jews, though these are, as usual, not specifically mentioned."[135] What is not so obvious is that the Ukrainian Nationalists also conducted *on their own* extensive pogroms whose object was not the elimination of only the Jewish people, but of the Polish and Russian people as well. "In many ways," states B. F. Sabrin, "Ukrainian Nationalist murderers surpassed their Nazi partners in perpetrating atrocities (Pogroms) against innocent people."[136]

3

Tales of Terror

I

Poland, the land of Gentry, lived
A lady much adored,—
She matched her strength with Muscovites,
The Sultan, and the Horde,
The Germans, too. Thus once it was...
But all things pass away.
The gentry boasted of their deeds
And feasted night and day...

Through Poland and Volynia
These factions rage amain,
In Litva and Moldavia
And on through vast Ukraine.
They spread abroad and quite forget
Man's liberty to keep;
They make the usurers their pals;
All things away they sweep.
Havoc and murder are their joy;
Churches they burn with zest...
And meanwhile all the haydamaks
Have had their weapons blest....

V

. . . .

Black are the steeds, already saddled there.
Where will they go? What riders will they bear?
Look! You will see!
Low hills the host engird.
Mute as if dead, they utter not a word.
These are the haydamaks ... at the alarm
The eagles have assembled, swift to harm
With blood and flame their enemies so fell...
They will give back to Poles their gifts of hell....

Raising his voice, the deacon cried:
"Death to the foeman! Hither stride
And take the knives! They have been bless'd!"
The heart grew chill at that request.
The bells broke out in noisy pealing;
The echo through the grove went reeling:
"They have been bless'd!" And loud of breath:
"Death to the Polish gentry, death!"
Each took his blade; these flashed their bane
To the far limits of Ukraine.[1]

The Polish "harvest of sorrow," the wholesale massacre of the Polish people in the province of Wołyń and the three provinces of Eastern Galicia (Lwów, Tarnopol and Stanisławów), began in the fall of 1942, just after the macabre summer of the Jewish Holocaust, and reached its zenith in the summer of 1943, when the Jews officially "ceased to exist" in the *Reichskommissariat Ukrainen* and the *Generalgouvernement* of Poland.

> The extermination of the Polish people who lived in Western Ukraine by the Ukrainian Nationalists began in Wołyń at the end of 1942, gradually moving from east to west. In February of 1943, the regions of Sarny, Kostopol, Równe, Zdołbunowo i Krzemieniec were most threatened. Until June 1943, it spread to the regions of Dubno and Łuck, in July to Horochów, Włodzimierz and Kowel. At the end of 1943 all of Wołyń became a territory of tragic occurrences. The Ukrainian fascists under the banner of the OUN, inciting the uninformed Ukrainian populace, turned their weapons against the Polish people.[2]

The reaping was conducted primarily by the Ukrainian Nationalists, under the veil of darkness and in broad daylight, in secrecy and in full view of witnesses, with the blessings of some Uniate and Orthodox clergy and the SS.

Three general pretexts were given for the massive murder of the Polish civilian population: (1) Harboring or aiding the Jews; (2) collaborating with the partisans; and (3) concealing firearms. But the real reason was stated clearly in a public proclamation, signed by Bandera himself, posted everywhere in Wołyń, and seen by almost everyone. "*Smert' L'akham, Zhydam, i Moskal-am*!"[3] it read. More personal notices were hung on Polish homes:

> Because the Polish government and the Polish people collaborate with the Bolsheviks and are bent on destroying the Ukrainian people on their own land, [name] is hereby called upon to move to native Polish soil within 5 days....[4]

Noncompliance was followed by the extermination of the Polish family and the burning of the house. Often, no warnings were given.

Death came in many forms, and many were the faces that it wore. Most often it had the face of a *Schutzmann*, a *Melnykowiec*, a *Banderowiec*, or a *Bulbowiec*. But sometimes it had the face of a next-door neighbor, a son, a husband, or a wife. In the general terror which pervaded the province of Wołyń during these years, the Polish people could trust no one but their own, even though salvation sometimes came from strange quarters—for not all Ukrainians and not all Ukrainian villages were sympathetic to the ways of the nationalist terrorists (and some of them paid dearly for their brotherly concern). In any case, one could not live under the protection of Wołyń's well-meaning Ukrainians forever.

As the terror intensified, five patterns of self-preservation emerged among the Polish civilian population.

Those who lived along the 1921 Polish-Soviet border sought refuge in the predominantly Ukrainian villages of Eastern Ukraine where they were well received.[5]

Those living in the interior were driven into the surrounding swamps and forests, where hunger, cold, and typhus awaited them. Or, they made their way to the large towns occupied by German garrisons—from which they were promptly dispatched to the slave-labor camps of Nazi Germany. Or, they sought the protection of the partisans in the civilian camps set up for fleeing refugees. Or, finally, if none of these options were feasible, or if they wished to remain on or near their own farmsteads, they joined one of the civil-defense centers organized in 1943 to protect the Polish people and their villages.

The resistance movement, such as it was in Wołyń, consisted primarily of (1) the partisans; (2) the remnants of the Polish Army, specifically the Twenty-seventh Wołyń Infantry Division of the Home Army (*27. Wołyńska Dywizja Piechoty Armii Krajowej*); and (3) the civil-defense units.

The largest and strongest of all the partisan groups were the Russian units (which included many Ukrainians) under the command of Nikita Khrushchev.[6] Others were predominantly Polish. The rest consisted of a mixed assortment of Russians, Poles, Jews, and Ukrainians who did not want to join the UPA.

The primary objective of all these groups was a program of anti-Nazi sabotage and diversionary tactics. They also offered protection to displaced civilians, hassled the extermination squads (*Einsatzgruppen*) at every turn,[7] and assisted the civil-defense units in their struggle with the Ukrainian Nationalists. Their home was the forests, hills, and swamps of Wołyń which they cohabited with the Ukrainian "partisans." Their presence in or near any village, however, was a mixed blessing, since the Germans were quick to respond with retaliatory expeditionary forces and air raids which usually levelled that village and sent its surviving residents scurrying into the nearest forests. The Germans never bothered to ask about the ethnic makeup of the population before bombarding a village with fire bombs.[8]

> The Russians now have an order for a partisan warfare behind the lines. This partisan warfare also has its advantages. It gives us the chance to eliminate everybody who is against us.[9]
>
> TAYLOR: Was an order issued by the highest authorities that the German soldiers who had committed offenses against the civilian population were not to be punished in a military court?
>
> VON DEM BACH: Yes, there was such an order. . . . The Dirlewanger Brigade consisted for the greater part of previously convicted criminals, among them murderers and burglars. These were introduced into the anti-partisan units partly as a result of Himmler's directives which said that among the purposes of the Russian campaign was the reduction of the Slav population by thirty million.[10]

At the height of the partisan movement in 1943-44, there were at least a half-million armed partisans in the Soviet Union. During the course of the partisan war, in Byelorussia alone, about one million partisans and those "associated" with them were killed.[11]

The *AK Wołyń* was formally organized in 1943, and its general mission was the same as that of the partisans, except that it also tried to coordinate the activities of the civil-defense units. However, its attempt to organize these units into para-military groups and to move them out into the forests met with bitter opposition since the very people and villages these units tried to protect would, thereby, be left stranded. It has been said that the very presence of the Polish Army in Wołyń—the army of the Polish government, the army whose mission was to eventually reunify Wołyń with the rest of Poland—exacerbated the nationalistic tempers of the Ukrainians and served to intensify the terror of their ways. There may be some truth to this assertion, but would life in Wołyń have been any safer without the AK's military, financial, and intelligence assistance?[12]

The civil-defense units began to emerge after the Ukrainian attacks on Polish households and villages. These units consisted of local inhabitants who simply wished to protect themselves and their families from such unprovoked attacks. Beginning at first as guard units stationed around their own villages using firearms saved from 1939, they later became organized into respectable forces whose aim was to protect not only this village or that, but a whole complex of villages and settlements in a given area. The Germans knew about the existence of these civil-defense units and generally did nothing about them. In fact, from time to time, the Germans would provide these units with arms and ammunition in the hope of drawing them into battle with the Russian partisans—a tactic which met with little success in Wołyń. Among these centers of self-defense were, in the Inspectorate of Równe: Młynsk, Huta Stepańska, Kostopol, Janowa Dolina, Zdołbunowo, and Ostróg; in the Inspectorate of Dubno: Pańska Dolina, Szumsk, and Krzemieniec; in the Inspectorate of Łuck: Przebraże, Rafałówka, Różyszcze, and regions of Sieliski and Włodzimierz; in the Inspectorate of Kowel: Zasmyk, Stara and Nowa Dąbrowa, Kupiczów, Rymcze, and Stary and Nowy Jagodzin.[13]

The heroic efforts of these civil-defense units met with varying degrees of success. Sometimes thousands of old people, women and children were saved. But just as often, without the assistance of the partisans and or the *AK Wołyń,* the smaller of these units perished together with the people they were so valiantly protecting. Size alone, however, was not the only determining factor in the survival of these centers. Huta Stepańska, with some 15,000 refugees, did not withstand the onslaught.[14] Przebraże, on the other hand, with about 20,000 people (including Jews and Ukrainians unsympathetic to the UPA), resisted until the end of the war.[15]

VI

. . . .

Terror moved through all Ukraine,
Through every field it spread;
Endlessly the blood flowed forth
And stained the steppes with red....

VIII

The sun had set. Throughout Ukraine
The flames their hunger glut;
And everywhere the gentry quaked,
In lofty buildings shut.
On gibbets in the villages
Unnumbered corpses hung;
These were the chiefs—the common sort
In nameless piles were flung.
The dogs and crows, upon the streets
And crossroads where they lay,
Devoured their flesh, pecked out their eyes,
And no one said them nay...
Only the children had been left
In village bivouacs,—
The women, with their oven-forks,
Had joined the haydamaks.[16]

[Złoczów, July 3, 1941] I saw that in the ditches, about 5 meters deep and 20 meters wide, stood and lay about 60–80 men, women, and children, predominantly Jewish. I heard the wailing and screaming of the children and women, hand grenades were bursting in their midst. Beyond the ditches waited many hundreds of people for execution. In

> front of the ditches stood 10–20 men in civilian clothes, who were throwing grenades into the ditch. . . . I found out from the SS soldiers, that they were Bandera's people. . . .[17]

Zofiówka was a small Jewish town located about ten kilometers from Przebraże (some seventy kilometers west-northwest of Ryświanka).[18] In August of 1942, about one month after Hitler moved his headquarters to Vinnitsa in the Ukraine and poisoned our air with rampaging evil, several SS men, together with eleven trucks of the Ukrainian *Schutzmann* police, arrived from Łuck and surrounded the town. The Jewish people were then led out, one group at a time, to a nearby forest and told to lie face down in previously prepared ditches. As they lay there, the *Schutzmann* walked along the pits and shot each person in the back of the head. Then the next group was brought in. . . . And so it went, group after group, mass grave after mass grave, until the whole town was emptied. As in Dubno, five thousand people perished that day in Zofiówka.

Yet there were escapes, and many Polish people suspected of "harboring Jews" were arrested. Among these was a certain forester by the name of Cezary Cybulski, who was denounced by Antoni Skirzewski's German wife for "harboring Jews" and for "collaborating with the partisans." Cybulski evaded the *Schutzmann* for a time; his son, Zygmunt, was arrested and shot. After his own subsequent capture, both Cybulski and his wife were cruelly tortured and also murdered.

Obórki was a small Polish village (about eighteen kilometers from Przebraże) whose isolation and good will made it an ideal way station for the constant stream of Jews, escaped Russian POWs, and partisans bound for the nearby forest.[19] Renowned for its heroic role in the underground movement, Obórki also bears the distinction of being the first Polish village to succumb to the terror of the Ukrainian Nationalists.

On November 11, 1942, a group of strangers claiming to be Russian partisans entered the village, requested some food, and afterwards departed in peace, asking not to be reported to the police or the people living in the forest. Two days later, a contingent of the Ukrainian *Black Police* descended on Obórki and arrested all but two of the men in the village. (The two in question managed to escape.) Of those arrested, one was shot; the sixteen others were beaten and taken to a nearby town by the name of Cumań, where they were later executed.

Meanwhile, a delegation of five women was sent to Cumań to report on the fate of the men. While they were gone, the Ukrainian police returned on November 15 and ordered all the remaining women to gather, with their children, in the house of Franciszek Trusiewicz for immediate "relocation." Then, they were taken in small groups to a nearby barn and systematically executed—all fifty of them.

When the party of women who went to Cumań returned (one stayed on for a few more days), they were also taken to the barn and murdered. Later, when the fifth woman of the delegation, Stanisława Trusiewicz, came back to Obórki, she found her village completely devastated by fire. In terror she went to the next village, Rudnik, to the house of an old Ukrainian friend. He greeted her by saying: "You cannot stay here . . . if they find you in my house, my whole family will perish."

That night, Stanisława was taken by him to Bogusława and placed under the protection of another Ukrainian, who took her to Silno and left her in the hands of a third Ukrainian with whom she remained throughout that winter. In the spring, he brought her to the Polish civil-defense center just forming in Przebraże.

The Polish colony of Parośle lay in a wooded area about twenty-two kilometers north-northeast of Huta Stepańska, which was located some fifty kilometers to our north-northwest.[20] On February 9, 1943, a group of armed men marched into Parośle claiming to be Russian partisans. The residents, taking them at their word, not only allowed them to remain in the colony but provided them with refreshments as well. That evening these same guests, who turned out to be Ukrainian Nationalists, surrounded the homes, and in the course of the unprovoked and unexpected attack that followed, 173 Polish people perished. Only two men and one six-year-old child managed to survive.

The details of that carnage almost defy description. Some infants were pierced with common kitchen knives and pinned to the tables. Several men were lashed to the point of having their skin removed, and others had their veins ripped out of their bodies. Women were not only raped but also had their breasts severed. Many of the victims were severely mutilated, their ears, noses, and lips cut off and their eyes gouged out, and many were decapitated.

After these deeds of terror, the Ukrainian Nationalists partook of food and drink at the home of the *sołtys* (chief administrator) and left the colony. Later, among the leftovers and empty bottles, the body of a twelve-month-old child was discovered pinned to the table with a bayonet; in its mouth was a half-eaten dill pickle.

According to another account of this same incident, after it was all over, the leader of the bandits told his men: "Behold your baptism of battle, Marksmen! You are the first in the name of the UPA to begin the bloody and holy war against the Poles and the Russians. *Khay zhyve samostiyna Ukraïna!* (Long live independent Ukraine!) Glory to Bandera!"

A mass grave was prepared for 137 of the deceased not far from another earlier mass grave from the days of the Khmelnytsky rebellion which also engulfed the residents of Parośle. The rest of the dead were buried in various other cemeteries by surviving family members.

Kazimirka was a small, predominantly Ukrainian village lying to the north of us between Kostopol and Sarny. This ancient village was renowned for its magnificent Roman Catholic Church with its three ponderous bells (the largest of which could be heard for many kilometers) and its famed painting of the Blessed Mother.[21] Like Our Lady of Częstochowa and Our Lady of Ostrobrama, Our Lady of Kazimirka was said to possess miraculous powers which she often used to alleviate the trials and tribulations of suffering mankind. Quickened by the majestic pealing of the bells, the faithful—not only from Wołyń, but from Polesie and Podole as well—flocked to the village church in order to avail themselves of her good graces.

In October 1942, Grzegorz Smułka, the Ukrainian *sołtys* of the village of Kazimirka, was ordered by the atheistic philistines of the Third Reich, in the name of their own Unholy Trinity, to have the bells taken down and brought to Stepań for immediate transport into the heart of Germany—the Krupp foundries, no doubt. All that precious metal was not to be wasted on pious ringing while there was a two-front war going on! Smułka dutifully relayed his orders to the Polish priest but added, on the side, that he would not be surprised if, in the course of that very night, the bells should happen to "disappear."

The ecstatic clergyman needed no further prompting. At midnight, Stanisław Domalewski and seven other husky men[22] from the nearby village of Karaczun met in secret at the belfry of the church. With them, they brought four of their village's strongest horses and two sturdy wagons. In no time at all, the ancient bells were muffled, dismantled, loaded on the wagons, and transported posthaste not to Stepań, but to Karaczun, where they were solemnly blessed, sprinkled with holy water, and buried in a field belonging to one of the men, about half a kilometer from the village. On the following morning, the entire area was plowed and sown over with winter wheat and rye to cover the traces of this strange funeral.

The secret of the bells was faithfully preserved during the remaining two and a half years of the war. The bells were saved! However, in 1945, when (after Yalta) Wołyń became a part of the Ukrainian Soviet Socialist Republic, the resurrection of the bells was indefinitely postponed by those involved, in the hope of Wołyń's eventual reunification with Poland and Poland's subsequent liberation from the Soviet Bloc. It was a vain hope, but the secret of the bells of Kazimirka, interred somewhere near the village of Karaczun, remained hidden throughout all these many years. For all Stanisław Domalewski knows, they are still there, ringing silently deep within the bowels of Mother Earth for the deceased and the displaced people of Wołyń.[23]

Shortly after this incident, Grzegorz Smułka, at a village meeting involving the Ukrainian delegates from Kazimirka, Karaczun, and Krzeszów, publicly voiced his opinion regarding the senseless fratricide which was going on in that vicinity.

"Brother Ukrainians," he said, "let us stop killing the Polish people in Wołyń. As we lived among them in peace for these twenty years, so now let them live in peace among us."

The very next day, Smułka—the Ukrainian *sołtys* of Kazimirka—was found brutally murdered.

In the spring of the following year, the 300-year-old church was burned to the ground. Miraculously, Our Lady of Kazimirka escaped the flames, was taken to Krzeszów, and from there to Przemyśl—where the human cargo bound for Nazi Germany was sorted out. As that was the end of the line for all excess baggage, this most illustrious exile of Wołyń was entrusted to one of the local parish churches for safekeeping.

Whether she survived the war or perished along with her faithful devotees (numbering into the hundreds of thousands) is difficult to say. But one thing is certain: such legends do not die easily, or fade from the collective memory of a determined people. I have heard it said that she emigrated to England along with some of the survivors. Perchance you have seen her there, arrayed in all her ancient splendor, with her sadly smiling countenance, and the pearl-shaped teardrops swimming in the far corners of her dark Wołynian eyes.

Ewa Hołubecki was an intensely devout ninety-year-old *babusieńka* who lived in the neighboring village of Pępków, a village of some sixty households, half of which were Ukrainian and half Polish.[24] Everyone in the vicinity knew this sweet lady and was familiar with her lifelong, noble attempt to embellish the legend of Our Lady of Kazimirka by claiming that the Blessed Mother honored her "portrait" by miraculously appearing in her own person on a stump near the parish church. She refrained, however, from claiming that she herself, unworthy sinner that she was, had actually seen the apparition. In fact, since no one in particular was ever mentioned as a witness, the miraculous incarnation of the Lady could never be contested.

When Ewa heard the tragic news that the church of Kazimirka was destroyed by fire, she decided to go and see for herself. "How could God and the Blessed Virgin permit such a thing! They are surely mistaken!" she must have thought.

Because of the increased Ukrainian activity in the area—by now there were almost daily reports of murders and burnings—the family tried to dissuade Ewa from her intended eight-kilometer journey.

"Do not go, grandmother!" they said. "The Ukrainians will kill you before you reach the church!" But their words fell on deaf ears.

"I am an old lady," she replied. "What would anyone want with me? And besides, I have known all these Ukrainian boys since they were small children and have always treated them like my own."

It was the truth. All the children in the village, Polish and Ukrainian alike, loved her as their own mother. And so she went to Kazimirka.

Just before Easter Sunday, in the year of 1943, Ewa Hołubecki's family found her body floating in the river near the village. A single bullet interrupted Ewa's final pilgrimage to Our Lady of Kazimirka.

Shortly after his grandmother's murder, Czesiek Kołosowski moved his family out of Kazimirka (where he was a miller) to live with his family of orientation in Pępkow. He urged his aging in-laws, who owned a small parcel of land on the outskirts of Kazimirka, to do the same for their own safety. But Edward and Ludwika Baczyński, who still had a young son at home, disregarded his advice.

"What would anyone want with us?" they said.

One evening, while visiting a neighbor, Ludwika heard her dogs barking. ("She heard the dogs barking. The dogs were barking. Oh, how they were barking!"—Ewa Kujański, Czesiek's sister, almost sang these Polish phrases as she continued her melancholy tale.) When Ludwika heard the dogs, she hurried home to see what was the matter. Even before she arrived on her premises, she saw horses galloping off in different directions. In the yard, various animals were running loose; the barn door had been flung open. On entering the house, she found it ransacked from top to bottom. Call as she may, there was no response either from her husband or son, both of whom were home when she had set out on her visit.

After searching the house and barn, she went into the pigsty. They were not there either . . . but as she was about to leave, she saw two piles of manure which seemed strangely out of place. Upon taking a closer look, she thought she saw traces of blood. When she picked up the pitchfork and moved some of the dung aside, her very worst fears were confirmed. There, in the piles of rotting manure, she uncovered her husband's bloody head and her son's mutilated arm. They had been murdered, dismembered, and buried under the manure.

Wild with grief and terror, Ludwika ran out of the pigsty and kept on running through the forest (thus skirting the very large Ukrainian village of Jabłonka) until she reached the village of Krzeszów. The armed guard surrounding this Polish village took her in and gave her lodging for the night. On the following morning, several armed men escorted Ludwika back to her house, dug out the remains of her husband and son, and gave them a proper burial under a nearby wayside shrine. They did not dare to bury them in Kazimirka's cemetery. After that, Ludwika was taken to Pępków to stay with her son-in-law, Czesiek, and his family of procreation and orientation.

Later that same day, two wagonloads of *Bulbowcy* came inquiring as to Ludwika Baczyński's whereabouts. Not finding her, they kicked and clubbed Czesiek until they thought he was dead, warned the family about the penalty for harboring fugitives, and returned into the dark forests from which they came. On the following day, Czesiek, his mother-in-law, his wife, and his son went to Karaczun, from where they were all shipped off to Germany as slaves of the Third Reich. Shortly thereafter, all the Polish residents of Pępków were confined to their quarters by the Ukrainians under the penalty of death. Nevertheless, at the risk of their lives, various families would still gather at night in their potato cellars to scrounge for food and to exchange news of the latest atrocities.

Meanwhile, the Germans called upon the Ukrainian terrorists to provide their war machine with more slaves, to round up all the village girls and to deliver them to Karaczun for transport into Germany. The *Bulbowcy* responded by felling trees along the road leading to the village and blamed the partisans for their inability to deliver the slaves on schedule. The German answer to this was the predictable air attack. Within minutes after the arrival of the planes, Pępków was leveled to the ground, and leaflets were dropped informing the survivors that the *Luftwaffe* would return if any more news of partisan activity was reported.

After this incident, every survivor in Pępków, Ukrainian and Polish alike, packed up what was left of his or her belongings and abandoned the burning village. Upon reaching the safety of the woods, the group split up according to nationality—the Ukrainians going in one direction, the Poles in another. ("It was as if God himself willed for this to happen. It was God's will. It is evident that God willed it so," sighed Mrs. Kujański.) Several of the Polish exiles, however, disagreed with the Lord and voiced their opinions that it would have been safer for them to continue traveling as a mixed group.

Be that as it may, the 150 Polish men, women, and children were now at risk. They were unarmed, without provisions beyond a few days' worth, near Jabłonka, and in the territory of the UPA. They could not remain in the forest. They could not continue to travel on unescorted. After a hasty meeting, it was decided that, while the group remained put, Marcel (Mrs. Kujański's brother) and Antek Jastrzemski would go to Krzeszów for help.

As the exiles waited for their deliverance, further distressing news reached their ears. Evidently, immediately after their departure, a contingent of armed Ukrainians descended on the burning Pępków and, finding themselves cheated of their quarry, proceeded to vent their anger upon the inhabitants of the surrounding countryside. (Mrs. Kujański recalled some of these instances of brutality.)

Mrs. Kujański's aunt (her father's elderly sister), together with her husband, her son, his wife, and their two small children—three generations—were all brutally murdered with axes and their bodies draped over the fence by their own house. (The village *sołtys'* sister, who was their next-door neighbor, witnessed this brutal slaying. She herself was Ukrainian, her brother, the *sołtys*, was married to a Polish girl.)

Kazik Bagiński had wed a Ukrainian girl against her parents' wishes. They were both very young and still very much in love. They had one small daughter. Mrs. Bagiński was visiting her mother when the Ukrainians attacked her home.

When she returned, she found her husband and her daughter axed to death and flung over the fence.

Mr. Jastrzemski, also married to a Ukrainian girl ("christened Polish," Mrs. Kujański added—meaning that she became a convert to Catholicism), was among those huddled in the forest with his wife and children. Before he left Pępków, his mother, Józia, had offered to take his beautiful horse to her brother on the outskirts of the village rather than to have the animal fall into German hands. She never returned, and now he found out why. While on her journey, she was caught by the Ukrainians and locked up in a cage. When they found her trying to dig her way out with her bare hands, she was executed and left in the cage which was to be her coffin. ("They tried to save their horse from the Germans," Mrs. Kujański said, "and so they gave up their mother to the Ukrainians."[25])

Mr. and Mrs. Hieronim Czetwertyński had eight children, one of whom was in the forced-labor camps of Germany. Fearing for the safety of his family, Mr. Czetwertyński took his wife and seven children to Równe. But when he found out that everyone there was being shipped off to Germany, he became even more frightened and returned to Pępków. All nine perished in the course of this same attack. They were butchered and flung into a mass grave in their own garden. Witnesses reported that their blood seeped up through the ground like a red spring. When the only surviving daughter heard this tragic news in Germany, she became suicidal.

("They killed many more people in the vicinity of Pępków," said Mrs. Kujański. "Today, I do not remember the other people's names or the circumstances of their tragic deaths.")

And so, terrified by the reports of what was going on in the surrounding area, the Polish exiles from the bombarded village waited for their deliverance. After several days, two horse-drawn wagons appeared near the encampment with a dozen or so armed men. They were not *Bulbowcy*, they were the rescuers from Krzeszów. As soon as the children, the elderly, and the remaining provisions were loaded on the wagons, the whole group was safely transported "by night, along black country roads" to the Polish village of Krzeszów.

Meanwhile, all the residents of Krzeszów, fearing a major onslaught by the UPA, were also preparing for a hasty departure. When all was ready, the combined Polish population of Pępków and Krzeszów set out with all their transportable staples, their cherished possessions, their cattle, horses, pigs, and sheep, to the next town, Karaczun, eight kilometers away. In Karaczun it was the same story all over again, the same as it was throughout all of Wołyń in the last week of July 1943.

The civilian population of these three villages, however, did not get very far. Their exodus—whether to one of the strongly defended Polish centers of resistance, or to the Russian border, or to one of the larger towns in the area—was abruptly cut short by the arrival of a heavily armed German transport. The roundup was now complete. All that remained was to confiscate the people's provisions and their animals, and to drive the helpless fugitives into the trucks and boxcars... And off to Równe... And off to Przemyśl... And off to Dachau, and the familiar physicals, the familiar showers, and the familiar ovens or forced-labor camps depending on whether one was Jew or gentile.

"After we were marched in front of the line of camp doctors," Mrs. Kujański said, "we were disinfected and placed in a small, dark, filthy cubicle where there were several young men on the verge of death. From time to time, we would take these young men outside for a breath of fresh air and so that they could see the sun. Not knowing what would become of us, we would gather each day in front of a small holy card of Our Lady of Kazimirka and pray—and pray."

The Kołosowski family spent two weeks in Dachau, and from there (on August 18, 1943) together with eighty other fortunate people, they were shipped to Rosenheim for factory work and farm labor, to dig trenches and to fix train rails, to work in German mines and to clean German offices and houses; in short, to become dismal slaves of the Third Reich.

Helena Piotrowiak (née: Przygrodzki), was born on October 20, 1930, in the village of Berezów Niżny, in the county of Kołomyja, the province of Stanisławów.[26] This particular village lay about 150 kilometers south of Lwów where, as in Wołyń, terrible, terrible things transpired both before and *after* the war. The largest town in the region was Kosów. It was a pretty area.

> Picturesque mountains covered with fir trees and criss-crossed by the swift-flowing Cheremosh River and winding mountain paths, the scenic green highlands abounding in flowers, and, of course, the hospitality of the Hutsuls hold an infinity of attractions for holiday-makers.[27]

Helena recalls that in 1941, when the German armies swept over the land, they were greeted by homemade signs, hung on "every other tree" along the roads, which read: "*Smert' L'akham. Smert' moskovs'ko-zhydivs'kiy komuni.*"[28]

In 1942, the saying "*Za San l'ashyi, po San nashyi!*"[29] became a commonplace.

In 1943, when Helena was in the sixth grade in Berezów Średni, her teacher, after being told by one of the students that she was Polish, said to Helena in front of the whole class: "What?! You come here to benefit from our education? Get out! Get out! Students, spit on her and throw her out of here!"

In that same year, her seventeen-year-old brother Michał was invited by a Ukrainian friend to a gathering of the young men of the village. In the course of the evening, the very same Ukrainian friend who had invited him took Michał by the shoulder and sang in a loud, clear voice for all to hear this commonly sung Ukrainian folk song:

> *Hej vy khloptsi, yunaky*
> *Nezabarom pryide pohrom na L'akhy*
> *Budem yikh rizaty na spys probyvaty*
> *Vychystym Ukraïnu vid smittya*
> *Todi na Ukraïni bude vilne zhyttya*[30]

Needless to say, after this threatening reception Michał left the party and went home. It was also in that year that the Ukrainians began to catch and murder Polish men, both young and old.

One day Antek, another good Ukrainian friend of Michał, the son of a Ukrainian neighbor named Vasyl Gienyk (called Vasyl "Popereznyczyn" in the village because his father was a forester[31]), came to Michał's house and said, "Anna [Helena's and Michał's mother's name], lock the door, cover all the windows with a cloth and nail them up with boards." This done, he took out a deck of cards, called Michał over and said, "Let's play cards."

After a time two more young Ukrainians carrying machine guns (*pepeszki*[32]) came to the house and banged on one of the covered windows. Both Anna and Helena went to the window, each drawing a section of the sheet to one side, and recognized the boy who did the knocking. It was Guścio, Michał's best friend, also a *Banderowiec*. To Anna he said, as if he did not know Helena's name, "Tell your daughter to get away from the window." He added, "Is Michał home?"

Helena moved aside and said nothing. Anna also said nothing. Meanwhile Antek crawled on his hands and knees to Anna's feet, tugged at her skirts and whispered, "Tell them Michał is not home. He is not home. He is not home." Anna said to the face in the window, "Michał is not home."

She knew then that there was a death warrant out for her son and that in his own way Antek came to warn them. She also knew that although Antek was himself a *Banderowiec* he did not have the heart to be party to his best friend's cold-blooded murder.

"Where is Michał?" Guścio insisted.

Anna replied, "He went to Andrzej's house." (Andrzej was Michał's Polish friend.)

So Guścio and his comrade left and went to Andrzej's house in search of Michał. Finding neither one of them there, they laid hold of Andrzej's mother, an infirm old hunchback who suffered from some trembling disease, and beat her so much so that she was bedridden for the next two weeks. Then they ransacked and robbed the house and left.

Later, Antek said to Michał, "I don't ever want to see you here again! Get out! I managed to save your life this time. Next time you might not be so lucky."

But Michał decided to stay on, keeping out of sight as much as possible.

Shortly thereafter Antek came to the Przygrodzki house again and said to Michał and his father, "Do not stay in your house tonight."

Michał left immediately, but Józef Przygrodzki wanted to remain and protect his family. To her stubborn father, Helena said, "Vasyl invited you to his house. Go there." This she repeated several times and finally added firmly: "He *told* you to go there!"

At last, he relented and went out. (All this happened around 11:00 P.M., three days before the Polish Easter, on Good Friday.[33]) In the house, there remained the mother, her three daughters, Helena (twelve), Rozalia (eleven), Anna (four), and their little brother Stefan, who was six years old.

No sooner did he leave when a group of armed *Banderowcy* surrounded the home. Pretending they were Polish partisans, one of the *Banderowcy* yelled in half-Polish, half-Ukrainian, "*Otwórz dveri!*" (Open the door!)

At the same time a shot rang out. Anna immediately complied with the order. The bandit then jumped into the house and, pointing his machine gun at her, yelled once more half in Polish half in Ukrainian, "*Gdzie twój cholovik?*" (Where is your man?)

Anna replied that he went to his uncle's house in Horodenka. She was then ordered to show the robber the place where her husband's boots were kept.

Meanwhile another bandit came over to where Helena and Rozalia were sleeping and uncovered Helena to her waist. She noticed that he had an army bag slung over his shoulder and that his hand was clasped around the handle of a long knife, the kind with which pigs were slaughtered in the village. The blade itself was still in the bag. Her eyes traveled slowly toward his face. She *knew* him. It was Myros' Drohomerecki; Myros', who lived in the same village as they; Myros', who married the daughter of their next-door neighbor.

"When he pulled the blanket off me," said Helena, "and I saw him reaching for his knife, I tried to shut my eyes because I knew I was going to die then and there. But I could not. Imagine! I could not close my eyes!"

At that very moment someone banged on the window so hard that Myros' turned around. Helena remembers that someone called to him and told him to come out. After a while, Myros' returned and came straight for her again. This time he just covered her up with the blanket which she could not do herself because she was paralyzed with fear. Myros' then went over to Stefan's bed and asked, "*To chlopak?*" (Is this a boy?)

"*Tak*," replied Anna.

"How old is he?" This time Anna said nothing; perhaps lying did not come easy to this very Christian soul, even in extreme circumstances such as these.

"Two," answered eleven-year-old Róża, unconstrained by Christian morality.

"He is two years old," she repeated emphatically, for she had heard that the Ukrainians did not kill boys under four years of age. Since it was dark and Stefan's head was completely shaven, the lie produced its desired effect. Myros' stepped away from the bedside of the six-year-old child who was too old to live and too young to die.

While this tense drama was going on, other Ukrainians came into the house and carried off everything they could find, which was everything except the bottle of vodka hidden under some goose feathers deep at the bottom of an old chest. (Anna raised geese, "whole flocks of them, fifty, sixty at a time," said Helena. The vodka was a "present" from the Germans for one of the cows which they stole sometime before that.) When everything was carried off one of the *Banderowcy* said again in half and half:

"*Zamknij dveri.*" (Close the door.)

And then they left.

After their departure, while Anna was lamenting over all their stolen belongings, Helena said, "Count your blessings, mother. Its a good thing they did not find the vodka. Who knows what would have happened then. And look there, and there, and there," she said, pointing through the windows to the houses burning brightly throughout the village.

This was the first organized attack on the Polish community in Berezów Niżny. All told, fourteen Polish households were attacked that night, and wherever a man—even a young man—was found on the premises, he was killed.

In one family they killed an old veteran of the First World War, Mr. Michał Przygrodzki. Mercifully for him, he was spared full awareness before his death—before his neck was sliced so that his head just dangled on the remaining skin and flesh—because he was already totally insane.[34]

In another household, they carved a Polish eagle on the chest of Stefan Milewski, and then they killed him.

In a third, they hacked Mikołaj Przygrodzki[35] to death with an axe.

In a fourth, they caught a young man who recently returned from Germany, Gienek by name. To punish him for pleading for his life, they cut his tongue out and stabbed him over and over again. But being a strong lad, Gienek did not die until 8:00 the following morning.[36]

In a fifth house, another young man, sixteen or seventeen years old, was also stabbed to death. In between the stabbings, his body was repeatedly splattered by liquified manure, such as the farmers used to increase the yield of their fields and gardens. Afterwards all the people wondered why they had killed him, since no one knew for sure whether his father was Polish or Ukrainian. His mother was a demented woman who had always been kept under lock and key by her own parents. One day this poor girl had escaped, only to come home pregnant—pregnant with the same Michał who now lay covered with blood and dung at her feet.

There were other casualties of that first attack, other stories which now, fifty years later, seem fantastic.

("It does not matter," said Mrs. Helena Przygrodzki Piotrowiak, "God knows that I speak the truth. Why would I make up such horrible stories?")

Meanwhile, when he saw the burning houses in the village, Józef Przygrodzki wanted to leave Vasyl's home in order to assist his own family.

"I must go back!" he said to Vasyl. "They are murdering my wife and children!"

"No!" said Vasyl, "If you go now, you will only make matters worse. You cannot save them. I will go myself and see what can be done. You will stay here."

Vasyl's wife, Anna, picked up a pail and said to Józef, "Come with me." And so, crouching by her billowing skirts, Józef Przygrodzki accompanied this Ukrainian Anna to the cow-shed (*obór*) where he was to spend the night.

Just as they reached the cow-shed ("The night was clear," remembered Helena, "and the moon was bright"), several *Banderowcy* happened to be passing by. Without further thought, Anna Gienyk immediately pulled up a stool and began to milk a cow. Józef took the hint and crawled in between her legs whereupon he was promptly covered by many layers of skirts. There he remained until the danger passed.

In the meantime, Vasyl went over, as he had promised, to the Przygrodzki house. Finding them all shaken but alive, he gave thanks to God and told them that their father was safely quartered in his cow-shed. He then returned home and told Józef the good news.

The very next morning, Józef Przygrodzki, together with his son Michał, left Berezów Niżny for the county town of Kołomyja. Once there, Michał signed up for the Polish Army and Józef took on any odd jobs that came his way in order to support himself.

From that time on, for as long as she could ("perhaps for one year, perhaps for one and a half") Helena would traverse the twenty-six kilometers to Kołomyja by foot, "sometimes once, sometimes twice a month," in rain or shine, in summer's heat and winter's cold, to see her father, to bring him food from the village, but most importantly, to share with him the letters which her brother sent home from the army. Needless to say, in 1943 and thereafter, that was always a dangerous and uncertain journey, especially for a Polish girl of twelve or thirteen summers.

At my bidding, Helena proceeded to recall one such journey in great detail.[37]

> One day as I was walking through a neighboring village by the name of Łucza, I saw that a house was on fire. When I got nearer, I saw a group

of *Banderowcy*. I saw them throw an eighteen-year-old girl into the flames because she refused to give them her scarves and dresses. For a young village girl, these things were very important. They were her wealth. I knew this particular girl and I was surprised because she was like they, a Ukrainian. They must have come to rob her. I quickly left that village.

Further down the road, I came across an old Polish woman who was lying dead in a pool of blood and beside her, in the ditch, there was an overturned wagon full of potatoes, cabbages, and other vegetables. This old lady would often come to our village to beg for food which she would then take to the town of Jabłonów where she lived. Later, when I told my mother of her death, she said that she was there that day and that she gave her some cabbages and potatoes.

I kept on walking to Kołomyja, twenty-four kilometers away. It was closer through the woods, but I was afraid of the bandits and kept to the roads and fields.

I saw a cart pulled by a very small and thin gray [*siwy koń*]. I have never seen such a poor animal in all my life! I still remember how he looked. The cart was loaded down with bags of salt which the two women, who rode on the wagon, got from saltworks up in our mountains and were taking home to Podole.

I asked them if I could go with them because I was afraid to continue on alone. They said that it would be all right, and so I walked besides the wagon since I did not want to add any more weight to it for the sake of that poor horse.

Huge chestnut trees grew beside that particular road on which we traveled and it was under one of these trees that we met two *Banderowcy* dressed in sheepskin coats without sleeves. On their heads they wore those *czapki mazepenkie z tryzubami*.[38] They also carried machine guns [*pepeszki*]. One of the *Banderowcy* asked the women what they had in the wagon.

"Salt," the women replied, "for which we exchanged some wheat."

Then the *Banderowiec* asked, "*Yakoyi natsiyi vy ye?*" (What is your nationality?)

They answered, "*My ukraïns'koi.*" (We're Ukrainian.)

And they let the women go.

They then came over to me. I was terrified. They were *Banderowcy*, after all, and in the bottom of my basket were the Polish letters from my brother which I was carrying to my father. My brother was then serving in the Polish Army.

"*A ty*," one asked me, "*yakoyi natsiyi?*" (And you, what nation?)

I answered, "*ukraïns'koi.*" [She gave me a knowing look.] Well, what was I to say?

He wanted to know where I was going: "*Kuda idesh?*" (Where are you going?)

I answered, "*Idu do Horodenky po yaru pshenytsyu na kutyu.*" (I'm going to Horodenka for some spring wheat for the *kutya*."[39])

The *Banderowiec* wanted to know: "*Ty znayesh khto my ye?*" (Do you know who we are?)

I answered, "*Lyudy.*" (People.)

He said, "*Diysn.*" (That's true.) "*My ye Banderivtsi.*" (We are *Banderowcy.*)

I said, "*Banderivtsi to lyudy.*" (*Banderowcy* are people.)

The *Banderowiec* let this remark pass to press his interrogation further:

"*Chy ty znayesh za shcho my Voyuyem?*" (Do you know what we are fighting for?)

I shrugged my shoulders and said nothing. One of them provided me with the answer: "*Za samostiynu Ukraïnu.*" (For an independent Ukraine.)

I said, "*Nay vam Boh pomahaye.*" (May God help you.) Well? What was I to say? [She added again. I smiled, knowing the double meaning of the phrase.]

"*Shcho vydila po dorozi yak ishla?*" (What did you see on the way as you were walking?), he continued to grill me.

"*Horila khata*" (a burning house), I replied.

And he: "*To z neba upala bomba na tu khatu.*" (A bomb fell on that house from heaven.) "*I shcho ty shche vydila?*" (And what else did you see?)

"*Ubytu zhinku*" (a murdered woman), I said.

He explained, "*Vona donosyla na NKVD.*" (She was an informant for the NKVD.) "*Yiy ne treba bulo donosyty na NKVD.*" (She should not have carried information to the NKVD.)

Then he said, "*Rosty kvitko lyudyam na potikhu.*" (Grow little flower. May you be a comfort to the people.) Imagine that! He called me a flower! It's a good thing he didn't examine the basket!

The other *Banderowiec* then added his own good wishes as well: "*Shchaslyvoyi dorohy, kvitko.*" (Happy journey, little flower.) And so my life was spared.

I then caught up with the two women and we traveled together to the village Stopczatów. There we spent the night in separate quarters and in the morning I went on to Kołomyja alone.

I saw my father, gave him the food and letters, and returned home that same day.

I kept going to see my father like this for some time—until one of our good Ukrainian friends told my mother that I was suspected of carrying information, of being an informant. This was generally a death warrant for which Polish people were killed "unto the ninth generation," as they used to say. And so I stopped visiting my father.

All this time, until 1946 when my father returned from Kołomyja with the Russian Army, we never slept in our house. In the evening we would either go over to our Ukrainian neighbors or we would sleep in the empty houses left behind by the Jews.

> Upon my father's return, we were transported under Russian guard to the interior of Poland, the province of Wrocław.

But this is not quite the end of Helena Przygrodzki Piotrowiak's story. There is a gruesome sequel. Her brother Michał survived the war but his Polish friend Andrzej was eventually caught and killed by the Ukrainians. Antek Gienyk, the Ukrainian friend who twice saved his life, because he could not kill his Polish neighbors left the *Banderowcy*, lived for a while with Michał's father in Kołomyja, and finally joined the Russian Army. When his Ukrainian cohort in Berezów Niżny found out about this, they executed both his parents, Vasyl and Anna Gienyk, and torched their home.

Helena recalls discovering their bodies:

> Sometime after their house was burnt, I saw two bodies hanging from a weeping willow. I ran over to see who they were because I thought that maybe the Ukrainians killed my mother and my sister. There I saw Vasyl and Anna suspended from a single nail under a weeping willow tree. It was a very large nail, this thick [Helena showed me her little finger] and about this long [she measured off a distance of about thirty centimeters with her hands]. Vasyl was dangling from that nail, his feet barely touching the ground. Dried blood was caked on his face and his long matted whiskers were also drenched with blood. On his chest hung a sign: "*Za zradu bat'kivshchyny*." [For betraying the fatherland.]
>
> Maybe Anna was hung there by his side on that nail, but by the time I saw her she must have slid down so that she was almost in a sitting position. Her stomach was slashed open and her exposed entrails just lay there in her lap.[40]

In 1972 Mrs. Helena Przygrodzki Piotrowiak took her family to visit her native village and the "picturesque mountains covered with fir trees and criss-crossed by the swift flowing Cheremosh River and winding mountain paths, the scenic green highlands abounding in flowers, and, of course, the hospitality of the Hutsuls."

While on her way from Kołomyja to Berezów, Niżny: "I saw that nail," she said. "After twenty-six years it was *still* there, *still* there," she repeated and then grew very quiet. . .

"And all at once, all those memories came flooding back, they all came back to me."

I said nothing.

"Then," she continued, "two days later, as we were walking over a bridge in Berezów Niżny, we saw a man approaching us from the opposite direction. He was tall, bent over, old—but I recognized him, I recognized him, I recognized him." She stopped again and her daughter, Danuta, who had heard these stories many times before and who now was helping me transcribe them, finished the sequence of her thoughts:

"It was Myros' Drohomerecki," she said.

Danuta continued:

> They both stopped, frozen in their tracks, and my mother's face turned completely white. I didn't know what was happening. They both exchanged long, meaningful glances. It was like a scene from one of those melodramatic films.
>
> And then we passed each other by and walked on.

"That man was Myros' Drohomerecki," said Helena, as if she hadn't heard a word her daughter said.

After that encounter, one of the aunts that they were visiting, Marysia Ficycz (married to a Ukrainian before the war), would never allow them to go out alone. "Many tourists," she told them, "perish in these parts."

After her six-year-old son was called *Polaku durnyi* (stupid Polak), and beaten on the back with sticks until welts appeared by the Ukrainian grandchildren of the aunt, Helena said to her, "I have suffered so much in my life at the hands of the Ukrainians, I don't need this." And she cut her visit short, packed her bags, and brought her family back to the United States. She has not been back to her village since, and I doubt very much that she will ever return to those "picturesque mountains . . . and, of course, the hospitality of the Hutsuls."

IX

It now grew dark. From Lisianka
Sprang up the light of fire;
And Zalizniak and Gonta lit
Their pipes in fashion dire,—
Grim was the way they lighted them!
Even the damned in hell
In such a manner cannot smoke!
Tikich in fashion fell
Is reddening with alien blood
And high above it blaze
The buildings and the houses all;
Thus Fate inflicts its ways
On nobles and on poor alike.
Out in the public square
Bold Zalizniak with Gonta stands
And shouts: "Their doom prepare!
Punish the Poles and make them weep!"
The lads do punish them.
Weeping and groans burst forth; one begs,
One curses to condemn;

Another prays, confessing all
His errors to a mate
Already dead. No one is spared,—
The ruthless mete out fate.
Like death itself, they take no thought
Of beauty, age, or youth
In gentle ladies, Jewish maids—
Their blood's a stream, forsooth.
Neither the crippled nor the old
Nor even children small
Remained alive; for none escaped
The wretched end for all.
All were laid low, and strewn pell-mell
Till not a soul alive
In Lisianka was left that day.
Now conflagrations strive
In lofty tongues of leaping flame
To reach to heaven's crown.
And Halayda ceased not to shout:
"Strike, strike the Poles all down!"
Corpses he slashes, mad with rage,
Hangs up the dead and burns them.
"Give me more Poles to kill, I say,
For punishment concerns them!
Give me more Poles! To drain their blood
I still would persevere!
A sea of blood were not enough!
Oksana, O my dear,
Where are you?" As he shouts, he leaps
To search the flaming glare.
Meanwhile the haydamaks have placed
Stout tables in the square,
And brought in food that they might sup,
Sought food on every side
To banquet while the light remained.
"Let us begin!" they cried.
They feast and round about them there
Red hell gleams maniac;
Hanging from rafters in the flames
The corpses crackle black.
The rafters flicker in the blaze
And burn along with them.
—"Drink, comrades drink! Pour out some more!
For such a requiem
May we with Polish gentry meet
Once more and end their reigns!"
And Zalizniak in one great breath

The mighty tankard drains.
—"To all your cursèd corpses now,
Your cursèd souls' bad end,
Once more I drink. Drink up, my lads!
Drink, Gonta, my good friend!" . . . [41]

Bear with me now as I relate the sad story of the Leonówka massacre, which also involved members of my extended family. It is but one more instance of the insanity which ruled our land at that time. Far be it from me to claim that this was the worst incident of the war or even in the history of my family. But it is representative of those days of terror in our immediate vicinity.

Picture in your mind's eye two quaint East European villages strung out along the same winding, quiet, country road within two kilometers of each other: Leonówka, a small Polish village of some thirty numbers,[42] with a store, a school, people in the streets, and many, many children; and Żalanka, a Ukrainian village of similar description, but without a school. That the relationship between these two villages was cordial before the war can be surmised from the fact that Żalanka's children were always welcome in Leonówka's red-brick schoolhouse, where Zofia Sigda taught grades 1–3, and her husband, Tomasz, taught grades 4–7 in the Polish language.[43]

My own family of orientation lived in Leonówka for some time before moving to Amelin and finally settling down in Ryświanka. My two surviving brothers were born there. Two of my father's brothers still lived there with their families in the early 1940s. One of these was Władysław, who passed away quite unexpectedly on February 2, 1942 after a severe asthma attack, and who left behind him his wife, Marcelina (née Bagiński), and seven children.

The date, fixed forever in the annals of human iniquity, was August 1, 1943. It was a Sunday. Marcelina went to her parish church in Tuczyn that day to attend Mass and to pray for her recently deceased husband. She also prayed for her children: Stanisława (called Stasia), a young lady of eighteen summers; Mirosława (thirteen), Zofia (eleven), Władysława (nine), Romalda (seven), Stefan (five), and her fair-haired child with an angelic face and long baby curls, named (at the insistence of his sisters) Waldymar—after a popular romance novel hero of that day. He was only three.

Not all the Piotrowski children were home that day. Stasia, the oldest, had been staying with her Aunt Franciszka Kuczyński (her mother's sister) who lived near Aleksandria. She recalls that one day the Gestapo came to her aunt's house looking for Jews and human slaves; they also raped young girls. Being well hidden, after their departure she was sent to a friendly Ukrainian's house in the village of Remel,[44] where she was to remain overnight in case they should return. She went, but, becoming frightened by the constant whispering in the household, she left the Ukrainians and made her way back on foot to her own home in Leonówka, some sixteen kilometers away. Just before August 1, she was sent to stay with Pawlina Prokopowiec, married to a German by the name of Bitner, who lived in the village of Kwasiłów on the other side of Równe.

Zofia, her sister, was also absent. That afternoon she had gone to her cousin's house (Adolf Bagiński) and had decided to remain there overnight. So at home there remained only Marcelina, her four youngest children, her daughter Mirosława, and her daughter's two visiting friends—a boy, Gienek Paśnieski (fifteen), whose family lived on the outskirts of the village, and a girl, Władzia Bagiński (thirteen), who lived next door.

It was that very night, at about eleven o'clock, that the cohort from Żalanka descended upon sleeping Leonówka. Whether this particular group of men consisted of the actual residents of Żalanka (as my cousin, Stasia, believes), or whether it was a contingent of the UPA using Żalanka as its base of operation, will perhaps never be known for certain. In any case, these hundred or so Ukrainians came well equipped with grenades, field rifles, and an assortment of axes, scythes, and swords.

Posting some men around the village, the rest threw themselves upon the first Polish household of Leonówka, the one closest to Żalanka, the home of Jan Bagiński, his seven-months-pregnant wife and eight of their children (their ninth, Władzia, was spending the night next door with the Piotrowskis.) A live grenade was flung through the window into the home of the sleeping family, and as the panic-stricken survivors emerged, they were slaughtered one by one. Only two children, Halina and Władysław, survived the carnage by hiding in the fields. On that particular night they slept in the hayloft of the barn.

The exploding grenade awakened Marcelina, her family, and their two young visitors. In horror, they saw their next-door neighbor's house go up in flames. In utter disbelief, they heard the death screams of the parents and the children with whom they played that very day. They all knew full well that they would be next.

As Mirosława, Gieniek, and Władzia (whose family was being burned and slaughtered next door) dove through an opening under the altar into the cellar, crawled through the tunnel, and ran out into the fields, Marselina threw each one of her darling babies out the nearest window, then dove out after them into the yard. Even as she scrambled to gather her dear little ones around her before running for safety, she perished. An axe-wielding Ukrainian cut her in half, and then in half again. Stefan, too, was killed outright, and fell beside his mother. Waldymar, the fair-haired child, the three-year-old named after the romantic hero of his day, was caught by a flying saber on the side of his head and fell bloody and unconscious to the ground. Romalda ran into the barn, where she had hidden so many times before, and there was pierced to death with an ordinary pitchfork. Władysława ran as fast as her little legs could carry her into the family orchard, only to be slaughtered by another scythe-wielding henchman.

Then, after the house and barn were both put to the torch, one of the men remembered that he had seen some children running toward the fields. The child-hunt began.

Mirosława and her two friends thought they could hide from the butchers by burying themselves deeply in the fresh-cut hay stacked up like sentry-shelters by their house. (How transparent to adults are the secret hiding places of our youth!) The terrible hunters searched every inch of the terrain, thrusting pitchforks into the hay stacks and turning them inside out as they went along. First, they found Gienek, the fifteen-year-old boy, and he was killed without a word of protest. Next, they found Władzia, the thirteen-year-old girl, and although she pleaded with them for her young life, she too was cut down with a bloodstained sword. Mirosława alone, somehow, managed to survive the carnage and lived to tell about it.

And so they proceeded from house to house, from family to family, from child to child until the entire village was utterly destroyed. Only those from the village and the houses beyond who were able to conceal themselves in the fields, woods, and the nearby marshes managed to survive. Stanisław Piotrowski (my father's brother), his wife, Marynia, and their four children were among these. Somehow, they were able to flee their home, reach the swamp, and thus, submerged waist-deep in mud and water, save their lives.[45]

At approximately 2:00 A.M., when the butchery was over and all of Leonówka stood in flames, the leader of those who called themselves "partisans" sounded a long victorious whistle which signaled the end of the siege, or rather the slaughter, and the return of the men to Żalanka; Żalanka which, in the Polish language, means "grief, sorrow, and anguish"; Żalanka which meant home and safe haven to the Ukrainians.

After the Ukrainians departed and all grew still as death, Mirosława left her shelter, bypassed her two slain childhood friends, and fearfully made her way back to her burning home. There, she beheld—and this memory of hers has never dimmed—the bloodied and dismembered bodies of her mother, her brothers, and her sisters. Amid the ocean of sorrow which overwhelmed this thirteen-year-old child, the only fleeting moment of joy—if that is the appropriate word to describe such an emotion—was the discovery that her youngest brother, Waldymar, with his bloodstained angelic face and his matted baby curls, was still alive. She lifted this feather of a child off the ground and pressed him to her sheltering bosom. Thus, they remained alone amid the fires of hell; sister and brother joined forever in that last heart-rending embrace . . . for even as she held him fast in her loving arms, his body went limp, and his little soul flew up to heaven.

As it was August and the barns were full of harvested grain and hay, the flames could be seen from far away. Zofia saw them from her cousin's house three kilometers away. We saw them, too, from about the same distance, rising above the tree tops of *Las Ryświanecki*. Stasia claims that, while at Pawlina's house, she had a dream that night about her mother, and that her house was on fire. When she awoke and looked in the direction of her home, she saw that the sky in the vicinity of Leonówka was all red, like a bright glowing ember in the night. She knew then that her own village was on fire. Perhaps it was the glow of her Leonówka that she saw at a distance of some thirty-three kilometers . . . but it also could have been the glow of any one of the many Polish villages burning, burning, burning night and day throughout Wołyń in those terrible months of July and August.

In the morning, when people from the surrounding countryside arrived in the village that was Leonówka to bury the remains of the deceased, the Ukrainians returned to drive them off. The bodies of the dead were left to lie there where they fell, under the red sky of August.

VI

. . . .

Meanwhile, it seems
None live here any more.
There's not a sound of cock or dog,
No voice of beast or fowl,
Save that far off, beyond the grove,
One hears the grey wolves howl. . . .

XI

. . . .

Only wild beasts upon the outskirts howl,
And into villages they boldly prowl,
Scenting the corpses. Not a man would bury
The Poles but let the hungry wolves make merry;
Till the snow covered with its silent weft
The tooth-scarred skeletons the wolves had left. . . .[46]

During this time we also lost my Uncle Hilary Bronowicki, who went one day to a neighboring Ukrainian's house and there was killed. After some time, when he failed to come home, Mania (his wife and my father's sister) became worried, and sent her son to fetch his father. He, too, was brutally murdered. When neither one returned, Mania—who had a wooden leg—went herself to see what had transpired. She arrived just in time to witness her husband and her son being lowered into a shallow grave by the people with whom they had lived as neighbors for so many years.

My mother's brother, Paweł, also met a similar fate. One evening at a neighbor's home, Paweł said, "There is not one Ukrainian house without a bandit." He did not know how right he was, for in that house there was a Ukrainian bandit among the men to whom he spoke. The following night, Paweł was dragged out of his house and clubbed to death. His wife, who was forced to watch, sustained a massive coronary and died as he was being beaten. Later, all their children were put to the sword.

My father's youngest brother, Edward,[47] narrowly escaped a similar fate when a Ukrainian neighbor's wife warned him not to come into their house, because her husband was waiting to kill him with an axe on the other side of the door. Edward was the godfather of one of their children! What happened to the rest of my many aunts and uncles during these terrible years God only knows. As far as I know, only Edward and my father, the youngest and the oldest of the Piotrowski children, survived the war.

Our nearest neighbor's son, Staszek, who married a Ukrainian girl before the war, also narrowly escaped his doom. When he was away, some Ukrainians came to his wife and ordered her to kill him (her own husband!) while he lay sleeping that very night. When he returned, she told him of the heartless visitation, whereupon he immediately left for Tuczyn just as he was, without taking anything for his journey. He was deported to Germany and survived the war, but he never went back to his home in Ryświanka again.

The husband of my sister Aniela (whom he met and married after the war) was born on March 25, 1913, in a predominantly Polish town by the name of Torczyn, about one hundred and ten kilometers due west of Ryświanka. Being a clever man, Dominik Tarnawski made his way quickly in this world, bought a house, and married a local girl, Helena, with whom he had two daughters and a son. Shortly after the German invasion, a group of Ukrainian bandits attacked his home at night. Dominik, thinking they were after him, jumped out of a window and began to run toward the forest. They shot at him and wounded him in the leg, but miraculously he somehow escaped.

His family was not so fortunate; the Ukrainians had not only come for him. First, they raped his wife. Then, they proceeded to execute her by tying her up to a nearby tree and cutting off her breasts. As she hung there bleeding to death, they began to hurl her two-year-old son against the house wall repeatedly until his spirit left his body. Finally, they shot her two daughters. When their bloody deeds were done and all had perished, they threw the bodies into a deep well in front of the house. Then, they set the house ablaze.

Dominik knew nothing of this until his parents, Anna and Hipolit Tarnawski, told him the tragic news a few days later. (It was they who retrieved the mutilated bodies of his family and, wrapping them in a sheet, gave them a proper burial.) After this, Dominik joined a group of Polish partisans organized against the Ukrainian attacks. Unfortunately, he was captured by the Germans, and for his partisan activity, he was sent to the extermination camp at Dachau. Because he was a shoemaker by profession, the Gestapo spared his life in exchange for his craft. Although he survived the death camp, he was never well again. After he married my sister, he named his first daughter Władysława—in honor of his murdered two-year-old son, Władysław. Until his early death at 55, Dominik often spoke to his wife and to his two daughters,

Władysława and Irena, about the tragic events at Torczyn. Never could he forget the cruel execution of his first wife and family.

VII

Throughout the length of our Ukraine
The church-bells raised their call;
The haydamaks raised up their cry:
"Death to the gentry! All!
Death to the gentry! Let's to work,
And warm the very clouds!"
The Smila region is aflame,
Wrapped in its reddened shrouds;
But Medvedivka is the first
To warm the startled sky.
All Smila's parish is ablaze,
The blood is flowing high,
While Korsun burns and Kaniv burns,
Cherkassy, Chihirin;
Down the Dark Highway sweeps the fire
As days of death begin.
Up to Uman the blood-stream flows;
Podilia bathes in fire
As Gonta makes a merry feast;
Zalizniak slakes his ire
Up in Cherkassy; likewise there
Yarema does his best;
One tempers thus his damask steel
And one his sword-blade bless'd.
"Good, good, my lads! Go to it now,
The evil foeman routing!
Good work, my boys!"—out in the square
Bold Zalizniak is shouting.
A hell surrounds him as he goes;
In that inferno set,
The haydamaks all beat about;
Yarema in a sweat,
A ghastly sight, hews down the foe—
Three, four, he makes them fall
In one fell swoop.—"Good work, my son!
The devil take them all!
By this you'll gain a paradise,
Or reach a captain's station.
Just keep it up! And forward, lads!"
Thus they, in wild elation,
In garrets and in storehouse bins,
In cellars, everywhere,

Mow down the foe, and loot his nest.
"Stop, lads! Your bodies spare,
For you are weary. Take a rest!"
The streets and the bazaars
Are strewn with corpses, wet with blood:
"Too few are yet their scars!
Their punishment must vaster be,
That their unchristian souls
May rise no more to vex our land!"
His force the square patrols. . .[48]

One by one the Polish villages of Wołyń fell into the hands of the Ukrainian Nationalists. One by one they were destroyed by fire and sword, and their inhabitants either killed, or driven into the hands of the awaiting Germans. Everyone's sad story was the same, differing only in the manner of its telling and the interpersonal details of each family's woes.

I have already described the first massacre at Obórki (November 13 and 15, 1942) and that of Parośle (February 9, 1943), where together, some 245 people perished. This was only the beginning. On Holy Thursday, April 22, 1943, a band of Ukrainian Nationalists surrounded the village of Zabara and, as in Leonówka, proceeded to set fire to the houses and execute the survivors. That night and into Good Friday, 750 people perished in Zabara.[49]

On Good Friday, April 23, of that same year, Janowa Dolina (in the county of Kostopol), which housed about 20,000 residents, a German garrison of about 1,000 soldiers, and a Polish self-defense unit, was attacked by the Ukrainian Nationalists at 1:00 A.M. In the mayhem that followed approximately 600 people died. The German soldiers did nothing to prevent the slaughter, choosing simply to remain in their barracks. The Polish civil-defense unit also did nothing—first, because no attack was expected given the presence of the Germans; and second, because in the presence of the Germans no one dared to bear arms.

June 16, 1943, marked the beginning of the siege of Huta Stepańska, another self-defense center in the county of Kostopol, where between 16,000 and 18,000 Polish people were gathered. After thirty-two hours of bitter fighting, on the morning of June 18, the civil-defense unit, fearing the worst, decided to break through the encirclement. In all, forty people perished during the standoff, and 300 more died while trying to escape. Jan Miszkiewicz (one of those interviewed, born in Huta Stepańska) clearly recalled the final stand at the three-story brick schoolhouse, the breakout of the civilians, and the Nazi roundup of some of the refugees at a railway station somewhere between Rafałowka and Sarny. Many, however, evaded the Nazis and either joined the growing partisan resistance movement or found their way to the safety of one or another local civil-defense center.

June 16, 1943, also marked the destruction of the Polish villages in the vicinity of Huta Stepańska, including Borek, Lady, Omelanka, Temne, Hały, Użenie, Perespa, Siedlisko, Ostrówki, Wykra, Zakuście, Wyrobki, Suszniki, Ziwka, and Szymonisko. Some of the residents of these villages managed to reach the protection of Huta Stepańska; others were killed trying.

On July 11, 1943, UPA members from Wołczak murdered the entire population of Dominipol: about sixty families, or about 490 people.

On that same day, as a group of Polish people gathered in the town church of Poryck for religious ceremonies, a grenade was tossed into the nave of the church and Ukrainian Nationalists opened fire on the faithful. Then, they entered the church and shot anyone who moved. Finally, they brought some straw, set fire to the church, and mined the walls. Fortunately, the walls withstood the blast and rain put out the fire. In all, 500 parishioners perished in and outside of this church. The same thing transpired on the same day in the villages of Chrynów and Kisielin. The next day, July 12, Poryck was attacked again, and many of the twenty survivors of the previous day were killed along with other Polish people in the town.

On July 13, 1943, about 150 Polish families or about 600 people perished in the day-long slaughter which transpired in the village of Gaj.

In that same month, 400 Polish people perished in Jadwipol near Równe.

On August 30, 1943, all the Polish residents of Wola Ostrowiecka were rounded up in the local schoolyard by the Ukrainian Nationalists. The men were taken five at a time to a barn where they were hacked to death. The women and children were then packed into the school, grenades were thrown through the windows, and the school was set on fire. In this way 529 people, including 220 children, were murdered.

The same thing happened to the men in Ostrówki (near Luboml) on the same day. There, the women and children were marched off to the woods, made to lie face down, and executed by shots to the head. Out of a total of 604 residents, 438 Polish people died that day, among whom were 146 children.

In magnitude alone, these were among the worst incidents of brutality, all involving 300 people or more in a mere handful of villages, adding up to a few thousand casualties. But there were many, many more. Relying on archival records of the *Polnische Hilfs-Komitee* which became accessible on June 4, 1989, Aleksander Korman states that a total of 52,274 buildings were burned by the OUN/UPA in the provinces of Lwów, Stanisławów, Tarnopol, Wołyń, and Rzeszów.[50] Since this total does not include information from all provincial counties, the actual devastation of Polish villages and settlements was probably much worse. To this must be added all the Polish losses of land, personal possessions, livestock, and their ultimate loss, the loss of their lives. In the final analysis, it may be impossible to ascertain the exact number of Jews, Russians, Poles, Ukrainians, and others who perished at the hands of the OUN/UPA. Even estimates from those years vary widely.

In 1944, during an audience with the Nazi governor of Galicia, Władysław Studnicki accused the Germans of allowing 200,000 Polish people to perish at the hands of the Ukrainian Nationalists in Galicia alone. The governor, SS Brigadeführer Otto Wächter, estimated the number to have been around 40,000. The chief of the German police and SS, General Thier, who was also present, set the number of those who died at 100,000.[51]

According to P.I. Lytwyn (1968), in Wołyń alone more than 165,000 Poles and Ukrainians were murdered by the Nazis in conjunction with the Ukrainian Nationalists during the years of occupation.[52]

Russian estimates set the number of Polish deaths at the hands of the Ukrainian Nationalists in Wołyń at 20,000. Polish estimates state that around 15,000 Poles were killed in Wołyń in 1943 alone, and between March of 1943 and June of 1944, over 40,000 people perished.[53]

Basing their conclusion on AK (Home Army) reports, Szcześniak and Szota estimate that between 60,000 and 80,000 Polish people were killed by the Ukrainian Nationalists in the regions of Polesie, Wołyń, Chełm, and Zasanie.[54]

Iaroslav Dashkevych, a Ukrainian historian from Lwów, states that anywhere between 70,000 and 80,000 "of truly and completely innocent [Polish] people, usually tortured in the most cruel fashion" perished in Poland's eastern territories.[55]

There are also the estimates of S. Dłuski (140,000), W. Krzemien (165,000 up until the fall of 1944), and J. Engelgard (300,000 to 400,000 Poles killed by the UPA alone).[56]

Perhaps the most authoritative recent source on this topic is the remarkable work of Józef Turowski and Władysław Siemaszko. Published in 1990 in the Polish language, *Crimes Perpetrated Against the Polish Population of Wołyń by the Ukrainian Nationalists, 1939–1945* is a chronological register of the places where these crimes took place as well as a necrology, a martyrology of those killed, who at times are mentioned by name. The entries are based on materials that have been collected over the span of the last thirty years by the Commission for the Investigation of Nazi Atrocities in Poland and include the results from an oral-history project initiated in 1985 by members of the Twenty-seventh Division AK. Each of the relatively short entries in this work is indexed for purposes of verification and further research. A rather large, folded map accompanies the publication indicating the places where these atrocities took place. In all about 1,000 Wołynian towns, villages, colonies, etc. are listed where slightly over 30,000 atrocities occurred.

This ambitious work concludes that the bloodiest month in Wołyń was July 1943, when about 20,000 people perished. The bloodiest days were July 11 and 12, accounting for about 12,000 murders. Although the register includes many isolated instances of mutilation, murder and pillage, the tolls for the largest numbers of people were as follows: 110 incidents involving the death of 50 to

100 people; 25 incidents of up to 200 people; and 13 incidents of 300 people or more.

The authors are quick to point out, however, that for a variety of understandable reasons, these statistics do not reveal the full extent of the atrocities. Their overall estimate for the province of Wołyń alone is that between 60,000 and 70,000 people perished in about 2,000 locations. They go on to state that if we take the overall atrocities of the OUN/UPA against the Polish population of Eastern Poland to be in the vicinity of 300,000 to 400,000, then Wołyń's losses were the highest of any other province. A summary of their findings appears in the following table:

NUMBER OF POLISH DEATHS AT THE HANDS OF THE UKRAINIAN NATIONALISTS IN WOŁYŃ BY COUNTIES BETWEEN 1939 AND 1944

County	Documented	Estimated
Dubno	1,900	6,800
Horochów	2,400	4,200
Kostopol	4,400	7,000
Kowel	3,350	7,300
Krzemieniec	3,000	5,100
Luboml	1,856	1,900
Łuck	4,000	11,300
Równe	1,000	7,400
Sarny	1,400	6,100
Włodzimierz	6,500	8,000
Zdołbunów	500	3,600
Total for Wołyń	**30,306**	**68,700**

Currently, some Polish authors (e.g. E. Prus, J. Czmuta, and A. Korman) set the total number of those who died at half a million.[57] In his May 19, 1992, statement while on a visit to Warsaw, Leonid Kravchuk, the president of the Ukraine, used the same estimate:

> We do not conceal and do not keep silent. During the Second World War Ukrainian chauvinists killed about half a million Polish people in the eastern regions of pre-September Poland. Likewise, for a number of years after the war Polish villages burned and people perished. Ukrainian chauvinism is an abscess on the healthy body of the Ukrainian nation, a pang of our conscience in respect to the Polish nation.[58]

Whatever the number, it was not so much the killings which filled the Polish people with such dread and terror, as the manner in which they were conducted. Stanisław Domalewski, one of the men who hid the bells of Kazimirka, recalls the first murder in his native village on the night of January 27-28, 1943: The axing of Mr. and Mrs. Podchorodecki and their five children. He also recalls the last murder of which he is aware, that of an eighty-year-old man by the name of Grzegorz Sawicki, who was found by his family in the bushes behind their house with his tongue cut off, his fingernails ripped out, and his remaining teeth knocked out. My brother Franek says, "The Ukrainians threw living human beings into flaming houses, or simply butchered them with knives, scythes, or axes."

> Most tragic of all was the manner in which these murders were carried out, usually combined with the benediction of the priest over the people and the blessing of the instruments of death—axes, scythes, pitchforks, swords, and firearms. No differentiation was made between men and women, between adults and children and the elderly. Often outnumbered, especially in the smaller settlements, the victims—the dead and the unconscious, although still alive—were thrown into wells, lakes, and rivers, they were impaled on posts, parts of their bodies were cut off—feet, hands, heads; women's breasts were severed. The bodies of living victims were eviscerated, exposing the entrails and leaving them for flies and worms. Children were pierced through with pitchforks, impaled on posts and fences. Bodies were sawed in half, eyes were plucked out, tongues and ears were cut off. People were chained to horses and their heads, arms and legs were thus ripped out of their sockets. The larger villages and settlements were first captured by force of arms and after their capitulation, the peasants were killed with axes, scythes, pitchforks, knives, swords. In this degenerate lunacy, even their own Ukrainian brothers who did not want to participate in the murder of the Polish people or who broke disciplinary regulations were slaughtered.[59]

And so these resurrected *haydamaks* continued their festival of blood in Western Ukraine until the end of the war, and beyond—1943 and 1944 being the worst years.

Perhaps it has occurred to some of my readers to ask: "What about Polish nationalism and fanaticism? Did not the Poles return fire for fire? Did they not slaughter the Ukrainians as well?" It is a legitimate question, the answer to which should not be placed in a footnote. I have asked myself that question many times.

The answer is that the general Polish population, as well as the AK, the partisans, and the self-defense units, were well aware of the distinction between the "Ukrainian people" and the "Ukrainian Nationalists," although it was often difficult to tell who was who. By and large, right up to the very end, Polish anger and rage was turned against the latter rather than the former.[60] However, there were exceptions, and hell had no fury as when Ukrainian and Polish nationalism embraced in the kiss of death.

Yes, there were Polish terrorists among certain detachments of the AK, but especially the terrorist detachments of WiN (*Wolność i Niezawisłość*—Freedom and Independence), NOW (*Narodowa Organizacja Wojskowa*—National Military Organization) and the NSZ (*Narodowe Siły Zbrojne*—National Armed Forces), who engaged in lawless plunder, murdered innocent Ukrainian civilians (specifically those along the river San), and destroyed their villages. In general, these wanton acts of terror, materially no different from those of the Ukrainian Nationalists, were condemned by the Polish Army as well as the general Polish population.

Among the vengeful acts of the Polish extremists was the attack on the Ukrainian village of Dobra (January 19, 1945), where thirty-three people were killed, as well as the attack on Sawków (April 4, 1945), in the course of which fifteen Ukrainians were shot and their possessions stolen. In that same month, there was an attack on Rudka, where six people perished. A similar incident occurred on May 18, 1945, in Dobcza, where forty people died, and at the beginning of June 1945, in the village of Piskorowice, where 300 Ukrainians were shot. At the end of 1945, the village of Pawłokoma was attacked and several hundred people were massacred.

The crowning point of all this terrorism was the brutal attack on the village of Wierzchowiny, where, on June 6, 1945, 250 bandits, now said to have been members of the NKVD, dressed in (and in disgrace of) the uniform of the Polish Army, in the space of two hours, slaughtered 194 Ukrainians, including sixty-five children under eleven years of age.[61] In a society governed by lawlessness, the Law of the Talon prevailed: an eye for an eye, a tooth for a tooth.

I would like to end this sad chapter of inhuman deeds by recording the following acts of brutality related to me by Mr. Stanisław Domalewski, who hailed from the predominantly Polish village of Karaczun, near Sarny, and whose wife's brother lived in our own town of Tuczyn.

> The first murder in our area occurred on January 27 or 28 of 1943. Seven people perished that night, the entire family of Mr. and Mrs. Podchorodecki. [Mentioned previously.] Mr. Podchorodecki was an overseer of the foresters in our area. The Ukrainians butchered them all with axes and left their bodies where they fell. When Mr. Podchorodecki's brother-in-law returned from church, he found their remains and gave them a Christian burial.
>
> By February 2, 1943, the news of this tragedy reached every village in our area. On that day, as we were coming home from church, we were informed that two more Polish families were attacked in Karaczun: the Mazurek and Malec families. Mr. Mazurek, who was also a forester and very old, his wife, and their two daughters were found lying on the floor of their home with their heads cut off and the blood already congealing. The bloody axe with which they were slaughtered was left lying by the doorway.

> There were seven persons in the Malec family. Four of them were axed to death, two of the boys were wounded and left for dead but survived, and Mr. Malec escaped. Later, he was deported to Germany with the rest of us. Believe me, after these incidents, I never took off my shoes!

Then he said, after making me turn off my tape recorder, "It was not until 1976, while on a visit to Poland, that I found out that these two families were murdered by the partisans."

"The partisans?" I asked. "Which partisans?"

He looked me straight in the eye and replied, "The Russian partisans."

"The Russian partisans?" I asked again in disbelief.

"Yes," he said. "The Poles, the Jews, the Ukrainians, and the Russians. They were the 'Russian' partisans."

How could they (any terrorists, all terrorists, then as now) do these things? How could anyone resort to such brutal means, devoid of fundamental human feelings? How could they torture defenseless civilians, murder them in cold blood, and desecrate their remains in such barbaric ways? How does one account for such savage cruelty in the human species? I do not know the answer, and neither do the survivors of these atrocities with whom I spoke.

Perhaps any one of the contemporary "Raskolnikovs" of this world, the moral relativists "to whom all things are allowable," of whom Dostoyevsky speaks so eloquently in the language of psychological literature, could tell us the secret of their insane hearts. But like their heroes of the past, they, too, only profess the language of the deed.

Theories of mass insanity seem to be too simplistic. Theories of the "banality of evil" leave me unconvinced. Theories of moral depravity latent in the human species, controlled by the social contract within rationally constructed societies, seem plausible, but leave a poor picture of the human race. Perhaps it is true that the worst possible political systems always call forth the worst possible array of human emotions. Without the backing of such corrupt systems of government, those who are so predisposed and who act upon their predispositions become labeled as psychopathic criminals and become subject to the sanction of the territory within which they operate. But more often than not, the fear of such sanctions compels these types into sterile conformity, and they become virtually indistinguishable from the rest of humankind.

A case in point is the all too familiar story of all those terrible Nazi torturers and Ukrainian concentration camp guards who subsequently crawled into the social fabric of their respective communities and became solid citizens, honest businessmen, faithful husbands, and loving fathers and grandfathers. God save us from such exemplary human beings! I will stop here, for I have already said too much about a subject that registers as a complete blank upon my mind.

VIII

. . . .

Such was the horror that prevailed
Throughout the whole Ukraine!
The slaughter was far worse than hell...
Why must these folk be slain?
For they are of one common stock.
Could they not live as brothers?
But no! it was against their will
That each should love the others!
They sought to shed a brother's blood,
They coveted his wealth;
Although their fields and barns were full,
They grudged a brother's health.
"Let's kill our brothers! Burn their homes!"
They spoke, and it was done.
It seemed an end! But for revenge
They left the orphan son,
Who grew to manhood full of tears
Until his tortured hands
Became unbound—and blood for blood
And pang for pang demands!
One's heart aches as these brother Slavs
Tear brother Slavs to bits.
Who is to blame for such a crime?—
The Polish Jesuits...[62]

In our vicinity, as elsewhere, stories abounded of Polish mothers being held by the Ukrainian Nationalists and forced to watch as their families were dismembered piece by piece; of pregnant women being eviscerated; of vivisected pregnant women having cats sewn into their bleeding abdomens; of Ukrainian husbands murdering their own Polish wives; of Ukrainian wives murdering their own Polish husbands; of Ukrainian fathers murdering their own sons in order to prevent them from murdering their own Polish mothers; of sons of Polish-Ukrainian heritage being sawed in half because, the Nationalists said, they were half Polish; of children being strung up on household fences; of helpless infants being dashed against buildings or hurled into burning houses. Were these, then, the worst instances of cruelty in the war? And if these were not, then what were?[63]

And so we were afraid, afraid for one another and for ourselves, knowing neither the day nor the hour of our own final sacrifice. Each night and day new fires were visible, rising high above our ever darkening landscape, and each day and night they grew more numerous and brighter. Nothing could deliver us from our growing fears save death itself. If they did not come for us yet, it was because Ryświanka was a Ukrainian village and the few Polish families scattered among its colony were not worth the effort. Our turn would surely come after the larger pools of Polish blood dried up . . . perhaps sooner.

XI. GONTA[64] IN UMAN

The days pass on, the fearful summer days,
And all of our Ukraine is still ablaze.
In villages, the naked children weep:
The parents are not there their charge to keep.
The yellow leaves in wooded vales grow dun;
The clouds prevail and cover up the sun.
Only wild beasts upon the outskirts howl,
And into villages they boldly prowl,
Scenting the corpses. Not a man would bury
The Poles but let the hungry wolves make merry;
Till the snow covered with its silent weft
The tooth-scarred skeletons the wolves had left.

The winter tempests did not check
The slaughter's hellish ires;
Poles froze to death, and Cossack bands
Kept warm at savage fires.
Then spring arose, to wake again
The black and sleepy earth;
Primrose and periwinkle spread
A coverlet of mirth;
In fields, the lark soared; in the grove,
The nightingale would sing
An early morning welcome to
The earth adorned with spring . . .
A veritable paradise!
For whom? Alas, for men . . .
Why do they fail to glance at it?
Why desecrate it then?
That beauty must be smeared with blood,
And lit with flames of ill;
Sunlight and flowers do not suffice;
Clouds must be thicker still.
Hell does not satisfy! . . . Mankind!
When will you be content
With all the good things that you have?
Why so malevolent?

Spring has not stopped the flow of blood
Nor turned man's wrath to joy.
How foul it is; yet thus it was
In the far days of Troy,

And so it will hereafter be.
The haydamaks bring doom;
Where'er they pass, the world's on fire
And blood beflecks the gloom.
Maksim has got himself a son
Most famed through all Ukraine;
Yarema's not his son, of course,
Yet dearest of his train.
Maksim assails the enemy;
Yarema ruthless rages:
No mortal fight by day or night
His savage blade assuages.
Thus none he misses, none he spares,
No, not a single soul,—
To avenge the saintly sacristan
He hews down every Pole.
And for his dear Oksana's wrongs
He smites with heart of hate.
While Maksim says: "Lay on, my son!
Before we meet our fate,
Let's have a merry time!"
They did:
And still the foemen fell;
The Polish corpses from Kiev
To Uman lay pell-mell.

In countless numbers, haydamaks
Ringed Uman with their ire
At midnight; and before the dawn
They'd set the place on fire.
They set the blaze and shouted loud:
"We'll smite the Poles, we swear!"
Again the national dragoons
Were mowed down in the square
And with them little children died,
Even the sick and maimed.
Mid shrieks and cries upon the square,
That in full frenzy flamed,
Stands Gonta in a sea of blood,
Maksim beside him stern;
Both cry: "Most royally, my lads,
You make them pay their turn!"

Then suddenly the haydamaks
Lead out a Jesuit
And two boys. "Gonta," says the priest,
"Your children I submit.

You slaughter us—then kill them too:
For they are Catholics!
Why do you pause! Why stay your hand?
Their years are eight and six.
Slay them, for they, to manhood grown,
Will see our debt is paid! . . . "
—"Kill the black dog! And these two pups
I'll kill with my own blade.
Summon assembly! Now confess!
What are you? Catholics?"
—"We are, because our mother was . . . "
—"God, let not mercy mix!
Be quiet, lads! I know, I know!"
The haydamaks attend.
—"My children—they are Catholics . . .
Our cause I'll not offend,
Lest any idle talk should say
That I am not your friend.
I swore, when this blest blade I took,
All Catholics to slay . . .
O sons of mine, dear sons of mine!
Would you were grown today!
Would you were slaughtering the Poles!"
—"Father, we will, we will!"
—"Alas, you may not live for that!
Curs'd be your mother still,
That woman of an alien faith,
My wife, who gave you birth!
Why did she fail to drown you both
Before night left the earth?
Less sin that were: you would have died
In Orthodoxy free!
But now, alas, my little sons,
You are a woe to me!
Kiss me, my children, kiss me!
Your slayer is not I
But my grim oath!" He swung his sword—
And thus the children die!
Slain, to the ground they fell, and spoke:
"Father!" in last salute.
"O father, father, we're not Poles!
"We're . . . " And their lips were mute.
—"Are we to bury them?"
—"Not so!
For Catholics were they . . .
O sons of mine, dear sons of mine,
Would you were grown today!

Would you were slaughtering the Poles,
Your mother most of all,
That wife of mine who bore you both
And doomed us to this fall!
Come, friend!"
Maksim was at his side;
Across the square they went;
And both cried out: "No mercy, men!
To not a Pole relent!"
They showed no mercy: Horribly
That Uman region flared;
In not a home, in not a church
Were any living spared—
All were cut down. The hands of death
All reason overrule
In Uman in despair that day!
The old Basilian school
Where Gonta's children had been taught
Great Gonta sets on fire:
"My children you have eaten up!"
He rages in his ire:
"You have devoured the tiny ones,
And taught them nothing good . . .
Tear down the walls!"
The haydamaks
Obeyed him where he stood;
They tore them down; they dashed the priests
On stones in frenzy fell;
And threw the schoolboys, still alive,
To perish down the well.

Till late at night the task of death went on
And not a soul remained. Now fierce and wan,
Gonta cried out: "Where are you, cannibals?
You ate my sons—the curse upon me falls!
How bitterly I weep, how lonely feel!
My precious children and my dearest weal!
Where from my fury do my foemen shrink?
Blood of the gentry I would gladly drink;
I want to see it redden all around,
To feast on it! Why can no wind be found
To blow me still more Poles? Weary am I,
And bitterly must weep! Ye stars on high,
Hide in the clouds! Your light I would not know!
I slew my children! . . . And my lot is woe!
Where can I now find peace?"
Thus Gonta cried

And rushed across the town from side to side.
In the square's blood, the troops their tables set,
And gathering such food as they could get,
Sat down to eat.... Their last grim slaughter this,
And their last supper!
—"Lads, be full of bliss!
Drink while you can! Strike while you have the chance!"
Shouts Zalizniak: "Give us a tune to dance,
You madcap kobzar, that the ground may sway!
Thus let my Cossacks finish off the day!"
And so the bard struck up a tuneful lay.

All dance. But where has Gonta gone?
He's left the merry throng.
Why does he not with Cossacks drink?
Why does he sing no song?
He is not there: at such a time,
He has no will to sing!
But who is this in mantle black
Through corpses rummaging?
He stops; he pulls a pile apart;
Dead Poles in tumbled rout
He searches; then, with sudden stoop,
Draws two small corpses out;
He takes them on his shoulders broad;
He steals across the square;
Over dead bodies, through the flames,
He seeks the dead to bear
Behind a Polish Catholic church.
'Tis Gonta, deep in dearth,
Who carries thus his little sons
To bury them in earth,
So that the tiny Cossack forms
The dogs may not devour.
Along the darkest streets he goes
Where flames have lost their lour;
He bore his little sons away,
So that no soul might see
The spot where they were laid to rest
Or mark his misery.

He bore the bodies to the field;
Pulls out the blessèd blade,
And with it, by the town's grim light,
A simple pit he made.
It shines upon his little sons;
All clothed, they seem asleep;

Why do they then afflict their sire
With horror stark and deep?
Why does he tremble like a thief
Who steals, or hides, a treasure?
Out of the streets of yonder town
Comes uproar beyond measure,
The shouting of the haydamaks—
But these he does not hear
While hollowing a resting-place
For his two children dear.
The task is done . . . He takes his boys;
He does not watch them, rather
Remembers as he lays them down:
"We are not Poles, O father!"
He lays them down; he then takes out
A cloth of silken gloss;
He kisses the dead children's eyes;
He signs them with a cross;
Above the Cossack children's heads
The silken cloth he swept;
Then pulled it off once more to gaze,
And bitterly he wept:
"O sons of mine, dear sons of mine!
Look now on our Ukraine,
Ah, look at her! Both you and I
Must die for her in pain.
And who will bury me at last?
In alien fields I'll be;
And who will weep above my bones?
Alas, my destiny,
My miserable destiny,
What means your fatal ire?
Why have you given me these sons?
And why not slain their sire?
Then would my sons have buried me—
Now I must bury them."
He kissed them, signed them with a cross—
Clods made their requiem.
—"Rest in your deep abode, my sons!
Your mother did not spread,
To soothe your bodies and your souls,
A newer, better bed.
Without sweet basil, without rue,
Rest little sons, my own,
And pray God that his punishment
May fall on me alone
For muddled plans and maddened sins

That in this world I mix!
Forgive me, sons, as I do you
For being Catholics!"

He smoothed the earth, replaced the turf,
And no one could detect
Where Gonta's Cossack children lay
And show them disrespect.
—"Rest, little sons, and wait for me.
I soon to you shall come.
For I have thus cut short your lives
And swift will be my doom!
I shall be slain . . . and soon, I trust!
Who'll bury me, I pray?
The haydamaks! . . . I'll join them now,
And plunge into the fray!"

Gonta was stooped; he stumbled much;
And walked in manner wild;
Flames lit his path; he blankly looked;
And horribly he smiled
As back he gazed upon the steppe;
With grief his throat did choke;
He wiped his tears . . . Then through the dark
He vanished in the smoke.

4

Farewell Forever, Ryświanka

As the Ukrainian attacks escalated, the men in our area began to organize civil-defense units and to join partisan groups, while their families began to take certain precautionary measures. At home, tunnels were dug leading from the interior of the houses to outside shelters. Continuous domestic watches were kept. Emergency supplies were buried in the fields. Children slept in barns. From the beginning of 1943, my family also took these precautions. My father and my two oldest sisters kept the nightly vigils in the fields and forests surrounding our house to warn us of approaching danger. Our shelter was located in the pine grove just behind the barn.

Meanwhile, on October 9, 1942, Hitler issued a personal order that a half-million young people between the ages of fifteen and thirty-five be transported from the Ukraine to Germany for forced labor. As a result of this order, many young people in our area were rounded up and deported. Felek Domalewski and his cousin Marysia were among the first conscripts. They were told that they were being taken to Germany for labor, that they would be paid for their work, and that in six months' time, they would be brought back home. Like so many others, Felek and Marysia managed to escape *en route* and returned to Ryświanka. To avoid being recaptured, they hid out in the forests, visiting their families under the cover of night, and staying only for short periods of time.

As the escapes mounted, the Nazis began to take harsh repressive measures against not only the escapees, but their families as well. Eventually, many simply went off to Germany without protest, like lambs to the slaughter. In May of 1943, three months before our own house went up in flames, my sisters Jasia (twenty-eight) and Aniela (twenty-one) were caught and deported. Two months later, the same fate befell my fifty-eight-year-old father. They had become slaves of the Third Reich. After this, until the Leonówka massacre, Stasia (nineteen) and Anna (seventeen) kept the watch in our behalf.

The Leonówka massacre (just three kilometers away) convinced us that we must consider the unthinkable. Immediately afterward, most of the Polish families in our neighborhood decided to abandon their homesteads and head for Tuczyn where, it was said, a German garrison was stationed. Such was our fear of the Ukrainian bands that we preferred to take our chances with the

Nazis! Moreover, what other alternative did we have? To stay put would have meant certain death.

Since we were without any means of transportation, it was decided that Stasia would go with the Domalewskis (she and Felek planned to marry upon their arrival in Tuczyn), and that Anna would go with the Gruntkowskis and return for us with their team of horses on the following day.

After their departure, only my fifty-one-year-old mother, my two brothers, Franek (twelve) and Janek (ten), and I remained at home. I was of the same age as my poor cousin Waldymar. Our situation was ominously similar to Marcelina's. With these thoughts in her mind, my mother asked our Polish neighbor to the east, Filip, if we could spend the night with his family. Since his house stood next to a Ukrainian home, it was unlikely that it would be burned. Our kind neighbor was more than gracious with his hospitality. He assured us that he and his four daughters would spend the night as sentries in case of an attack. He, too, was much troubled by what had been transpiring in our area.

At about eleven o'clock that night, as we all tossed and turned uneasily in our beds, Filip's daughters ran into the house, yelling and screaming that our home and barn were on fire. So this was the day and the hour!

All was instinct now. In the twinkle of an eye there was not a living soul left on the premises. My mother grabbed me, still asleep, and we all ran out and kept on running until we collapsed in a potato field some sixty meters from the conflagration. We saw then that our flaming house was completely surrounded by Ukrainians . . . and that they had axes.

We were so close we could feel the heat and hear the mournful lowing of the cattle and the unearthly sounds of the other animals trapped within the barn. They were desperately thrashing about. They were being burned alive. We heard the sound of broken glass. We saw our house and barn disintegrating before our very eyes. We smelled the awful scent of burning flesh.

It was at that most inopportune moment that I, frightened as I was, began to cry. The night was clear and the moon was so bright one could find the proverbial needle in any one of the many haystacks surrounding our house; and if one could find a needle in a haystack, one could all the more easily find four crouching figures in a potato field. Moreover, the flaming house and barn were like two huge torches which lit up the whole countryside and turned the night into day.

What mother does not know the fine art of quieting a despairing child? And so Maria Piotrowski began to tell me a story about sheep. I am told that as a child I entertained a healthy respect for those wooly creatures. At the age of three the terror of sheep had more power to deter my tears than the events of the night had to inspire them. So, despite the felt agitation of my family, the night, the black fields, the shrieking animals, and the burning barn and house, I stopped crying. For the moment, at least, we were safe.

I have often wondered what she was thinking then, my poor, dear mother, seeing her own home going up in smoke and flames—that home that she swept daily and nurtured like her own child. How she loved that house! How many memories did she lose that night—or gain? Our homeless *Burek*—where was he now? Our dear *Bociek*—where will he build his nest? Our cruel swallows—barns were so scarce these days! The work, the joy, the grief, the sorrow, all mingled with the flames and smoke rising, rising to the moon and stars.

"What shall we do now?" she must have thought. "And where shall we go? . . . And where is my husband? . . . And what has become of my four oldest daughters? . . . And what am I to do with these three young boys of mine? . . . And will they ever reach full manhood?"

Did she perhaps think of poor Marcelina, and Waldymar, and Stefan, and Romalda, and Władysława, and Hilary, and Paweł, and his wife, and their slain children?

Did she sing? My mother always sang. Did she sing "Gorzkie Żale?"

Did she think of the time when she was almost devoured by the hungry wolves, or of the old *babusieńka* with her amulets and herbs, or God, or the devil?

Did she become a little girl again, playing in the sweet memories of her bygone nineteenth-century days?

Mother, what did you think out there in that potato field, seeing your home go up in flames and knowing that only by the grace of God were we here *in this desolate field and not* there *inside the house? How I wish I could ask you that one question now! I have never in my life known, nor will I ever know, a more important question. Oh Mother, please tell me the story of the sheep once more.*

I think it was my brother Franek who disturbed her quietly racing thoughts with the sobering news that we were still at risk. It was so bright; shelter must be found.

We had not gone very far from where we were, when my mother suggested that we hide in one of the haystacks in our field. (Perhaps she did not want to leave at all.)

"No, mother, they will surely find us here. It is still too close. Remember Gienek and Władzia," someone must have said.

And so we went on into the night a little further until we reached the small forest bordering our property, called *Ochrona*, which means "Shelter." There, we fell beneath the sprawling branches of an evergreen tree—the type that spreads its limbs low upon the ground for little frightened animals to hide beneath, the type under which *Krasnoludki* dwell, the type which children often use in their games of hide and seek. Yes, that was the type!

At about midnight (but who could say exactly when it was?) we heard the sounds of hurried footsteps coming in our direction along the road which separated *Ochrona* from our potato field. We held our breath in panic as six armed men ran past our hiding place in the direction of our house. They, too, must have been Ukrainians zeroing in for the final kill. God only knows how they missed seeing us, for at the time, we did not realize just how close we were to the road.

After several more attentive hours, as the fire continued to dance in the pupils of our unblinking eyes, the gruff voices of the men mingled with the soft murmuring of the pines, then faded in the distance. When all grew silent as the grave, some of us finally surrendered ourselves to the welcome tides of sleep in the vain hope that upon awakening, all this horror would prove to have been nothing more than a bad midsummer night's dream.

We remained in our forest shelter the whole night through, until the first rays of sunlight appeared over the horizon and fell on the smoldering ashes which had been our house and barn only the day before. Even then we were in no hurry, as we no longer had anywhere to go. Now, the whole wide world was our home: everywhere and nowhere. The road was no more than two meters from the tree, so we followed that to our neighbor's house, where we planned to spend the night.

When we arrived at Filip's we found that, although all the windows were broken, no one was hurt and the house was still intact. They were much relieved to see us safe and sound.

The time had finally come to bid farewell to our Ryświanka. We could no longer even think of waiting for Anna to return with Gruntkowski's team of horses. Perhaps she would never come. We would walk. We urged our neighbor to come with us, since he and his family would most certainly be the next target of attack—but to no avail. He was of an unyielding disposition. Neither he nor his family, he said, would ever abandon their ancestral home. They were resolved to stay and confront the devil that they knew, rather than the unknown demons to the west. Since we were all doomed anyway, they preferred to die here in Ryświanka. So be it. We embraced them all there, near their doorstep, near their fields and meadows, on the graveyard of their own choosing, and prepared for our departure.[1]

As we hurried to dig out our emergency provisions from fields and woods, we realized that our cache did not contain extra footwear. Who would think of hiding *trepy?* No matter, we would walk barefooted as we had the evening before to Filip's house.

At the very moment of our departure, the unimaginable transpired. We saw a lone, unarmed figure coming slowly toward us all. It was our Ukrainian neighbor, Pasichnyk. And just when we thought that we had finally caught a glimpse of the devil that we knew, he metamorphosed before our unbelieving eyes into an angel of mercy.

He was a mild-mannered man, a compassionate man, a man of genuine sympathy and good will. We could all see the painful expression in his face as he drew nearer. We could feel his deep sorrow for our recent tragedy. We could sense his heartfelt regret for what his people had done. He was a good man—like the passer-by who once put down his basket of eggs to help our Savior bear his cross. It was he who saved our lives that day.

Mr. Pasichnyk offered to take us to Tuczyn himself, but when his wife saw him harnessing the horses and realized what he was about to do, she said to him in the presence of my mother, "You will not get anywhere because the road you must take leads through the forest where the bandits are lying in ambush and you will perish along with them."

It was a sobering thought, and although the eight-kilometer trip was very long by foot, we all realized that it was much safer to proceed that way. Before we left, he warned us not to take the main road through the woods:

"Do not go that way, Piotrowska!" he said. "The woods are full of bandits! You will be killed! Rather, take the winding footpath through the fields, the one which skirts the forests and the Ukrainian village on the other side. It is much longer, but it is much safer too."

The forests he referred to were our own *Ochrona* and *Las Ryświanecki*; the village was our own Ryświanka. So, we took his neighborly advice and left. Never will we forget our kind Ukrainian friend.

> From our village . . . the "Kulaks" were driven out on foot. They took what they could carry on their backs: bedding, clothing. . . . They marched along in a column and looked back at their huts, and their bodies still held the warmth from their own stoves. What pain they must have suffered! After all, they had been born in those houses; they had given their daughters in marriage in those cabins. They had heated up their stoves, and the cabbage soup they had cooked was left there behind them. The milk had not been drunk, and smoke was still rising from their chimneys.[2]

We were not much different from the "Kulaks" except that our warmth did not come from our stove, and the smoke, still rising, did not emanate from our chimney. I can see the grim procession even now: the elegant, half-century-old woman with two large parcels strapped securely to her strong shoulders; her twelve-year-old son with his heavy load; his ten-year-old brother; and on his back a small, three-year-old child, all barefooted, all silent, all trudging warily southward across the Ukrainian landscape toward an unknown destiny.

It was early August, the season of the harvest. As we walked on and on, we watched Ukrainian families pause to consider this strange migration of four displaced persons, before returning to their systematic mowing, mowing, mowing of their verdant fields, pregnant with life-sustaining bounty. What did they think of us? What did we think of them? (We left just in the nick of time, for we learned subsequently that two or three days later, no one could pass that way unescorted without being killed.)

At one point in our journey, the oppressive heat of August finally took its toll, and I would not be consoled for lack of water. Moreover, our poor feet were blistering from the hot, sandy soil which we had just crossed, and bleeding from the stubble of a recently-mown hay field. We needed to rest and to refresh ourselves with cool, clear water. What were we to do? Should we risk it?

It was my mother who decided that we should wait there in the fields, while she would go to the nearest house to ask for water. She went, she asked, she thanked the kind Ukrainians, and then she returned—to the great relief of the three of us who were hiding in the waist-high wheat. We drank to our hearts' content and so, refreshed by water, and more so by the milk of human kindness, we proceeded on the rest of our eight-kilometer journey to Tuczyn, where we expected to find our sister Anna and the newlyweds, Stasia and Felek Domalewski.

Evening had fallen by the time we reached the town. All was ominously quiet. There were no lights. There was no movement in the deserted streets. It soon became apparent to us that Tuczyn was a ghost town. A population of 3,000 people vanished into thin air![3] As we proceeded from house to house down main street, we noticed some motor vehicles preparing for departure on the other side of the town. It was a small contingent of the SS.

In a spirit of that bravery born of desperation, my mother left us hiding once again and ventured forth alone to find out what was to be done. She was told by the SS that all the people in Tuczyn were taken to Równe "for protection." We were to wait here until more people gathered. A transport would be sent to take us there also.

As we waited we saw them coming, one family at a time: all the displaced people from our territory, all the homeless souls, all the grave-faced parents, all the frightened children—all just like us. Within a span of three hours, about seventy-five of us gathered and waited for the transport which would never come. We were then commanded by the SS to begin walking once more to the next town called Szubków, three kilometers away.

Although most of us were already exhausted, this moonlit, midnight journey was much easier to endure. We were no longer alone; there was human solidarity and social discourse to accompany us. Moreover, some of the people had means of transportation and one kind soul offered to take me in his wagon. Even though the rest of my family had to continue on foot, at least they were relieved of the burden of having to carry a three-year-old child. By the time we reached Szubków we numbered in the hundreds, picking up other displaced persons as we walked along.

We arrived there early in the morning. Unlike Tuczyn, this town was bristling with people. Our first thoughts were to look for Anna, Stasia, and

Felek Domalewski. As we moved through the dense crowds, a German transport rumbled through the streets and stopped in the middle of the town. All were ordered to line up for departure to Równe. Our search was cut short by this unexpected turn of events. We got in line with the rest.

Meanwhile, unknown to us, Anna was already in Równe awaiting deportation. Just as we arrived in the city, a freight train full of people was leaving the station. Anna was to have been on that train, but being forewarned by the neighbor with whom she left Ryświanka, she hid in his small apartment to avoid leaving without us.[4]

We spent several anxious days and nights in that formerly Jewish city, among the constantly mushrooming throng of Wołyń's refugees, near the heavily guarded, barbed-wired compounds wherein thousands upon thousands of Russian prisoners of war were being detained and were dying of starvation. While we waited, we searched the crowds for signs of familiar faces, we inquired after our sisters and Felek Domalewski, and we prayed.

On the morning of our own scheduled departure, as Anna was surveying the human tapestry of helpless deportees being prodded like cattle into the transports, she saw us! We were about to board the train.

In desperation, she flung open the second-story window behind which she kept her daily watch, and was about to leap out when she realized the formidable distance to the earth below. Without so much as a thought, she climbed out of the window, scrambled onto the nearby tree, made her way down to its lowest branch . . . and despaired of ever reaching the ground without a mishap. Just then she heard the encouraging voice of a man who had been silently observing her heroic acrobatics.

"Jump!" he said, "I will catch you."

So Anna closed her eyes, slid off the limb, and landed in the arms of a perfect stranger. Then, without so much as a word of thanks, she rushed off, fought her way through the pressing crowd, and leapt onto the already departing train.

Ours was a bittersweet reunion in that evil-smelling, congested boxcar. To be sure, we were together, and we realized that at long last all our troubles with the Ukrainians were over. But we also realized that the five of us were on a train bound for Nazi Germany, and that we were perhaps leaving our beloved homeland forever. The five of us . . . but where were Stasia and Felek, whom we expected to find along the way?

Stasia and Felek, and Jasia, and Aniela, and father Józef were now lost to us, and it would be a long, long time before we would see any of them again.

XII. Epilogue

. . . .

The haydamaks had sown their rye
In their Ukrainian fields,

And yet the harvest was not theirs:
An alien takes the yields.
The crop of justice is not ripe;
And evil chokes the grain;
The haydamaks must all disperse
And separate with pain:
Some to their homes, to forests some,
A knife in every legging;
Even today they have a name
For slashing more than begging .... [5]

REFUGEE SCREENING COMMISSION REPORT
ON UKRAINIANS IN SURRENDERED ENEMY PERSONNEL
(SEP) CAMP NO. 374 ITALY

LACAB/18 RSC/RIC 21 February 1947

1. This camp consists entirely of male Ukrainians who were either captured in German uniform or were working in Germany as civilians and attached themselves to the 1st Ukrainian Division shortly before its surrender....

...On the crucial point whether any of them are Soviet citizens by our definition we have no evidence other than that supplied by the men themselves. Many of the places which they have given as their place of birth and/or habitual residence are small villages and hamlets which are not likely to be marked on any but the largest maps; but I think we can safely assume that the great majority of those born after 1919 were born in Poland, and were resident in Poland on 1st September 1939, and that the great majority of those born before Poland existed were not resident in the Soviet Union on 1st September 1939. The general impression which we have formed of all the men in the camp is favourable, as they strike us all as being decent, simple-minded sort of people. The national emblem of the Ukraine, in the form of a trident, is freely displayed all over the camp, and the inmates clearly regard themselves as a homogeneous unit, unconnected either with Russia or Poland, and do not seem conscious of having done any wrong....

A. It seems likely that the great majority, at least of the men, are not Soviet citizens by our definition. It must, however, be borne in mind that an official Soviet Mission has questioned nearly all of them, and that the Soviet Government merely regards nearly all of them as Soviet citizens; and that there *may* be among them a number who are Soviet citizens by our definition. We may, therefore, if we get them all accepted as DPs render ourselves liable to a valid charge of sheltering Russian traitors. (It might be worthwhile noting in this connection that on the nationality issue these men are really having the best of both worlds. They do not qualify as Soviet citizens because their places of birth and/or habitual domicile on 1.9.39 were in Poland, and they therefore by our definition escape all punishment by the Russians for their having assisted the enemy; and they are not presumably eligible now for punishment by the Polish authorities because that part of the country from which they came is no longer part of Poland.)

B. The great majority of them voluntarily enlisted in the German Armed Forces and fought against our Allies, Soviet Russia and Jugoslavia. There are some grounds for believing that some of those whom we have questioned have stated that they were volunteers, because if they said that they had been conscripted they would then be told that they would have nothing to fear if they returned to the Ukraine. The number of volunteers may thus be smaller than would at first appear. Nonetheless, also allowing for intimidation, and dislike of forced labour, the majority for our purpose must be regarded as volunteers. There are, therefore, prima facie grounds for classifying them as traitors, i.e., as ineligible for IRO status according to the 1st section of paragraph two of the definition sheet. The term "traitor" is vague and has been defined for our guidance by Professor Royse as embodying, among other things, "civilians who voluntarily offer their services to the enemy and, in general sense, people who gave aid and comfort to the enemy." This definition undoubtedly applies to most, if not all, of these Ukrainians.

C. We must, however, I think take into account their motives for having voluntarily offered their services to the enemy, even though by so doing one might be able, as a reductio absurdum [sic], to prove Quisling himself as eligible for IRO assistance. There seem to be four main reasons for their having taken this step:

a. The hope of securing a genuinely independent Ukraine.
b. Without knowing exactly what they were doing, e.g., because other Ukrainians whom they knew had already volunteered.
c. As a preferable alternative to forced labour, etc., or to living in Soviet-controlled territory.
d. To have a smack at the Russians, whom they always refer to as "Bolsheviks".

They probably were not, and certainly do not now seem to be at heart pro–German, and the fact that they did give aid and comfort to the Germans can fairly be considered to have been incidental and not fundamental.

D. The desire among their leaders for an independent Ukraine, naive and unreal as it is, is nonetheless genuine.

E. They are obsessed by a terror and hatred, bordering in some cases almost on hysteria, of Soviet Russia. It seems clear that when the Russians occupied Eastern Poland in 1939-40 many of these people's wives and families were ruthlessly taken away from their homes to Siberia and other remote parts of the Soviet Union and have not been seen or heard of since. They also seem to have suffered a good deal at the hands of the Red Army during the Russo-German campaign, and also on occasion at the hands of the Germans.

F. None of them wish to return to the Ukraine, with the exception of one man, who, after securing an interview with one of the Commissioners and stating to him that he did wish to return to the Ukraine, was subsequently found to be suffering from the last stages of consumption and was not expected to live very much longer. He is now in the hospital.

G. No one in the camp has been sentenced by any British military authority to one year's imprisonment or over. Their behaviour indeed since their surrender to us has been exemplary. They have not indulged in any subversive activities, nor do I think they will do so in the future. They seem resigned to the fact that there is now no place in Europe for them and that those of them who have wives and families in the Soviet Union will never see them again. We must not, however, expect most of them ever to become well disposed toward the Soviet Union.

12. I am not competent from here to judge the issue as far as our relations with the Soviet Union (or with Poland) are concerned; nor do I know whether our policy is to interpret strictly or liberally the instructions as to who is eligible for DP status and who not. I can only speak from the experience gained from our actually having seen the men and from humanitarian instincts common to us all; and on this basis and taking into account the long time that has elapsed from the end of the war, I recommend most strongly that all these Ukrainians should be classified as DPs. . . .

(signed) D. Haldane Porter
Refugee Screening Commission
In charge S.E.P. Camp 374[6]

BOOK II

GERMANY

5

In the Eye of Satan

The county of Równe was served by the Lwów-Wilno Railroad with junctions in the larger cities connecting both East and West. Our particular transport was an ordinary freight train, the kind used before the war to move cattle, farm produce, machinery and various other marketable commodities from place to place. All the boxcars had sturdy sliding doors which could be locked from the outside; some had windows, but without panes.

In the 1930s, such trains were used to transport the *Kulaks* to the "special settlements" in the Urals. During the war, such trains were used to transport the Jews to the extermination camps and human slaves to and from the forced-labor camps. A description of an encounter at Brest Litovsk (September 1942) between a returning transport of exhausted workers and fresh "recruits" from Russia bound for Germany, is found in the Rosenberg files:

> Because of the corpses in the trainload of returning laborers a catastrophe might have occurred. . . . [I]n this train women gave birth to babies who were thrown out of the windows during the journey. Persons having tuberculosis and venereal diseases rode in the same car. Dying people lay in freight cars without straw, and one of the dead was thrown on the railway embankment. The same must have occurred in other returning transports.[1]

This would be a description of us, if we survived slavery. But for now, we were the "fresh" recruits, barefooted and hungry, hugging our small parcels of clothing and packed like sardines inside the stifling boxcars at the beginning of August 1943. Due to the oppressive heat, our lengthy confinement, and the lack of sanitary conditions, many people became gravely ill in the course of the three-week journey to Essen. Among these were my brother Franek and myself. Fortunately, we recovered; others were not so lucky.

The inordinately lengthy trip was due to our frequent stops to pick up still other "passengers" along the way, as well as to the interminable delays caused by partisan activity and the eastward transportation of German soldiers, supplies, and equipment. When the train stopped, sometimes we were allowed out under guard, but usually the doors remained shut and bolted.

In the first two weeks of that grueling journey, everyone told and retold his or her own sad story, everyone sympathized and sympathized again and again with one another. But in the last week, an ominous silence descended on the train as if an unseen hand yanked on an invisible choke collar around each person's neck. Those who were not ill or exhausted simply withdrew into the privacy of their own thoughts about the past as well as the future. We were, after all, far from home, in the heart of Nazi Germany: Satan's other eye.

> ESSEN. City. (1939 pop. 666,743) . . . Situated in a rich coal field, it is the industrial hub of the Ruhr, a great steel-mfg. center (pig iron, steel, steel products). Other mfg.: chemicals, textiles (cloth, silk), glass, furniture. Coke ovens, cement and brickworks. Brewing. Coal mined in suburbs, including Borbeck, Katernberg, Kray, Ruttenscheidt, Steele, and Stopenberg. Founded in 9th cent., when it had a rapid industrial rise after Friedrich Krupp built 1st steel plant here c. 1810 and began to develop the coal field. Towards end of 19th cent., Krupp concern started building its model workers' colonies (at suburb of Altendorf) near the ever-expanding steel plant. Trunk lines were constructed to connect city with rest of the Ruhr . . . its port on Rhine-Herne Canal is at Altenessen. A center of Ger. war industry, city was about 75% destroyed by Allied aerial attacks in Second World War; its ancient minster was damaged.[2]

(The vengeful destruction of this German city began shortly before our arrival, and ended while we were there.)

Adam Schmidt, a German railway employee at Essen, described us well at the Nuremberg trial:

> In the middle of 1941, there came the first workers from Poland, Galicien, and from Polish Ukraine. They arrived in freight trains which were built for transportation of potatoes, construction materials, and cattle, and they were employed in Krupp Industries.
>
> It was shocking for every honest German to see how these people were pushed, trampled upon, and generally treated. I could see with my own eyes how the sick, who could hardly walk, were brought to work.
>
> The same treatment was applied to the "Ost" [*Ostarbeiter*] workers, who came to Essen in the middle of 1942.[3]

The same procedure was applied to us in 1943. After disembarking in Essen, we were taken to a nearby heavily guarded collection camp consisting of plain wooden barracks surrounded by a high barbed-wired fence. There, we were first "disinfected" by being sprayed with DDT, and were then issued the so-called *Holt* shoes, or *trepy*—as we used to call them—which consisted of a wooden base and leather bindings. We wore them without socks.

Next, the *Oberlagerführung* (Foreign Workers' Camp Administration) selected the ablest from among our ranks, and handed them over to the waiting industrial police for factory work. If they were chosen for the Krupp works, the largest manufacturer of Germany's guns, tanks and ammunition, they received Krupp blankets stamped with three interlocking wheels and the firm's blue, yellow-striped prison uniforms. The next ablest were handed over to the waiting farmers for agricultural labor. Then, Germans who needed domestic help claimed whomever they wanted. Finally, those who were left (and we were among these)—the old and the young, the infirm and the feeble, the lame, and even the blind—were told to wait. The indiscriminate *Menschenjagden* (the Fritz Sauckel dragnet) swept us all into Essen. Factory owners complained about all the "inferior" workers being shipped to them by Sauckel: "We really get the rejects only. Just now 600 Russians, consisting of 450 women and 150 juveniles ... arrived" (summer 1942).[4] But what was to be done? More and more Germans were required for the war effort, and many able-bodied prisoners of war and Jews had already been exterminated.

> At that time [1941] we did not value the mass of humanity as we value it today, as raw material, as labor. What after all, thinking in terms of generations, is not to be regretted but is now deplorable by reason of the loss of labor, is that the prisoners died in tens and hundreds of thousands of exhaustion and hunger.[5]

In Essen, foreign workers were rare for about two and a half years after the beginning of the war. By the end of 1943, however, the city thronged with foreigners. According to the Nuremberg files, Alfried Krupp von Bohlen und Halbach, the chief slavedealer, was personally responsible for "about 100,000 persons exploited as slaves by the Krupp factories in Germany, in countries alien to them, and in concentration camps."[6] An undated document, discovered after the fall of Essen, revealed that the *Gusstahlfabrik* alone employed about 75,000 slaves. After the labor crisis of 1942, the revised Nazi policy was "extermination through work."

In keeping with the German ethnocentric ideology, each ethnic group was assigned its own distinctive mark of identification: Jews wore yellow cloth-tags; Russians, the initials "SR" (Soviet Russia); Poles, the black letter "P" on a yellow patch; other eastern slaves, "OST"; other nationalities, blue, red, or green-on-white armbands. Names were replaced with numbers. As punishment for minor infractions or simply as additional humiliation, some people's heads were shaved.

Life in the collection camps was led under extremely primitive conditions, below the level of subsistence, in unsanitary surroundings, amid disease and physical abuse. Moreover, during the air raids, our only source of protection was the shallow trenches dug by previous inmates. If protein had not been so difficult to obtain, already by the fall of 1943, we would have been fed "cat and horsemeat," as *Reichsmarschall* Göring recommended. It was just as well that we were spared that benign indignity, for by the testimony of German doctors, all the meat rations were contaminated.[7] Of course, given our poor diet, inhaling the tubercle bacilli could also cause death. The elevated rates of pulmonary tuberculosis would not subside in Europe until 1947. Such, then, was our introduction to Nazi Germany. It was much worse than anyone had ever expected.

After our relatively short stay in the collection camp, we were relocated into various "housing" facilities throughout the city. Like the factory workers, some of us were placed in buildings, others in makeshift huts and tents on school playgrounds and parking lots, and still others among the ever growing ruins of Essen—all of us in full view of the German civilians who later would deny any knowledge of the existence of such camps.

The camps varied in their security measures as well as in their conditions of life. Fritz Führer, a former Krupp camp commandant, once explained to the astonished Nuremberg tribunal: "I can say that the Dechenschule camp did not give the impression that it was a prison, except that it was surrounded by barbed-wired fences, and that guards were at the gate, and there were armed guards patrolling the grounds."[8] Other places had high brick walls with makeshift guard towers. Still others were left relatively unguarded.

Dr. Wilhelm Jaeger, the senior doctor for Krupp slave employees, commented on the conditions of life in one such work camp containing six hundred Jewish women imported from Buchenwald under the "extermination through work" program:

> Upon my first visit I found these females suffering from open festering wounds and other diseases. I was the first doctor they had seen for at least a fortnight. . . . There were no medical supplies. . . . They had no shoes and went about in their bare feet. The sole clothing of each consisted of a sack with holes for their arms and head. Their hair was shorn. The camp was surrounded by barbed wire and closely guarded by S.S. guards.
>
> The amount of food in the camp was extremely meager and of very poor quality. One could not enter the barracks without being attacked by fleas. . . . I got large boils on my arms and the rest of my body from them.[9]

Dr. Jaeger's next description is a composite report on eight camps inhabited by Russian and Polish workers:

> The clothing of the Eastern workers was likewise completely inadequate. They worked and slept in the same clothing in which they had arrived from the East. Virtually all of them had no overcoats and were compelled to use their blankets as coats in cold and rainy weather. In view of the shortage of shoes many workers were forced to go to work in their bare feet, even in winter.

> Sanitary conditions were atrocious. At Kramerplatz only ten children's toilets were available for 1,200 inhabitants. . . . Excretion contaminated the entire floors of these lavatories. . . . The Tartars and Kirghiz suffered most; they collapsed like flies [from] bad housing, the poor quality and insufficient quantity of food, overwork and insufficient rest.
>
> These workers were likewise afflicted with spotted fever. Lice, the carrier of the disease, together with countless fleas, bugs and other vermin tortured the inhabitants of these camps. . . . At times the water supply at the camps was shut off for periods of from eight to fourteen days.[10]

If we were better off than the residents of Krupp's 138 slave labor camps, it was because—considered "worthless" from the outset—we were placed as a family in a camp-building which was relatively unguarded. Our appointed place of residence was a classroom, which we shared with six other Polish families of similar description, on the sixth floor of an "L" shaped corner building called *Schule Steinmetzfir*. All together, about 300 people occupied this former schoolhouse, the Ukrainians in one wing, the Poles in the other.

It was a strange twist of fate that brought us together at Essen where we were equally enslaved. We remained here for one whole year, until the building was bombed out from under us.

Each "able-bodied" resident of the *Schule Steinmetzfir* was given a specific task to perform, in accordance with the German saying: "*Keine Arbeit, Kein Fressen*."[11] My mother worked as a cleaning woman in the local police station; I always went with her. She surprised us from time to time by bringing home German marks, which she said one of her kind employers gave her. She kept this small amount of money on her person at all times, saving it for an emergency which, except on rare occasions, did not include the purchase of food when we complained of hunger.

My sister, Anna, worked in the disinfecting "lavatories" where new recruits were brought daily to be deloused with DDT. Many of these included not only European and East European civilians, but also harshly guarded prisoners of war, especially the French. She also cleaned German administrative office buildings.

Franek and Janek, who were still children themselves, worked on construction (mixing cement, assisting bricklayers, for instance), within about a ten-kilometer radius of the schoolhouse. Since no transportation was provided, they had to walk both to and from the assigned work in summer and in winter. Franek recalls:

> We were sent out to do various jobs. The work was very difficult. We dressed in rags and wore wooden shoes or none at all. In winter we froze and if we got wet we just stayed wet. Moreover we were always hungry.

Had I been two years older, I would have joined my brothers the following February instead of hiding in my mother's skirts. "In 1944, children as young as six years of age were being assigned to work."[12]

In between these "normal" tasks, everyone was also required to help clear the streets of fallen debris after the air attacks which were constant and terrifying. According to Adolf Trockel, as the bombings mounted, "mostly they had to lug bricks and corrugated iron sheets. This hard physical work had to be done in cold weather, in inadequate clothing, without gloves or protective clothing of any kind."[13] He should have added: "and without proper rest or nutrition."

Our daily regimen began at 4:30 A.M. with rising. Work started promptly at 5:00 A.M. and ended at 6:00 P.M. without any breaks. No clothing was issued so that one never had a change of clothes and slept in whatever he or she had on that day. Sometimes there was no water to drink, never mind to bathe or wash clothes with. If one got wet in the course of the day, one simply stayed that way until the clothes dried on one's back. This was especially hard to bear in the late fall, winter, and early spring months, for the schoolhouse was unheated. At night, we also had to contend with fleas, lice, and bedbugs of which we were never free . . . besides the falling bombs. Franek says, "During the day we had to do hard labor and suffer from cold and hunger. At night, we could not sleep because of the bombs and the vermin which we could not get rid of."

Our daily food rations were the same as those of the Krupp factory workers: one tin cup of the dirty, evil-tasting *Bunkersuppe* (bunker soup) per person per day, supplemented by one wafer-thin piece of bread spread with jam or margarine. Upon returning to our respective camps after a thirteen-hour workday, we were required to stand in line for this vile *Fressen*. One production-minded Krupp foreman wrote:

> What these men call a day's ration is a complete puzzle to me. The food was a puzzle too, because they ladled out the thinnest of already watery soup. It was literally water with a handful of turnips, and it looked like dish water. . . . The people have to work for us. Good, but care must be taken to see that they get at least the bare necessities. I have seen a few figures in the camp, and a cold shudder actually ran up and down my spine. I met one there, and he looked as though he'd got barber's rash. . . . If this continues, we shall all be contaminated. It is a pity, when just at this moment the motto is "increased production." Something must be done to keep the people capable of production.[14]

The soup, which contained perhaps 350 calories, consisted of water, cabbage leaves, and pieces of turnips. A Nuremberg testimony corroborates the foreman's observations, and our own experience:

> The warm meal consisted of soup, the cold one of bread with jam or margarine. The so-called "bunker soup" that was served at Krupp was not touched by many German workmen. After the air raids in October of 1944, however, even this was no longer available.[15]

According to Franek:

> For nourishment they gave us some kind of soup so filthy that although we were starving, it was impossible to bring it up to our lips without holding our noses. Besides this, they also gave us a pound of bread to be divided among eight people.

One survivor remembers "pitchforking dirty, decaying spinach from a wagon directly into the cooking pots," and that "disease and dysentery were rife" in the various compounds.

At one point of the Nuremberg trial Dr. Rohlfs testified that under Krupp care, the "deplorable physical condition" of the incoming workers, which had been "certainly caused by the strains of transport and perhaps also during their stay in the collection camps," had been dramatically ameliorated. Max Mandellaub, an American attorney, cross-examined the witness:

> Q. Can [you] here state, under oath, that the situation of the prisoners of war in Essen, and particularly that of the Russian prisoners of war, was satisfactory?
>
> A: Yes, it was satisfactory, as far as possible under then prevailing conditions.
>
> Q: You said . . . the Russians had a rate of sickness of 35 percent. If I remember correctly, that must have been 35 percent.
>
> A: Yes.
>
> Q: This percentage then was reduced to 6 percent. Is that correct?
>
> A: Yes, I remember this figure very decidedly.
>
> Q: Of what date?
>
> A: I am afraid I can't say that. We were successful in reducing the rate of illness in the case of the Russians to such an extent that the percentage of illness fluctuated around 6 percent.
>
> Q: How many cases of death did you have?
>
> A: I'm afraid I can't give you any figures for that . . . because of extreme weakness and exhaustion many of them died.
>
> Q: Is it therefore correct to assume that part of this reduction of illness in the case of Russian prisoners of war might also be caused by death?
>
> A: Yes, of course. . . .[16]

The general cause of death in those days was malnutrition, although it was often called by other names, such as tuberculosis and "acting according to regulations." On April 29, 1944, for example, a Russian prisoner of war, Sergei Schosow, was shot to death by a guard because, while assigned to a work detail (*Arbeitsabteilung*) to clear away the rubble of a bombed-out bakery, he reached for a piece of bread.

In the middle of one student's testimony of how truckloads of malnourished men vanished from the *Neerfeldschule* camp never to be seen again, the Krupp defense lawyer chose to focus, instead, on an incident involving a mouse which the student happened to mention:

> Q: Can you describe in detail how you caught the mouse?
>
> A: Yes. We were terribly hungry in those days . . . we became a little bit crazy, so to speak, and were looking for anything that could be eaten. And we saw other prisoners eating, and just seeing one chewing made us more hungry for something. And they said, "Well, you can eat it, too." Well, there were lots of those mice in the straw beds, and my friend and I, we got one, and although we didn't eat it with appetite, we did try to.
>
> Q: You caught the mouse with your own hands?
>
> A: Yes, of course I did.
>
> Q. And on the following day, as you say, you cooked it in the factory?
>
> A: Yes.
>
> Q: Did you have the possibility of doing so?
>
> A: Yes. Near the works we found some wood and we made a fire. Sometimes we were allowed to make a fire when it was terribly cold, and in the iron saucepan which we always carried with us when there was something to put in it we, so to say, fried it in order not to eat it raw.
>
> Q: I'd like to ask one more question on this subject. A mouse has a skin. Did you skin the mouse before you cooked it?
>
> A: Of course, we ate only the meat.
>
> Q: Did you have tools to do that?
>
> A: Well, not tools, but pieces of glass and little iron pieces we could always find around the grounds.[17]

The poor diet in these camps had nothing to do with the lack of provisions. There was food all around us, in every bakery, butcher shop, and grocery store in Essen. The granaries of Germany were never as full as they were in the early 1940s—with the plundered bounty of all the occupied territories. Rather, the starvation diet was a matter of policy, the policy of planned systematic extermination—not only of individuals but also, as it was said, of generations. There is no other explanation.

At this point I must apologize for grouping all these nationalities, all these multi-colored tags, armbands, and badges, all the "voluntary" (*Freiwillige*) workers, and the conscripted ones, all the prisoners of war and the enslaved civilians, all the "able-bodied" workers and the "undesirable" ones—into one vast category and speaking of them as if they were a homogenous group of people. In fact, although these various and sundry subtleties may have fitted well into the official party line, they were soon lost upon the employers, the foremen, the guards, and the general German population. Given the swirling mass of foreigners and the mass confusion in Essen especially in 1944 and the early months of 1945, everyone decided to settle for simplicity.

Only three general rules were adopted, but there were many exceptions: (1) The Jews were to be treated in the worst possible way; (2) the Russians in the next worst possible way; and (3) the people from the East were to be treated worse than the people from the West, Germany being the line of demarcation. The differential enforcement of these general rules was often more a function of the personalities involved than of the directives of the Third Reich. In reality, we were all treated as if we were the same. If one was not German, one was an *Untermensch*. If one was an *Untermensch*, one did not receive food stamps. If one did not receive food stamps, one was fed "bunker soup." If one was given "bunker soup" (*Fressen,* animal feed), one was always hungry in *Essen* (the ironic German verb "to eat"). We were not German; we did not receive food stamps; we were fed "bunker soup"; we were always hungry in Essen where we worked.

My brother Franek maintains that from time to time POWs would share their food (what food?) with the starving families, but I do not know how this was possible. Dr. Jaeger once described the conditions of the French prisoners of war (note rule number 3 above) in an Essen camp as follows:

> Its inhabitants were kept for nearly half a year in dog kennels, urinals and in old baking houses. The dog kennels were three feet high, nine feet long, six feet wide. Five men slept in each of them. The prisoners had to crawl into these kennels on all fours.... There was no water in the camp.[18]

My sister Anna claims that sometimes the German soldiers themselves took pity on us and gave us some of their own food stamps, telling us to say that we found them blowing in the wind or in some bombed-out store. This I would find even more incredible (but less incredible than my mother being given German marks at the police station) were it not for the fact that my fair sister was a sweet nineteen-year-old in 1944. But even granted that all these family recollections are accurate, what possible difference would such isolated acts of kindness make to a starving population? How long could the very recipients of such sporadic charity survive amid the squalor, cold, and misery of tubercular Essen?

I know for a fact, however, that some German soldiers were rather fond of photographing us and at least one of them actually gave us copies of the prints. (This is no small matter, for there were cases of people being severely beaten for trying to keep snapshots of their family, e.g. Hendrik Scholtens, the same nineteen-year-old student who ate the mouse.)

I have in my possession several pictures taken of us at Essen. One is of my mother seated stiffly on a wooden chair in front of the *Schule Steinmetzfir* steps, holding me on her lap. I am clutching the only toy I had, a plain rubber ball. It is a very sad picture of a mother and son.

The next picture was taken in 1944 and we are all in it: I, still clutching the rubber ball and standing in front of my mother, my two brothers in the middle, and Anna on their right. This fractured family portrait tells the whole story of our experience with the war. On the reverse side there is a message dictated by my mother and written by my sister for the intended recipient, my father, to whom it was never sent: "As a remembrance to our father in exile, I am sending our likeness. Your beloved wife together with the children separated from you. Do not forget your family. Essen. 2-14-1944."

Perhaps we knew then, that our father was enslaved near us on a farm in Bremen. After the war, he told us that he was also brought to Essen, where he was recruited for farm labor. He was one of the two and a half million slave farm workers of Nazi Germany.

It is widely held that the life of the farm laborers was better than that of the city factory workers. This, however, is a matter of opinion. When we were reunited in 1946, my sixty-one-year-old father spoke of having been beaten and of having his teeth knocked out. A German directive entitled "Treatment of Foreign Farm Workers of Polish Nationality," dated March 6, 1941, stated:

> Farm workers of Polish nationality no longer have the right to complain, and thus no complaints will be accepted by any official agency.... The visit of churches is strictly prohibited.... Visits to theaters, motion pictures or other cultural entertainment are strictly prohibited.
>
> Sexual intercourse with women and girls is strictly prohibited.
>
> Arbitrary change of employment is strictly prohibited. The farm workers have to labor as long as is demanded by the employer. There are no time limits to the working time.
>
> Every employer has the right to give corporal punishment to his farm workers.... They should, if possible, be removed from the community of the home and they can be quartered in stables, etc. No remorse whatever should restrict such action.[19]

Furthermore, sexual intercourse with German females was punishable by death. The use of "railroads, busses, or other public conveyance" was prohibited to prevent farm slave workers from escaping, and "special treatment" was to be meted out for "severe violations against discipline, including work refusal or loafing at work." According to Himmler's directive of February 20, 1942, in such cases:

> Special treatment is requested. Special treatment is hanging. It should not take place in the immediate vicinity of the camp. A certain number [however] should attend the special treatment.[20]

Miraculously, although my father did escape from the farm to which he was confined, and although he was later caught, he was neither hanged nor condemned to a concentration camp. Instead, he was thrown in prison, where he remained until the end of the war. Needless to say, after our reunion and until his death at age seventy-eight in 1962, my father was never again the same man who was taken from us in Ryświanka.

For a few months after our arrival in Essen we also knew of the whereabouts of Aniela and Janina, but our brief correspondence was suddenly broken off at the beginning of 1944.

Added to the pain of family separation, indignity, hard labor, constant hunger, lice, illness, and cold weather, were the wailing sirens and the falling bombs. The following three-month British tallies provide us with a good indicator of the magnitude and the scope of the R.A.F. activity in the Ruhr:

> August 1944: During August R.A.F. Bomber Command is out on 30 days and 26 nights, flying 10,000 daylight sorties to drop 40,000 tons of bombs, and dropping 25,000 tons of bombs at night. . . .
>
> September 1944: R.A.F. Bomber Command operates every day and 24 nights, dropping 52,400 tons of bombs, 37,400 tons by day, 15,000 by night; 21,000 tons are dropped on Germany and some German towns previously bombed strategically are now targets as supply and communications centers for German armies. . . .
>
> October 1944: R.A.F. Bomber Command drops 50,000 tons of bombs on Germany during month and 10,000 tons on Occupied Territory; major attacks are made on 15 German towns. . . .[21]

The results of this all-out, round-the-clock bombardment were evaluated by the *United States Strategic Bombing Survey*:

> Prior to the summer of 1943, air raids had no appreciable effect either on German munitions production or on the national output in general. . . .

> The effects ... became more noticeable from the summer of 1943 onward.... For the first four months of 1944 the A.A.F., capable for the first time of carrying out repeated attacks deep into Germany, concentrated its strength on aircrafts and ball-bearing targets. During the attacks beginning in February, about 90 per cent of German fighter production was attacked and 70 per cent destroyed....[22]

Doubtlessly, the Allied air power contributed to the collapse of Germany. In respect to the effects of the bombing on productivity, however, a curious paradox emerges which has never been adequately explained. Judging by the captured Ruhr's wartime performance records, as the air raids increased so did German production until the very end of the war. The recuperative power of Germany was indeed astonishing! According to Willi Schlieker, the number three man in the Ministerium for Armament and War Production, "as the bombings grew, so did German production, until on the very eve of defeat, when Germany had collapsed within, the Ruhr was producing more than ever before." The *Ruhrgebiet*, he went on to say,

> ultimately collapsed, not because of the bombing of plants, mills and mines but because the railway exits were so clogged with blowouts, breaks, and burned-out locomotives that they could not carry away the 30,000 tons of finished goods the Ruhr produced every day. The Ruhr strangled finally, in January and February 1945, on its own production; it did not cave in under blast.[23]

The *Survey* drew a similar conclusion. "The attack on transportation," it stated, "beginning in September 1944, was the most important single cause of Germany's ultimate collapse."[24]

Bearing all this in mind, one wonders, then, about the nature and intent of the continuous saturation bombing of German cities. According to the *Survey*:

> 24 per cent—nearly one-fourth the total tonnage dropped [2,700,000 tons], and almost twice the weight of bombs launched against all manufacturing targets together—was dropped in attacks against large cities.... In sheer destructiveness these raids far outstripped all other forms of attack.[25]
>
> During the period from October 1939 to May 1945 the Allied Air Forces, primarily the R.A.F., dropped over one-half million tons of high explosives, incendiaries, and fragmentation bombs ... on 61 cities.... These cities included 25,000,000 people.... [A]ttacks are estimated to have totally destroyed or heavily damaged 3,600,000 dwelling units, accounting for 20 per cent of Germany's total residential units, and to have

> rendered homeless 7,500,000 people. They killed about 300,000 people and injured some 780,000.[26]

One after another, the great cities of Germany—Hamburg, Frankfurt, Hanover, Munich, Stuttgart, Nuremberg, Berlin, and fifty others—were systematically destroyed, their damage ranging from 30 to 80 percent. Of all the cities in the Ruhr, Essen and Dortmund were hit the hardest. To be sure, many of the cities contained military targets, such as the eighty-one factories of the *Gusstahlfabrik* complex in Essen, but the bombing was not limited to these installations. And even if it were, according to the *Survey*, the *Gusstahlfabrik* "as an ordnance target . . . undoubtedly received more attention than was justified by its importance."[27]

The real nature of the bombing of cities was revealed by Winston Churchill in a note sent to Stalin after the spring 1944 thousand-bomber raid on Essen:

> We sent 348 bombers to Essen on Saturday, casting 900 tons of bombs in order to increase the damage to Krupp's, which was again effectively hit, and to carry ruin into the southwestern part of the city which had previously suffered little.[28]

The southwestern suburbs were entirely residential. The R.A.F. raids (it was a British show) were clearly aimed at terrorizing the German population. The main objective of what Churchill once had called "the hideous process of bombing open cities from the air" and "an experimental horror" was, in his own words: "To make the enemy burn and bleed in every way."[29] After Rotterdam and Coventry, the British had little compunction about bombing German cities and turning them into a heaping mass of rubble. It was a case of vengeful "moral bombing." (Compare the 600 acres of obliterated London with the nearly 6,500 acres of downtown Berlin.) The survey summarized the intent of this "moral bombing" as follows:

> It was believed that city attacks offered a means of destroying German civilian morale. It was believed that if the morale of industrial workers could be affected, or if laborers could be diverted from the factories to other purposes, such as caring for their families, repairing damage to their homes . . . war production would suffer.[30]

As we already saw, the productivity of the Ruhr *increased* in the face of this misguided strategy, and Essen was bitterly defended to the very end. Only the morale of the helpless, shelterless slaves was adversely affected. The *Survey* concludes:

> The mental reaction of the German people to air attack is significant. Under ruthless Nazi control they showed surprising resistance to the terror and hardship of repeated air attack, to the destruction of their homes and belongings, and to the conditions under which they were reduced to live.[31]

Major General J.F.C. Fuller called the air strikes a "massacre of civilian populations."[32] Chester Wilmot wrote that "in cities like Cologne and Essen there was nothing left to burn, and the blast bombs, which caused such havoc when the buildings were intact . . . did little more than convulse the rubble."[33] More often than not it was we who were the "rubble."

> On March 5, 1943, Essen and the Krupp works received its first big bombing. Two years later, on March 11, 1945, the last and greatest blow was to fall on both. In between, the bombers came regularly. The monotony of this form of warfare made a habit of terror. The missiles did not distinguish between the just and the unjust, nor did they spare the innocent, and they seldom landed on the guilty.[34]

The bombs inevitably landed on the shelterless camps. A Krupp housing administrator conceded at Nuremberg that "the camps were without exception in the areas which were most affected." According to a report sent to Alfried Krupp later in the war, three camps were "partially destroyed," thirty-two "destroyed," and twenty-two "twice destroyed." None were left intact. On the night of October 23, 1944, alone, 820 people were killed and 643 wounded.[35]

> As the many fires broke through the roofs of buildings there rose a column of heated air more than two and a half miles high and one and a half miles in diameter. . . . This column was turbulent and was fed at its base by inrushing cooler ground-surface air. One and one and a half [sic] miles from the fire this draft increased the wind velocity from eleven to thirty-three miles per hour. At the edge of the area the velocities must have been appreciably greater, as trees three feet in diameter were uprooted. In a short time the temperature reached the ignition point for all combustibles and the entire area was ablaze. In such fires complete burn-out occurred; that is, no trace of combustible material remained and only after two days were the areas cool enough to approach.[36]

The heavy, immoral bombardment of Essen did not begin until the Battle of the Ruhr in the spring of 1943. (Essen was virtually untouched in the early years of the war.) On the night of the first major strike, March 5, 1943, 908 tons of bombs fell on the city. By the autumn of that year, 6,929 tons were dropped. During the raid of October 23-24, 1944, 4,522 tons of bombs fell. The last and the worst of the fifty-five air raids on Essen transpired on March 11, 1945, four days after the American army crossed the Rhine. It was after this attack that the *Gusstahlfabrik* complex was finally paralyzed. In these many missions of death, at times strung out over several successive days (twice exceeding a total of 10,000 tons), both incendiary (phosphorous) bombs and the explosive "block busters"—as heavy as 8,000 pounds—were used.

Given the devastating nature of such bombs, no one was ever completely safe in Essen except those in the deep (over 100 feet) underground *Kruppbunker* at Villa Hugel, the castle on the hill—which was never hit. Some, however, were more safe than others. In this matter the German racist ideology again prevailed. The native population was provided with more or less adequate air raid shelters from which everyone else was excluded. The slaves were allowed to use basements, but more often, shallow slit trenches (*Splittergraben*). The Jews had to stay where they were and take it. One Jewish survivor recalls:

> When there was an air raid, we were the only ones expressly forbidden to go into the air raid shelter; we just had to stay where we were, exposed to the air raid and without any sort of protection.[37]

In the beginning, because of the heavy fortifications around the Ruhr, the air raids were usually conducted at night. Each time the sirens sounded (and they sounded often), my mother would grab me and we would all scramble headlong down the six flights of stairs to the basement, our "bomb shelter." During these times I would usually cry, so much so that everyone began to call me *syrena* (siren), at which point I would wail all the louder.

But I was not the only one to give expression to my fears in that dark, scarcely subterranean shelter. As the bombs pounded the city into massive heaps of rubble, we clung to one another for dear life. Each new explosion sent spine-chilling shivers down our backs and caused us to duck instinctively as if in response to an unfelt shock wave. Some trembled continually. All prayed: "Our Father who art in heaven... Thy kingdom come. Thy will be done on earth ... forgive us our trespasses ... and deliver us from evil. Amen. Hail Mary ... Holy Mary ... pray for us sinners now and at the hour of our death. Amen. *Ojcze Nasz* ... *Zdrowaś Mario* ... *Ojcze Nasz* ... *Zdrowaś Mario* ... *Ojcze Nasz*..." and on and on and on—if for no other reason than, by that quiet murmuring, to drown out the reverberating thunder of the falling bombs.

The bombs falling on churches ... Our Father...; on brothels ... Hail Mary...; on hospitals ... Our Father...; on cemeteries ... Hail Mary...; on academies of science and institutes of art and culture ... Our Father...; on houses ... Hail Mary...; on schools ... Our Father...; and on the living and the dead, on masters and slaves, soldiers and civilians, the old and the young, women and children, innocent and guilty alike... Lord have mercy on us... *Boże zmiłuj się nad nami*... *Gospodi pomiluy*... *Hospody po—my—luy!* But for the most part, the God of Abraham, Isaac, and Jacob was uncompassionately silent while the victorious Gods of War reigned terror upon the trembling earth

It was amazing how after each bombing our *Schule Steinmetzfir* remained standing while all around us buildings toppled like dominoes. After a while, the residents came to believe that the British actually knew that our schoolhouse was occupied by refugees and spared it on purpose. Perhaps it was with this thought in mind that eventually many began to delay their six-flight trip to the basement shelter, trying to extend their rest period for as long as possible. In time even Anna, Franek, and Janek refused to budge until they heard the concussion of the first bombs. Only then would they run for cover and join us in the basement. My mother always responded immediately to the warning sirens. I had no choice in the matter.

Actually, there was no real need to hurry. The routine was quite predictable: first, the sirens; then, the unmistakable artillery of the 88s around the Ruhr manned by the 100,000 German troops; then, the black Pathfinders (twin-engine R.A.F. Mosquitoes) which would outline the target areas of Essen with red and green signal flares ("Christmas trees"); and finally, about ten minutes later, the Lancaster bombardiers with their tons of bombs. This was the time to hide. If one survived until the second blast of sirens, one thanked the Lord, and went outside to see precisely why one was still alive.

Once, as we came out of our *Schule Steinmetzfir*, there, half buried in the sidewalk by the foundation behind which we huddled, was a live bomb, its tail sticking prominently out of the earth. After we were evacuated, a detonation team arrived and defused the ticking mechanism, much to everyone's relief. This particular bomb was said to have a delayed fuse—the type which would not explode on impact, but later, when all resumed their normal rounds of activity. Many bombs simply failed to explode for various reasons. After the last attack on Essen, over 700 such unexploded bombs were found among the debris.

In spite of all these dangers and hardships, the five of us somehow managed not only to stay alive but also to remain together throughout that first fall, winter and spring of 1943-44. That summer, however, Anna was taken away, and we thought we had lost our last sister forever. She recalls:

> In July, all the young girls were taken from each family to dig trenches for German soldiers near the Holland border. [Some one hundred kilometers away.] I was one of these. However, because of the constant air raids we were not able to dig, so they gave us to the local farmers as field hands and domestics. After several weeks I, together with my girlfriend, Władzia, decided to run away and make our way back to Essen. We took some clothes, removed the "P" [for Polish] which we always had to carry on the left side of our bosoms and with the money my mother gave me before I left, we bought two train tickets to Essen.

> When we got off near the city, we saw that one half of it was completely destroyed. Not one building was left standing. The other half was still there, but all the windows were broken and the doors were blown off their hinges. As we made our way through the rubble we began to cry, thinking that our families had perished. Then, we met an acquaintance, Franuś, who told us that everyone was all right and offered to take us to the new camp where our families were now living.
>
> It took us all night to reach our destination because of the air raids. Each time the sirens went off we had to look for shelter and remain there until it was safe again. When we finally reached the new camp, we were very happy to be reunited with our families once more. Mother said: "All the other mothers were lamenting for their daughters, but I prayed because I somehow knew that you were all right and that we would see each other again."

While Anna was milking cows and cleaning houses, in the middle of the Battle of Hamburg—on July 25 and 30—Bomber Command ordered two more strikes on Essen. The whole city shook as bombs fell everywhere all at once. This time our poor schoolhouse was not spared. Three bombs in succession landed on the Ukrainian side of the building, killing over half of the 300 people in the *Schule Steinmetzfir*, turning that part of the basement into another mass grave. Miraculously, we were saved again. The following chilling description of that week's events in Hamburg applies to the raids on Essen as well:

> Eyewitnesses describe how the holocaust was so terrible that the air was sucked into it from outside the perimeter of the fire. Many were suffocated or shrivelled up by the intense heat. Others were drowned on throwing themselves into the canals that run through the city. Days later, when nearby cellars were opened, thousands were found to have perished as though cooked in an oven.[38]

It was immediately after this incident that we were relocated into the second camp-building where we would spend the following fall, winter, and part of spring, 1945. This camp was also a schoolhouse. It was called *Beisingschule*. The date of transfer on Franek's work papers reads August 1, 1944. Its distance from the first camp was about eight kilometers.

In running away from the farm to join us, Anna clearly violated both the injunction against the slaves' use of public transportation and the slave-labor commissar's (Fritz Sauckel's) decree:

> There is no claim to free time. Female domestic workers from the East may leave the household only to take care of domestic tasks.[39]

For either one of these infractions, Anna could have been subjected to "special treatment," or sent to a concentration camp, if she had been caught. It was said that people were often sent to these camps for the slightest deviation from the rules set down by the rule-abiding Nazis.

Once in *Beisingschule*, for example, Anna got caught in an air strike and was unable to return to the premises before the gates in our walled-in building were locked at 9:00 P.M. When she returned, around 11:00 P.M., she tried to sneak into the building through a bathroom window which was too high for her to reach. A non–rule abiding German neighbor saw her trying to scramble up the wall and came to her assistance. Hearing of her dilemma, he first warned her that if she were caught, she would be sent to the concentration camp; then, while his wife held a crate, he helped Anna to squeeze through the window to safety. She also could have been sent away earlier that day for removing the "P" from her bosom and seeking refuge in the course of the air raid in a German bomb shelter rather than one designated for the slaves.

Our life in *Beisingschule* was similar to our life in *Schule Steinmetzfir* except that now, in late 1944, there was more bombing, more work, less food . . . and also the hope of liberation.

> June 6, 1944—"Overlord," the allied invasion of the Normandy coastline.
>
> July 20, 1944—Hitler is wounded in an assassination attempt at "Wolf's Lair" in East Prussia.
>
> September 17, 1944—Allied airborne army lands in Holland. On the very border of Germany, the Allied advance subsides.
>
> December 16, 1944—Germans launch a counter-offensive. Battle of the Bulge.
>
> February 23, 1945—"Grenade," the operation of the U.S. Ninth Army driving toward the Rhine.
>
> March 7, 1945—The U.S. Army crosses the Rhine over the bridge at Remagen.

After crossing the Rhine, the Allies began to encircle the Ruhr, the industrial heart of Germany. The continual air attack culminated in the third week of March 1945, when about 42,000 sorties were flown over the area, destroying everything in sight and reducing the mighty blast furnaces of the Krupp works throughout the Ruhr to ruins.

The Führer's response to all of this was an order to transform the Ruhr into a "fortress" and to defend it at all costs. To this end he recruited every available

German including the elderly and even the physically unfit. This savage but hopeless resistance was quickly crushed when, on April 1, 1945, Simpson's U.S. Ninth Army (advancing from the north above Essen) and Hodges' U.S. First Army (advancing from the east) effected a juncture at Lippstadt, thus surrounding Field Marshal Model's troops in an eighty-mile circle. In the following two weeks the defenders of the Ruhr were systematically annihilated, and about 400,000 Germans were taken as prisoners of war.

Meanwhile, on March 19, Hitler, anticipating defeat, issued his infamous "scorched earth" directive for the destruction of Germany ("all industrial plants, all important electrical facilities, water works, gas works, food stores and clothing stores; all bridges, all railway and communication installations, all waterways, all ships, all freight cars and all locomotives"). To Albert Speer, the Minister of Armament and War Production (who would not carry out this insane directive), Hitler said:

> If the war is to be lost, the nation also will perish. This fate is inevitable. There is no need to consider the basis even of a most primitive existence any longer. On the contrary, it is better to destroy even that, and to destroy it ourselves. The nation has proved itself weak, and the future belongs solely to the stronger eastern nation. Besides, those who remain after the battle are of little value; for the good ones have fallen.[40]

After Remagen, but all the more so after these senseless orders to destroy everything and to shoot those who would not comply, a kind of deeper insanity—reminiscent of the last-minute execution of prisoners of war by the NKVD before the Nazi invasion of Western Ukraine—swept through the slave camps of Essen:

> Toward the end of that winter, when two feet of snow had blanketed the Reich and Germans without face masks had suffered constant headaches, Ukrainian women in unheated barracks were awakened at 4 a.m. (for no reason whatever) by icy jets of water. Once the prisoners were up, guards attacked them with solid rubber hoses, lashing at their breasts. Male slaves were struck in the groin, and few were left unbruised, for beatings had now been incorporated into the daily routine.[41]

On March 23, another insane directive, this time by the Führer's secretary, Martin Bormann, aimed at the destruction of the German people and the enslaved masses. No German property would be surrendered to the Allies, not even the *Herrenvolk* or its emaciated chattels. An order is an order. Speer at Nuremberg:

> The Bormann decree aimed at bringing the population to the center of the Reich from both East and West, and the foreign workers and

> prisoners of war were to be included. These millions of people were to be sent upon their trek on foot. No provisions for their existence had been made, nor could it be carried out in view of the situation. It would have resulted in an unimaginable hunger catastrophe.[42]

Like the "scorched earth" decree, this too was disregarded—as far as the German population was concerned. The evacuation of the slaves from Essen actually began a week before the Bormann decree. On March 17, a fifty-coach train procured by Heinrich Lehmann, the director of the Krupp *Arbeitseinsatz* (Bureau of Labor Procurement and Recruitment), stopped at the intact Bochum terminal and added 500 more Jewish women from one of Krupp's labor camps to its 1,800 "passengers" bound for Buchenwald.[43]

While all this was going on around us, oblivious to the last-minute insane decrees ordering our destruction, we prayed and hoped for a speedy delivery. At one point, the Allies were so close to the city we could hear their artillery and even their machine-gun fire. We knew that it was only a matter of days before our liberation. Then, in the beginning of April—quite unexpectedly—we were ordered to proceed to the nearest functioning railway station, loaded on cattle cars, and whisked away to an unknown destination. The Allies entered Essen on April 9, 1945.

Although we did not know it at the time, our trip would end in Meiningen, a large town in central Germany over 250 kilometers from Essen. Judging by the way in which we were simply dumped there in the mass confusion of the final month of war, Meiningen was not meant to be our ultimate destination. To the north, Gotha was just forty-five kilometers away; Buchenwald, a few kilometers further; Nordhausen lay beyond that. To the south, but much further, lay Dachau. These and the thirty other principal extermination camps were meant to be the final resting places for all the slaves of the Third Reich.

It was no favor to us to be left in Meiningen, however. Although it was without gas chambers, this camp, too, was a death camp. In fact, it would not be stretching the truth to state that all the concentration and forced-labor camps in Nazi Germany and its occupied territories were extermination camps—differing only in their means of execution.

6

Meiningen, Ach Meiningen

Contrary to the Bormann decree, we were allowed to board a southeast-bound train for Central Germany. The night we left it was cold and snowing. Except for the few additional rags some people found in the ruins after the bombings, our winter clothing was the same as our summer's—the same we had worn since August 1943.

The cattle cars in which we were being transported were also similar to those which first brought us to Essen. As we suffered from the heat before, so now we suffered from the cold as the freezing night wind whistled through the broken boxcar windows, blowing snow on all the huddled and desolate travelers. This was the end of the war. Supposedly we had come to Germany to work. Why then in God's name didn't they just let us remain in Essen? Why this trip away from the front? Many of us would find out soon enough. Having survived the terror of the work camps and the terror of the bombs, we would now be called upon three times to perish in the middle of nowhere just before the end of World War II.

In a continuing effort to disrupt the flow of German troops and supplies, the Allies bombed every train they saw. The white crosses on the boxcars, indicating the presence of civilians, were meaningless now. Indeed, our transport was filled with retreating German soldiers unworthy of *der Führer*. Due to the triple bombardment and the necessity of having to make repairs (it was amazing how quickly they were done!), the trip to Meiningen took about five days. Franek describes the journey:

> The Germans made us walk about five kilometers to the train station where they put all the families on the train. It was cold and there was still snow on the ground. There was a window in our boxcar which was broken. I remember standing by that window all night long and holding some rag I found over it so that the snow would not blow on us.
>
> Finally, we came to a station in the mountains and were told to get out. This is when I saw the German soldiers. I suppose they thought the train would not be bombed because it was a civilian transport.
>
> Then, a few small reconnaissance planes appeared overhead. They must have seen the soldiers too because about ten or fifteen minutes

> later, the bombers arrived and started to bomb the train . . . small bombs but very many of them.
>
> When the people saw the bombers, they began to run in every direction. I also ran for my life. But in my confusion, instead of running away from the train like the others, I found myself running along the track, away from the approaching aircraft behind us. Then I saw a large sheet of metal, perhaps blown off another train, lying on the side of the track. As I dove under it, I heard the bombs hit and felt the rocks bounce off the metal sheet over my head. The wind from the bombs was so strong I had to hold on with both hands so as not to be blown away.
>
> Many people were caught by the falling bombs as they were running. Many died and many were wounded. Fortunately, nothing happened to us. We had to stay there for a few days until the repairs were made.
>
> When we were bombed the second time, the same thing happened. People started to run again, but this time there was a tunnel in the side of the hill in which to hide so that many of us escaped without injury. I got to the tunnel just as the bombs began to fall.
>
> The third time I almost got killed. When the train stopped, everyone headed uphill towards a partially finished shelter. As I was running I could see the people trying to crowd in. Everyone was pushing and shoving since it was a small shelter. I knew I couldn't make it in time, so just before the bombs hit, I fell flat on the ground and grabbed hold of a small tree.
>
> After the blast, when I looked up, the shelter and the people were gone. A bomb landed right in that spot; about 100 people perished.

During these attacks, my fifty-four-year-old mother, whose remarkable strength was weakened by hard work and starvation (she often shared her food with us), could not run very fast; nor did she try to. During the first air attack, she decided that she and I would take our chances under the train, come what might. Janek, who had just turned twelve that March and therefore could already think for himself, decided to remain with us. Like Franek, my sister Anna always ran for cover. She describes the last bombardment as follows:

> As soon as the train stopped, people jumped off and began running in every direction. I also ran and found myself climbing a steep hill. Then the bombs began to drop while the circling planes sprayed us with machine-gun fire. I fell flat on the ground and covered my head with the large shawl I had. One bomb exploded so near that I bounced off the earth and was bombarded with flying rocks and gravel.
>
> I lay there until the planes departed, then I got up unhurt. All around me were people who were terribly mutilated by the bombs. They were screaming and begging for help. As I made my way back to the train, I kept looking for my family among those wounded and the dead. When I reached the train, I found out that everyone was safe and sound. We all had a good cry because we were still alive. After the third raid, there were not many left of those who began the journey.

Five years of age at the time, I, too, remember the carnage. The dismembered cadavers, the unattached arms, legs and heads, the pools of blood in the patches of the white snow, the screams of the wounded and dying—a child is not likely ever to forget such a scene.

For the third time they fixed those damned rails again, salvaged the few remaining boxcars and people, and loaded us on. Were it not for the bizarre circumstances surrounding that ill-fated trip, the determination of the Nazis to deliver the "passengers" to their appointed destination would have been most admirable. And so, having escaped death three more times, terrified, worn out, and hungry, we finally arrived at Meiningen.

Meiningen, Ach Meiningen—with your memorials to Brahms and Jean Paul; with your nineteenth-century dramatic academy and stock company theater; with your Hans von Bülow and your famous orchestra—how dark you were, how unaesthetic, how un-compassionate in April of 1945!

Could you not have shared a little bread with us, so as to prevent us from littering your proud streets with our rotting corpses? Could you not have given us some clothing, so as to spare yourself the shame of gazing upon our nakedness? Could you not have given us a little medicine in those last few days of the war, so as to prevent us from spreading our diseases to the four corners of your world?

There was food in your stores. There was medicine in your apothecaries. There was excess clothing in the crates and boxes of your railroad cars standing in full view of suffering mankind. But there was no kindness in your cold and unfeeling heart. Like the rest of Germany, you were neither magnanimous in time of victory, nor repentant in time of defeat. Hell must be like you!

The wooden barracks into which we were dumped were packed with people in varying stages of decay. Many ethnic groups were represented, but predominantly the French. The political ideology of segregating the different nationalities was finally abandoned! Each day we were given ten tablespoons of soup per person and one pound of bread for twenty people. In the last week before the end of the war, we were not fed at all. Anna recalls:

> In the barracks where we were quartered, there were already about twenty-five Frenchmen who were dying of hunger. A German matron would bring us some soup and bread once a day in the evening. We had to line up for our portion of the food and it often happened that just as it would be our turn to receive the soup, there would be none left.
>
> One day, the people at the end of the line thought they would not get anything so they threw themselves on the kettle and spilled its contents on the floor which they then began to lick. The German matron became very angry at this breach of discipline and the next day she did not come at all.

It was at this time that mother took out the German marks which she was saving so that we could buy some food. Mother had a good heart and she would always share whatever we had with the others.

The pangs of hunger were so bad that at one point the people began to eat the spring grasses, dandelions, roots, and weeds. I remember their swollen bellies and emaciated faces. I recall those beset by typhus and dysentery; how valiantly they suffered; how they held their stomachs; how, racked with diarrhea, they ran outside to relieve themselves; and how they fell over dead even as they were running. A child is not likely ever to forget this spectacle either.

While we were in Meiningen, the town was bombed several times, but no one in our camp bothered to hide anymore. We no longer feared death. It was life that worried us.

Unbelievable as it may sound, even as people were starving and dying like flies everywhere, Germans would come looking for workers. This time they *asked* if anyone wanted to work. After several weeks, Franek and Janek finally volunteered. To stay put meant certain death; perhaps they could find something in the city of Meiningen to prolong their life. I wished they had taken me with them. I did not want to continue watching people die of hunger.

Fortune smiled upon us once again. As my two brothers were cleaning the stock company theater, they saw a piece of paper blowing in the wind among the ruins. Pursuing a hunch, they chased the paper down . . . and discovered the lifesaving food stamps with which they were able to purchase some bread. In the last week of our captivity, all food had to be kept hidden and eaten in secret. During this time, the last vestiges of humanity disappeared in the camp; people killed for mere scraps of food. Thanks to my brothers' lucky break the five of us survived until the very end.

April 25, 1945—The American and the Russian Armed Forces meet at Torgau on the Elbe, 120 kilometers from Berlin.

April 30, 1945—Adolf Hitler, because of whom 50 million people died,[1] commits suicide in his underground bunker.

May 2, 1945—The Fall of Berlin to the First White Russian and the First Ukrainian Armies.

May 7, 1945—Germany surrenders unconditionally. "With this signature the German people and the German Armed Forces are, for better or worse, delivered into the hands of the victors. . . . In this hour I can only express the hope that the victor will treat them with generosity." [General Jodl after signing the capitulation in a little red schoolhouse at Reims.]

With that signature, although scarcely alive, we were finally liberated; so were all those enslaved in German households and on German farms; so were all those in German forced-labor camps; so were all those in Buchenwald, Bergen-Belsen, Dachau, Lublin-Maidanek, Treblinka, Auschwitz, Gotha, Erla, Nordhausen, Ohrdruff, Luckenwalde, Ganow and Oberusel—some of the worst Nazi death camps—minus the 10,000,000 who perished therein, and so were already liberated forever.

The extent of the Nazi program of genocide shocked the world. People were horrified when they learned of the sadistic medical experiments involving amputations, injections with gasoline, exposure to freezing temperatures and decompression chambers (simulating altitudes of 70,000 feet), sealing of glass, rags and dirt into wounds to simulate battlefield conditions, and vivisections—including those carried out on pregnant women. (But who would believe such things?)

People were horrified when they learned of the mass murders to the accompaniment of music played by the prisoners, of the bleaching of human skulls for souvenirs, of the use of human skin for lamp shades, handbags, and gloves. (But who would believe such things?)

People were horrified when they were told that the bodies of those gassed in the "shower baths" (*Brausebad*) were subjected to further shame by having their hair removed and gold extracted from their teeth; that prisoners were cooked in heated asbestos-lined cells to make them talk; that the still alive were thrown upon carts loaded with the already dead, and taken to the crematories; that no one, including the children, was spared. The Nuremberg indictment in respect to the children is the saddest one of all:

> Along with adults the Nazi conspirators mercilessly destroyed even children. They killed them with their parents in groups and alone. They killed them in children's homes and hospitals, burying the living in the graves, throwing them into flames, stabbing them with bayonets, poisoning them, conducting experiments upon them, extracting their blood for the use of the German army, throwing them into prison and Gestapo torture chambers and concentration camps where the children died from hunger, torture, and epidemic disease.[2]

(But who would believe such terrible, terrible things?)

So that the Allies would not be accused of propaganda, congressional committees, the news media, historians, and even 1,200 "well-fed and well-dressed" German civilians were taken on tours through the death camps.

> In the Little Camp, where prisoners slept 16 to a shelf, an infraction of discipline—particularly an attempt to escape—not infrequently resulted in all 16 being condemned. Such persons were immediately marched on foot to a small door in the fence of the back yard at a point immediately adjacent to the incinerator building. . . .

The condemned prisoners, on being hurried and pushed through the door in the fence, inevitably fell into a shaft and crashed 13 feet down to the cement floor. This ... was the strangling room. As they hit the floor they were garroted with a short double-end noose by S.S. guards and hung on hooks along the side walls, about 6½ feet above the floor, the row of hooks being 45 or 50 in number.[3]

There surged around me an evil-smelling crowd; men and boys reached out to touch me. They were in rags and remnants of uniforms. Death had already marked many of them....

When I entered one of the barracks, men crowded around, tried to lift me to their shoulders. They were too weak. Most of them could not get out of bed. I was told that this building had once stabled 80 horses. There were 1,200 men in it, five to a bunk. The stink was beyond all description....

I pray you to believe what I have said about Buchenwald. I reported what I saw and heard, but only part of it. For most of it, I have no words.

Dead men are plentiful in war, but the living dead—more than 20,000 of them in one camp ... and the country around was pleasing to the eye, and the Germans were well-fed and well-dressed....[4]

I went to Belsen. It was a vast area surrounded by barbed wire.... Outside the camp, which is amidst bushes, pines, and heather, all fairly recently planted, were great notices in red letters: *Danger—Typhus*....

Next day some men of the Yeomanry arrived. The people crowded around them, kissing their hands and feet—and dying from weakness. Corpses in every state of decay were lying around, piled up on top of each other in heaps....

About 35,000 corpses were reckoned, more actually than the living. Of the living there were about 30,000....

The S.S. men were driven and pushed along and made to ride on top of the loaded corpses and then shove them into their great mass open graves. They were so tired that they fell exhausted among the corpses. Jeering crowds collected around them, and they had to be kept under strong guard....

The next morning I left this hellhole, the camp. As I left, I had myself deloused.... This is what you are fighting. None of this is propaganda. This is the plain and simple truth.[5]

The German people saw all this today, and they wept. Those who didn't weep were ashamed. They said they didn't know about it....

Some Germans were skeptical at first, as if this show had been staged for their benefit, but they were soon convinced.... Men turned white and women turned away. It was too much for them.

These persons, who had been fed on Nazi propaganda since 1933, were beginning to see the light. They were seeing with their own eyes what no quantity of American propaganda could convince them of. Here was what their own government had perpetrated.[6]

This was the government which now pleaded that the Allies treat "the German people and the German Armed Forces . . . with generosity." William Shirer describes the fate of the key members of that government, now behind bars at Nuremberg:

> At eleven minutes past 1 A.M. on October 16, 1946, Ribbentrop mounted the gallows in the execution chamber of the Nuremberg prison, and he was followed at short intervals by Keitel, Kaltenbrunner, Rosenberg, Frank, Frick, Streicher, Seyss-Inquart, Sauckel and Jodl.
>
> But not by Hermann Goering. He cheated the hangman. Two hours before his turn would have come he swallowed a vial of poison that had been smuggled into his cell. Like the Fuehrer, Adolf Hitler, and his rival for the succession, Heinrich Himmler, he had succeeded at the last hour in choosing the way in which he would depart this earth, on which he, like the other two, had made such a murderous impact.[7]

In Meiningen, May 1945, our conquering heroes came in American Army trucks. There was never a more welcome sight in all the world! We were too weak to cheer, but in our hearts we greeted the troops with a panegyric of love. After five and a half years of hell, the dove of peace finally returned upon the earth and bore us skyward on its wings of hope. Freedom never suited us so well as here, in Meiningen.

As the convoy slowly made its way through the camp, the GIs divested themselves of their last packs of chewing gum and their last candy bars. Those who were not lucky enough to receive these treats knew that soon there would be more. There was—a lot more; too much more and too soon. When food became available some literally threw themselves upon it and ate until they became ill. Some died therefrom. It was difficult to control our famished bodies. It was difficult *not* to eat. Yet somehow we even survived this, our final encounter with the yawning jaws of death.

There were some who could not eat at all. These were the first to receive medical attention . . . then all the rest. We were allowed to bathe. Our festering wounds were cleaned and bandaged. Shots of penicillin were dispensed. Hands and feet were treated. In the entire camp there was virtually no one who did not need and who did not receive some form of medical aid from our angels of mercy.

When we were all fed, when we were all treated, when we were all fed again, we were allowed to rest and to enjoy the quiet sounds of spring. And as we rested and listened, we heard the sounds of silence. No more guns, no more artillery, no more exploding bombs—nothing but silence on the Western front, the welcomed silence of peace. The war was really at an end, and those of us who were here, in Meiningen, survived.

After making sure that her family was well taken care of and well provided for, my mother, who had never left my side for the entire duration of the war (or was it the other way around?), left us alone and headed for the idle coaches full of unclaimed clothing. Like a veteran bargain-hunter, she picked out what we needed, according to our sizes and her tastes, and when she returned we had clean clothes and shoes! We would be well dressed! We would be slaves no more! For the remainder of her life—and she lived until she was ninety-two—no one would ever accuse my mother of not being a smart dresser.

Perhaps it was thievery. But what was it in comparison to the Nazi plunder of Europe? In currency alone, according to the *U.S. Strategic Bombing Survey*, a total of 104 billion marks ($26,000,000,000) was extorted from the conquered nations. (The price of all the exported raw materials, manufactured goods, food and labor will never be known!) What was it in comparison to the wholesale looting of Europe's priceless art treasures? What was it in comparison to the $250,000,000 Nazi hoard discovered by Patton's troops in the lower levels of a salt mine? What was it in comparison to Heinrich Himmler's million dollars stashed away in a barn near Berchtesgaden? Like so many other architects of the Third Reich, this head of the Gestapo, this murdering destroyer of Lidice, this exterminator of Jews had been, after all, a greedy little man.

So history will forgive my mother for the few clothes she took from that abandoned train. It is the only war reparation my family ever received from Nazi Germany—or ever wants.

In Meiningen, though free, we were not ever completely at peace. Uppermost in our minds were thoughts about the other half of our family, our three sisters and our father. Were they still alive? If so, where were they and how were we to find them? These thoughts were shared by everyone in the camp. There was not one person there, not one family, who did not lose someone, somewhere throughout the war. A Polish interpreter eased our mind somewhat by telling us that provisions were being made whereby families would be reunited, but we had to wait awhile until things settled down a bit.

We remained in Meiningen for another month, but the camp looked different now. All the dead were buried, all the living resurrected. The barracks were cleaned and sanitized. Regular meals were provided. Frequent bathing was encouraged. One could remain in the bathroom for as long as one wished. Neither *Aufstehen!*, nor *Links! Rechts!*, nor *Raus! Appell!*, nor *Stücke!*, nor *Schweinhund!* was ever heard by anyone again.

Our captors were all gone. The scourge of Nazi Germany was over. Soon we would be reunited with our family, and we would all go back home to resume our interrupted lives in free Poland, perhaps even in Ryświanka—or so we thought.

7

Of Displaced Persons

After we recuperated sufficiently to travel, an American convoy took us about fifty kilometers north to a large camp located in Eisenach—where Johann Sebastian Bach was born, where Luther lived, and where, in 1869 (at the Congress of Eisenach), August Bebel and Wilhelm Liebknecht founded the German Social Democratic party. There, we were advised, in keeping with the postwar policy for displaced persons, to prepare for transport to our respective countries of origin. We signed up for Poland. While we waited for our transport, we made frequent inquiries regarding the whereabouts of the rest of our family.

The horrendous task of finding the millions of persons who had disappeared during the war was originally handled by the Central Tracing Bureau of the UNRRA (United Nations Relief and Rehabilitation Administration). Since the operations of the Central Tracing Bureau were limited to Germany, the PC-IRO (Preparatory Commission for the International Refugee Organization) created an International Tracing Service (ITS) to operate on a worldwide scale and to coordinate the activities of all national tracing bureaus. (The work of the ITS was handled by the PC-IRO from June 1, 1947, until January 1, 1948, when the ITS was formally established.)[1]

The functions of the ITS included reuniting families by locating lost relatives; providing evidence or proof of death (needed for legal purposes such as remarriage or adoption); finding children kidnapped by the Nazis for the Germanization program; assembling all documents and other information concerning missing persons; and preparing such publications as the two volume *Catalogue of Camps and Prisons in Germany and Germany-Occupied Territories, September 1939 to May 1945* and its *Supplement*—in order to help determine categories of prisoners for compensation purposes.

Inquiries concerning missing persons were forwarded to the ITS headquarters at Arolsen, Germany, where a central card index was maintained. Lists of missing persons were then published and promulgated throughout the displaced persons camps as well as in the press. This information was also broadcast over German radio stations and over Radio Vatican at Rome. In addition, ITS arranged for the showing of photographic slides of missing persons in thousands of European cinemas.

In its relentless search for information, the ITS canvassed records of concentration camps, prisons, the German civil administration, and war-time hospitals. They pored over transport lists and walked among graves. By the end of 1949, ITS accumulated between seventy and eighty tons of material in respect to the first three categories alone. Its search for missing children (reckoned to be in the hundreds of thousands) involved the investigation of children's homes, foster homes, and adoption records. By the end of 1949, the investigation of institutions alone involved the screening of 190,996 children. In that year, 1,996 unaccompanied children of 23 nationalities were located, and a balance of 18,945 known but unsolved cases, involving children of thirty nationalities, remained.

In 1950, when the master card index contained 10,538,358 cards of information and some 28,000 new cards were being inserted daily, the General Council of IRO resolved that the ITS should gradually reduce its activities and transfer its operation and master card index to the Allied High Commission by March 1951. The Child Search Branch ceased registering new cases on April 1, 1950, but its work on children already found continued until August 31. In September, the Child Search Headquarters in Esslington was closed and the records transferred to Arolsen, where a small Child Tracing Unit was retained.

By the time the ITS suspended its operation, only my father was found, and that was under UNRRA. News of my three sisters, who survived the war and returned to Poland, would not reach us until 1958 by means of a bizarre coincidence totally unrelated to the official channels. Meanwhile, for fourteen years we grieved our Stasia, Jasia, and Aniela, thinking that they had all perished during the war—and they thought the same about us.

While in Eisenach, we were at liberty to move about. For some, this privilege proved to be catastrophic. As can be imagined, after the war, armaments were scattered over the entire length and breadth of Germany. Well into the 1950s, people were still being blown to smithereens when, while plowing their fields or digging their gardens, a buried grenade or a mine would explode in their faces. Thus, sociopolitical, economic, and psychological consequences haunted the German people long after 1945!

In our area, a compound was established just on the outskirts of the city, and various instruments of war were dumped there. Among these were defused bombs, live German grenades, live ammunition of every description together with the guns which fired it, disabled artillery, vehicles, and even tanks. These instruments of terror held a peculiar fascination for all the civilians who survived them, but especially the children. Although we all knew better, the adults went there daily to inspect the arsenal and the children went there to "play" war. Since the compound was unfenced and unguarded, access was easy. Therefore, hardly a day went by without someone getting hurt outside of Eisenach. The weapons did not know the war was over. They followed their own inner logic.

Unknown to my family, at five years of age, I and my friends (now, there was even time for friendship) would visit the compound often. Sometimes we would collect armloads of long-handled grenades, proceed to the nearest bridge and heave them into the waters below. When they exploded we would watch the fish surface and flow away with the current. Sometimes we would play inside the tanks. They were so impressive with all their levers, switches, buttons, and revolving turrets. It was fun to see what mechanical devices responded to our touch. Once, however, when one of the tanks fired a volley of shells, we were frightened out of our childish wits.

Our favorite pastime in the munitions compound consisted of collecting heaps of aimless shells, removing their deadly points with knives or by wedging them against something and pushing downwards, and emptying out the powder. After we had a bucketful, we would make a trail to some object we wished to blow sky high (a German bridge, munitions factory, city, etc.) or to a mound of powder some distance removed (a bunker). We would then find safe refuge, light the powder, and watch the snakelike flame dart towards its objective. Then we would duck, hold our ears, and afterwards inspect the success of our "brave" ventures. I suppose in time we, too, would have made good soldiers. Boys who play with firearms generally grow up—in troubled times—to become warriors. It has always been that way. It is that way still.

By the time the transports for Poland arrived, my family had accumulated quite an impressive collection of clothing and other useful items. Thanks to the tireless efforts of the UNRRA, we even had some luggage and a trunk. When the news reached us that an American convoy was on its way, people lined up for hours in advance, and when the trucks arrived, there was a mad scramble to get on board. We tried in vain. When the dust settled, we were still standing on German soil. One by one the trucks left without us, each loaded beyond capacity with those who had the strongest elbows. This happened on two separate occasions. We began to despair of ever seeing our Ryświanka again. Then, by a stroke of unbelievable luck, we somehow found ourselves on a truck of the third convoy. In the mad scramble to get on board, however, Anna was left behind. After all was said and done, no more room could be found for my sister and her luggage. There was only one thing to do: we got off the truck.

Before the next transport arrived, we received some very disturbing news about our fatherland. The Poland we had left, we were told, was no longer a free country; in fact, it was no longer even Poland! The boundaries had been moved again! We were informed that during the February 4–12, 1945, Conference at Yalta, President Roosevelt, Prime Minister Churchill, and Generalissimo Stalin decreed that the eastern frontier of Poland would (more or less) follow the 1919 Curzon Line. This meant that the territory from which we hailed was now a part of the URSR (*Ukraïns'ka Radyans'ka Sotsialistychna Respublika*—Ukrainian Soviet Socialist Republic).

In spite of the Polish government-in-exile's unwillingness to enter into an alliance with the Soviet Union and its rupture of diplomatic relations with it, the Yalta decision in effect gave Poland to the Communists. Thus, while the Western Allies fought for "victory," for the defeat of Nazism, the Soviets fought, in addition, for political expansionism. With the collapse of Germany assured, the Yalta Conference placed into Russian hands unprecedented power over the neighboring nations.

Having achieved all his objectives with little difficulty—in respect not only to Poland but to Europe and Asia as well—the ever-benevolent Stalin agreed to allow representation from the government-in-exile in Poland's Communist regime, an agreement which he never honored. The fate of a nation was determined in four little paragraphs:

VII. Poland

The following Declaration on Poland was agreed by the Conference:

A new situation has been created in Poland as a result of her complete liberation by the Red Army. This calls for the establishment of a Polish Provisional Government which can be more broadly based than was possible before the recent liberation of the Western part of Poland. The Provisional Government which is now functioning in Poland should therefore be reorganized on a broader democratic basis with the inclusion of democratic leaders from Poland itself and from Poles abroad. This new Government should then be called the Polish Provisional Government of National Unity.

M. Molotov, Mr. Harriman and Sir A. Clark Kerr are authorised as a commission to consult in the first instance in Moscow with members of the present Provisional Government and with other Polish democratic leaders from within Poland and from abroad, with a view to the reorganisation of the present Government along the above lines. This Polish Provisional Government of National Unity shall be pledged to the holding of free and unfettered elections as soon as possible on the basis of universal suffrage and secret ballot. In these elections all democratic and anti–Nazi parties shall have the right to take part and to put forward candidates.

When a Polish Provisional Government of National Unity has been properly formed in conformity with the above, the Government of the U.S.S.R., which now maintains diplomatic relations with the present Provisional Government of Poland, and the Government of the United Kingdom and the Government of the U.S.A. will establish diplomatic relations with the new Polish Provisional Government of National Unity, and will exchange Ambassadors by whose reports the respective Governments will be kept informed about the situation in Poland.

The three Heads of Government consider that the Eastern frontier of Poland should follow the Curzon Line with digressions from it in some

> regions of five to eight kilometres in favour of Poland. They recognise that Poland must receive substantial accessions of territory in the North and West. They feel that the opinion of the new Polish Provisional Government of National Unity should be sought in due course on the extent of these accessions and that the final delimitation of the Western frontier of Poland should thereafter await the Peace Conference.[2]

Almost immediately after its promulgation, the section on Poland drew heavy criticism. Many believed that the whole Yalta Conference represented a shameless sellout of America's friends and that it would be responsible for many of the world's future ills. Yalta, it was said, paved the way for Russia's postwar domination of all of Eastern and half of Central Europe. Others argued that the Western Allies gave no more to Stalin than he already had or could have easily taken. A British historian, Chester Wilmot, concluded: "The real issue for the world and for the future is not what Stalin would or could have taken, but what he was given the right to take. This agreement provided Stalin with a moral cloak for his aggressive designs."[3] Be that as it may, the Yalta Agreement dealt a deathblow to Poland's hopes for independence and democracy. It also demoralized the remaining opposition to the Communist rule in Europe.

To my family it meant returning either to Ryświanka, which was now a part of the URSR, or to Poland, which was now also under Soviet domination. Neither proposition appealed to us. We had had our fill of tyranny. In our pardonable ignorance, we could not distinguish between Communism and National Socialism. The UNRRA report of May 1946 entitled "Why the Displaced Persons [82 percent] Refuse To Go Home" states our case well:

> With very few exceptions, the Poles in the U.S. and British Zones gave political reasons for their negative votes in the repatriation poll.... In general, the Poles who quoted political reasons can be broken down into three groups....
>
> The second group consists of people who have private political reasons for fearing repatriation. The largest number in this group are those whose homes were located east of the Curzon line in that part of Poland which has been annexed to Russia. The loss of their homes to Russia makes them feel an even stronger nationalistic tie with Poland, so that they invariably refuse to return to their homes and become Soviet citizens. If any of them would agree to go back to Poland they would probably be sent to the newly annexed western provinces which are now being settled by the Poles. This cannot properly be called repatriation, but rather "pioneering" in an unfamiliar land, far from friends and relatives. Most of the DPs now being maintained in camps in Germany seem to lack a pioneering spirit to set forth and build a new home and a new life in an area where conditions are reported to be difficult.[4]

As we waited in Eisenach, new reports reached us that the Poland we had known had changed beyond recognition. The conditions of life which were being described (hunger, fear, lack of adequate housing, and so on) reminded us of Nazi Germany. It would be difficult without our father. Moreover, we were told that the American transports would take us only as far as the Polish border. What became of us after that was up to the SSSR (*Soyuz Sovietskikh Sotsialisticheskich Respublik*—Union of Soviet Socialist Republics). After hearing these distressing reports, we decided to wait it out. First, we would renew our efforts to locate the other members of our family, and then we would consider emigration.

As it turned out, we were not the only ones to follow this course of action. On the basis of the 1931 Polish census, Casimir Smogorzewski estimated that 3,914,000 Poles resided in the area between the 1921 Treaty of Riga frontier and the Curzon Line.[5] Most of them were now either displaced or dead. Of those alive, many did not want to live under the Soviet regime either in the Ukraine or in Poland. This pattern repeated itself in respect to every Soviet-occupied territory, creating a serious refugee crisis in Europe with which the United Nations had to contend. As we will see shortly, given the original membership of the UN, this was not a simple matter.

I wish I could state that after our five and a half years of sheer hell under the Soviets, the Ukrainian Nationalists, and the Nazis, life under the American occupation was a bed of roses. Such, I am sad to say, was not the case; far from it. As it would be unseemly for me to complain about our treatment at the hands of our liberators (and in truth they really were), I will defer to a higher, official authority who will state our case in a much better and more convincing way than any one of us could possibly do. Here, then, is a confidential report from those years which provides a fairly accurate description of what life was like in the various displaced persons' camps in West Germany. I quote it at length.

THE CONDITION OF DISPLACED PERSONS
SEPTEMBER 1946

REPORT OF THE EXECUTIVE STAFF OF THE UNITED NATIONS RELIEF AND REHABILITATION ADMINISTRATION (UNRRA), U.S. ZONE HEADQUARTERS, TO THE DIRECTOR GENERAL OF UNRRA

The purpose of this report and of this action is to bring to the personal attention of the Director General of UNRRA a realistic view of the deplorable and rapidly deteriorating position of the Displaced Persons in the U.S. Zone of Occupation in Germany. For the reasons which are explained further herein, it is the conclusion of the Executive Staff of UNRRA U.S. Zone Headquarters that immediate action is required by the highest level of authority to initiate steps for the earliest possible *removal of non-repatriable Displaced Persons and Refugees from Germany*.

It is the conclusion of UNRRA U.S. Zone personnel that the ideology which ineradicably permeates the minds of the German people is successfully exerted with such consistent pressure upon the Military Government and the Army of Occupation as to render them incapable of securing for the DP a safe haven in Germany; that to retain them in Germany for any protracted length of time, under any conditions, would be to perpetuate the crimes of Nazism and the injustices of other circumstances which have caused them to be uprooted from their normal lives, with the loss of relatives, friends and possessions; that to oblige them to continue their present form of existence would be to contribute to the creation of a "barrack race," a demoralized, hopeless mass of stranded humanity.

The agencies upon whom it had been expected that the responsibility for resettlement would fall, have proven inadequate to meet the situation. It is known that the Economic and Social Council of UNO [United Nations Organization] have recognized the seriousness and urgency of the problem, but unfortunately the plans of this body do not call for any form of initial action before September 1946.

It therefore remains for UNRRA, who has lived in close human touch with these unfortunate people for many months, to take the initiatives in their behalf. While it may be argued that such action does not come within the scope of UNRRA responsibility as governed by its charter and resolutions, it is the consensus of the UNRRA personnel in the field that, because of the effort which has been put forth, and in order not to shatter the last remaining hope and faith which the DPs are placing in it, there *has* developed the inescapable moral obligation and responsibility upon UNRRA to see the problem through, either directly or indirectly.

It has therefore been resolved to place before the Director General of UNRRA the urgent request that he take the lead in developing a solution for the Displaced Persons in Germany. Known as a man of direct, forceful action, unfettered by political or diplomatic considerations, but bound rather by strong human instincts to the sufferings of oppressed and downtrodden people, it is hoped that he will use his strength and prestige to awaken world consciousness to the urgency of this need; that he will take direct and energetic action with the Governments of Canada, Australia, New Zealand, Brazil, and any other interested nations to hasten the opening of their gates to these people; that he will take steps to spur the Economic and Social Council of UNO into more rapid action on their behalf; and that he will take necessary action with the Government of the United States in order that, pending their final resettlement, the genuine DP and refugees in Germany will be given asylum, hospitality and protection in the true spirit of American tradition.

I. GENERAL SITUATION OF DP, U.S. MILITARY AND GERMAN AUTHORITIES

. . . In countries other than Germany and not under military occupation, the lot of the DP is not critical. He lives among former Allies with fairly equal economic, educational and general living opportunities. His ultimate settlement can be a plan of the future, without causing him undue suffering and hardships in the meanwhile.

The DP and refugees remaining in Germany, whether in camps or in the community, do not have such an equal chance. They are living in a country hostile to them, which is itself being subjected to a punitive economy under military control with lowered standards of living and restricted occupational and educational opportunities. They are held in the greatest contempt by the Germans, who lose no opportunity to discredit them in the eyes of the American Military Authorities. The effect of this derogatory influence has been strong and widespread to the point where it has seeped up from the operating levels to even the highest military echelons. The DP problem has always been a nuisance to the Army. With redeployment and the introduction of new, untrained and unoriented military personnel, there is now an almost complete lack of knowledge and understanding of the factors which created the DP situation in the first place; and the subjection of the Americans [sic] mind to German influence has been such that there is even less human sympathy and consideration than there is understanding. The DP are generally considered by military personnel as "lousy Poles" and "Goddam DP" who should be sent back where they came from whether they like it or not.

The combat troops who originally liberated the DP, who saw the conditions to which they had been subjected, were human and considerate in their treatment of them. The directives of General Eisenhower, reflecting the policies of the U.S. Government and people, recognized the DP on the level of Allied citizens and decreed that, pending final repatriation or resettlement, they would be cared for on a high standard at the expense of the German community, and that *priority* was to be given to their requirements over those of the Germans.

Insofar as it has affected and continues to affect the DP situation, we can state authoritatively that the U.S. military establishment has broken down completely. The directives of General Eisenhower have not been and are not being properly implemented in the field. The majority of officials are woefully ignorant of the problem and the few officers remaining who have knowledge of, and sympathy for it are unable to make their influence felt at the troop level. Occasional instances of sympathetic and cooperative treatment by military authorities at the field level are usually the product of the individual intelligence and humanity of a particular officer and of his resistance to German influence.

That the contempt for the DP and forgetfulness of his proper status has also permeated the higher military echelons, is evidenced by recent policies. Most revealing of the loss of regard toward the DP, and of the absence of elemental psychological understanding, is the granting of authority for the use of German police in carrying out raids and searches in DP installations. That the average DP has long been subjected to German brutal force is established fact. That he will resent and resist the intrusion of this, to him, same brutal force into his so-called "liberated" situation, is a foregone conclusion.

This policy has provoked several serious situations, and has culminated in the incident at Stuttgart, where over 200 armed German police, under the supervision of a few MP [military police] troops with *no* commissioned officer, using a number of dogs on leashes, surrounded and attempted to search a camp of approximately 1,500 Polish-Jewish Displaced Persons. This resulted in the shooting to death by the German police of one Polish-Jew (survivor of a concentration camp and only recently reunited with his wife and two children) and the wounding by gunshot of three other DPs.

Another activity carried out on the basis of military necessity has been the wholesale transferring of DP populations from one camp to another. That this is a policy of subtle coercion toward repatriation has been confirmed by the statements of high officers who did not want the DP to become too "settled" in their living conditions.

Further to this attitude is the evident and proclaimed desire of the military to "liquidate" the DP problem by integrating DPs into the German community. This has taken the form of more or less official announcements in the press relative to the imminent closing of DP camps and various instructions given by U.S. officers at field level that UNRRA DP camps were to be closed as of certain dates, without any indication as to the future fate of the DP.

Another indication is the great emphasis which is being placed on the criminality of DPs. Continuous allegations by German civil authorities of black market activities of DPs, and the general conclusion that DP camps are largely populated by collaborators, by SS, etc., have created the tendency to class all remaining DPs as criminals and collaborators. These allegations and conclusions are founded more on assumptions than on facts. On the allegations of black market activities, and sometimes possession of arms, shake-down raids have been carried out at some time or other in almost every DP camp in the U.S. Zone. These have often been carried out by U.S. troops, untrained, unoriented, and undisciplined, without adequate officer supervision, in the crudest and roughest manner, with deliberate destruction and theft by the troops of DPs' personal possessions. These raids have in general failed to produce the evidence of large-scale black market activities by DPs as would justify such violent action. Likewise, what screening has been accomplished thus far has failed to reveal any large percentage of collaborators or otherwise undeserving persons in DP camps which would factually sustain the general assumption which is being taken.

The deterioration of the Military attitude toward the DPs, and the arbitrary, provoking and often violent actions which are being taken against them, have served to place them again in the position of inferiority and baseness, in the eyes of the Germans, that they occupied under the Nazi regime; this time, however, with the apparent concurrence of the Americans. More and more authority is being delegated to the German

Civil Government and the DPs are receiving proportionately less and less protection from the U.S. Military.

Living in an uncertain status, lacking any clearly defined juridical rights and representation, the DP in his contacts with German authorities is again the victim of discriminations and ruthless treatment.

II. PRESENT LIVING CONDITIONS AND MORALE OF DPS IN THE U.S. ZONE

The living conditions of DPs and their material and spiritual lot can be generally estimated as being about ten percent of the requirements necessary to achieve a minimum acceptable standard.

Most of the DPs live in former troops barracks, often partially destroyed, in primitive conditions of housing and feeding. The directives of General Eisenhower calling for the provision of normal living accommodations, even at the expense of German housing, were intended to restore to the DPs some opportunity for the home life which had been denied them for many years. These directives always met with resistance by Military Government and have been implemented only to an insignificant degree. This fact is self-evident since the DPs have continued to live in the most demoralizing conditions of overcrowding, with large numbers of people in single rooms, often with mixed sexes, mixed families and with children of all ages observers of adult intimacies. Within the compass of one room, without separation or privacy of any kind, are affected by groups of people the daily activities of dressing and undressing, of eating and sleeping, and of conjugal relations. These barracks constructed only for the use of regimented men are totally inadequate in the basic requirements of sanitation. The waste disposal, washing facilities and toilets were intended for a population of men, not women and children. The difficulties in obtaining materials and tools for alterations have prevented any substantial degree of correction of these conditions. Only by virtue of the initiative and persistence of UNRRA team personnel were some of the badly damaged barracks repaired sufficiently to enable the DPs to withstand the past winter. The facilities for food preparation and messing are equally dismal. While sufficient food is provided to retain average health (not, however, for workers) the lack of balance, the monotony of diet, and the method of preparation, dispensation, contribute to the general despondency. The DP diet contains very little, if any, fresh foods of any kind. Military Government regulations forbid the procurement of fresh foods, other than potatoes from indigenous sources for DPs. Any efforts by the DPs to secure such foods independently are immediately attacked by M.G. [Military Government] and German authorities as black marketing activities.

There are few facilities which can be adapted to use as central messes and this idea is generally resisted by the DP; for, although his main meal usually consists of the eternal soup or stew, in which most of the available ingredients are combined, he prefers to carry it in a container of any description to the room where, supplemented by some dry rations, on a box or other flat surface, he goes through the parody of setting the family table.

The DP's clothing is not calculated to restore or sustain this self respect. He has been provided with a covering for his body, generally a second hand, ill fitting garment. The legal issue has been limited to a single item, i.e., one trouser, one jacket, one dress, one pair of shoes, without due allowance for cleaning, mending or replacement, resulting in considerable difficulty in making ends meet. This condition has been particularly demoralizing for the women. Independent efforts by the DP to obtain supplementary clothing are again attacked as black market activities; in fact, items of clothing legitimately possessed by the DP are often confiscated by U.S. troops or German police during shakedown raids. The German civilian is still unusually well dressed and presents a neat respectable appearance. In contrast the DP looks like a bum, and this difference does not fail to make its impression on the U.S. troop. The German looks like a gentleman (or a lady) and the U.S. soldier accepts him as such; the DP man or woman looks like a bum or a tramp and that is the way they are regarded. The medical aspect of the care for DP has been far in advance of any other. Fortunately, UNRRA was able to discharge directly this professional service by having doctors on its teams; but even here, the difficulties of securing medical supplies and instruments for DP use have been a great obstacle to an adequate program. Until recently, UNRRA's medical services were limited to camp infirmaries, to deliveries, inoculations and minor injuries. Patients suffering from major illnesses or requiring surgical treatment were generally placed in German hospitals, with varying degrees of acceptance by the Germans. At present, however, UNRRA has direct administrative control of hospitals for DP to the extent of nine thousand beds, which is resulting in a great improvement for hospitalized cases.

It is a tribute to the zeal of UNRRA medical personnel that no serious outbreak of disease has occurred among DP. It is also significant that the program has been successful, in the one field of professional work where UNRRA services could be directly applied in the field, without great dependency on the military organization.

The foregoing paragraphs have dealt with the basic physical requirements to sustain life and health among the DP and the shabby manner in which they are met.

Even more serious are the tremendous deficiencies in those aspects of a normal life which develop character and spiritual values, i.e., employment opportunities, work incentives, education, vocational training, religion and recreation; and as long as the DP remain in Germany their possibilities for realizing these activities are non-existent.

Understandably enough the DP refuse to work for Germans or under German supervision, the latter being generally a condition of working for the Army. They have no desire to assist in the reconstruction of Germany, nor to be again subjected to German regimentation and discrimination against foreigners. There is plenty of hard labor to be done in Germany, but the DP who are highly trained professional and technical people (especially the Balts), such as engineers, scientists, architects, lawyers, doctors, teachers and scholars, administrators, etc., have no prospect whatsoever of following their individual pursuits or of establishing themselves once more with any degree of independence.

The maximum employment of DP has been between 12 and 14%. All but a very few of these work in assembly center administration, maintenance and workshops. On the principle that the Germans must bear the cost of DP maintenance, directives provide that the wages of such workers must be paid by the Bürgermeisters. This policy is meeting with growing resistance on the part of Bürgermeisters and Military Government.

Army directives have always stated that priority in employment be given to DPs, yet consistent discrimination has been practiced against this group by all Army echelons. This, the one possibility for acceptable employment outside of assembly centers, has never been realized. The UNRRA Employment Branch presented to the Displaced Persons Division at USFET a practical operating procedure for DP employment pools in October 1945. This division took no action until 13 March 1946, despite constant urging of this branch. On this date, a directive was again issued stressing the priority to be given DPs in employment by the Army. In view of the delegation of procurement responsibility to German civil authorities and of their recognized antagonistic attitude toward the DP, its effective implementation is not probable.

It is now a year since their liberation, and the majority of DPs have remained in comparative idleness. That they are idle by nature cannot be accepted, since the nationalities they represent are traditionally hard workers; but lacking adequate opportunities, motivation of private family life and responsibility, incentives of remuneration in convertable currencies, supplementary workers' rations and, most important, a future for which to strive, it is inevitable that every passing day adds to the deterioration of character, self-respect and the urge for independence.

Equally discouraging in effect are the extreme limitations in educational and training opportunities. The desire for education is unusually high and UNRRA welfare personnel have exploited existent possibilities to the fullest extent. However, it is estimated that only about five per cent of the children, youth and adults are having their educational and training needs properly fulfilled to desirable standards. The lack of space for school facilities, inability to procure adequate books and school supplies and the dearth of teachers, particularly in the Polish and Jewish groups, have all contributed to this deplorable situation. German high schools, technical schools and universities have been ordered to make available ten per cent of their enrollment to DPs, but here again exists a language barrier, since these schools are conducted in German and [there is] the natural reluctance of the DP to accept German-style education, even under Military Government supervision. In any case, these facilities would meet only about one-tenth of the need.

Opportunities for vocational training are equally limited by lack of machinery and materials, with obvious reluctance on the part of Military Government to make such facilities available for DPs. A case in point was the action considered necessary by Military Government to forbid supplies of leather for DP centers. This leather was being used in cobbler workshops, set up in centers for two purposes; to repair shoes and for apprentice cobblers. DP shoes subsequently had to be sent to German factories for repair.

Religion and recreation have found a measure of native self-expression, despite dire limitations of facilities and materials. Because of its suppression under the Germans, religion assumed greater significance than ever for these people. Psychologically, the DP has had to cope with the effect of years aimed at the degradation of the human spirit, and with the months since liberation spent under conditions which have afforded little opportunities for private family living, little chance for constructive employment, little hope for the future. Serious handicaps have been the absence of a Greek Orthodox Church in Germany, of synagogues, and of facilities for Roman Catholics, notably the Poles, who do not choose to use churches frequented by the Germans. Spiritual leadership is also lacking as well as materials such as bibles, prayerbooks, etc. UNRRA and the voluntary agencies are doing all in their power to facilitate religious services and the observance of major religious holidays, the first such holidays to be observed since the war began.

The recreational activities of the DP instinctively take the forms best calculated to buoy their flagging spirits. National zeal is manifest through their music, dramatics, crafts, legend and lore. The exuberance of children and youth finds expression in sports and games, under any conditions.

This bright spot of cultural recovery, while serving to hide the tragedy and hopelessness which lie in their hearts, is also an indication of their ability to adjust and of their potential contribution to any community in which they may live and work with equal freedom and opportunity.

At this stage, the morale of the Displaced Persons is at its lowest ebb. The change of attitude and treatment by the U.S. Military leaves them utterly bewildered. The incomprehensible moves of entire population from one camp to another, abruptly destroying whatever meager roots they may have established, fills them with dismay. The increase of German authority over them and the announced prospect of their being dumped into the German community and left to their own resources, is draining their very last hopes. Their faith in UNRRA is dying, for they cannot understand that the U.S. Military are the only responsible and commanding authority as far as the DPs are concerned.

The U.S. Immigration program, at first a light on the horizon, is being recognized in all its inadequacy, and the silence of other nations on the subject of refuge fills them with despair.

On every side, the future is dark and forbidding. The job that started with liberation, in all its glorious, humanitarian brightness, has been left

> to drift and disintegrate. The world of charity and understanding is breaking faith with a part of humanity.
>
> But the job *must* be completed. The impoverished "little people," caught like grains of sand between the millstones of power, cannot be left to the "tender mercies" of a German populace, nor to the degrading effects of substandard institutional living. They *must* be removed from Germany and given the ordinary opportunities of human beings.
>
> Every sincere UNRRA employee feels in his heart, "It is up to UNRRA to take the lead and point the way"—now, urgently, without delay.[6]

While the UNRRA wrestled with the problem of the displaced persons and the refugees, we were being loaded onto various transports and dispersed throughout Germany. First, we were taken to one camp, then to another, and another—until, by the end of 1945, we had been shuffled around like checkers through about twenty different residences. Sometimes we would be told to board a truck which would take us a hundred kilometers in one direction only to turn around and bring us right back to the spot from which we started out.

Meanwhile, Europe's economy was in shambles and the agencies responsible for the care and maintenance of the displaced persons and refugees found themselves hard pressed due to the sudden and massive influx of new cases. Although in good hands, we again experienced hunger; not like the hunger in Nazi Germany, but ordinary, common hunger, like that of someone who has not eaten for a day or so. At times, we were also cold. Even when we were bundled up in blankets, winter travel in army trucks left a lot to be desired. We often regretted owning all our newly acquired capitalistic paraphernalia. Travel was so much simpler when one had absolutely nothing.

After "touring" much of Germany for a period of about six months, we were brought (at the beginning of 1946) to majestic Bad Reichenhall, and much to our surprise, allowed to remain at the foothills of the Bavarian Alps until the fall of 1947. Life in this famous summer and winter resort in Upper Bavaria was not hard to take at all. For the first time in many years, we discovered the pure tranquillity of peacetime existence. My brother, Janek, recalls one incident from those bygone days:

> Bad Reichenhall was a camp formerly occupied by German soldiers. The barracks and compound were surrounded by a tall barbed-wire fence. We liked to play soccer in the compound but soccer balls were hard to come by. We therefore cut the ends off the footballs which the Americans gave us, stuffed them with old rags and used these instead.
>
> One day I made a deal with a German boy who used to watch us play. I agreed to swap six bars of chocolate (we received a candy bar every other day in school) for a good soccer ball. When I finally saved up enough bars, each with the ends nibbled off, I slipped them through a hole in the fence to the German who promised to bring me the ball the next day.

> Much to my disappointment, that was the last I saw of him. I should have known better than to trust a German.

In Bad Reichenhall schools were established for the refugee children's much-neglected education. While Franek and Janek participated in an accelerated grammar school program which promoted them to the next class every six months, I attended kindergarten. As I recall, we played a lot and went on long hikes up to the surrounding mountains. It was a nice way to begin my long academic career.

Since Anna was too old for school, she spent all her time being courted—with good success. On April 21, 1946, she married Stefan Piwowarski, who wore an American uniform, displayed an affected American accent, and claimed to have relations in America. It was all a big lie, but Anna fell for this handsome devil nonetheless. In time, he turned out to be such a bad husband and father that even the Roman Catholic Church assented to annul her on-and-off marriage of some twenty years. But in Bad Reichenhall, Stefan was the best thing that ever happened to Anna, and so we rejoiced in her good fortune and ours. It was the first family wedding we ever attended.

With Anna married and the three boys in school, my mother finally had some peace and quiet, but not for long. In September 1946, our long lost father finally came back to us. He was very thin. He had aged beyond recognition. He did not say much about his captivity; nor did we ask. It was good to have him with us once again. Although we did not know it at the time, our three sisters were also safe and sound in Poland. In spite of the fact that our fate was still undecided, we began to live a little, to attend social gatherings and dances and other people's weddings.

I have three memorable photographs from Bad Reichenhall. The first is of Anna and my mother, two strong Polish women without whom we would not have survived the war. The second is of Anna, Stefan, and myself with my arm around a German shepherd of whom I was deathly afraid. The third is of my entire family, minus my three sisters. In this picture Anna is holding her several-month-old firstborn child, Zofia. In all these photographs we are well dressed, some of us are smiling, and all, except for my father, are a picture of health.

In Bad Reichenhall we also made many friends who would be of great assistance to us once we reached America. But America was still a long way off. The UN proceedings were slowly determining not only our future, but the future of all the people in Europe who did not want to or could not go back home.

In general, these people could be divided into three categories: Refugees, displaced persons, and stateless persons. Unfortunately, since this typology was not always mutually exclusive, it proved to be a stumbling block in some of the UN proceedings. Initially (February 16, 1946), the word "refugee" referred to "a person who has left, or who is outside of, his country of nationality or of former habitual residence, and who is a victim of the nazi, fascist, or falangist regimes, or who was considered a refugee before the outbreak of the Second World War for reasons of race, religion, nationality, or political opinion." The term "displaced person" designated "an individual who has been deported from his country of nationality or former habitual residence to undertake forced labor, or has been deported for racial, religious, or political reasons."[7]

In its 1948-49 proceedings, the UN placed the category of "displaced persons" under the category of "refugee" and began considering the relation of the latter category to that of "statelessness." Statelessness could be either *de jure* or *de facto*. *De jure* statelessness included persons who were deprived of their nationality by their countries. *De facto* statelessness included persons who were political exiles as well as non-repatriable persons. The causes of statelessness included "failure to acquire nationality at birth, loss of nationality through marriage or dissolution of marriage, voluntary renunciation of nationality, and deprivation of nationality."[8] Stateless persons, in short, were those who did not enjoy the protection of any government.

In 1950 the UN urged the elimination of statelessness and broadened the definition of "refugee" to include any person who

> [A]s a result of events occurring before 1 January 1951, and owing to well-founded fear of being persecuted for reasons of race, religion, nationality or political opinion, is outside the country of his nationality and is unable or, owing to such fear or for reasons other than personal convenience, is unwilling to avail himself of the protection of that country; or who, not having a nationality and being outside the country of his former habitual residence, is unable or, owing to such fear or for reasons other than personal convenience, is unwilling to return to it.[9]

As is *perfectly* clear, according to these guidelines—pending our acquisition of nationality—we were displaced persons from 1945 to 1947, "de facto" stateless refugees from 1948 to 1949, and just plain refugees in 1950.

Initially, the task of dealing with Europe's refugees, displaced and stateless persons was handled by the IGC (Inter-governmental Committee on Refugees) and the UNRRA (United Nations Relief and Rehabilitation Administration). Established in 1938, the IGC was charged with providing for the legal protection, maintenance, and resettlement of the victims of Nazi persecution in Germany and Austria. It subsequently expanded its program to include (by July 1946) all non-repatriable refugees and displaced persons.

The UNRRA was an organization established on November 9, 1943, by the unofficial UN to deal with similar matters. (Although not formally established until 1945, the United Nations charter dates back to conferences [1941–45] held by nations opposed to the fascist coalition of Germany, Japan, Italy and their satellites.) The work of the IGC and the UNRRA was furthermore supplemented by over sixty voluntary societies which provided relief and specialized services.

On January 23, 1946, the United Kingdom delegation introduced a proposal noting that the numbers of the refugees had outgrown the machinery previously established for their aid. The delegation proposed that the Economic and Social Council of the UN apply itself to thorough study of the problem.

Two days later, the Yugoslav delegation presented an alternative proposal which urged the Assembly to consider the problem of displaced persons as non-existent since the defeat of the fascist countries meant that displaced persons could return to their home countries. International, organized assistance to such persons was therefore unnecessary. Any arrangements for refugees or displaced persons should be made by agreement between the countries of origin and the countries of residence. Further, the delegation proposed that any displaced person who had not reported for repatriation within four months' time should be ineligible for both international and state assistance.

Representatives of the Byelorussian SSR, Poland, the USSR, and the Ukrainian SSR echoed the Yugoslav proposal and furthermore argued that "assistance by an international organization to persons unwilling to return to their own countries for political reasons would tend to perpetuate the refugee problem instead of solving it." Moreover, they held that it was important to distinguish between "genuine victims" of fascism, who should be returned to their own countries, and other displaced persons such as "Quislings, war criminals, traitors, Fascists and undemocratic elements who opposed the governments of their countries"[10] and were therefore not deserving of aid as refugees.

At the same time the Arab States weighed in with remarks against "political Zionism," claiming that although they sympathized with the Jewish victims of fascism, this problem was unrelated to the problem of Palestine. Jews who had left Europe "as a matter of personal preference" should not be considered refugees.[11]

While the above delegations were voicing their opinions as to the desirability of creating an international body to deal with the refugee question, another group of representatives (included the United States and the United Kingdom) argued that human considerations should take precedence over political ones. They reminded their colleagues of the problem of political dissidents who were not fascists, war criminals, or traitors. Forcing such persons to return to their home countries would violate the right of asylum for political dissidents, which, this group noted, was a basic human right as defined by the Charter of the United Nations.

In addition to this, the Soviet delegation introduced a resolution which contained the following provisions concerning refugee camps:

> No propaganda should be permitted in refugee camps against the interests of the Organization of the United Nations or her Members, nor propaganda against returning to their native countries.
>
> The personnel of refugee camps should be comprised mainly of representatives of States concerned, whose citizens are the refugees.[12]

After lengthy deliberations, on February 12, the UN General Assembly adopted a resolution which referred the refugee problem to the Economic and Social Council for thorough examination and recommended that

> No refugees or displaced persons who have finally and definitely, in complete freedom and after receiving full knowledge of the facts, including adequate information from the governments of their countries of origin, expressed valid objections to returning to their countries . . . shall be compelled to return to their country or origin. The future of such refugees or displaced persons shall become the concern of whatever international body may be recognized or established . . . except in cases where the government of the country where they are established has made arrangement with this body to assume the complete cost of their maintenance and the responsibility for their protection.
>
> The main task concerning displaced persons is to encourage and assist in every possible way their early return to their countries of origin.[13]

The proposed Soviet amendment that resettlement of refugees should not take place without the consent of the country of origin as well as the country of resettlement was rejected along with the recommendations quoted above concerning "propaganda" in the refugee camps.

The Economic and Social Council answered this resolution by establishing a Special Committee on Refugees and Displaced Persons. The committee, in turn, recommended that a specialized agency, the IRO (International Refugee Organization), be established to address the problem. The Council also drafted a Constitution of the IRO and submitted it for a general debate on November 4, 1946.

As before, there was disagreement between the countries from which most of the refugees and displaced persons had come (Byelorussian SSR, Poland, Ukrainian SSR, USSR, and Yugoslavia), and the countries administering the camps as well as those interested in resettlement.

The countries of origin held that repatriation was the only practical way to deal with persons displaced by the war. Resettling such persons in other countries should not be the focus or the duty of the IRO. As for persons who refused to return to their countries for political reasons, they should be of no concern to the IRO. The countries of origin also claimed that persons hostile to their governments were carrying on an active propaganda campaign against repatriation. They demanded that the Constitution of IRO include measures to suppress such propaganda.

The countries administering the camp and those interested in resettlement opposed the recommendations of the countries of origin, arguing that repatriation should never be compulsory and that those who did not wish to return were indeed the proper concern of IRO. For these people, resettlement was the only answer. In reference to the charge of propaganda, the governments responsible for the administration of the camps argued for the right of free speech, pointing out that representatives of the countries of origin were given sufficient facilities and opportunity to speak on behalf of their governments within the camps.

All in all, sixty-five amendments were submitted by the various delegations, and seventeen lengthy meetings were devoted to examining these amendments, before the General Assembly approved the Constitution of IRO on December 15, 1946. The IRO, however, would not come into existence until at least fifteen countries accepted the constitution and put up their share of the $151,060,500 operational budget. Since this was unlikely to happen before June 30, 1947, when both IGC and UNRRA were to terminate their activities, to avoid any breach in the continuity of operations, an interim arrangement provided for the establishment of a Preparatory Commission (PC-IRO) which would carry on the work until the IRO was established (August 20, 1948).

Needless to say, the countries of origin opposed the institution of the PC-IRO. When the Agreement on Interim Measures came up for vote, the USSR regarded it as unsatisfactory and suggested further examination by the Economic Council. Yugoslavia and Poland argued that the PC-IRO would, in effect, have all the powers of the IRO while not being bound by its Constitution since the latter was not yet in force. This would create a "dangerous situation," they claimed, whereby the provisional organization might tend to become permanent.

Despite such specious arguments, the PC-IRO was established. On July 1, 1947, the PC-IRO would assume "operational responsibility for the refugees and displaced persons eligible for assistance under the terms of the IRO Constitution."[14] There was much work to be done.

By 1947, of the approximately 8,000,000 displaced persons at the time of liberation, over 6,500,000 had returned to their homelands. The remainder was divided as follows:

	Number	*Percent*
Poles	370,000	29
Balts (Estonians, Latvians, Lithuanians)	194,000	15
Yugoslavs	77,000	6
U.S.S.R.	30,000	2
Stateless and Undetermined	98,000	8
Jews	229,000	18
Other	281,000	22
Total	1,279,000	100[15]

Of this total, two-thirds lived in the assembly camps of West Germany, Austria, and Italy, and the rest outside of these camps but mainly in these same countries.

When the PC-IRO came into existence it took over the care and maintenance of over 705,000 persons, including 626,000 in the assembly centers previously under the care of the UNRRA (552,000 in Germany alone, of whom 192,000 were Polish and 107,000 were Ukrainian); 8,980 outside of the assembly centers, who had been the responsibility of the IGC; and 9,300 refugees (mostly European Jews) in China.

In addition to these, there were approximately 900,000 other persons in various countries who met the IRO's eligibility requirements for care, maintenance, legal protection, or help with repatriation or resettlement. At the inception of the Preparatory Commission's operations, this group constituted a frighteningly large body of potential applicants for aid. Faced with these numbers and yet provided with a very limited budget, the Executive Secretary decided (on July 2, 1947) that further admissions to care and maintenance would be limited to those who could prove that without such aid they would face genuine hardship. In October the PC-IRO approved this "freeze order" but instructed the Executive Secretary to be as broad as possible with its definition of "hardship."

According to the IRO Constitution:

> The functions of the Organization to be carried out in accordance with the purposes and the principles of the Charter of the United Nations, shall be: the repatriation; the identification, registration and classification; the care and assistance; the legal and political protection; the transport; the re-settlement and re-establishment, in countries able and willing to receive them, of persons who are the concern of the Organization. . . .[16]

With this in mind PC-IRO (IRO as of August 20, 1948) care and maintenance involved "a comprehensive program offering food, clothing, personal items, health services, hospital care, employment and vocational training, education, individual counseling, and child welfare services and assistance."[17] This was done in conjunction with a network of some eighty voluntary societies in various countries.

Moreover, immunization programs were preventing epidemics among the refugee populations. Smallpox, typhoid, diphtheria, typhus, cholera, and yellow fever were all controlled through immunization. Daily medical services were also provided by the IRO, along with concentrated efforts in such areas as tuberculosis control and medical processing of refugees for resettlement. In their endeavors, the small IRO medical staff had the help and support of some 2,500 refugee physicians and 2,000 refugee nurses.

Finally, IRO tried to provide a dietary level of 1,900 calories daily for persons in camps. To insure good diets for children, schools, children's centers, summer camps, and youth clubs began to offer supplementary rations provided by IRO. However, because of the rise in the overall caloric diet in the countries in which refugee camps were located, the General Council directed (September 1948) that the diet of camp refugees should not exceed the caloric level of the diet common to persons in the surrounding areas.

As of September 21, 1948, IRO was operating a total of 672 installations, including 538 assembly centers (330 in West Germany alone), 58 hospitals and sanatoria, 3 convalescent homes, 2 rehabilitation centers, 8 vocational training centers, 22 children's centers, 8 children's convalescent and nutrition centers, 5 admission control centers, 6 repatriation centers, 7 resettlement centers, and 15 embarkation, staging, and transit centers.[18]

In 1950, to transport refugees resettling overseas, IRO maintained a chartered fleet of some 36 vessels, booked space on commercial ships and aircraft, and operated an average of 35 trains every month.

During IRO operations from July 1947 to December 1949, 68,778 persons were repatriated to their countries of origin, and 688,284 refugees were resettled in various other countries (United States: 149,971; Australia: 105,352). Moreover, in these thirty months, IRO provided assistance to 1,431,000 refugees; of these, approximately 938,000 had received care and maintenance, and the rest received only such services as legal protection or resettlement assistance.

As the termination date of IRO approached (originally June 30, 1950, but later extended to March 31, 1951), a number of deadlines were established: (1) No new applications after August 31, 1949. (2) No new admissions to care and maintenance after December 31, 1949, in the assembly centers. (3) No care and maintenance by the IRO after June 30, 1950, except for persons in the process of repatriation or resettlement and those requiring permanent assistance such as institutional care. As these deadlines passed, the caseload of IRO declined from 318,323 on January 1, 1950, to 80,905 on December 31, 1950. (The responsibility for the remaining refugees was passed on to the local authorities in Western Europe.)

As the caseload of IRO began to diminish, the proportion of its "difficult" cases increased. This included the resettlement of the aged and the sick refugees who could not be admitted by overseas resettlement countries under existing immigration legislation. The beginnings of this problem were already observed in a report to the General Assembly dated June 10, 1948. While commending various countries for their efforts in resolving the refugee problem, the report stressed the unfortunate tendency of certain governments to accept only the most able-bodied refugees for resettlement in their countries. These exclusionary policies would eventually leave the IRO to deal with all the older, handicapped, or disabled refugees who were not welcomed for resettlement.

The report decried such closed-door policies and urged the member nations to extend open arms to family groups, which would include the elderly, the ill, and the disabled.

Compounding the problem of finding a place for these last displaced persons, in 1950 the Australian program came to a halt. Before closing down, that program had absorbed 170,453 refugees.

Thanks to the cooperation of various governments, individuals, volunteer societies, public and private organizations, even these hurdles were eventually, although not completely, overcome. In 1950, the President of the United States signed an amendment to the Displaced Persons Act that opened the door to another 108,000 IRO eligible refugees (thus allowing a total of 313,000 to enter the United States under this Act). New Zealand and Canada also liberalized their immigration policies. Many other countries volunteered to accept even individuals in need of permanent care.

The result of all this concerted effort was that in 1950, 2,917 persons were successfully repatriated (972 were Poles), and 191,119 persons were resettled. (The monthly average for that year was 16,170, as against 29,166 in 1949, the most active year.) Of these, a significant number belonged to the "Institutional Hard Core," those excluded from resettlement by countries unwilling to accept ill or disabled refugees. As of July 1, 1950, 15,319 persons requiring permanent care were numbered among these difficult cases, along with 7,509 members of their families. By December 31 that number had been reduced to 7,833 persons and 3,469 family members.

Meanwhile, throughout the existence of the IRO, the representatives of the Soviet bloc charged that the refugees and the displaced persons were being prevented from returning to their homes through intimidation and false propaganda concerning conditions in Eastern Europe. They claimed that the countries seeking to resettle refugees hoped to derive financial and economic advantage from the immigration of foreign labor. They charged that children especially were being prevented from returning to their countries of origin.

The Soviets accused the United States specifically of utilizing relief assistance as a political and economic weapon and even as a means of securing military bases (in Greece and Turkey, for example). The assembly camps, according to the Soviet delegations, were nothing more than hotbeds of propaganda and terrorism (directed against the Eastern European states) as well as reservoirs of cheap labor. Despite previous Assembly resolutions, they claimed, the emphasis had been shifted from repatriation to resettlement.

Time and time again the Assembly restated its position that freedom of speech was guaranteed by the UN Constitution and that compulsory repatriation was unethical and unacceptable. Time and time again it reminded the Soviet bloc that it had heard these unfounded objections many times before and that it objected both to their objections and to the spirit in which they were given. A case in point is the discussion at the 228th meeting of the Third Committee on May 12, 1949:

> The Committee first considered a draft resolution submitted by the representative of Poland (A/C.3/513) which, *inter alia*, asked:
>
> (a) that an end should be put to all propaganda and pressure to dissuade refugees from returning to their countries of origin;
> (b) that repatriation be encouraged and completed by 1950;
> (c) that emigrating refugees should be protected against exploitation and that, to that end, emigration should be regulated by bilateral agreements between the emigrant's country of origin and the country to which he was emigrating;
> (d) that the emigrant's right of return to his country of origin, at the expense of the country of immigration, should be guaranteed;
> (e) that all Polish children in Germany should be repatriated.
>
> During the debate the representatives of the Byelorussian SSR, Poland, the Ukrainian SSR and Yugoslavia, *inter alia*, claimed that nothing had been done to implement the Assembly's resolution 8 (I), which had called for an early return of the refugees to their countries of origin. Resettlement had been substituted for repatriation by IRO on the pretext that the refugees did not want to return. Repatriation officers had been unable to establish contacts in the camps, and pamphlets were being distributed by a number of countries which portrayed false conditions in the Eastern European countries, and encouraged emigration instead of repatriation. The USSR had proposed, at the eighth session of the Economic and Social Council . . . that an international investigation should be conducted by a qualified commission to ascertain the conditions in both the capitalistic countries and in the people's democracies, but this proposal had been rejected. There were a number of missions recruiting workers for overseas countries, including the United States, Canada, Brazil, Argentina, Venezuela, Bolivia, Chile, Peru, Uruguay and Australia. The result of this had been a breakdown in repatriation. During the second part of 1948, 4,000 had been repatriated as against 130,000 resettled abroad. Many children who could have been repatriated were still in the British and American zones of Germany. The representative of the USSR particularly wished to know by what right orphans had been sent to countries other than those of their origin. Some 70,000 Ukrainians, and 400,000 Soviet citizens, as well as citizens of other countries, were still in repatriation camps.
>
> Moreover, conditions in the camps were very poor. Refugees were being gathered into semi-military formations, such as the "security guards" in the western zones of Germany and Austria, and in United States military camps in France. These groups were becoming hotbeds of fascism

and war propaganda. Former collaborators and traitors were housed in the camps and in many instances were in a position to terrorize the refugees if they as much as indicated a wish to be repatriated. When these countries had sent investigation groups, false conditions had been staged. Yugoslavia had submitted proof and had asked for an investigation but had been turned down.

Concerning resettlement, it was stated that only refugees in the best of health were taken, and usually their families were not permitted to accompany them. Intellectuals were for the most part excluded. IRO was presiding over a cheap labour market for Western Europe and overseas. In Belgium, France, Canada, the Netherlands and the United Kingdom, the representatives of Poland and the USSR claimed, the refugees did harder work than the local people, were paid less and were badly housed.

In reply to these accusations, the representative of the United Kingdom stated that in 1945 the only solution contemplated had been repatriation. It was primarily the refugees from Eastern Europe who did not want to return to their countries of origin that had created the present problem. The representatives of the United Kingdom and Canada both stressed that repatriation missions had been given free access to the displaced persons camps, but held that displaced persons should not be forced to yield to representatives of these missions.

The representatives of the Philippines and Egypt, while agreeing that refugees should be given full freedom to decide whether or not they wanted to return to their countries of origin, stressed that there were those who had chosen not to, and that they should not be forced to go.

The representative of the United Kingdom stated that more than 3,000 children had been repatriated from the British zone and that only 1,044 remained. He felt that repatriation would go faster if Poland, for example, would facilitate the exchange of information. It was necessary to have indisputable proof of nationality and family before repatriating the children.

Concerning admission of refugees, the representative of France stated that his country had admitted 15,000 workers and 35,000 men and women unable to work. Actually many others had crossed the border in a clandestine manner. The representative of Australia stated that Australia's doors were wide open, while the representative of Venezuela said that his country preferred family groups and, in fact, had taken 14,000 persons.

In answer to the charge that conditions were very poor for the refugees that had emigrated, the representatives of the United Kingdom and France stated that these accusations had not been and could not be verified. These representatives, as well as those of Argentina, Canada, and Uruguay, claimed that working and living conditions were the same for refugees as for nationals, and that they were protected by the same social laws. The representative of Venezuela pointed out that it took time to settle large groups, but that conditions improved daily and the

> majority of the immigrants were satisfied. In reply to an accusation that many refugees now wanted to leave the countries to which they had been sent, the representative of the Netherlands stated that, in the case of the workers who had come to the Netherlands, some now wished to leave, not because they were disappointed but because they wished to emigrate overseas. At the time they had been sent to the Netherlands that opportunity had not been available.
>
> The draft resolution submitted by Poland (A/C.3/513) was rejected by 6 votes in favor, to 19 against, with 11 abstentions. Several representatives stated that they objected to it primarily because of the spirit in which it had been offered.[19]

Thus, while the Polish Government was desperately trying to repatriate us, the United Nations was trying just as desperately (in accordance with our wishes) to resettle us. Fortunately for us, in the end, the good guys won.

In the fall of 1947 the residents of Bad Reichenhall were transferred to another assembly camp in Gablingen, West Bavaria—about fifty kilometers from the now deserted Dachau. This was to be our last refugee camp in Germany; but we would not leave Europe until 1950. In spite of our willingness to emigrate, it seems that no sponsors could be found either for us or for the Piwowarski family. (Anna's oldest child, Zofia, was born on October 26, 1947; Stanisław was born in May 1949.) As the Germans did not want us for lack of workers, so now we ran into the same roadblock with the worldwide community. An old man, an elderly woman, two teenagers, and a small boy stood no better chance of emigrating than a young couple with one child and another one on the way. Fortunately for us, however, the pressure to empty the refugee camps by 1950 (the projected year in which the IRO would be dissolved) became intense. When an affidavit of support was offered to us in 1950 from Australia, we accepted it immediately. We would go to Australia.

The preparations for emigration (physicals, verbal examinations, passports, and so on) were to be made in nearby Augsburg, an ancient German city recuperating from its 50 percent destruction. After all the bureaucratic red tape was taken care of, we waited patiently for the transport to Bremen, the port from which we were to depart. Since I still have all our passport pictures with "Australia" typed on the back and our signatures underneath, it is clear that we did not get there. The reason why we did not emigrate to Australia had to do with my oldest brother Franek who, just before our departure, happened to have fallen in love with a refugee girl bound for the United States. (Camp life was certainly conducive to romantic liaisons, especially in my family!) And as if this were not bad enough, a certain clergyman by the name of Fr. Wiertel told Franek that in Australia we would never be able to make enough money to return to Poland (when and if it became free) or to ever reach America.

Such being the case, Franek came home one day and informed us that he was not about to go to Australia. We could go without him if we wanted to; he was going to Michigan, U.S.A. (for that is where the girl's family emigrated). No one could believe it, but since he would not back down, there was only one thing to do: We told the IRO authorities that we were sorry, but we had changed our mind. We would wait for a sponsorship from America. They said, "Fine"—and gave our affidavit of support to another, less choosy family.

I must confess that at age nine, I also had my first "affair" in Gablingen, but with much more drastic consequences. If my memory serves me right, we must have been caught red-handed (and red-faced as well!) while playing "doctor" by the girl's watchdog of a mother. Judging by the raging storm which followed, either the "gynecologist's" pants or the "patient's" panties were nowhere to be found.

When the poor girl's mother confronted my own with her well-founded accusation, Maria Piotrowski surprised me more than she ever realized by taking my side, upbraiding the shocked lady for her prudishness, and dismissing the whole affair as innocent child's play—which is what it was. And that was that! But never in my wildest dreams would I have passed up a chance to emigrate because of "some girl." Of course, there may be a difference in the way we love at nine and at nineteen.

Fortunately for us, the same priest who dissuaded Franek from Australia was able to get us a sponsor from Rensselaer, Indiana, through the NCWC (National Catholic Welfare Conference). Unfortunately for Franek, however, after we settled in America and he located his true love and wrote her a long letter stating his intentions, she wrote back:

> Dear Franek. I didn't know you were in love with me and now it's too late. I am engaged to be married to the farmer's son with whom we're staying.

After that letter, Franek would remain a bachelor for a very long time.

Meanwhile, Anna and Stefan procured an affidavit from a sponsor in the Polish-sounding state of Oklahoma. Having no idea of the distances between Indiana and Oklahoma, we rejoiced at the prospect of our reunion in America. This was all too good to be true! If only our three sisters were here to share our joy! After another trip to Augsburg, we bade farewell to Anna and her family (they would not leave for some time yet) and on March 16, 1950, departed for Camp Grohn, the largest IRO embarkation center in West Germany, housing over 5,000 displaced persons. After ten days, we were transferred to Bremen, Germany's oldest port city and one of the hardest hit targets of Allied bombing.

In Bremerhaven, an impressive American ship, the USAT *General R. M. Blatchford*, was already waiting for us in the harbor. This particular steamer was an army troop transport chartered by the IRO just for us. Its passenger list contained 1,222 names of displaced persons from the American, British, and French zones of occupation in Germany and Austria. It would deliver us all in ten days' time to New York City. Thus ended our five and a half years of captivity, indignity, and terror, and another five of wandering, waiting, and uncertainty. What would the "sweet land of liberty" be like?

Amelin, 1928: The funeral of the author's grandfather. Top, left-right: Józia Bagiński, Franciszek Piotrowski, Stanisław Piotrowski, Edward Piotrowski, Józef Piotrowski (author's father). Bottom, left-right: Władysław Piotrowski; son of Mania Piotrowski (small boy in front); Marcelina Piotrowski, holding baby Mirosława; Mania; Hilary (Mania's husband), Antosia Piotrowski (author's cousin), Maria Piotrowski (author's grandmother).

Maria Piotrowski (author's mother), Ostróg, 1930.

Top: Nazi Germany, 1943. Bottom: Deportations from Poland's eastern territories to the Soviet Union, 1940–41.

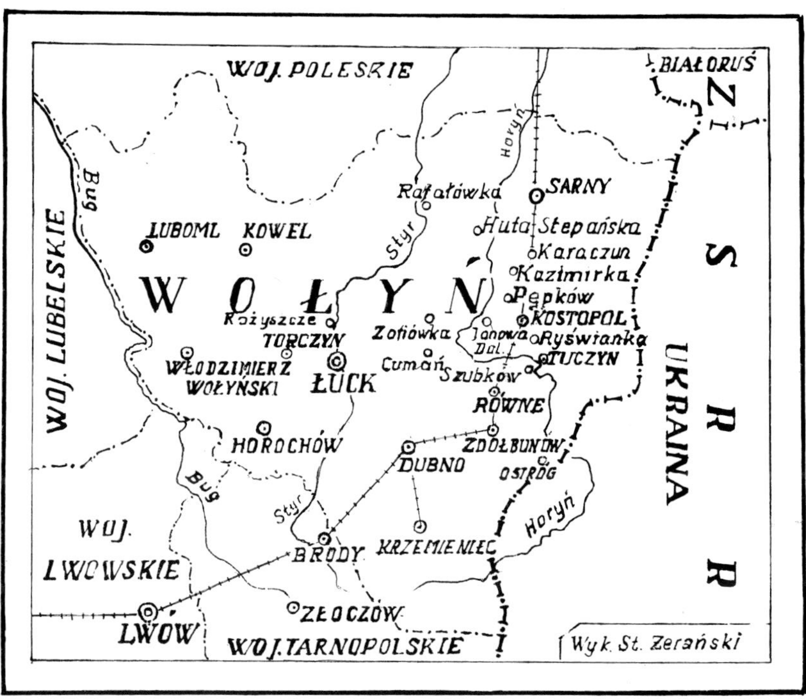

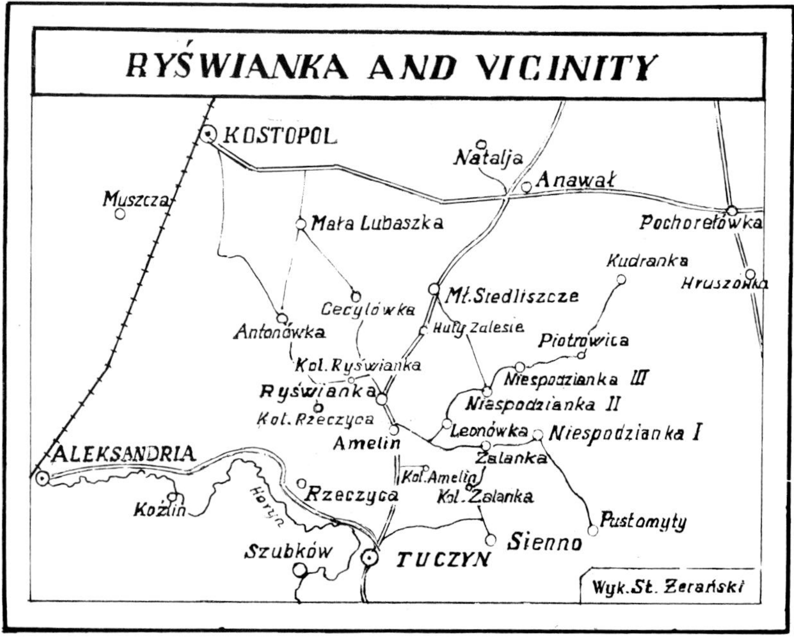

Top: The province of Wołyń, 1943. Bottom: Ryświanka and vincinity, 1943.

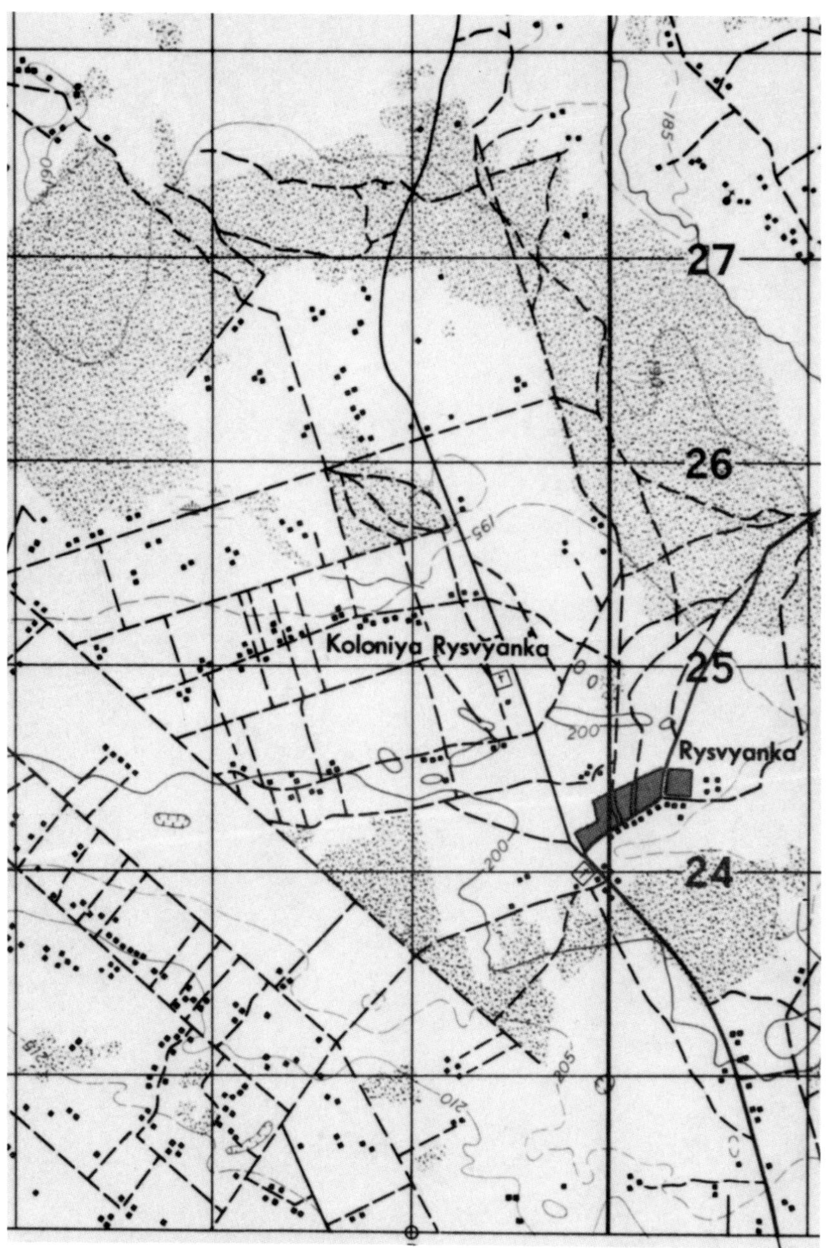

Ryświanka and colony.

Top: A village set on fire by the Banderowcy. Bottom: Members of the UPA in three different uniforms, left to right: Nazi SD (Security Service), Ukrainian police, and German police. Photos courtesy of Antoni Szcześniak.

Top: An early Christian symbol of the Holy Trinity. Minus the white figure in back, the trident became a symbol of Ukrainian independence and an emblem of the Ukrainian Nationalists. Bottom: A group of Banderowcy in a Ukrainian village. Photos courtesy of the Wojskowy Instytut Historyczny (top) and Antoni Szcześniak (bottom).

Maria Piotrowski and son Tadeusz (the author), Essen, 1943, on steps of the Schule Steinmetzfir, where the author's family were held as forced laborers.

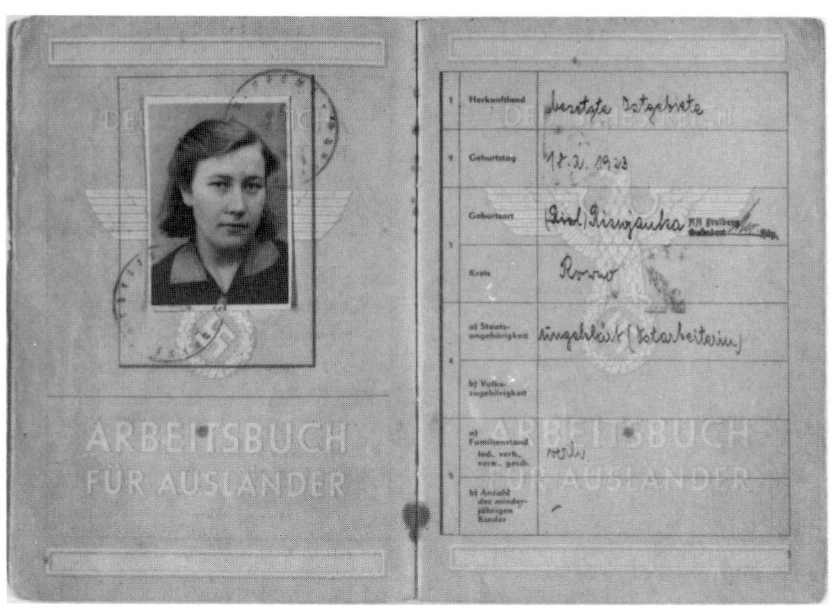

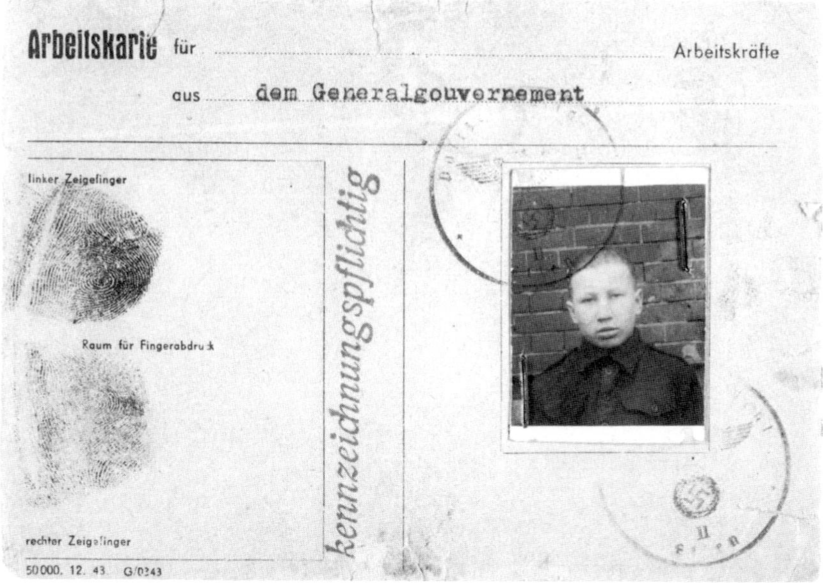

Top: Pages 2 and 3 from the workbook of Stasia Piotrowski (author's sister), Nazi Germany, 1943. Bottom: Work card of Franek Piotrowski (author's brother), Nazi Germany (Essen), 1943.

Tadeusz Piotrowski, Essen, 1944.

Author's family at Schule Steinmetzfir, Essen, 1944: Anna, Jan, Franek, Maria, Tadeusz (author).

Top: Tadeusz (center) with sister Anna and her first husband, Stefan Piwowarski, Bad Reichenhall, 1947. Bottom: Bad Reichenhall photo of author's family, excepting the three oldest daughters, whose whereabouts were then unknown. Front: Józef, Tadeusz, Maria. Back: Jan, Anna with infant daughter Zofia, Franek.

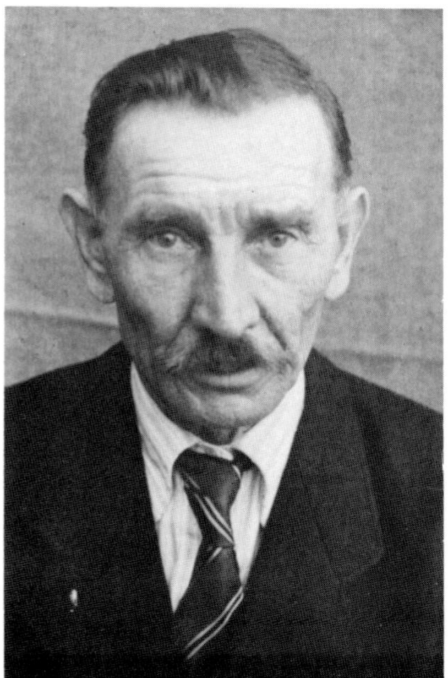

Top: Wedding photo of author's cousin Stasia Piotrowski Plaza and Jan Plaza, July 1, 1945. Stasia Piotrowski was 18 when her family was murdered in the Leonówka massacre. Bottom: Passport photos of author's parents, Józef and Maria, 1950.

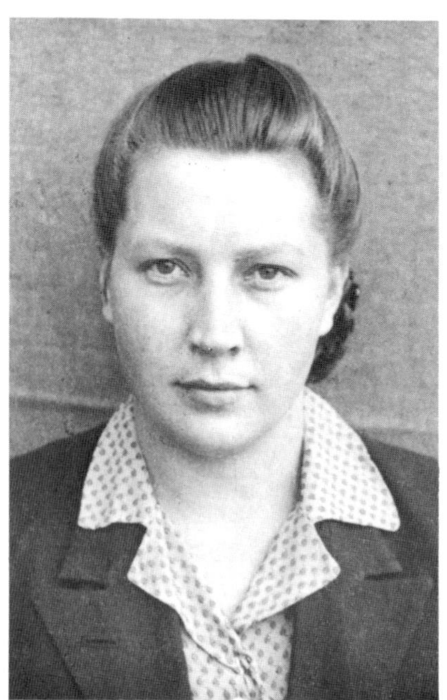

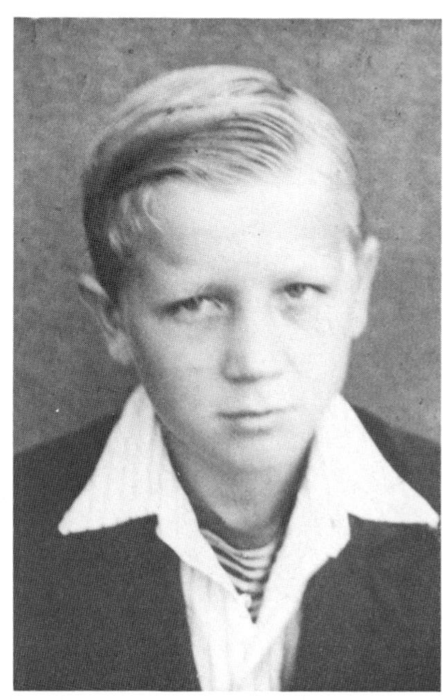

Passport photos, 1950, clockwise from top left: Franek, Jan, Tadeusz, Anna.

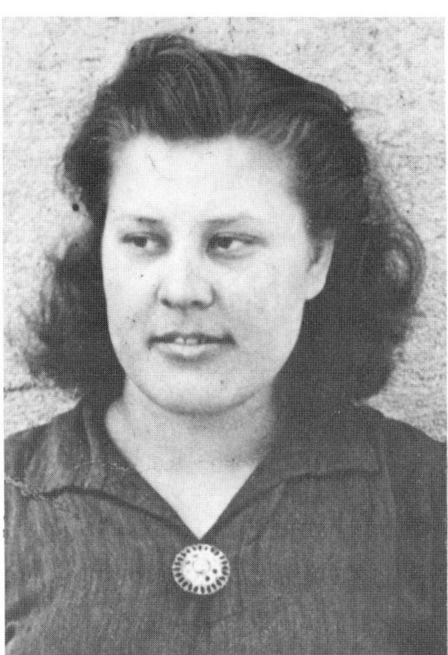

Author's three oldest sisters, whom the family located by chance in 1958 after a separation of 15 years. Top: Stasia, with husband, Felek Domalewski, and son, Bronek. Bottom left: Aniela. Bottom right: Janina.

Top: Author with his family in Poland, 1968. On bench, left to right: Aniela, Stasia, Janina. Standing: Franek, Tadeusz. Bottom: Author dances with his mother at the wedding of his sister Anna and Ryszard Pedowski, 1979.

BOOK III

A M E R I C A

8

Sweet Land of Liberty

> For the sea has not lost its magic and its mystery, and those who go down to it in ships must still battle against elemental odds. [Ralph D. Paine]

Mr. Paine did not pen these lines in 1919 with us in mind. To be sure, in 1950, when we crossed the Atlantic, the "magic and the mystery" still prevailed, but the "battle against [the] elemental odds" for us was long past. Our ahistoric attitude toward the ocean admitted no terror. We went "down to it in ships" like sinners to the river Jordan. It would take all the churning water of the Atlantic to cleanse our bloodstained souls and heal our wounded spirits.

On March 26, 1950, with mixed emotions we bade farewell to battle-scarred Europe and steamed off toward a continent to us as yet unknown. I had just turned ten.

After a day's journey, for the first time in my life, I was surprised to discover nothing on the vast horizon between wet earth and sky. The sheer magnitude of that enormous emptiness bespoke of hope and promise. We were as if suspended for a time upon this *tabula rasa*, between the firmament and *terra firma*, on the horizontal axis between the primordial elements of water and of air. We hovered for a time, poised at the junctures of being and nothingness, essence and existence, good and evil, in anxious anticipation of another try at paradise.

Our voyage was a catharsis, a period of grace to gaze upon the mighty emptiness of the sea and be refreshed; to wonder at its majesty and power and be uplifted; to contemplate the eternal void of nothingness from which all things came to be and unto which all must eventually return; to grasp at once the final truth, the etiology and eschatology of our existence in perfect equanimity of body and of mind. Today, when I gaze upon the sea, I still think of those ten happy days of voyaging—and I miss them so.

Externally our trip across the ocean was unusually uneventful. There was nothing of those incessant Odyssean battles with the swinging surges and the boisterous winds; nothing of Lord Jim's great trials and tribulations. The awesome peace and the tranquillity of order upon the glistening sea happily deprived my mother of her final opportunity to reassure us with that frequently spoken phrase of hers: "God has not brought us all this way, only to let us perish here..."—whereupon she would add the appropriate place or time. (In this case, it would have been: "upon the sea.") After leaving Europe, she had never had the occasion to use that phrase again, nor for that matter, has any one of us. But once it was most reassuring. It seemed to have such a ring of truth.

Oh, there were a few times upon the open sea when our ship heaved (and the people too), shuddered, and sank again into the yawning abyss left by the swelling tides. I rather enjoyed the roller coaster ride. Others must speak for themselves.

There were also times when the sea was as calm as the surface of a looking glass. It was then that we saw the flying fishes and the myriads of happy dolphins racing with the ship and leading us like princely escorts to America's shores.

During the long journey I somehow managed to make good friends with the captain (or he with me), spending many happy moments with him on the bridge and often sporting his white captain's hat upon my head—until the envious wind took it off one day and flung it into the sea. I am happy to report that this misadventure did not cost our friendship. To this day, and for that reason alone, I take my hat off to all captains of great ships.

And so we sailed. With each nautical mile, our thoughts turned more and more from what was to what would be; from our former years of trial, to the unknown challenges of a new existence; from the Old World to the New, until, on the final day of our voyage, all eyes were focused firmly on the West. High upon the bridge, the captain pointed to a happy, smiling island in the sun and said: "That, my lad, is your new home!"

At our journey's end, on April 4, 1950, we saw the Lady of the Harbor, the grand and eloquent Lady with the burning torch of freedom held aloft and the lines from Emma Lazarus' famous poem engraved beneath her feet:

> Give me your tired, your poor,
> Your huddled masses yearning to breathe free,
> The wretched refuse of your teeming shore,
> Send these, the homeless, tempest tossed, to me:
> I lift my lamp beside the golden door.

It did not matter that we did not know the verse. We saw the welcoming look in Liberty's strong, kind face, and we were comforted.

The magnificent skyline of New York City loomed ahead. It was *all* there—no decomposing heaps of rubble; no half-charred, half-chewed-up buildings in desperate need of reconstruction; so unlike Europe, so mercifully preserved from the hungry jaws of war! No one on board, save perhaps the crew, had seen such a sight in over a decade. No one will ever forget that first and lasting impression of the New World, engineered to outlast war itself!

When the steamship's motors were finally stilled, we were asked to disembark, one person at a time, and to proceed through U.S. Immigration and Customs. The scene was reminiscent of an ancient pilgrimage to the Holy Land: a stream of people hailing from assorted nations, stopping from time to time to kneel and pray and to kiss the earth beneath their feet, waiting to be reintegrated into life.

That is how we became the permanent residents of a continent thousands of miles removed from our native land. That is how America became our new home, and the home of our children, and the home of our children's children as yet unborn. Our sentiments, on that day, became commingled with the panegyric of countless generations which both preceded us and would follow us unto these shores:

> My Country, 'tis of thee,
> Sweet Land of Liberty,
> Of thee I sing.

After receiving our clearance and our papers, we were all greeted by Catholic Relief Service volunteers, who poured us cups of steaming coffee, stuffed us with doughnuts, and gave us two dollars each. We were then ushered into large waiting halls, and those with known sponsors and known destinations were dispatched speedily on their way.

Our own departure was somewhat delayed due to the fact that our particular sponsor only signed to obtain us passage to America. Since there were so many displaced persons at that time in Europe, and since one could not emigrate without a sponsor, this was a common practice. It was correctly assumed that once here, people would either make their own way, or someone else would pick up the sponsorship. In our case, it proved to be the latter. Our new sponsor's name, we were informed, was Mr. John Thompson. A one-way railway ticket would take us to our new home in America: a lazy Southern town on the gentle banks of the Ohio River, called Owensboro.

9

To Kill a Hummingbird

The train we boarded was unlike any of those German boxcar transports which bandied us about in Europe. Comparatively speaking, it was a first-class luxury train replete with upholstered seats, bathroom facilities, dining rooms, and even sleeping compartments. It was heated, and its huge, tinted windows allowed us to watch the world as it flew by: the industrial complex of New Jersey, the majestic Appalachian Mountains of Pennsylvania, the endless forests of West Virginia, and the rolling countryside of Kentucky—until we reached the Indiana line. I wonder what my mother thought of those endless tracts of uninhabited terrain. Perhaps that He would not let us perish there either!

The train left us standing in the middle of the night at the most desolate train station imaginable. Since no one was there to greet us, we began to wonder whether it was the right place after all. As we waited on the deserted platform wondering what was to become of us, an old ramshackle slop truck pulled up to the station, and out of the cab came Mrs. Thompson. Since we were the only people there (and unmistakably foreign), she recognized us immediately, and running up gave us a good hearty handshake. Although she spoke a mile a minute (no doubt trying to explain how the spring-flooded roadways impeded her passage and accounted for her lateness), we said not a word, not out of any discourtesy, but because we could not speak English.

Soon we were loaded on: my father and my two brothers hugging the large and recently scrubbed slop tank on the back of the truck for warmth and safety, and my mother and I safe inside the heated cab with Mrs. Thompson. It was on that trip that both I and my mother received our first lesson in the enigmatic language called English.

"Moon," said Mrs. Thompson, pointing to the fuzzy patch of light up in the sky.

"Moon," I repeated and got it on the first try.

After several unsuccessful attempts and after a good deal of laughter, my mother just gave up. (She gave up on English altogether shortly thereafter, and chose to stick to her native tongue for the remainder of her long life. It was much easier that way for her, and it gave us a reason to keep up with our Polish.)

Upon our arrival at the farmstead, located just on the outskirts of the town of Owensboro, Kentucky, we were greeted by the entire Thompson family, who had stayed up late into the night to wait for us. We were flattered by this simple gesture of good will. It was a good sign. So this was Mr. Thompson and his eight children!

During the introductions, it soon became apparent that no one could pronounce my name. Joseph, Mary, Frank and John were common, international names—but Tadeusz? What could one do with that without an interpreter or at least a Polish-English dictionary? After many tries and sundry variations, we finally settled on a close phonetic equivalent: "Tadeos," which resembled both "adios" and "rodeos," both words within the Thompsons' frame of reference. And so I was, and still am, in those backwoods of Kentucky, called by that right and proper Western-sounding appellation of "Tadeos."

On the following morning, after a most refreshing sleep and a hearty country breakfast, we were taken to a little five-room house about a half mile from where we spent the night. This was to be our residence. The house was located on the main road leading into Owensboro. Across the way lived our only neighbors, an older, taciturn couple who strangely kept to themselves the whole time we were there. (Or perhaps it was we, ourselves, who minded our own business!) Behind our house was a small garden and a large barn used for curing tobacco. Adjacent to the barn were the Thompsons' fields, and beyond these lay their house. Except for the flatness of the land, the expansiveness of the farm, and the mild climate, we were once more in familiar surroundings.

Our house resembled a rather large cabin which was perhaps once used to quarter field hands during the farm's more prosperous days. It was a shaky, wooden structure painted dull red. I suppose well-to-do folks might have referred to it as a "shack" or a "shanty"—but there were no tracks to separate us from them. Inside, was an old-fashioned kitchen with a wood stove, a dining-room table, and a spacious pantry. Two bedrooms adjoined a small living room. It was without heat or plumbing. (In winter, standing water would freeze inside the cabin.) The outhouse, with its marvelously crescented door, stood about fifty feet from the back entrance. The well, with its top-mounted, chug-a-lugging pump, was conveniently located in the overgrown backyard. And best of all, it came equipped with electricity and a car-chasing dog, which I promptly named "Blackie" for self-evident reasons. By today's standards, the homestead was rather rustic, but what did it matter to us? It was, after all, our very own, and we made the most of it.

Many years after we left the farm, we learned—much to our regret—that the little red house in which we spent our first two memorable years in America had perished in the midst of a fire, though under much different circumstances than our Ryświanka home.

For as long as it lasted, life was good to us down on the farm. My mother tended house and garden, I went off to pursue my long overdue education, and my father and two teenage brothers worked the 250-acre farm from sunrise to sunset for two dollars and fifty cents a day.

Now one may suppose that even in the fifties, two dollars and fifty cents a day constituted a mighty poor exchange for three hands of honest labor, which translated into 150 hours and more per week. A confirmed Marxist might call it "capitalistic exploitation" and worse. But it was not. Our situation manifested all the classic indicators of what sociologists are wont to call "relative deprivation." First of all, those two dollars and fifty cents were more than we had ever earned before. Secondly, we had a house and garden. Thirdly, the work itself was that kind of honest toil which carried with it its own intrinsic rewards. (On this one point my father and my bothers may choose to quibble.) And fourthly, although the Thompsons were poor themselves, they never hesitated to share all that they had with us. For all these reasons and more, we are still much indebted to them even to this day.

For me, the ten-year-old, blond-haired, blue-eyed, foreign kid, school was an experience which I am not likely ever to forget. Recall that I never went to school, except sporadically after the war in between our various journeyings from one refugee camp to another. For all practical purposes, then, I was illiterate; and even if I weren't, it wouldn't have mattered, since I didn't speak English and no one outside of my family spoke Polish or any of the other languages we knew. For this reason, my mother wanted me to begin my education in the first grade—with the six-year-olds!

The wise nuns, however, said, "No, Ma'am, he should be with his own peers."

And so, against my mother's better judgment, I was assigned to the fourth grade, and spared four years of indignity and embarrassment.

Each morning I would be picked up by a yellow school bus and transported to a rural Catholic grammar school some fifteen miles from where we lived. I was the first one on the bus and the last one off, and the trip took over an hour.

Holy Rosary school stood like a mighty fortress high on a windy hill. One could never miss it, for on the steep bank overlooking the main thoroughfare was a rocky, painstakingly fashioned, heart-shaped outline of the familiarly monotonous pattern of Our Fathers and Hail Marys.

A serpentine road constituted the only avenue of access to the crest of the hill where, instead of a fortified bunker, a disarming, humble country church graced the rolling plateau. Off to one side, a winding footpath led downward to a grotto where each spring, the Queen of May (a distant relation to Our Lady of Kazimirka) would be crowned anew.

An asphalt ribbon, interrupted here and there by a series of steps, ran to the sun-bathed schoolhouse. There were playing fields and meadows all around. During the recesses and extended lunch hours, the one hundred or so children from the surrounding countryside dotted the hills like little lambkins foraging in the sun. In time, although I missed the constant companionship of my mother, I learned to love that country school. Would that there were more such pleasant schools throughout America!

At Holy Rosary, I must have been the teacher's pet. I still recall being so accused by an envious student who, although native born, received lower grades than I from the good nuns. As far as I can recall, this incident constituted my only bad experience with anybody in the entire vicinity, but I must admit that he spoke the truth. I knew absolutely nothing of reading, writing, or arithmetic. My knowledge was of a different sort: the type taught in *Schule Steinmetzfir* and *Beisingschule*, the type not easily communicated to those who have never been hungry, thirsty, or on the verge of death. But it did me very little good at Holy Rosary school.

I recall that the nuns spent a lot of time with me, as did my fellow students. "Walk," they would write in chalk upon the blackboard, then proceed to walk until I grasped the meaning of the term. Since no one had a Polish-English dictionary, this is the way in which I learned the rudiments of the English language. I learned so well that by the end of the first year my mind was in total confusion as to what was English and what was Polish. People looked benignly upon this strangely versed child, and my poor mother often said, "*O jej!*" Even now, after all these years, I still do all my arithmetic calculations and my spelling, the last bastions of linguistic resistance, in my native tongue.

Besides the challenge of the English language, other phenomena also occupied my time: for instance, the confounding enigma of how the American children were able to blow those gigantic pink bubbles which burst upon their noses. I had never heard of bubble gum! The American troops who liberated us chewed only regular Wrigley's. Finally, when my curiosity got the best of me, I asked one of the Schell boys, a nearby neighbor, to divulge his secret, but he was good naturedly reluctant. After a few days, he took me into his family garden, pointed to the peanut plants and said, "Chew these."

I did.

"Now blow."

I did.

"Blow harder."

I did that, too, but the peanuts and the shells simply would not coalesce into the gummy substance which he was chewing so avariciously. Besides, the color was all wrong!

"Oh," said Tommy Schell with a knowing look, "You shouldn't chew them with the shells. Here, try some of these."

I took the shelled peanuts which he offered, I chewed and I spluttered, until Tommy could no longer contain himself and burst out in a fit of laughter—and so did I, at my own naiveté. For my reward he bestowed upon me a whole packet of Bazooka bubble gum. The secret was finally laid completely bare!

But I had my revenge. Once, while going to school on the bus, this same sporting neighbor offered me a dime for one stick of Wrigley's chewing gum. I would not accept because I thought the dime, being smaller than a penny, was worth less. After much pleading on his part, I relented and agreed to the exchange. The word got out, but the next day I was prepared—having first checked on the value of the dime. I boarded the bus with three packs of gum and protested vehemently each time Tommy or someone else suggested another such "unfair" exchange. (In the end, however, they somehow always managed to "extort" the gum from me.) I must have gone through twenty packs of gum before they all realized what was going on. It was not the first time that feigned ignorance on my part paid off!

With ten dollars at my disposal (minus the initial investment of five cents a pack), I had accumulated a small fortune indeed. So I bought me a gun: a hundred-shot, Sears-special B.B. gun, with three hundred rounds of ammunition. I missed my war toys so! The time had come for me to be a boy, to hunt and fish and romp unto my heart's content, unworried, in the safety of the surrounding woods and meadows.

It was the purchase of the gun, combined with a typical fifth grade assignment, that constitutes my most vivid memory of my childhood in America.

"Go out into the woods, observe nature, and write down what you see and hear," the assignment read.

But then again, I was not a typical boy, far from it! And had I not just bought a new Daisy air rifle and three hundred rounds of ammo? What possible sense could there be going into the woods armed with a pen and pencil, and besides, what would I do to pass the time if I found nothing to observe or document?

These compelling questions led to the inevitable arming of this ten-year-old boy in search of either knowledge or adventure. Little did I know that both lay in store: the adventure leading to knowledge, knowledge to wisdom, and all melting into a long-remembered episode—for who knows what will be remembered when we are old, and what lost forever?

So there I was, a formidable, knowledge-seeking hunter in the middle of the vast wilderness behind my home. As I sat on the predestined fallen limb, listening and looking for nature to reveal herself, I was continually distracted by strange sounds and darting little animals who kept making weird noises and producing tingling sensations in my right-hand trigger finger. After a time I stuck my paper and pen in my pocket, and still a little later my Daisy slipped off my shoulder and landed on my lap, and before I knew it, a hundred rounds of ammunition found their way into the empty chamber.

Then, fate struck its inexorable blow! Just as I was surveying the endless spaghetti of boughs and branches around me over the notched sight-finder on the Daisy, lo and behold, a stupid little hummingbird appeared out of nowhere and froze in my line of fire. I pleaded and begged him to fly away, I warned him of his peril, I remonstrated with his arguments of free will—I didn't own the woods and he had the right to be where he was and so on and so forth—until at last all this *inner* discussion became too unbearable for my boyish brain. So I just pulled the trigger.

My last thoughts on the matter and the recklessness on which I based my action can be summed up simply: He was so small, and quick, and far away, that I would probably miss him.

But I did not.

I thought I saw him dart off to one side as the muffled sound exploded from my rifle, and I breathed a sigh of relief when he vanished from my sights. But then, to my eternal consternation, there lay his little body, all a-quiver, and there were signs of blood. He did not get away, he flew into the line of fire; he was not grazed, he was dying.

My thoughts ran pell-mell like dry leaves on a breezy autumn day. My heart throbbed like a symphony of jungle drums, my eyes began to water, my body froze, then melted as I sprang to my feet and rushed to save the little harmless bird. I panicked even more when I finally held him in my hands and his little head would not align itself with the rest of his tiny body. The gaping hole was clearly visible. The B.B. had caught him in the belly.

As I ran through the woods and reached the clearing beyond which lay my house, I tried to think of all the emergency procedures I had learned about in school—first aid, tourniquets; but it was all no good; none of it applied to fatally wounded hummingbirds.

After what seemed an endless journey, I crossed the field, and after what seemed endless hours of running, I reached my house and breathlessly implored my oldest brother to save our lives. Frank was a practical sort of man; he would know what to do, he would not fail us in our hour of need.

And then the hour of separation between the generations struck. In all his wisdom at nineteen years of age, Frank looked at the plight of the stricken bird and said calmly,

"Give him to the cat."

I realize now of what little consequence the passing of a single hummingbird must have been to a man who had seen the face of death so many times and for so long. But at that time, in that safe place, in that peaceful sanctuary of Owensboro, Kentucky, his statement appeared to me utterly heartless. All the horror of my own life in Europe paled in comparison to the impending death of this little American hummingbird for which I alone bore all the blame. The other horror had been done unto me.

I took the bird away from Frank, glanced around to see if the cat had heard what he said, and proceeded to do the best I could, which involved a simple washing, force feeding, and splashing of drops of water on his parched beak. It was in the course of his treatment that my patient died. I knew I could do no more.

The burial was a traditional, back-yard affair, inherited from the collective consciousness of my race, with all the attendant ceremonies which befit a fallen hero. My own immediate thoughts on the matter can be best summarized by my son's written reflections (at age seven) on his first encounter with immortal death, that of his namesake Angel fish. He wrote:

Poem

"My Fish"

I have some fish.
There are eight of them.
One died.
And I put it in the stream.
I could not keep My mind off him.
I named him after me.
by Andrzej

My very sentiments, the sentiments of every boy as he wrestles with the agony of death.

The next day in school, the good nun asked, "Who would like to share with us some of the things that you have learned from your trip to the woods yesterday?" I did not volunteer.

I have many other vivid recollections of my stay at the Owensboro farmstead: the neighborly gatherings after church, which allowed children an hour or so of socializing as well; the annual country fairs in the nearby grove, with whole sides of mutton sizzling over hand-dug pits and all you could eat for two dollars; the hay wagon, blackberry-picking trips of late summer days; my dog Blackie, who chased cars, was hit and nursed back into health, only to resume his car-chasing days and then be killed in front of my eyes by a combine; the public lynching to which we were all invited, an invitation we politely declined, having already had a share of death to last us a lifetime; my best friend, Bobby Higdon, to whose house I used to ride my old bicycle—a full twenty miles away—and whom I missed so after our departure from the Thompsons; and finally, at age ten, my second love, the one to whom I gave my favorite Papermate pen with the two hearts on the clip as a sign of true love always. I wonder if fair Kathleen ever got the message?

My most happy memory by far is of our joyful reunion with my sister Anna and her family. They left Bremen three months after us (July 1950) on the *General Hann*, which brought them to New Orleans. Since their Oklahoma sponsor failed to show, they spent a good month in a hotel waiting for some other arrangements to be made. Thereafter, they were relocated to Nebraska and several months later (November 1950) came to live within five miles of us on Mr. Charles Hayden's homestead. Mr. Hayden was a kind and prosperous agriculturalist, and his willingness to give them all a home stemmed more from his good will towards us, than from any need on his part.

After only one year with the Haydens, Stefan became restless and so, one day, simply vanished out of sight—abandoning his two children and his pregnant wife. Without question, there was only one thing to do: We took them all in to live with us. When Helen was born on January 6, 1952, the little red cabin on the Thompson farmstead housed nine happy people. Now I had two nieces and one nephew—perhaps more, but we did not know at that time of the whereabouts of our three oldest sisters or even whether they were still alive.

We stayed with the Thompsons for a full two years, until they finally succumbed to the American version of collectivization and sold out to Mr. Hayden. Even with our help, the small farm they had hoped to save proved to be a liability. Eventually, Mr. Hayden bought out all the failing, smaller farms in the area while allowing the people to remain on their former homesteads and work for him if they so chose. For many, this proved to be a congenial arrangement. The Thompsons, however, decided to move on, and so did we.

In the summer of 1952, the same inexorable fate which summoned the disenfranchised agriculturalists to the great cities of Europe during the time of the Industrial Revolution, and in America sowed the grapes of wrath, now beckoned to us. We packed up our belongings, and with the kind assistance of one of our neighbors, relocated to the town of Owensboro.

Although great strides have been made in Owensboro, Kentucky, since the 1950s, at that time it could not be counted among the great and prosperous cities of America. But then again, neither was it Dickens' London, nor one of Steinbeck's California encampments. I suppose one could call it "marginally economically depressed." In fact, in the immediate neighborhood of our residence, the only uplifting sight was the "Holy Roller" church, which I frequently eyed from a safe distance.

Our house, with a dirt floor, was situated about twenty feet from two sets of commercial railroad tracks, on the other side of which was the clay-pipe factory in which my brothers worked for one dollar an hour. Anna and my father procured work in a nearby convalescent home, she as a cook, he as a custodian. I peddled papers. With all these cash-paying enterprises, we were now in a position to save some real money.

Two highlights stand out in my mind relative to my first gainful employment. The first was the all-expense-paid, three-day trip with the managing editor of an Owensboro newspaper to St. Louis—a prize for the largest number of new subscribers acquired by a paperboy. While there, he wound up attending one of the numerous conventions always transpiring in St. Louis, and I wound up spending all my time at the amusement park. So, a good time was had by all!

The second incident happened on one of my collection routes when a well-meaning African-American matron plied me with milk and cookies and proceeded for a span of two precious hours to try to convert me to Baptist Christianity. May the Lord forgive me, but I found the milk and cookies much more to my liking than her endless references to the "Good Book" and her message of salvation. When she was through, I thanked her for her trouble and left an uncontrite sinner. Moreover, I subsequently even harbored ill will toward that lady who, while preaching redemption, always managed not to pay me for her papers.

While in Owensboro, I was also summoned weekly to the church rectory, where another well-meaning soul, the parish priest, proceeded with great pains to enlighten me on my human sexuality. May God forgive me again, but during those long, embarrassing sessions which I had no use for in the least, my mind kept wandering off to the earthly banks of the Ohio River where I used to spend my Saturday afternoons before he took an interest in my spiritual well-being and God knows what else.

My favorite pastime in Owensboro consisted of making bows and arrows. (This was after I became an inveterate fan of Nabisco's "Straight Arrow," and after the incident with the hummingbird and my trusty Daisy.) The arrows were easily made, but the fine art of making bows proved to be most elusive. I spent endless hours whittling and chiseling, soaking and scraping any piece of wood which happened to come my way. What didn't I do to get that perfect bow! Alas, all my endeavors had but one result: a broken stick. This insane compulsion on my part proved to be so nerve-wracking to my brothers that they went out one day and bought me a brand-new, factory-made, bow-and-arrow set. It was *so* good that not only did I give up making bows and arrows forever, but I also gave up using them altogether. It was the worst present I have ever received from anybody at any time.

We did not stay in the town of Owensboro for very long; otherwise I'd have more recollections. Well, I do have a few more: for instance, the time I tried to protest the making of my first Holy Communion on the grounds that I was a most unworthy sinner. This did not bother the parish priest as much as the fact that I had no record of my baptism. Since all our family records perished in the war, we were not even sure of our own ages—never mind the dates of such relatively minor events like marriages and baptisms. Moreover, heartened by the absence of documentation, over the years, my father developed a penchant for adding or subtracting years of our lives, thus rearranging nature's chronological order to suit our momentary exigencies both here and in Germany.

So when the priest asked me, "Were you, then, baptized?" not ever having given the matter much thought, I gave him my standard reply: "I'll have to ask my mother, she'd know."

My mother had always had a most remarkable memory. Even on her deathbed at the age of ninety-two (but she could have been younger or older), she would sing and, when her voice gave out, recite entire Polish ballads and songs learned in early childhood, verse by verse, rhyme by rhyme, for endless hours. So when I asked her regarding my baptism, I was very much surprised by her reply. She assured me that in Poland it was the custom to baptize children about three weeks after birth, although in my case it may have been sooner or later. Since her mind was filled with more pressing issues in those days, she could not give me the exact information which I requested. My dilemma, since I could not give this answer to the priest, was resolved by our official chronicler, my father, who provided me not only with the date but the hour as well.

The whole matter was finally settled by having both my parents sign, or to be more precise, affix their shaky X's to an affidavit of baptism. Thus, being sufficiently distracted by the bureaucratic requirement of having to establish my Christian standing (the priest would not do it twice), I forgot all about my primary concern and received the Holy Eucharist, unworthy as I was.

As I began to say, we did not remain in this town very long. My salvation from Owensboro proselytism came in the form of an old Chevrolet purchased for three hundred dollars with the family's accumulated savings. Leaving the rest of us in Owensboro, my two brothers headed for Chicago. This pattern was typical of earlier immigrants to America: the oldest son or father would come over first, save some money, and send for the rest of the family later. Since Chicago was much closer than Europe, after several months of separation, my brothers came back Owensboro in the same old Chevrolet, but the news they brought with them was not encouraging.

Although they were able to find work immediately, they had not been able to find suitable living quarters for our "extended" nine-member family. It seemed there was some sort of prejudice on the part of Chicagoan landlords when it came to families with young children—or at least on the part of those landlords whose rents we could afford. Since the wages were much higher in Chicago than in Owensboro, it was decided that Anna would accompany my brothers on their way back, and when an apartment was found, they would return for the rest of us. Although it seemed to take forever, in three months' time that old Chevrolet came rolling into Owensboro once again, this time to take us all to our new home in the "Windy City," where, we were told, there were more Polish people than in Warsaw.

10

The Slings of Fortune

The trip to Chicago, Illinois, will forever stand out in my mind. As there was no one to say good-bye to in Owensboro, after cramming our few transportable belongings into the Chevy, we just took off. The year was 1953.

I do not know if we looked strange traversing the prairies of Indiana and the Land of Lincoln in our old jalopy, but I know we were ecstatic. The gentle winds of summer were never so capricious, the smiling sun never so coquettish as on that day, playing with our moods and dispositions as if they were their very own. We sang, we laughed, we chattered as lovers often do on their honeymoons. We were in love, after all, with life again.

It was Chicago's Lake Shore Drive which finally stilled our boisterous spirits, inspiring us with both awe and trepidation. Now *this* was a city! Never before had I encountered so many cars at such fast speeds in so many different lanes. At thirteen years of age, I once again clung to my mother's skirts.

The basement apartment on South 23rd Street was fully furnished. Not only was there a floor, there were plush carpets on top of it. (I took off my shoes.) Not only were there windows in the step-down apartment, but full-length curtains as well. There were *three* bedrooms. There was a bathroom with a toilet, tub, and shower. There was a full-sized kitchen with a gas stove and running water. There was furniture: a dining-room table, chairs, sofas, recliners. There was—there was—I am almost afraid to say it now, there was a *television set!* I could have told you then how it felt to be *nouveau riche*, to have arrived. "Relative deprivation" will do it every time. Never have I been so well off; never will I be so again! (Now, when I feel down and out, when I am inundated with bills and hassled by creditors, I just add a little relative deprivation to my life and right away I feel a whole lot better.)

In three short years after coming to Chicago, we bought our first home in America: an impressive three-flat apartment building (with a rented basement, naturally) on Chicago's North side. It stood like a mansion towering over Hoyne Avenue in a section of the city known as "Little Poland": Damen, North, and Milwaukee. While my mother and my father (who were now too old for work) took care of the house and children, my sister and my brothers labored in a factory called Wells Gardener. Later, Ann was laid off, but she secured another position with the American Spring Company. John also changed his job to work for the Schwinn Bicycle Company, where, having gone to night school for his eduction, he would later become a reliable general maintenance engineer. Frank took a machinist position with a small Chicago firm and later joined my brother, John, at Schwinn. I just kept on going to school.

As we once got used to poverty, so now we got used to our relative affluence. Although our circumstances kept changing around us, I would like to think that we remained the same. The city life appealed to us. Work was plentiful, there was public transportation, the church and school were just down the street, and there were many, many Polish people—some of whom we knew from the refugee camps in Germany and some from Wołyń. Once in Chicago, it was not difficult to find even distant relatives and friends.

And so it happened that one day, thirteen years after the end of World War II (in 1958), while Ann was washing her hands in the bathroom of the American Spring Company before going home, a co-worker became unwittingly enthralled with her countenance to the point of staring. Ann, becoming aware of the stranger's gaze, looked into the mirror—and as their eyes met, they recognized the familial bond in one another. It was Stasia Piotrowski Plaza, our first cousin, daughter of Marcelina, sister to the family slaughtered in the Leonówka massacre. They both stood there looking at each other for what seemed like eternity before their bodies and their souls mingled in a fast embrace.

Stasia Plaza presented us with the most joyful news we had heard since 1946, when we found our father through the UNRRA: that our three oldest sisters, whom we had not seen since 1943 and presumed dead, were alive, and well, and living with their own families in Poland. Moreover, she was able to provide us with the addresses of our Jasia, Stasia, and Aniela. Miraculously, with the grim specter of death raging all around us, we had somehow all survived the eye of that threefold storm unscathed. The time had finally come to renew our family ties with one another.

In 1958, I was eighteen and away in my final year of boarding school. Although I faithfully corresponded with each one of them by mail, another ten years would pass before I would get my chance to see my three long-lost sisters once more, for it took that long to become a Franciscan priest of the Most Holy Order of the Assumption B.V.M. Province of Friars Minor—and they would not let me out!

Meanwhile, our chain of correspondence was quickly followed by several family visitations to our country of origin. Finally, we were able to piece together our collective history during the Second World War under the Soviets, the Nazis, the Ukrainian Nationalists, and the American occupation forces—a history shared by so many other displaced persons.

Mindful of my sisters' comments that the events of their lives during the war years might not readily lend themselves to verbal expression (the same can be said for all victims of World War II), the history of my sisters' exile—remembered and set down in their own words half a century after the events of which I speak—is as follows.[1]

Janina

I was born on December 1, 1914, just after my father, Józef, was conscripted into the Polish Army. I was therefore raised by my mother as well as my maternal grandparents and uncles with whom I was left while she worked. I have been told by my mother that as an infant, I was simply unbearable and cried so much that one day my uncle Staszek swung my cradle, which was suspended from the rafters, so hard that I fell out and landed in a pile of rags near the front door.

When my father returned from the war, I was already five years old. I did not know him at all and, in spite of my mother's pleading, refused to call him "Father." Whether this was due to my stupidity or stubbornness, I do not recall. I only know that I was not his favorite child.

My mother, however, was very good to me and always shielded me with her own body from my father's anger and his stinging belt. I loved my mother and the very thought of her having to die someday brought tears to my eyes and sadness to my young heart. Although she is no longer alive, I love her still. I only regret that we could not be together for so many years during and after the Second World War. But that was neither my fault nor hers.

My father did not allow me to go to school because, being the oldest, I was expected to help out around the house, farm, and garden. How I envied my sisters, Aniela and Stasia, who attended school! Often I would take Aniela's notebooks and, in my spare time, rewrite all her lessons in between the lines with a stub of a pencil that I somehow acquired. Out in the meadows, while pasturing cows, I would practice my penmanship on splinters of wood. When the time came, however, mother did send me to religion classes so that I could make my first confession and communion with all the others.

When I turned thirteen, I was sent into service: to live with and to work for a certain Mr. Tofil Bagiński, who came from America and bought a farm in our area. He had two sons and two daughters, but since they were much older than I, they were not much company. While there, I was very unhappy and lonely. I watched with envy as young people my age gathered together on Sundays and during their free time to socialize and have a good time while I, from morning to dusk, had to chase after Mr. Bagiński's cows. Finally, when I became fifteen, I told my father that I did not want to remain there any longer and came home.

No sooner did I cross the threshold, than my father hired me out again to a veteran who lived with his wife near Osada Krechowiecka. They had a son, but he was away in school. Mr. Karol Olszewski was a wealthy man employing two field hands, two domestic servants, the cook, and myself.

Besides doing all the household chores, I was also required to milk their seven cows, work in the fields, and tend the garden. It was a very large plot of land, and in the spring I had to turn it over myself with a spade. It was hard work! Moreover, the mistress of the house was extremely miserly and so, except for the cook, we were always hungry. The field hands were often starved to the point of not being able to work at all. No wonder there was a constant turnover in their ranks![2]

Although all this was difficult for me, I stayed on for a full year as agreed upon by the proprietor and my father. I was told that if I left before the year was out, my family would not receive the potatoes and grain—the contractual payment for my labor.

After this I went to work for the mayor, Mr. Podchorski, another wealthy man who had a wife, three children (with a governess), two field hands and two servant girls. This time I was the cook and so life was much easier to bear. Generally, I would rise at 4:00 A.M., milk the cows, prepare the daily meals, clean up, and retire between 11:00 P.M. and midnight.

While in Mr. Podchorski's service, Kazimierz Rudkowski, the foreman—an educated man with three years of high school to his name—fell madly in love with me. This marked the beginning of my amorous adventures. To tell the truth, I liked him as well, for he composed such beautiful verses, which my sisters enjoyed reading immensely whenever I came home to visit. In time, I collected an entire volume of his wonderfully romantic poetry!

Once, when my mother came to see me, my ardent admirer began to plead for my hand, but my mother said that I was too young to marry and so nothing came of it. (I was sixteen at the time and he, ten years my senior.) Be that as it may, we continued to see each other and he continued to compose until Mr. Podchorski discovered our secret and dismissed my dear poet from his service for courting a girl beneath his own social standing.

Shortly thereafter, I also left (or perhaps was dismissed) to work for a couple by the name of Schroeder, in Babin, a small town nearby. The work was not difficult, but again the lady of the house failed to feed me properly. While there, I became acquainted with an elegant bachelor who worked in the town sugar factory. Actually, not wishing to appear too forward, I did not see that much of him, but when the factory season ended, he surprised me by sending a letter of proposal requesting permission to meet my parents in order to ask for my hand in marriage.

After leaving Mr. Schroeder's service, I showed the letter to my mother, Mother told Father, and Father flew into a fit of anger. I was still sixteen and, so, left well enough alone. I never answered the letter, and the elegant

Janina *(continued)*

bachelor, not knowing where I came from or where I lived, could not pursue his intended proposal of marriage. So it ended.

Again I was sent into service. And so it went until the beginning of the war when all those who hired people (the gentry) were deported to Siberia. In all these years I never worked for myself; always for the good of the family. Whatever I received, I shared with them. Mother knows this best. Whenever she came to visit me, she would never leave with empty hands. What I could give, I gave willingly. In all this time, if I came home at all, it was only for a brief visit and off to work for someone else again. Sometimes, when I saw my brothers sprouting like beans and my sisters quickly turning into fair ladies, I wished I could remain with them—but it was never to be.

Just before the war, I was employed by a family in Ostróg, a large town near the Russian border. This family was not very good to me, but I managed to make many dear friends in the town. One young man, in particular, struck my fancy—but off he went to war and I never saw him again. This was a frequent occurrence in those days, as any girl from Ostróg will tell you.

After my service there, I came home again; home was now Ryświanka. How good it was to be back, to attend dances with my sisters, to be with my parents, to meet our neighbors, and to be courted by Antek Domalewski and Olek Łebedź, the local Ukrainian teacher of the Russian language, of whom my father never did approve. There now being four girls in the house (the others having also returned from service), we never lacked good company. It was wonderful, but it did not last.

Again, and for the last time, I went to work for Mr. Bagiński in Trostaniec. Having lost his wife in a tragic set of circumstances, Mr. Bagiński was an elderly widower with a fourteen-year-old daughter and two sons. He owned over twenty hectares of land, cattle, horses, and many, many pigs. That is to say, he was a very wealthy man—but also very kind. As the mistress of his house, I was kept very busy cooking for the family and all his hired help, but I was also happy there. I was well liked, respected, and made many, many friends. Stasia loved to visit me while I lived in Trostaniec, and she often stayed as long as she possibly could.

Added to all this good fortune, the landlord's eighteen-year-old son, Józek, fell madly in love with me, although I was seven years his senior. And that would have been all right except that Władzio, the landlord's godchild—one year younger than I—used to visit me every evening and loved me no less. But this was already late in 1939, so they took them both off to war and I returned again to Ryświanka.

After several years and many changes in our beloved Poland, Władzio—quite miraculously—reappeared in our vicinity and came to see me at home. His visit happily coincided with our annual and last celebration of the *Andrzejki*. The year was 1942. Władzio came bearing a bottle of vodka, which was very scarce in those days, and which endeared him to my father immediately. "Never pass this way without stopping in for a visit," he told him.

Meanwhile, we girls were all preparing to go over to Gruntkowski's to celebrate the *Andrzejki*, and so we invited Władzio to come along. Pretending to be sleepy from his journey, Władzio declined, but urged us all to go on without him. Strangely enough, Father, for the first time in his life, decided to accompany us.

As usual, we all had a wonderful time and returned home around midnight to find Władzio wide awake and in a friendly and talkative mood. Being in good spirits ourselves, we sat up the whole night talking, but mostly listening to Władzio's terrible stories of the war and the fields of corpses [*trupy*[3]] upon which he trod to and from battle. As far as I can remember, this was the last happy celebration in our neighborhood, for already many Ukrainian bands were on the prowl, and the Germans were conscripting people for forced labor.

Early in the following year, Aniela and I were among those marked for deportation to Germany. When news of this reached Władzio, he sent his sister to beg me not to go away. He offered to hide me in his own house (about thirteen kilometers from us), to marry me, and—if worse came to worse—to join me in exile.

I relayed this news to my mother and she to my father. (I never spoke to him directly but always through my mother.) He told me that if I did not go, the Germans were sure to revenge themselves on the entire family. Since I could not allow this to happen, I decided to do as I was told.

I prepared myself for the departure with mixed feelings, but took heart when the Germans told us that we were only going for six months, after which we would be returned and others would be recruited to take our place. (Later, we found out that they only said this so that we would not be tempted to run away.) I thought to myself: "Half a year is not such a long time. It will pass quickly and I will return." As we boarded the German transport on the appointed day, I changed my mind about going and wanted to jump off along the route and hide in the woods. Only the fear of the consequences to my family and of my father prevented me from doing so.

The trucks first brought us to Tuczyn, and after a few days, another transport took us to Równe. It was there that we saw a great mass of humanity, all prisoners of war, behind barbed-wire fences. They were all terribly hungry and put out their hands in the hope of obtaining some bread from the passersby. We had some provisions that my mother gave us for our journey, but what was that for so many people! (Aniela felt so sorry for them that she practically gave away everything she had.) We watched with great sadness as they dug in the earth for roots and ate the leaves off the trees. We watched with horror as the Nazis beat them with rubber truncheons for no apparent reason. We mourned for them as they collapsed and died from starvation and disease.

After several days of having to witness the agony of the Russian prisoners

Janina *(continued)*

of war, we were loaded on a freight train and shipped off to Germany. During the journey, we were given soup to eat which was worse than the slop we fed to pigs. It consisted of water, unwashed turnips, and sand. Due to this diet I became very ill. My body swelled to twice its size, and my face broke out in a rash. My eyes were so puffy I could scarcely see.

When we arrived at our destination, Würzburg, we were allowed to spend the night in some wooden barracks. The floor was to be our bed, but in spite of our utter exhaustion no one could sleep due to the lice and flea infestation. In the morning, Germans arrived from factories and farmsteads, and began to sort us out according to their pleasure. Here, in Würzburg, Aniela and I parted company, each being forced to go in a different direction. I, myself, was taken to a small village where I was put to work without pay and with just enough food to keep me from starving to death.

After a few months, I was transferred to an airplane ammunition factory in Schweinfurt am Main. Our labor camp was located some distance from the factory itself, and each barrack within it was packed to capacity. The women in our camp were separated each according to her nationality. I had to wear "OST" because I was from the East near the Russian border. The Germans said that I was, therefore, Russian and treated me accordingly. Polish people had it a little better. During the air raids, however, we often became mixed up and had to be resorted again.

We worked in three shifts. Each worker was allowed only four hours of rest in a twenty-four-hour period. There was no time off. My particular shift was roused each morning at 4:00 A.M. and lined up four abreast, like soldiers, in a long column along which every few meters were Nazis armed with machine guns and revolvers to prevent escapes. We were then marched to the train, loaded on, and unloaded at the factory—a very large, low, one-story building. The roof of the factory was completely covered with grass and various bushes for purposes of camouflage.

Our evening rations consisted of turnip soup. Sometimes we would be given two very small, unpeeled potatoes or an unsavory stew in which we often found parts of frogs and God knows what else. Everything smelled horrible, and all leftovers were reheated time and time again. For breakfast we received a slice of bread, spread with some margarine or marmalade (which could be consumed in two bites) and black, unsweetened coffee. Sometimes I would hide a small piece of this bread for later, when I would be famished, but when I looked for it again it was usually gone; someone would inevitably steal and eat it. Given the nature of this nourishment and our long hours of work, it is no wonder that we were always hungry. Our heads were reeling for lack of food and from the hard labor. We were anemic; we were often on the point of complete physical exhaustion.

The machine to which I was assigned stood near a large window. Beyond the window, on both sides of the street, were spacious sidewalks. While working, I would often gaze out of the window at the people who were walking about, smiling, engaging each other in lively conversation, free, and evidently quite happy. Many of these Germans were of my own age. It was at such times that I missed my family and my country of birth the most. I longed for home, for my parents, for my sisters and brothers—especially the youngest, who always ran with open arms to greet each of his sisters as they returned from the various domestic services, and to kiss them and hug them as if there were no tomorrow. Once, when he spent an undue amount of time hugging and kissing Stasia, I said: "Tadziu, leave a kiss for me." He then reached out, felt his lips with his little fingers and said, "There's one left. There's one left."

At such times I was often tempted to go back to Poland on foot—and would have, except that the roads were crawling with Nazis and I did not know how to swim.

In the beginning, Father, who was now also in Germany, somehow obtained my address and wrote me a letter in which he complained of his mistreatment and the hard labor he was forced to endure. He asked me to write often and explained that it was difficult for him to do so, since he never learned how to write. I did write: long, rambling letters to Father, and Aniela, and to my family in Poland, but after a few months there were no replies from Poland and all my addresses were destroyed during one of the air raids, so that our correspondence ceased.

When the air raids on Schweinfurt began,[4] we were allowed to seek shelter in the basement of a tall cement building. True, it protected us from the bomb fragments, but everyone knew that if a bomb should happen to fall on the building itself, we would be buried alive by all that cement.

Later, when transportation became a problem, our camp was moved to within walking distance of the factory. Sometimes the bombers came as we were returning from work. Then, a general panic would set in. People would break out of the marching column and seek shelter wherever they could. Often we fled over the dead and the dying, through flames and flying debris, and many would return to the barracks covered with blood from bomb fragments, suffering from first-degree burns, or distended from the shock of the explosions.

One time, just as my shift left the factory, before we were able to get out of the town, the alarm sounded and almost immediately bombs started falling around us like hail. Everyone scattered to the four winds and I found myself alone, surrounded by flames on all sides. In desperation, I wrapped my head with an old coat that I had, and dashed through the fire to safety. When I looked up, the sky around me was as red as blood. The entire town stood in flames. Never have I witnessed such a terrifying sight in all of my life!

At another time, the air raid sirens began wailing while we were already in the camp barracks. We all waited for the inevitable attack on the city, thinking that we were safe, being some distance away. However, the wind was very

Janina *(continued)*

strong that day and many of the bombs missed the city entirely, landing in the fields near our camp. In the course of the bombing, one of our barracks caught on fire, but was soon put out, and the exhausted workers retired to get some much needed sleep. Almost three peaceful hours elapsed and then, without the slightest warning, phosphorous, incendiary bombs began to hail right on top of our barracks.

Those who could fled the wooden buildings and threw themselves into the covered trench in the yard, which served as our bomb shelter. The trench was about fifty meters long with wooden entrances at each end. It resembled a root cellar, like that in which we used to store potatoes for the winter. I, too, wanted to run to the trench, but by this time, the yard was a burning inferno and the shelter was unapproachable. Even so, many tried desperately to reach it. Some succeeded, but most were covered with phosphorus and burned to death as they ran across the compound.

Looking around, I saw a small building near where I stood and ran there for cover. Fortunately, this building had a basement where a number of people were already huddled. Outside, we could hear the bombs striking all around us like thunder, only more often. And we, we ran from corner to corner, each praying in her own way for salvation. I prayed, too, but I was no longer thinking of life. I prayed for the forgiveness of my sins and for eternal salvation. Then, I simply waited for the bomb with my name to fall.

It came crashing through the roof of the building and the floor as well, and landed in the middle of the basement about five meters from the corners where we were huddled. We gazed upon this messenger of death and held our breath, waiting for the inevitable. But it did not explode. It simply hung there motionless, like some deadly metallic cobra, coiled and waiting for someone to move. Since there was nowhere else to go, we stayed with that live bomb and stared at it until the air raid was over. Then, ever so slowly, we all hurried past that terrifying instrument of death to freedom, or rather, continued slavery.

After leaving the bomb and the shelter, I made my way to the trench which was now completely sealed off with debris on one end and bodies on the other. Through the earth, I could hear the moaning of the few despairing survivors. In the course of the bombing, one of the entrances caught on fire from the phosphorus and those inside who could not escape in time, simply burned to death or suffocated from smoke inhalation. Moreover, some of the old rags, which the Russian girls always dragged with them into the shelters, also caught on fire and smoldered into deadly smoke.

From my barrack, only I and two other girls survived. The remainder went into the trench, and there they perished. Later, the Germans uncovered the trench, dragged out the cadavers, and laid them in long rows. Then, they searched each body and confiscated everything of value, including watches, pins, necklaces, and wedding rings.

During this attack, many men were also killed. Across the way from us was a camp for predominantly French prisoners of war. They stood without shelter behind barbed-wire fences and perished with the falling bombs.

It was after this last attack that I decided to escape from the camp and go to Würzburg to look for Aniela. In the general confusion which followed, I knew that if I did not return to my barrack, I would be presumed dead, and so they would not bother looking for me. For my journey I took two loaves of bread from the burned-out magazine, and while it was still dark, I set out on the thirty-five kilometer trip to Würzburg.

I walked for the remainder of the night and throughout the next day, avoiding the military and all people in general. Finally, toward the late afternoon, my legs began to give out. I felt extremely tired and was on the verge of complete exhaustion. With my last ounce of energy, I reached a German village and decided to ask for lodging.

I came to one house and knocked on the door. When the German lady opened it, I asked her in German whether I could spend the night in some corner of her house. But the lady was very unfriendly and told me curtly that there was no room, and that she received no one, and had nothing to give me. So I went away empty-handed and still without a place to sleep. I walked aimlessly about the village for some time, until I gathered enough courage to knock on another door. This time the lady told me that they lived in fear themselves, and had to hide in their own basement during the air raids. She could not let me stay.

What was there to do? I simply began walking again, not knowing where I was going or why, until I chanced upon another village. There, in the dark street under a dim light, I saw a man with a kind face, and so I approached him. I explained that I was running away from the bombs and that I was on my way to Würzburg but that, since it was already night, I needed a place to rest. He said: "Good. I know an older woman who has a weak heart and has three sons and whose husband is off to war. She has one prisoner of war who works for her on the farm, but she could use a girl around the house as well."

I said no more, thinking that I would simply go there, spend the night, and resume my trip to Würzburg in the morning. When we entered the house, I found a well-disposed lady who, although she was German, immediately took pity on me, gave me a good supper, and a bed such as I had never slept in all my life, or so it seemed to me after all of my hardships and exhaustion.

When I got up in the morning it was already late. In the doorway of my bedroom stood Antek Futoma, the prisoner of war the kind gentleman told me about. As he proceeded to give me a polite bow, the thought occurred to me that I knew him from somewhere before. I *knew* him as he was then and there, and even his clothes seemed familiar. And then I remembered.

Before the war, while we were still in Poland, my sisters and I wanted desperately to know whom we were destined to marry. To this end we engaged

Janina *(continued)*

in various fortune-telling games and even went so far as to consult the Gypsies, each of whom told us something different. We all had many suitors who respected us, went with us to dances, *Andrzejki*, and *wieczorki*, but none of whom was in any hurry to propose marriage. Perhaps it was better that way. Moreover, even if any one of them did become serious about us, we changed our minds often about whom *we* wanted to marry. We were, after all, young; and then, there was news of war.

In any case, I recall a dream I once had as a young girl. I was in a deep, dark forest, which I took to mean a foreign land. A road led through this forest, and about a meter above the road ran a long thread which unwound from a spool at my side. A long thread meant a long journey. At the end of the thread stood Antek, just as I saw him there on the German farmstead, stooping near my doorway, weary from all his battles, labors, slavery, and submission, and in the same clothes as he appeared at the end of that thread.

How odd, I thought, that of all the boys and men I had ever known and loved, he should be the one chosen by God for me—whether I consented to it or not. And so it began. He raved over me and did not care that I was indifferent towards him, avoided him, and refused to speak to him. But since we lived under the same roof and had to work together, I could not always get my way.

In the same German village there were other Polish prisoners of war and laborers. There was Julek Gabrys, for instance, from Kraków, who was three years my junior; a handsome, good man who also took a liking towards me. He came to the house after work to visit me and to take me to dances, which the Polish people were allowed to conduct in that village. We became good friends, but when, after the war, Julek proposed marriage, Antek vowed to kill himself. One time Julek just barely saved his life. After that, not wishing to have Antek's death on his conscience, he gave me up. It was then that I decided to live with, and subsequently to marry Antek—but not for some time.

Needless to say, I did not continue my trip to Würzburg. This was not only because of Antek and Julek, but also because it was said that the Germans were patrolling the area for escapees in order to return them to factory work. So I remained in the village until the very end of the war.

After our liberation, I and Antek went to Aschaffenburg, where we found Aniela and her Dominik. There we remained until 1946. Although it was possible to emigrate abroad, I had no desire to continue my travels into foreign lands. I wanted to be reunited with my family, and to see my mother again whom I missed most of all. And so, I waited for news about my family from the Red Cross.

Finally, in May of 1946, when my son, Tadeusz, was six months old, I and Antek left for Poland. Once there, we received a post-German house with one cow and some land in Międzylesie. After some time, I was able to locate Aniela and Stasia through the Red Cross, and also found out much later that the rest of my family had emigrated to America. How I regretted this turn of events, but it was already too late.

There is much more to be told, but that belongs to my private sphere. About these matters I do not wish to speak because no one would believe me anyway. I was never sent to an extermination camp because I always bore patiently come what may. I witnessed how they would hang Polish people in the city streets for the merest infractions, or how they would send them off to the gas ovens. No, I survived because I became that to which I was reduced in Nazi Germany: *pokorne ciele* [a submissive calf].

In time, I had two more children, Halina and Anna, by Antek. Even after I found out that he was already married, I continued to live with the father of my children, and married him when he became a widower. He was not the worst of men. In his youth he was a splendid marksman, and later received many military medals of distinction which he was allowed to wear, and often did when he donned his army uniform. He was a very capable man, and whatever he set his mind to do, that he accomplished. There was nothing he could not do. He was a hard worker and thrifty in his ways. In this we were of like disposition.

My Antek died in 1975 at the age of seventy-four—two years before I came to America. Now I am an old widow. Everything has passed, but we must continue to live on until our appointed hour.

Aniela

I was born on June 20, 1921, in Cecylówka. As a small child, I grew up with my parents and sisters on a colony by the name of Natalja. We lived in a small wooden house with a thatched roof. I remember that there was a barn and a large orchard connected with the property. After a while, my father sold our house and moved to Anował, and from there to Leonówka, where he rented a room from his brother, Stanisław. Next, we moved to Amelin, where we lived for several more years. Near us lived my father's parents and family, including my father's married brother, Franciszek. I and Stasia went to school which was located about five kilometers from our house. I remember that during the winters we had to trudge through snow up to our waists.

The land was very sandy in Amelin, and we were often very poor. For this reason, our parents sent us girls into service. None of us, therefore, ever completed grammar school. Life was hard, so father decided to sell our house again and move to Ryświanka. Here, the land was not better, but worse. Near us lived such Polish families as Gruntkowski, Domalewski, Urbański, Filip, Dzikoński; and Ukrainian families, such as Omel'ko, Mykyta, Voronka, and Pasichnyk. One Jewish family, which owned a store, also lived nearby. There, we all lived together until the Second World War.

Aniela *(continued)*

How happy we were in our humble home in Ryświanka until the terrible war scattered our family to the four winds. Exile put an end to our carefree existence and burdened our hearts with sadness and deep longing for the bygone days of our childhood.

When the German armies invaded our territory they began to round up all the young people for forced labor. I and Janina were among those conscripted. Before we left Ryświanka in May of 1943, Mother, with my three-year-old brother in her arms, came to bid us farewell. It was a sad parting.

A German transport picked us up at Filip's house, the rendezvous point for our vicinity, and brought us to Tuczyn, where we remained for two days. While there, many of the young people escaped, but I and Janina, being afraid of the Gestapo, did not attempt it.

From Tuczyn they transported us to Równe, where we remained for another three or four days. Then, we were loaded onto a freight train and taken to Würzburg, Germany. On our week-long journey we were promised that we would be returned safely home that fall after our tenure of paid work. Well, we thought, at least we would earn some money for the family.

When we arrived in Würzburg we were told to disembark and wait. Shortly thereafter, many Germans arrived from factories and farms and began to sort us out like animals according to our looks and strength. It was at this time that I and my sister became separated from each other. This forced parting constituted a sad experience for us both.

I was taken to a farm in Meidbron, near Würzburg, where I was put to work in the fields. The name of the proprietor was Ambrose Keller. I had to work barefooted and bareheaded from sunrise to sunset, without pay; only for the clothes on my back and my food. It was hard labor, and the farmer's wife was very mean to me. I wrote many letters to Janina and back home, but I know that the German matron did not give me all the replies. I always cried when I wrote home. I always asked about my precious three-year-old brother, whom I missed very much. One day, Anna sent me his picture, which I still treasure. In it, he is standing near a building[5] and in his outstretched hand is a small apple "for *Lela*"—for that is how he used to call me. How sad I was. Words cannot express how much I longed for Ryświanka and my family. Words cannot describe all that we have lived through.

In October of that year, some high-ranking Germans came and rounded up about sixty of us from the various farms. They took us all to Würzburg to work in a munitions factory which manufactured machine-gun belts. There were many of us here both from Poland and Russia. The Germans claimed that the people from our area were from Russia and proceeded to treat us accordingly. The work was very fatiguing and the food was very meager, but we tried to cheer one another up so as not to think about our condition.

In April 1944 I was taken to an airplane factory some twenty kilometers from Würzburg, and here I worked until 1945. I lived in a two-story building with many other people. We worked at night and had to walk to the factory, which was some distance away. Along the way, we used to gather and eat the apples which we found on the ground because we were constantly hungry. Each day we received three small potatoes, a little margarine, and some bland cabbage soup. I remember that one German boss, an old man, took pity on me and, from time to time, would throw me a piece of bread. He always did this very secretively so that no one would notice.

During the air raids we hid in a potato cellar where sometimes we would find a carrot or a potato, which we would eat raw. Most of the time, however, we just fell asleep on the straw until the air raid was over.

Because of the hard ten-hour night shift and the lack of food, we became emaciated and spiritless. During work we were so tired we'd yawn and sometimes fall asleep. If we were caught napping or did not work fast enough, a German supervisor, who patrolled the work benches, would hit us with a rubber truncheon so hard we could feel the pain for a long time.

When we became ill or completely worn out, the Germans would bring in new replacements and hand us back to the farmers. This is what happened to me. I stayed on a farm until May 1945, when the Americans liberated us. When we heard them coming, we all ran out to greet them, and we were very happy. I was then taken back to Würzburg, where I and others were placed in a city hospital administered by American medical personnel.

After I recovered, I was taken to Aschaffenburg and placed in some army barracks. There I met Dominik Tarnawski, who was from our vicinity in Poland and whose wife and family were brutally murdered by the Ukrainians.[6] We fell in love and married. Our daughter, Władysława, was born on April 2, 1946.

While we were in Aschaffenburg, many Polish families decided to emigrate to America, England, and other countries. Dominik, however, wished to return to Poland. He was ill from his mistreatment at Dachau and tired of his five-year exile. He longed to go back home. Meanwhile, it was being announced that everything awaited those who would return. But, as we found out too late, only poverty and hard times awaited us. Dominik was very sorry that he had come back, but once there, it was impossible for us to leave.

Before we departed for Poland, I met Janina, who told me that she, too, was going home. Neither she nor I knew anything about the rest of our family. We presumed that if they were still alive, they would also return and that we would all find each other in Poland. We left Germany in November of 1946. Through the Polish Red Cross, I was able to locate Janina and Stasia, but try as I might, I received no word as to the whereabouts of the rest of my family. It was not until I received their letters in 1958 that I knew they were all right.

My husband, Dominik, died of a heart attack in 1968 at age fifty-five. His life experiences were beyond the human capacity to endure. He was a good husband, provider, and father.

Aniela *(continued)*

Throughout my life I have always felt a deep bitterness and regret that we could not remain together as a family unit; that I was separated from my mother, father, sisters and brothers. Even now a great distance divides us still. We have become strangers to one another.

Stasia

In days gone by, in the province of Wołyń, beyond the Bug River, on the Ukraine, there were a number of Polish villages such as Cecylówka, Leonówka, and Kudranka. There were also a number of Ukrainian villages, such as Rzeczyca, Żalanka, and Ryświanka. Many Jewish people lived in the area but, being predominantly shopkeepers and traders by profession, they tended to inhabit the larger towns and cities such as Tuczyn, Kostopol, Równe, and Lwów.

It was in this general vicinity, near the village of Ryświanka, that my father purchased a small parcel of land together with a pine grove which provided us with firewood in the winter and wild mushrooms in the summer. Flowers surrounded our house, and we had a garden as well. Beyond the garden grew wheat and potatoes, but due to the poor condition of the soil, the yield was never sufficient to support our large family. For this reason, we were often sent into other people's employ.

I became a servant at the age of seven, pasturing geese and cows for the well-to-do proprietors during the summer months. In winter, I was sent to school but never graduated since, as I became older, the length of service increased. Like my sisters, I always sent the few *złoty* which I received as payment for my work to my father to help defray family expenses. This is how it was before the outbreak of the Second World War.

When the Russians invaded our land in 1939, they took pity on some of the poorer families in the area, and I recall that my father received a certain sum of rubles with which he bought us clothes. All the rich people, however—that is to say, all those for whom we worked—were unjustly expropriated and sent into Siberian exile.

It was at this time that I and my sisters returned home from service. Being between the ages of fourteen and twenty-five, we girls entertained the usual secrets of youth, and often got on our mother's nerves with our constant whispering and gossip. Our brothers, being quite a bit younger than we, never concerned themselves with our affairs, and spent their time playing games of their own devising in the yard, fields, and woods. Although we were poorer than ever before, at least we were together and happy.

Much of my and my sisters' happiness in those days stemmed from living near the Domalewski family, a fine, upstanding family with a widowed mother, one girl (Placyda)—and four boys. As we had four girls in ours, it was only natural that much neighborly visitation took place. Eventually, I became engaged to Felek (born in 1915), and Antek planned to marry Janina. The other two boys, Józek and Felicjan, went off to war.

My fiancé also served in the Polish Army (*Ochrona Pogranicza*) for a while and consequently wore a grey uniform resembling that of the police. When the Russians came into our area, they thought that he was a member of the militia and called him several times for hearings before the NKVD. During these proceedings, Felek was very much afraid that they would ship him off to Siberia, but somehow, he was finally able to clarify the situation and they left him alone. All in all, while our parents worried about the events of the war, we children were making the most of our youth and enjoying our homecoming immensely.

Our happiness, however, did not last very long. In 1941, the German armies marched through our land and began to deport all the young people to forced-labor camps. Many of our neighbors' children, including Gruntkowski's two oldest sons, were among the first conscripts. Felek and his cousin, Marysia Dzikoński, were also conscripted but escaped in transit and came home, where they went into hiding and lived in the woods for over a year. If they came to visit us, it was only at night and for short periods of time. Later, we found out that the Germans would often murder the families of the escapees out of revenge, but somehow their families were spared. In time, my two sisters, Aniela and Janina, as well as my father, were also deported.

Meanwhile, under Nazi instigation, the Ukrainians began to kill all the Polish people in our area, beginning with the most recent arrivals. As a precaution, many Polish families began to keep nightly watches and constructed secret tunnels leading from underneath the makeshift altars to shelters in their gardens, orchards, and fields. Toward the end, people often slept in these underground passageways. My father took similar precautions. Our shelter was located in the woods behind the barn and was covered with logs and branches. Just before our own exile, we used to sleep in this shelter for fear of being murdered in the middle of the night.

When the Ukrainians began to surround and burn entire Polish settlements—such as the one at Leonówka where the family of our cousin, Stasia, was brutally murdered—everyone in our neighborhood decided to seek protection in the town of Tuczyn. I went with the Domalewski family and Anna with the Gruntkowskis.

How sad we were to leave our house, our lands, our dear animals, and our barns full of recently harvested hay and grain. Felek was especially heartbroken to leave behind his three young colts which he had raised so lovingly, as well as the two old family horses. My heart, on the other hand, went out to my poor mother and my young brothers—all that now remained of my family. There was no one to help them, since our neighbors' wagons were full of baggage and children and everyone was looking out for themselves. Being without a husband

Stasia *(continued)*

or means of transportation, my mother was left alone and defenseless to face the murdering Ukrainians and the Nazis. To us she said, "I have never harmed anyone in my whole life, why should they want to kill me and my children?" And so we left.

Once we arrived in Tuczyn, Felek and I procured a hasty wedding as the German transports were already waiting to take us to Równe. In Równe we were loaded on a freight train and deported in congested boxcars to Nazi Germany—and poverty, and hunger, and unimaginable filth.

After many delays and a difficult journey, we finally arrived in a village by the name of Helbigsdorf near Freiberg, in Lower Saxony. There, we were sorted like animals: some going to factories, others to farms, and still others to dig trenches for German soldiers. Since the Domalewski family included two healthy males, Felek and Antek, we were put to work in a saw mill. The men ran the mill, while the women operated the machinery which turned out wooden truncheons. My first assignment required me to lug heavy boards from the mill to an upstairs workshop, but when my pregnancy became obvious, I was reassigned to a lighter job.

For nourishment, we were given a bowl of foul-smelling turnip soup, coffee, and bread. I lived mostly on the black, unsweetened coffee because I gave my small portion of bread to Felek to keep him alive. As for the soup, being with child, I could not stomach its terrible stench and could not even force myself to eat it. Hunger was rife in our camp, and many died for lack of food.

Due to our hard labor, poor diet, and the unsanitary conditions of camp life, a typhus epidemic broke out, and among those who succumbed to it were my mother-in-law and Antek. They were both taken to the camp hospital, from which only my mother-in-law returned.

Antek was a brave, stout man, as strong as an ox, but evidently he crossed his captors once too often. One of our neighbors, who was quartered across the hall from him, told us of his bloodcurdling screams as the Nazi doctors proceeded to murder him in cold blood, there in the hospital. Another man, by the name of Antoni Babiszkiewicz, who was once our neighbor in Leonówka and had a large family, was confined to an empty barrack for complaining of hunger, and there was starved to death. When, at the pleading of his family, they finally opened the door, he was already half-eaten by rats. There were many such inhuman occurrences in our camp, but we were powerless to resist.

After an uneasy pregnancy and much worry, my labor pains began on the night of January 10, 1944, in the presence of the sixty people who occupied the barrack. When the German matron who guarded us was called in, she began to yell and scream at me, telling me to wait until the morning when I could be taken to the hospital. This, however, was my worst fear because no one giving birth ever returned to us from there. After a while, when it became clear that the baby would not wait, the German matron called for help and had me transferred to the same deserted barrack where the late Mr. Babiszkiewicz had been devoured by the rats.

While I was giving birth, Felek kept peeking through a small window, and the German guard kept striking my legs with a wooden truncheon and ordering me to hurry up because she was tired and wanted to get some sleep. Finally, at 4:00 A.M., my child was delivered, and the German matron lifted him up to the window so that Felek could see his firstborn son. He weighed four kilograms and was such a quiet and beautiful little baby that everyone fell in love with him immediately. Even the German matron became partial to him, and later brought him the milk and cookies which helped to keep him alive until the end of the war.

Meanwhile, I had enough milk in my breasts not only to feed my own baby, but also, in spite of Felek's protests, the infant of another woman who had died in childbirth.[7] And all the while I myself was hungry; oh, so very hungry!

Somehow, my father found out my address, wrote me a letter, and even sent me a care package which contained some dried bread. How delicious it was! How nourishing! I did not know the whereabouts of anyone else in my family at this time, and eventually, even the correspondence with my father was broken off.

Although I went back to work about two weeks after childbirth, I was allowed to breastfeed my infant every three hours. While I worked, the baby had to remain in the barrack alone. I worried about him a great deal because of the rats and his lack of care. When he began to crawl, I made a kind of a halter for him and fastened him by means of a leash to a little wagon. One day, when I returned from work, I found him tangled in the strap, hanging upside down—and laughing.

After this episode, I refused to leave my son alone and demanded that either I or someone else be allowed to stay with him during working hours. I raised such a fuss that they finally allowed my mother-in-law, who had a broken arm, to watch over him. Even the German matron would check on him from time to time to make sure he was all right.

By the grace of God, we survived in that forced-labor camp until 1945, when the Russian army swept through Germany and liberated all the workers. Immediately after this, since all the trains were inoperative, we were told to begin walking back to our own country. So we set out for Poland on foot. On our way we chanced upon some post–German horses which we caught and harnessed to an old farm wagon. We loaded our children, the ill, and our few belongings on the wagon and marched behind it.

Along the way I would milk the cows which were grazing in the meadows, and we even slaughtered a few of these just to remind ourselves of the taste of meat. At this time there were many abandoned farms in the area, since the

Stasia *(continued)*

German residents decided to flee to the western frontier rather than to surrender to the Russians. We therefore slept in their barns, cooked in their fields, and bathed in their streams without fear of reprisal.

As we walked on, we split up into smaller and smaller groups until, finally, only our immediate family remained. Every time we found a horse, the Russian soldiers would take it away. This happened time and time again. At last, Felek found a horse with an injured leg to which he took a great liking. It was a young, smart, and beautiful animal, and must have reminded him of his three abandoned colts. To prevent the injury from healing too rapidly, Felek would sprinkle salt on it from time to time. Thinking the horse was lame, the Russians did not try to take him from us and so, after traveling all summer, we came to Poland in the fall of 1945.

Once there, we reported to one of the many repatriation centers charged with the resettlement of displaced persons. Since we could not go back to Ryświanka, which was now a part of Russia, they gave us an abandoned farm near Piotrkowa, in the village of Kamocin. However, when we arrived to claim the property, we found it to be already occupied by a local inhabitant who refused to leave. So, we went back to the resettlement center, and the police were sent to evict the illegal settler. Before he left, however, Mr. Kasperski vowed to throw us "Russians" off the land—for that is how we used to be called in those days, being from the Ukraine.

And so we began to farm. The location was ideal, the buildings were beautiful, the soil was black and rich. Moreover, we were given a post–German cow, and we already had our prize horse from the journey. The following spring we plowed and seeded the fields, and when the fall arrived, we harvested the crop and filled the barn. Meanwhile, I became pregnant with my second child.

It was all too good to last. Incited by the evicted occupant of the farm, a group of armed men invaded our property on three separate occasions and robbed us of all our possessions: our crops, our clothes, our money, and finally, even our beautiful horse. After each raid, they threatened to kill us unless we "Russians" got off their land. During the last raid, I became so frightened that I held on to my son for dear life. My brave Bronek said to them, "You bandits! You better not take our horse!" at which point one of the bandits aimed his revolver at him and I went into hysterics—and into labor. Eventually, they left with the horse, but without harming us. In the course of that same night (February 26, 1946), my second child, Krysia, was born.

All this was too much for us to bear. A few days after my delivery, we borrowed a team of horses from one of our neighbors, and departed for Łódź to live with one of Felek's brothers, who eventually left us his apartment and moved westward. Here we remained until the present day, and here both I and Felek made a life for ourselves and our family which, in time, also included Renia, my second daughter (born on August 11, 1956).

Meanwhile, it took me almost two years after leaving Germany to find out that Janina and Aniela were safe and sound and living in Poland. Much later, I also learned that my mother, my father, my sister Anna, and my three brothers were also alive and well, but alas, separated from us by a wide ocean.

Enough of all these bittersweet memories. All of this happened so very long ago, as if in a dream which, like a soap bubble, suddenly burst upon the water and is now gone. Now, there is only sadness, old age, and death for which there is no cure.

My husband, Felek, passed away on October 15, 1980. My youngest child, Renia, died on January 18, 1981, at the age of twenty-five. My daughter, Krysia, has been in and out of sanitoriums for most of her adult life. I am now seventy, I live alone. And I await the end of all this dreaming.

11

Reunion

My own reunion with my three sisters, as well as with my country of origin, transpired in a month-long trip during the summer of 1968 with my brother, Frank. I would have preferred to retrace my steps by sea and land, but in the interest of time, we decided to take a swift jet plane. The two-hour layover in Germany provoked some thoughts on my part, but the rickety old twin-engine plane which set us down on Polish soil gave me the jitters.

We were greeted at the tiny Warsaw airport by Stasia, Felek and their oldest daughter, Krysia—and what a reunion that was! Stasia was now in her mid-forties. Somehow, judging by the only picture I had of her, taken when she was a young girl, I had imagined she would look different—like my mother, perhaps. But this middle-aged lady was indeed my sister and I, her little brother, received in ten minutes' time all the affection she had been saving for me for the past twenty-five long years. This was Frank's second trip to Poland, but he was greeted just as warmly.

After our prolonged airport rendezvous, we took a cab to their tiny apartment in Łódź, where we met their son, Bronek, and daughter, Renia. Using Łódź as our base, we then proceeded to visit and revisit our two other sisters and, in a roundabout way, to tour all of Poland.

Aniela, "Lela," who had recently lost her husband, Dominik, lived in Chorzów with her two daughters, Władzia and Irena. Here, too, we received a most cordial reception from family, friends, and neighbors.

Janina, "Jasia," my oldest sister and my senior by twenty-five years, lived in Wrocław with her three children, Tadeusz, Halina, and Anna. In time, although several of my nephews and nieces came to visit, she would be the only one of my three long-lost sisters to rejoin us in Chicago.

While in Poland, we arranged for a general family reunion in Łódź and again in the village of Starkowa, where some of my distant relatives resided. In the final two weeks we toured our native country under the able guidance of Krysia and Bronek.

In our travels we visited Wawel, Zakopane, Pieniny, Przełom Dunajca, Starkowa, Wambierzyce, Gdańsk, Sopot, Mazury, Warsaw (Warszawa in Polish), and Oświęcim (Auschwitz)—with the wrought-iron sign above its entrance proclaiming *Arbeit Macht Frei* (work makes one free); with the two blown-up crematoria, the death ovens; with the obelisk monument and the multilingual, flower-bestrewn plaques which read: "Four million people suffered and died here at the hands of the Nazi murderers between the years 1940 and 1945"; with the sign at the front entrance in Russian, French, English, and German which said: "Let us keep silence here. This is the world's greatest cemetery." Blessed be Oświęcim, now and forever. Amen.

In all our travels, although we found the people always well disposed toward us, we were appalled by the catastrophic economic condition of the country itself. After all this time, there were still many signs of devastation especially in the cities. The housing shortage was such that, whether married or single, one had to wait ten years before qualifying for an apartment. Food was scarce. Political intrigue was rife, usually carried on outdoors for, as we were told, the "walls had ears." Police patrolled the streets with submachine guns and made frequent spot-checks of all citizens and tourists. We were told to report to the police station in every town we visited. We were told not to take pictures of landscapes and factories. We were told that we were ex-Russian citizens, since Ryświanka now lay in the Russian sector of Europe. We were watched and followed. Our initial chauffeur we dismissed when we found out he was a card-carrying Party member and a member of the secret police, no less—information which he himself did not volunteer.

Once, our new chauffeur made a wrong turn and wound up about three hundred feet away from the Czechoslovakian border. When he realized his mistake, he told us to wait in the car and to keep quiet, while he ran up to the approaching, machine-gun–carrying border guards to explain his error. After one hour, we were finally allowed to depart, being thankful that the episode did not end with our arrest. This was, after all, 1968!

Once, on a serpentine, mountainous road in Zakopane, the chauffeur almost killed us when the brakes failed on his old *Warszawa*—the only make of car anybody drove, manufactured in Russia. Half of our trip consisted of the mechanical maintenance of his Communist car!

Yet in spite of the dangers from the state, its chauffeurs, and its automobiles, we managed to have a wonderful time. Despite the chronic poverty of the country, it was rich in cultural heritage beyond words. It was not the cultural heritage, however, which made the most profound impact upon me. The profoundest impact resulted from the mere fact of my being back in Poland. It manifested itself visibly one day in the form of my long crying spell.

We were in the small village of Starkowa, all of us: Frank, my sisters, their families and friends, and I. It was evening. The sky hung low, and the last rays of sunshine were rapidly vanishing under the western horizon. We were just getting ready to sit down to supper, when a sweet voice began to hum, and then to sing, a melancholy folk song which I had never heard before. It was the Polish version of "Careless Love" called "*Wesoła Wiosenka*" (Cheerful Springtime). The haunting, minor key melody cut through my soul like a knife. Tears welled up in my eyes, and I began to cry.

They saw me crying. Felek put his strong arms around me.

"Cry, cry," he said. "You are back in the bosom of your fatherland now. Cry to your heart's content."

And so I did. In order to spare everyone (especially myself) the embarrassment, I went outdoors—but not before banging my head on the low-hung doorway. My niece, Krysia, accompanied me, and we just out walked into the open fields. No one came looking for us, and when my last tear was gone, I returned Krysia's smile, and went back inside to drink that good old Polish vodka. I may add that although food was always scarce in Poland, there was always plenty of vodka.

I found it most difficult preaching to my people in the country churches where I celebrated Mass. It was not so much that I would choke up after a few words; it was because I thought *they* should be the ones preaching to *me*. What could I have possibly said to them that they didn't already know, these old faithful people, long abandoned by their Christian God. If I had been brave enough, I would have told them about the death of God. Perhaps they knew that, too.

I will relate only one instance of creeping secularization. We were sipping coffee—served in a glass with all the coffee grounds—in a small village cafe where about two dozen people were watching "Zorro" on the only TV set in town. (The dialogue was in Polish!) Outside, on the village street, a funeral procession was winding its way to the local cemetery. Before the advent of TV, *everyone* would have been a part of that mournful pilgrimage, weeping and wailing for their dearly departed. ("*Ciężko ci na świat iść, ciężko i odchodzić.*") It was the traditional thing to do. It was always so. And here they sat, watching "Zorro."

We were not allowed to revisit Wołyń, but no matter; there was nothing in this playground of Satan but sad memories of days gone by. Most of the villages about which I wrote had disappeared without leaving so much as a trace of their ever having existed. None of the people, whom I have called by name, lived there any more; they were either deceased or displaced forever. Perhaps the very bells of Kazimirka, buried somewhere near Karaczun, had also ceased their mournful knelling.

(I now imagine Wołyń—after the Chernobyl nuclear reactor disaster of 1986, a few hundred kilometers to the east—as a wasteland of prairies and windblown deserts which the refugees in my story traversed, of forests and quagmires in which they hid from danger, of ponds, rivers and lakes which they navigated in their relentless search for safety, and of ghost towns from which they were once deported to the forced-labor camps of Nazi Germany. I also imagine it as a vast cemetery of mass graves—like those exhumed in 1992, containing the earthly remains of 1,700 innocent victims, including 500 children, of the OUN/UPA. On the map, it now belongs to *Samostiyna Ukraïna*, but as a reliquary of ancient and sad memories spanning a thousand years, it really belongs to us all.)

After our thirty days were up, in spite of my recently acquired American citizenship, I did not want to leave Poland. The last days, spent in the old section of Warsaw near the Warsaw ghetto, were the most heart-rending. In 1968, they were still carting away the rubble of the war in wheelbarrows! I wished I could have stayed for a few more days, just a few more. Unlike Frank, I did not have to rush back "home." Our departure, however, could not be delayed.

So, back I came—with four hundred photographs, so that I would never forget my precious moments in Poland. Back I came—with a small piece of brick from one of the blown-up crematoria in Auschwitz, so that I would not forget all those who perished there. Back I came—with a film container full of bloodstained Polish soil, so that from time to time I could kiss the ground from which I came and unto which I will return. Back I came—but my heart is still in Poland, among the rubble of the war.

Afterword

Objectively speaking, perhaps there is such a dimension as time. But in the realm of human consciousness, there is only the eternal moment, the great, all-embracing present, the everlasting here-and-now. Just as there is no sound apart from the ear, no sight apart from the eye, so there is no history apart from living memory, no time apart from human consciousness. One can deny many things, but not the centrality of man in the otherwise meaningless commingling of essence and existence.

Objectively speaking, perhaps there is such a dimension as freedom. But in the realm of human experience, it only exists in the eternal moment, the great, all-embracing present, the everlasting here-and-now. Once spent, that precious fragment of existence enters the domain of living memory and human consciousness, and becomes subject to the inexorable laws of historical necessity.

And so, the necessary war must continue in all its magnitude in the living memory of its survivors. It cannot end, it will not end until the last remnant—Jew or gentile—is no more. Only then will that moment of time cease, that moment of agony end once and for all. Then, the world will be set free at last of that horror that was, is Nazi Germany. But until the last child of the war disappears from the face of the earth, the drama must continue unabated and unchanged, in accordance with the laws of historical necessity, and the script set forth by those pursuing freely a terrible course of action in the timeless past.

Come Panie Domalewski, come old man:

Wołają do nas te rdzawe dzwony
Prawie czas je wykopać.

Notes

Chapter 1: Ryświanka

1. In Tuczyn, there was one Polish Roman Catholic church, three Jewish synagogues, two Ukrainian Orthodox churches, and one Lutheran church. The Lutheran church was attended by the German population from the so-called "German colonies" surrounding the town. After the Soviet invasion of 1939, all the Germans in our area were repatriated and their lands given to Ukrainian settlers from Galicia.

2. The story of the stork is one of those special family memories which, although not easily forgotten, lends itself readily to subsequent elaboration. Therefore, I am not surprised that there are several versions of this tale, each representing a subjective perception of how things appeared to be over fifty years ago. Since my own recollection does not reach back that far, I shall here, as elsewhere, rely on the collective memory of my family of orientation, which does. In fact, that collective consciousness spans a full century and then some.

3. Philip T. Weller, S.T.D. (ed.), *The Roman Ritual* (Milwaukee: Bruce, 1964), pp. 415–16. What we heard, but did not understand, was the following: "*Pax huic domui, et omnibus habitantibus in ea. OREMUS. Exaudi nos, Domine sancte, Pater omnipotens, aeterne Deus: et sicut domos Hebraeorum in exitu de Aegypto, agni sanguine linitas (quod pascha nostrum, in quo immolatus est Christus, figurabat), ab Angelo percutiente custodisti; ita mittere digneris sanctum Angelum tuum de coelis, qui custodiat, foveat, protegat, visitet, atque defendat omnes habitantes in hoc habitaculo. Per eumdem Christum Dominum nostrum. Amen.*" From the *Ritual of Piotrków*, 1623 and 1629 (approval dates). The full reference is as follows: *Ritualis, Pars Altera, De Caeremoniis Ecclesiasticis Ex Decreto Synodi Provinc. Petricoviensis Ad Uniformem Ecclesiarum Regni Poloniae Usum, Accuratissime Edita* (Cracoviae: Saec. Congr. Missionis Domus Stradomiensis, 1885), pp. 445–46.

4. For an interesting set of rubrics to complement the *Ritual of Piotrków, op. cit.*, see Biskup Ant. Jul. Nowowiejski (ed.), *Ceremoniał Parafjalny, Przewodnik Liturgiczny dla Duchowieństwa Pasterstwem Dusz Zajętego*, Vol. II, sixth edition (Płock: Kurjera Płockiego i Mazura, 1923), esp. pp. 114–16, which deal with the paschal season.

5. ". . . and after having drunk to excess, they were scarcely able to return to raise Christ the Lord from the sepulchre, yes, were even unfit to celebrate the sacrifice of the Mass on that festive day itself, with great scandal [to the faithful] and disgrace to the clergy." From the Synod of Płock, 1793. In Nowowiejski (ed.), *op. cit.*, pp. 218–19.

6. And no wonder, there was even a blessing for more holy water!

7. "And I was there among the guests, drinking both mead and wine
And what I saw and what I heard, I placed within this rhyme."— From some ancient ending to a rhyming yarn.

8. "How many elements are there?" we would tease our mother. "Five," she would reply. "Earth, air, water, fire, and salt."

9. These same slats and fenceposts would serve another purpose in 1943 and 1944.

10. At least the grand larders of the *polskie pany* in whose employ my sisters spent their childhood as domestic servants. Our humble household was much less endowed. But we had the wood, the warm hearths, and the snow, to be sure!

11. "Guest in the house, God in the house."

12. "I bring this harvest into God's house.
May this grain be fruitful,
From each peck, ten bushels yield."

13. "And I bring hay,
To place under Jesus' head and knee."

14. A thin wafer of unleavened bread, like that used in the Catholic communion service, but larger.

15. "Praise be to Jesus Christ. We wish you this Christmas that, by the grace of God, you may live to see another Christmas in happiness and in health. May your calves thrive like fir trees in the forest and may your domestic fowl be as numerous as the pests of summer."—Words from far away and long ago.

16. You know: "Renia did not feed me for three days"; "Ala forgot to close the barn door last night"; "Andrzej never mucks out my stall." Etc., etc., *ad nauseam*.

17. "Sprinkle me . . . ," etc. From the Catholic ritual of sprinkling the faithful with holy water.

18. *The Roman Ritual, op. cit.*, p. 412.

19. "Holy God, holy mighty-one, holy and immortal
Have mercy on us. (3x)

"From wind, hunger, fire and war
Deliver us, O Lord. (3x)

"From a sudden and unexpected death
Preserve us, O Lord. (3x)

"We sinners plead with you, O Lord,
Hear us, O Lord." (3x)

In Laurentius Grabski (ed.), *Ecclesiasticum Polonicis* (Gnesnae: Joannis B. Lange, 1895), pp. 171–72. (Translation mine.)

20. "On entering life and leaving, we are torn.
If the choice was ours to make, we would not be born,
We would wish to skip this war, which calls itself life,
We would stay with Mother Earth and by-pass this strife."

Maria Konopnicka, "W Dolinie Skawy," in *Zbiór Nowel i Obrazków* (Pittsburgh, Pa.: Związek Polek w Ameryce, 1945), p. 456. (Translation mine.)

21. "Beyond the mountains, beyond the forests, beyond the seven rivers, there lived. . ."

22. *Nazi Conspiracy and Aggression* (hereafter: *NCA*), 10 vols. (Washington: U.S. Government Printing Office, 1946), Vol. IV, pp. 553–54. (Nuremberg Document 2233-C-PS.) Hereafter, N.D. will stand for Nuremberg Document.

23. A symbol of Ukrainian independence, the Hetman's trident was the emblem of the Ukrainian Nationalists. The so-called Hetmanate was a seventeenth-century autonomous Cossack body politic.

24. Irena Grudzinska-Gross and Jan Tomasz Gross (eds.), *War Through Children's Eyes: The Soviet Occupation of Poland and the Deportations, 1939–1941*

(Stanford: Hoover Institution Press, 1981), p. 203. This work provides 120 moving accounts written by children of the Soviet occupation of eastern Poland. This quoted passage and those which follow come from the section (pp. 169–213) which deals specifically with the province of Wołyń.

25. *Ibid.*, p. 211.
26. *Ibid.*, p. 201.
27. *Ibid.*, p. 171.
28. *Ibid.*, p. 169.
29. *Ibid.*, p. 181.
30. *Ibid.*, p. 198.
31. *Ibid.*, p. 178.
32. *Ibid.*, p. 185.
33. *Ibid.*, p. 193.
34. *Ibid.*, p. 180.
35. *Ibid.*, p. 190.
36. *Ibid.*, p. 191.
37. *Ibid.*, p. 175.
38. *Ibid.*, p. 196.
39. The legendary Ukrainian folk hero Taras Bulba, whose name Borovets took, supposedly killed his own son for falling in love with a Polish girl:

> "Well, what are we going to do now?" said Taras, looking him straight in the eyes. But Andrii could make no reply to this, and stood with his eyes fixed on the ground.
> "Well, son; did your Lyakhs help you?"
> Andrii made no answer.
> "To think that you should be such a traitor! that you should betray your faith! betray your comrades! Dismount from your horse!"
> Obedient as a child, he dismounted, and stood before Taras more dead than alive.
> "Stand still, do not move! I gave you life, I will also kill you!" said Taras, and, retreating a step backwards, he brought his gun up to his shoulder. Andrii was white as a sheet; his lips moved gently, and he uttered a name; but it was not the name of his native land, nor of his mother, nor his brother; it was the name of the beautiful Pole. Taras fired.

From Nikolay Gogol, *Taras Bulba,* trans. by C.J. Hogarth (New York: Dutton, 1977), pp. 106–107.

Several authors, including Klym Dmytruk, "Role of the Catholic and Orthodox Clergy During the Nazi Occupation" in B.F. Sabrin (ed.), *Alliance for Murder: The Nazi-Ukrainian Nationalist Partnership in Genocide* (New York: Sarpedon, 1991), p. 259, and Edward Prus, *Herosi spod znaku tryzuba: Konowalec, Bandera, Szuchewycz* (Warszawa: Instytut Wydawniczy Związków Zawodowych, 1985), p. 116, attest to the fact that Bandera was the son of a Greek Catholic (i.e. Ukrainian Catholic) priest.

40. The first and last stanza of Konopnicka's poem, *op. cit.*, pp. 456, 460. (Translation mine.)

> "Welcomed is the good death and the easy end,
> Welcomed is the quiet grave to which me you send,
> You must now return, your own road to trod,
> While I rest in peace in the bosom of God."

Chapter 2: Dies Irae

1. From the outset let me state clearly and unambiguously that not all Ukrainians were nationalists, or fascists, or Nazi-nationalist collaborators, or Nazi-nationalist sympathizers—even in Wołyń, the hotbed of extreme Ukrainian nationalism, the epicenter of the Nazi-Ukrainian Nationalist alliance, and the pupil of the eye of the storm. Those who were, placed the attainment of national sovereignty above all else, including common decency and morality. For them, the end justified the means, any and all means. Their rampant fascist fanaticism not only embraced in a *danse macabre* all non–Ukrainians—Jews, Russians, Poles, Gypsies, together with all other ethnic or religious groups—it also turned its venom, perhaps with greater self-righteous vehemence, against the Ukrainian people and even fellow-nationals who did not espouse the cause of the OUN/UPA. All of these suffered at their hands; all of these, together with their homes, villages and towns, were "ethnically cleansed," were "pacified," were subjected to "special action," "hay action," murder, pillage, rape, and systematic "liquidation." Words fail when such radical evil visits humanity from time to time. Silence and memory alone can fill the void left by the universal sigh of humanity when confronted by evidence of such satanic visitations.

2. In William Shirer, *The Rise and Fall of the Third Reich* (Greenwich, Conn.: Fawcett, 1960), p. 611.

3. *Ibid.*, p. 839.

4. *Trials of War Criminals Before the Nuremberg Military Tribunals* (hereafter: *TWC*), 15 vols. (Washington: U.S. Government Printing Office, 1951–52), Vol. XII, p. 1086.

5. *Trial of the Major War Criminals Before the International Military Tribunal* (hereafter: *TMWC*), 42 vols. (published at Nuremberg in 1949), Vol. XV, p. 350.

6. *Ibid.*, Vol. X, p. 519.

7. *Documents on German Foreign Policy 1918–45* (hereafter: *DGFP*), Series D, 1937–45, 10 vols. (Washington: U.S. Department of State, 1957), Vol. VIII. Files of the German Foreign Office, Schulenburg Dispatch, September 10, pp. 76–77. In Shirer, *op. cit.*, p. 831.

8. *TWC*, Documentary Survey by Vice-Admiral Ossman, Vol. XXXIV, p. 674. See Ihor Kamenetsky, *Hitler's Occupation of Ukraine 1941–1944* (Milwaukee: Marquette University Press, 1956), pp. 19–20.

9. Schulenburg Dispatch, September 10, as quoted by Shirer, *op. cit.*, p.832.

10. *Ibid.*, p. 835. For the text of the treaty and secret protocols, see Schulenburg Dispatch, September 10, pp. 164–68.

11. "Dear mother, do not be afraid. Please let the girls stay a little while longer. They'll go right in."

12. In Alexander Werth, *Russia at War 1941–1945* (New York: Dutton, 1964), pp. 58–59.

13. German-appointed Hetman of the Ukraine in 1918.

14. Head of an ephemeral Ukrainian nationalist government in 1918. Known for his banditry and anti–Semitic pogroms, he was assassinated in Paris by Samuel Schwartzbard, a Jew, in 1928.

15. And all of these armies to be followed shortly by the German Army; the Polish Home Army (AK); a mixed assortment of various pro–Nazi armies such as the Russian Liberation Army (ROA), the Ukrainian Liberation Army (UVV), and the Ukrainian National Army (UNA); and finally, the Red Army once more in 1944 . . . which was to remain in Wołyń for nearly half a century.

16. The Soviets consistently denied their part in these massacres until April 13,

1990—forty-seven years to the day when the Nazis shocked the world with their announcement of the discovery of the mass graves of some 10,000 slain Polish officers in the Katyn forest near Smolensk. Among these was Jan Zimny, the husband of my aunt's (Anna Łoś Piotrowski's) sister, Weronika. Weronika and her son, Zbigniew, were then exiled to Archangel.

17. Needless to say, none of these ambitious undertakings could have been carried out without the widespread assistance of local collaborators. Among these were the Ukrainian Nationalists and the Jews who, as members of the Soviet organs of oppression, helped identify and apprehend those marked for deportation, imprisonment, or execution. See Edward Prus, *Banderowcy-Defekt Historii* (Wrocław: Semper Fidelis, 1992), pp. 50, 74; Norman Davies, "Poles and Jews: An Exchange," *The New York Review of Books* (April 9, 1987); and Karol Liszewski, *Wojna Polsko-Sowiecka 1939r.* (London: Polish Cultural Foundation, 1986).

18. Grudzińska-Gross and Gross (eds.), *op cit.,* p. xxiii.

19. Orest Subtelny, "The Soviet Occupation of Western Ukraine, 1939–41: An Overview," in Yury Boshyk (ed.), *Ukraine During World War II* (Edmonton: Canadian Institute of Ukrainian Studies, 1986), p. 12. For additional information regarding these atrocities, see Grudzińska-Gross and Gross (eds.), *op. cit.,* p. 254, n. 63.

20. *The Third Reich,* "Barbarossa" (Alexandria, Virginia: Time-Life, 1990), p. 17.

21. *NCA*, Vol. III, pp. 525–26 (N.D. 710–PS).

22. Otto Ohlendorf's testimony at Nuremberg, *TMWC*, Vol. IV, pp. 311–23. The *Einsatzgruppen* were first organized in 1939 by Himmler and Heydrich to follow the German armies into Poland with the intention of rounding up all Jews and placing them in ghettos for the "final solution."

23. *Ibid.*

24. Sworn affidavit at Nuremberg of Herman Graebe, a German engineer, who witnessed the *Einsatz* commandos, supported by Ukrainian militia, liquidating the entire Jewish population (some 5,000) of a town by the name of Dubno in Wołyń. Dubno lay about seventy kilometers southwest of Ryświanka. *NCA*, Vol. V, pp. 696–99 (N.D. 2992-PS).

25. Rudolf Hoess' affidavit at Nuremberg, *NCA*, Vol. VI, pp. 787–90 (N.D. 3868-PS).

26. Richard Lukas, *Forgotten Holocaust* (N.Y.: Hippocrene, 1990), p. 38; Richard Natkiel, *Atlas of the 20th Century* (New York: Facts on File, 1982), p. 92.

27. *Hitler's Secret Conversations, 1941–1944* (New York: Farrar, Straus and Young, 1953), p. 501.

28. A summary of a letter written by Martin Bormann to Rosenberg. *NCA*, Vol. VIII, p. 53 (N.D. R-36).

29. Erich Koch, *Reichskommissar* for the Ukraine, in a speech at Kiev on March 5, 1943. *Ibid.*, Vol. III, pp. 798–99 (N.D. 1130-PS).

30. Bormann's memorandum on Hitler's plans. Quoted in *TMWC*, Vol. VII, pp. 224–26 (N.D. USSR 172).

31. Hans Frank, Governor General of Poland, quoting Hitler. *Ibid.*, pp. 468–69.

32. Hans Frank, *NCA*, Vol. VII, pp. 420–21 (N.D.s EC-344-16 and -17). In the dock at Nuremberg: "There was . . . Hans Frank, the Nazi Inquisitor in Poland . . . having become in the end contrite and, as he said, having rediscovered God, whose forgiveness he begged. . . ." Shirer, *op. cit.*, p. 1482.

33. Memorandum from Rosenberg's files. *NCA*, Vol. III, pp. 71–73 (N.D. 031-PS).

34. Report by a member of the Political Department in the *Ostministerium* for October 25, 1942. *TWC*, Vol. XXV, p. 331.

35. From Rosenberg's files; a letter from a German official to Governor Frank. *NCA*, Vol. IV, p. 80 (N.D. 1526-PS).

36. See Table II in Alexander Dallin, *German Rule in Russia, 1941–1945* (London: Macmillan, 1957), p. 452. In addition, millions perished at the hands of the Nazis in the Ukraine. Who does not remember the massive executions in Babi Yar (195,000 people), or in Równe where, between 1941 and 1942, 99,000 civilians were tortured and killed? See *Nacisticka okupace Europy...*, Vol. 1 (Praha: Nase vojsko, 1966), p. 196.

37. These dates are relative. Although reports of sporadic Ukrainian attacks appear as early as September 1939, the Polish slaughter actually began in the fall of 1942 and continued until the end of the war. The extermination of the Jews was orchestrated by the SS with the active participation of the Ukrainian auxiliary police, which had close ties with the Ukrainian Nationalist movement. The chief of the police, Roman Shukhevych, was a militant leader in the OUN-B (the Bandera faction) and later became the head of the UPA. In the spring of 1943, thousands of Ukrainians deserted the police force and joined the UPA. For additional information on Ukrainian anti-Semitism, see Raul Hilberg, *The Destruction of the European Jews* (Chicago: Quadrangle, 1961), Martin Gilbert, *The Holocaust: The Jewish Tragedy* (Glasgow: Collins, 1986), and especially Sabrin (ed.), *op. cit.* The latter contains many personal testimonies, eyewitness accounts, photographs and documents which detail, as the subtitle states, "The Nazi–Ukrainian Nationalist Partnership in Genocide."

38. My brother Franek.

39. My sister Anna.

40. See the "Introduction" by Piotr Stachiewicz to Michał Fijałka's *27 Wołyńska Dywizja Piechoty AK* (Warszawa: Instytut Wydawniczy Pax, 1986), and pp. 44–48, as well as the "Introduction" by Stanisław Wroński to Henryk Cybulski's *Czerwone Noce* (Warszawa: Wydaw. Min. Obrony Narodowej, 1966; 4th edition, 1977). The statistical tables in this section come from the *Mały Rocznik Statystyczny 1939* (Warszawa: 1939), as cited by Stachiewicz, p. 10. I have taken the liberty of correcting one calculation error in the second table. See Wroński in Cybulski, *op. cit.*, p. 8, for a similar table.

41. As quoted by Wroński in Cybulski, *op. cit.*, p. 11. (Translation mine.)

42. Wroński (*ibid.*, p. 13) states the illiteracy rate to have been 77.4 percent among the Ukrainians and 68.9 percent among the entire population of Wołyń. Stachiewicz (in Fiałka, *op cit.*, p. 11) includes a statistical table which shows it to have been 47.8 percent among all the residents of both towns (18.1 percent) and villages (52.3 percent), and adds that, given the Polish government's orientation toward public education, it is not unreasonable to deduce that the majority of the illiterates were Ukrainian. This table also reveals that of the overall percentage (47.8 percent), the rate of illiteracy among women (62.3 percent) was almost twice that of the men (32.2 percent).

43. The corresponding figure for Judaism in the province of Wołyń (1939) was 10.0 percent. In towns, the percentages were: Roman Catholic, 25.7 percent; Orthodox, 23.5 percent; Jewish, 49.1 percent; other, 1.7 percent. In the villages, they were: Roman Catholic, 14.9 percent; Orthodox, 76.2 percent; Jewish, 4.6 percent; other, 4.3 percent. Stachiewicz in Fijałka, *op. cit.*, p. 10.

44. Wroński in Cybulski, *op. cit.*, p. 13.

45. Paul Robert Magocsi, *Galicia: A Historical Survey and Bibliographic Guide* (Toronto: University of Toronto Press in association with the Canadian Institute of Ukrainian Studies and the Harvard Ukrainian Research Institute, 1983), p. 175.

46. *Ibid.*, p. 178.

47. *Ibid.* According to a report by T. Gwiazdowski (August 4, 1938), during June and July of 1938, 91 Orthodox churches, 10 chapels, and 26 houses of prayer were disassembled in the province of Lublin. See Wroński in Cybulski, *op. cit.*, p. 13.

48. Bereza Kartuska was a Polish concentration camp wherein all kinds of political prisoners were detained without the benefit of any legal proceedings. Founded in 1934 by Piłsudski's *sanacja* ("sanitation" regime), Bereza Kartuska housed 725 inmates in May of 1936, among whom were 420 Communists, 227 OUN members, 64 activists of the National Party, 6 members of the People's Party, and 3 criminals. J. Żarnowski, *Polska Partia Socjalistyczna w latach 1935–1939* (Warszawa: Książka i Wiedza, 1965), p. 159.

49. For a different perspective on Polish-Ukrainian relations during the inter-war years, see Edward Prus, *Bluff XX Wieku* (London: Koło Lwowian, 1992), pp. 29–88.

50. Stanisław Domalewski, one of those interviewed. He also recalls seeing a sign addressed to the Red Army on the gate of the village of Horodziec which read, "*Vytayemo brativ*" (We welcome our brothers).

51. Otto Bräutigam's confidential report to his superiors of October 25, 1942. Text in *NCA*, Vol. III, pp. 242–51.

52. General Heinz Guderian, *Panzer Leader* (New York: Dutton, 1952), pp. 193–94.

53. Erich Kern, *Dance of Death*, translated by P. Findlay (London: Collins, 1951), p. 102.

54. *The Goebbels Diaries*, translated by Louis P. Lochner (New York: Fireside, 1948), p. 185.

55. A.M. Andriievs'kyi, *Katekhyzys abo nastavlennia V derzhavnii nautsi dlia ukraïns'koho Het'mantsia-Derzhavnyka* (*A Catechism or Position on State Science for the Ukrainian Adherent to the Hetman State*) (Berlin, August 15, 1940), p. 3.

56. According to Hilberg: "In addition to the Baltic *Selbstschutz* used by *Einsatzgruppe A*, a Ukrainian militia (*Militz*) was operating in the areas of *Einsatzgruppen C* and *D*. The Ukrainian auxiliaries appeared on the scene in August, 1941, and *Einsatzgruppe C* found itself compelled to make use of them because it was repeatedly diverted from its main task to fight the 'partisan nuisance.' Moving with speed, the *Einsatzgruppe* organized a network of local Ukrainian militias, making them partly self-financing by drawing upon Jewish money to pay their salaries. The Ukrainians were used principally for dirty work—thus *Einsatzkommando 4a* went so far as to confine itself to the shooting of adults while commanding its Ukrainian helpers to shoot children." Hilberg, *op. cit.*, p. 205. See also p. 204.

57. "Little is known about the guard forces of Belzec and Sobibor," states Hilberg, "except that they numbered in the hundreds and that, again, they were mostly Ukrainian." *Ibid.*, p. 585.

58. See Robert Conquest, *The Harvest of Sorrow* (New York: Oxford University Press, 1986).

59. It may be noted that although Poland, using the occasion offered by Russia's civil strife, did annex regions of Lithuania, White Russia and Western Ukraine, it also supported the Ukrainian counterrevolutionary movement after World War I and offered military assistance to the Ukraine in its quest for independence from Bolshevik Russia.

The April 21, 1920, treaty of alliance between Poland and Ukraine resulted in the Piłsudski-Petliura march on Kiev (April 24) during the Polish-Russian war. This action almost ended in a disaster for Poland. In its counterattack, the Red Army had actually reached the suburbs of Warsaw only to be turned back by Polish forces.

60. "The Ukrainians were involved in the fate of Polish Jewry as perpetrators. The SS and Police employed Ukrainian units in ghetto-clearing operations, not only in the Galician district but also in such places as the Warsaw ghetto and the Lublin ghetto.

The Ukrainians have never been considered pro-Jewish (the Ukraine had been the scene of intermittent pogroms and oppressions for three hundred years); on the other hand, these people had no stomach for the long-range systematic German destruction process. Short violence followed by confession and absolution is one thing; organized killing is quite another." Hilberg, *op. cit.*, pp. 329–30. In respect to the Ukrainian Nationalists, however, there is little doubt that they and the Nazis were of like mind *and* disposition.

61. Bräutigam, "Aufzeichnung," Oct. 25, 1942. *TMWC*, Vol. XXV, p. 340 (N.D. 294-PS). In Dallin, *op. cit.*, p. 108.

62. Alfred Rosenberg, *Der Zukunftsweg einer deutschen Aussenpolitik* (Munich: F. Eher, 1927), p. 97. In Dallin, *op. cit.*, p. 108.

63. Rosenberg, "Denkschrift Nr. 2" (April 7, 1941), Document 1018-PS, pp. 29–30. In Dallin, *op. cit.*, p. 109.

64. *Ibid.*

65. In Antoni Szcześniak and Wiesław Szota, *Droga do Nikąd: działalność Organizacji Ukraińskich Nacjonalistów i jej Likwidacja w Polsce* (Warszawa: Wydaw. Min. Obrony Narodowej, 1973), p. 106. (Translation mine.)

According to Dallin, *op. cit.*, pp. 119–20, n. 4, the text of the declaration of independence is available in two versions. One concludes with the words: "Long live the leader of the OUN, Stepan Bandera!" The other includes the phrase: "Glory to the heroic German Army and its Führer, Adolf Hitler!"

For a translation of a typewritten copy of the "Act of Proclamation of the Ukrainian State," see John A. Armstrong, *Ukrainian Nationalism* (Littleton, Co.: Ukrainian Academic, 1980), pp. 79–80. However, none of the words quoted in the text above appear in that version. In his footnote 14, *ibid.*, Armstrong directs the reader to a printed version of the *Akt* in Mirchuk and other versions in Pan'kivs'kyi. Just how many versions there are and why so many, he does not say; an interesting and telling anomaly since most nations—as far as I know—have only one declaration of independence. See also S.V. Savchuk, "Akt proholoshennia Ukraïns'koi Derzhavy' 30-ho chervnia 1941 roku," *Novyi Litopys 1*, no. 1 (1961), pp. 3–25. Copies of the "Akt," circulated in Lwów and elsewhere in 1941, can be found in the Tsentral'nyi Derzhauni Arkhiv Zhovtnevoyi Revolutsiyi in Kiev, f. 1, spr. 5, ark. 3.

66. In Szcześniak and Szota, *op. cit.*, p. 106.

67. In Armstrong, *op. cit.,* p. 81. Andrei Roman Sheptytsky (1865–1944), Metropolitan of the Ukrainian (Greek) Catholic Church, was a descendent of a family which was counted among the Polish nobility (*ibid.*, p. 9) and the brother of the Polish general Stanisław Szeptycki, as well as the grandson of Aleksander Fredro (Szcześniak and Szota, *op. cit.*, p. 105, n. 120). He regarded himself as a Ukrainian and was a lifelong, ardent supporter of Ukrainian nationalism. The latter authors refer to him as the "uncrowned king" of the Ukrainian Nationalists.

Numerous references can be cited to the effect that the Metropolitan welcomed the Third Reich as a friend of the Ukrainian people (e.g. his congratulatory letter to Adolf Hitler, quoted in Sabrin (ed.), *op. cit.*, p. 50) and that the Third Reich welcomed his support as well (e.g. the letter of April 29, 1943, describing the transfer of funds—360,000 złoty—from the Nazi Administration of the *Generalgouvernement* to the treasury of the Metropolitan, *ibid.*, p. 258). However, I would not go so far as to say that the Metropolitan, who after all saved a number of Jewish children and wrote a pastoral letter in 1942 entitled "*Ne ubyi*" (Thou Shalt Not Kill), supported the murder of innocent civilians. See Taras Hunczak, "Ukrainian-Jewish Relations during the Soviet and Nazi Occupations," in Boshyk (ed.), *op. cit.*, pp. 49–51. See also Szcześniak and Szota, *op. cit.*, p. 174.

The latter state that some of the Ukrainian clergy, following the example of some of their leaders, blessed the extremists as well as their implements of death and exhorted the faithful to exterminate all non–Ukrainians. To illustrate their point, they cite a fragment of one sermon which was preached in those days in a small village church: ". . . *Dorogije parafiana! Jak szczo w zbiżu spotkajet zile, szczo z tym zile treba zrobyty? Nu, ot baczyte, Lachy, ce tože takie zile w naszym ukraińskim zbiżu. Treba nam ce zile wyrizaty z koriniami, na czysto, szczob nykały wie ne dorosło. . . .*" (Dear parishioners! When you find weeds among the wheat, what is to be done with those weeds? Well, look here, the Poles are also such weeds in our Ukrainian wheat. We must tear those weeds out by the roots, completely, so that they will never reach maturity.) From Z. Bogdanowicz, "Kronika" nr. 4–5, January 28, 1967. In *ibid.*, p. 175 and n. 97. (Translation mine.) See also Dmytruk in Sabrin (ed.), *op. cit.*, pp. 259–64.

68. German military counterintelligence service headed by Wilhelm Canaris (d.o.b. January 1, 1887), who served as a German officer during World War I. In 1935, he became the chief of the *Abwehr*. After the failed assassination attempt on Hitler's life (July 11, 1944), he was imprisoned, sent subsequently to the concentration camp in Flossenburg and, on April 9, 1945, "liquidated" by the SS. See Szcześniak and Szota, *op. cit.*, p. 62, n. 147.

69. Chief of the SP and SD, Report on Events in the USSR, No. 15, July 7, 1941, NO 5154. In Armstrong, *op. cit.*, p. 87, n.39.

70. In Alexander Werth, *op. cit.*, p. 788.

71. In Dallin, *op. cit.*, p. 123.

72. Adolf Hitler, July 16, 1941. *TWC,* N.D. 221-L.

73. Erich Koch's Inauguration Speech, Równe, September, 1941. In Kamenetsky, *op. cit.*, p. 35.

74. Otto Bräutigam's memorandum of October 25, 1942. Text in *NCA*, Vol. III, pp. 242–51 (N.D. 294-PS).

75. *Ibid.* In Kamenetsky *op. cit.*, p. 60.

76. After the head of the OUN (formerly the head of the UVO), Ievhen Konovalets, was assassinated in 1938 (most probably) by a Soviet agent, Andrii Melnyk became its new leader. Meanwhile the younger, more radical contingent of the OUN began to challenge the leadership and the direction of the organization and to win some support among its progressively military-minded membership. These included Stepan Bandera, Mykola Lebed, Roman Shukhevych, and Iaroslav Stetsko.

With the invasion of Poland and their release from Polish jails, these younger members denounced Melnyk and the OUN directorate and in February 1940 established a rival Revolutionary Directorate headed by Stepan Bandera. From this time on, the Melnyk contingent became known as the OUN-M, whereas the Bandera contingent was known as the OUN-B. We knew the first as *Melnykowcy*, and the second as *Banderowcy*. If we had to choose which one of these we would prefer to murder our family, I suppose we would choose the former.

OUN-M maintained two "training" camps in Wołyń: one south of Krzemieniec and another one near Włodzimierz. The OUN-B operated in Polesie (the province north of Wołyń) as well as in Wołyń itself. In the spring of 1943, these factions united into the UPA under the leadership of Roman Shukhevych, the former commander of the pro–Nazi Ukrainian auxiliary police.

Meanwhile, the Taras Bovovets ("Taras Bulba") contingent (organized in 1940) also operated in Wołyń, in the regions of Sarny, Kostopol, and Ludwipol near Równe—in other words, in my family's back yard. "Bulba's" troops, the infamous *Bulbowcy*, were said to be the first (in 1941) to call themselves the UPA. It was also they who initiated the brutal attacks on the civilian Polish population of Wołyń.

77. See Dallin, *op cit.*, pp. 114–22; also Magocsi, *op. cit.*, pp. 211–12.

78. Canaris, "Kriegstagebuchaufzeichnung über die Konferenz im Führerzug in Ilnau am 12.9.1939," N.D. 3047-PS. See also Lahousen, testimony, *TMWC*, Vol. II, pp. 448, 478, and Vol. III, p. 21. In Dallin, *op. cit.,* p. 115.

79. Kamenetsky, *op. cit.*, p. 9.

80. For the three categories in the preceding paragraphs, see Peter J. Potichnyj, "Ukrainians in World War II Military Formations: An Overview," in Boshyk (ed.), *op. cit.*, pp. 62–64. According to Potichnyj, "Since the war's fiercest battles were on Ukrainian territory, it is not surprising that Ukrainians fought in various armies and military formations, in large numbers and on all fronts." Aside from the military and paramilitary units mentioned above, there were also 4.5 million Ukrainian citizens in the Soviet Army, thousands in the Polish, Romanian, Hungarian, Serbian, American and Canadian armies (40,000 in the last), 160,000 in the Soviet partisans, in Tito's Yugoslav partisans, in Czech units attached to the Allied forces, in Polish units which advanced with the Soviets into Poland, and even in the French Resistance.

Some of the Ukrainian units in the second category mentioned in the text were used by the Nazis in the "final solution." For instance, see Hilberg, *op. cit.,* p. 330, n. 92, on the use of the *Baudienst* for this purpose.

81. Dallin, *op. cit.*, p. 119. The same can be said for the grander Soviet-Nazi conspiracy as evidenced by the Non-Aggression Pact of August 24, 1939, which allowed Hitler to initiate World War II.

82. These time frames come from Szcześniak and Szota, *op. cit.*, pp. 64–65. I have changed their last date (July 1944) to: "End of the War."

83. Stachiewicz in Fijałka, *op. cit.*, p. 13.

84. Armstrong, *op. cit.*, p. 73.

85. Dallin, *op. cit.*, p. 115.

86. Armstrong, *op. cit.*, p. 75, and also see his footnote 6.

87. See Stachiewicz in Fijałka, *op. cit.*, p. 14. The *Nachtigall* battalion, consisting predominantly of Ukrainian volunteers, operated under the Brandenburg Division which reported directly to Canaris. It was organized by Roman Shukhevych, and trained in Neuhammer in Silesia. When Germany invaded Russia, the *Nachtigall*, consisting of about 1,000 men, advanced with the *Wehrmacht* to the Galician capital of Lwów and reached it on June 30, 1941, the very day that the Ukrainian declaration of independence was being read over the radio by Iaroslav Stetsko.

Relying on Drożdżyński and Zaborowski as well as Cyprian Sawicki, Szcześniak and Szota state that upon entering Lwów, the *Nachtigall* tortured and executed fifty-one professors together with members of their families, and one hundred Polish students. In the following days, the SS in conjunction with the *Nachtigall* murdered about 3,000 of the Polish intelligentsia. At the same time, there appeared on the streets of Lwów civil patrol units of the OUN, which pretended to be a part of the Ukrainian militia and which proceeded to torture and kill both Polish and Jewish civilians. After Lwów, the *Nachtigall* marched on Złoczów, Tarnopol, Satanów, Proskurów, and finally Vinnitsa. See Szcześniak and Szota, *op. cit.*, pp. 108–10 and n. 126. See also Aleksander Korman, *Z Krwawych Dni Lwowa, 1941 Roku* (London: Koło Lwowian, 1989). Cyprian Sawicki's work is called *Ludzie i sprawy Norymbergi* (Poznań: Wydawn. Poznańskie, 1967). For eyewitness accounts of *Nachtigall* members' participation in the Lwów massacre of Jews, see Aleksander Drożdżyński and Jan Zaborowski, *Oberländer, Przez Ostferschung, wywiad i NSDAP do rządu NRF* (Poznań: Wydawnictwo Zachodnie, 1960).

Armstrong questions these "alleged eyewitness assertions" and states that "since . . . the numerous Ukrainian interpreters for German formations like the military field police . . . wore similar uniforms, they may well have been the real culprits." Moreover, he is of the opinion that this particular work (*Oberländer*) was written to "discredit the German officer Theodor Oberländer, who had supervised 'Nachtigall,' and at the time of publication was a member of the cabinet of the Federal Republic of Germany." He adds: "I have not been able to find any corroborating evidence indicating involvement of 'Nachtigall' members, specifically, in anti-Semitic atrocities." Armstrong, *op. cit.*, p. 54 and n.12, and p. 56, 1990 edition.

According to Dallin (*op. cit.*, p. 119 and n.2): "During the following days of chaos [in Lwów], it became obvious to the Germans that Bandera's followers, *including those in the 'Nightingale'* regiment, were displaying considerable initiative, conducting purges and pogroms." (Emphasis mine.) His references on the excesses of the *Banderowcy* in respect to the Russians, Poles, and Jews include: W. Diewerge (ed.), *Deutsche Soldaten sehen die Sowjetunion* (Berlin: Limpert, 1941), p. 45; Einsatzgruppen Reports, July 16, August 9, and 28, 1941; and Petro Yarovyi, "K desiatoi godovshchine velikoi provokatsii," in *Sotsialisticheskii Vestnik* (New York), Vol. XXXI (1951), pp. 138–49. For additional information on the role of this death battalion in the extermination of the Jews in Lwów and elsewhere see Sabrin (ed.), *op. cit.*, p. 8, and Dmytruk in *ibid.*, p. 260.

88. Kamenetsky, *op. cit.*, p. 55; also, Magocsi, *op. cit.*, p. 213.

89. Werth, *op. cit.*, p. 601. Born in Galicia in 1909, Stepan Bandera was an active member of the UVO and, later, of the OUN. In 1932 he was appointed as the regional director of the OUN by E. I. Konovalets. Working closely with the Third Reich, Bandera ("*Sera*") was the organizer of the fifth column on Polish soil. For his part in the assassination of Minister Pieracki, he was condemned to death by the Polish authorities. His sentence was subsequently commuted to life in prison. Freed in 1939 by the Germans, Bandera became one of the leaders of the OUN directorate and served as an officer in the infamous *Nachtigall* battalion. After the announcement of the Ukrainian declaration of independence (June 30, 1941), he was arrested by German authorities until mid–1944. Following his release he lived in Turkey and in Italy. Returning to West Germany shortly after the war, he resumed his leadership of the OUN. The USSR, in turn, proclaimed him to be a war criminal and attempted to extradite him, only to be prevented from doing so by the American occupation authorities. When the UPA was being "liquidated" by the Polish Army, Bandera resided in Munich near Kreitniayerstrasse under the name of "Stefan Popiel." On October 15, 1959, Stepan Bandera was murdered. See Szcześniak and Szota, *op. cit.*, p. 82, n. 58.

90. Kamenetsky, *op. cit.*, p. 55.

91. Armstrong, *op. cit.*, p. 111.

92. Werth, *op. cit.*, pp. 613–14.

93. Stachiewicz in Fijałka, *op. cit.*, p. 14.

94. The term SS is an abbreviation for *Schutzstaffel* (Hitler's Elite Guard, the Blackshirts). The *Allgemeine* (General) *SS* began in the 1920s as Hitler's personal bodyguard unit and ended up as Himmler's powerful secret service. The *Waffen-SS*, originally an elite Nazi para-military organization, developed into a military force consisting of thirty-eight divisions. Like the *Allgemeine-SS*, the *Waffen-SS* originally recruited only "racially pure" Aryans. After the battle of Stalingrad (January 1943), however, nineteen of its divisions were composed mostly of non–Germans. See Myroslav Yurkevich, "Galician Ukrainians in German Military Formations and in the German Administration," in Boshyk, *op. cit.*, p. 75. For a treatise on the *SS Galizien,* see Aleksander Korman, *Nieukarane Zbrodnie SS–Galizien z Lat 1943–1945* (London: Koło Lwowian, 1989).

95. Many of these interesting details along with the appropriate documentation can be found in Armstrong, *op. cit.*, pp. 170–74. For information on the role of the church in Ukrainian nationalism see his chapter VIII. See also John S. Reshetar, "Ukrainian Nationalism and the Orthodox Church," *American Slavic and East European*

Review, Vol. X (Feb. 1951), pp. 43–45; Friedrich Heyer, *Die Orthodoxe Kirche in der Ukraine von 1917 bis 1945* (Koln-Braunsfeld: Verlagsgesellschaft Rudolf Muller, 1953); Dmytruk in Sabrin (ed.), *op. cit.,* pp. 259–64; and A. Korman, *Piąte Przykazanie Boskie: Nie Zabijaj!* (London: Koło Lwowian, 1989). The Metropolitan's words to Kubiiovych come from Volodymyr Kubiiovych, *Meni 70* (Paryzh: Naukove Tovarystvo in Shevchenka, 1970), p. 61.

Kubiiovych's proclamation contains the following words: "Side by side with the heroic army of Greater Germany . . . we too come forth to battle our greatest national foe and threat to all civilization. The cause is sacred and great and therefore it demands of us great efforts and sacrifices." Source: *Krakivski Visti* (*Cracow News*), May 16, 1943. The text of the proclamation can be found in Boshyk (ed.), *op. cit.*, pp. 183–85.

96. Armstrong, *op. cit.*, p. 175.

97. Fijałka, *op. cit.*, p. 44. The founding date of the UPA is held to be October 14, 1942, the day on which Vasyl Sydor was sent to Wołyń by the OUN directorate to form the first Ukrainian Nationalist "partisan" contingents.

98. Roman Shukhevych ("Taras Chuprynka") was born in 1907 in the town of Krakowiec in the county of Jarosław. In 1923, he entered the ranks of the UVO and participated in a number of terrorist activities including the assassination of S. Sobiński, a school administrator. He joined the OUN in 1929 and in 1933 organized, among others, the attack on the Russian consulate in Lwów. Many of his skills in this respect came from the *Abwehr* "training" course which he took in Germany. In 1934, after the assassination of Minister Pieracki, he was incarcerated in Bereza Kartuska for six years. After his release in 1938, he became an officer in the OUN and in 1941, as major "Tur," organized and headed the Ukrainian staff of the *Nachtigall*.

In the general crackdown on the OUN, he was first arrested by the German authorities, then released and appointed as the commandant of the Ukrainian auxiliary police. In August of 1943, the OUN III Congress appointed him as the head of the OUN directorate. In September of that year, he became the Commander in Chief of the UPA. In July 1944 he was made the secretary general of the UHVR (*Ukrainska Holovna Vyzvolna Rada*, Ukrainian Supreme Liberation Council, established in that month and year) by which he was given the rank of "general" on February 9, 1946. He was killed in a battle between the UPA and the Russian armed forces on March 5, 1950, in the village of Bilohorszcza near Lwów. See Szcześniak and Szota, *op. cit.*, p. 141–42, n. 10.

99. Born in 1909, in Bystrzyca, Wołyń, Taras Borovets completed four years of formal education, served as a noncommissioned officer in the Polish Army, and owned and operated two stone quarries in the Kostopol area which he purchased upon receiving an inheritance from the USA. Before the war, Borovets was imprisoned in Bereza Kartuska by the Polish government for his connections with the Ukrainian Nationalists. When the Russian armies marched through Wołyń, Borovets left for Warsaw, where he was regarded as a confirmed fascist. When the German armies marched through Wołyń, he returned, voluntarily entered a police battalion organized by the SS, changed his name to coincide with that of a legendary Ukrainian freedom fighter ("Taras Bulba"), proclaimed himself to be the head Ukrainian hetman, began a newspaper called *Haydamak* (How revealing!), contacted the *Wehrmacht* and secured an authorization to organize his *Poliska Sich* (Polessian stronghold, later a territorial subdivision of the UPA). The manifest purpose of this organization was diversionary: initially to promote a general uprising and to wage war on the anti-German partisans in Wołyń. The success of his venture can be gauged by the rapid expansion of his small but brutal group into an impressive but rather irregular and equally brutal band of several thousand men.

In the general crackdown on the OUN when the Germans ordered him to lay down his arms (1942), he and his men absconded to the woods from which they commenced to terrorize the villages and settlements of Wołyń. Among the thousands of civilians tortured and slain were also Ukrainians sympathetic to the plight of their Polish, Jewish, Russian, and other ethnic neighbors. See Stachiewicz in Fijałka, *op cit.*, p. 14, and Szcześniak and Szota, *op. cit.*, p. 161, n. 61.

100. Armstrong, *op. cit.*, pp. 153–54.

101. *Ibid.*, p. 178.

102. *Ibid.*, pp. 179–80. Hung by the soviets after the war.

103. In Armstrong, p. 182.

104. *Ibid.*, p. 183.

105. Armstrong, *op. cit.*, p. 185.

106. For a bibliography on postwar Ukrainian nationalism, see Magocsi, *op. cit.*, chapter 9. According to Magocsi, the most comprehensive Polish history of postwar UPA military activity is in Szcześniak and Szota, *op. cit.* Armstrong, *op. cit.*, also has a chapter (XIII) on this topic.

Armstrong's book, *Ukrainian Nationalism*, was first published by the Columbia University Press in 1955, and again in 1963. The Ukrainian Academic Press reprinted the second edition in 1980, and published a third, revised edition in 1990. In reading through Armstrong's initial treatment of Ukrainian nationalism (the 1980 edition; the 1990 edition was not yet in print), I was constantly troubled by what I perceived to be his two major sins, one scholarly and the other scholarly and humanitarian—both "sins of omission."

For one, in the 728 footnotes (many of which provide multiple references) I could find less than a handful of Polish names, no Polish references in the 14 pages of bibliography, and no references whatsoever to any Polish archives, newspapers or periodical files. His references were predominantly Ukrainian and to a lesser extent, English, Russian, and German. Does it not stand to reason that if there is any truth to the "alleged" Ukrainian Nationalist atrocities against the Polish people, the very first place to look would be the archives of the injured party in whose interest it would be to collect, preserve, and share whatever documentary evidence it could get its hands on in regard to the organization which did it so much harm? Moreover, not one of the 73 persons interviewed was Polish, nor was it stated that any of the other "very large number of persons . . . who furnished a useful hint or an impression of the wartime scene" (p. 332) were Polish. I found all this to be rather strange.

Secondly, although the author covered a wide range of topics, only occasional and usually oblique references were made to the consequences of Ukrainian nationalism for the Polish, Russian, Jewish and other ethnic populations. I felt that, if not an entire chapter, then at least a good portion of the chapter entitled "Perspectives on Wartime Nationalism" should have been devoted to this topic. What I took to be a deliberate skirting of a fundamental issue seemed more than strange to me: I considered it morally and intellectually reprehensible. It's as if an author came out with a brilliant history of the Third Reich and failed to mention that there were some pretty nasty goings-on involving millions of people. In a sense, it seemed even more reprehensible than that because at least, by 1955 and subsequently, everyone knew what Nazi Germany was all about and an author could assume the "given." But how many people, excluding those involved, knew of the terrible consequences of Ukrainian nationalism for the non–Ukrainian as well as the Ukrainian population of Poland and the Ukraine?

When the *revised* edition of *Ukrainian Nationalism* came out in 1990, Armstrong got what few authors seldom get: a second chance to rewrite history. Having had 35 years to give the matter some thought, Armstrong certainly could have availed himself of this golden opportunity to add that missing chapter. Instead, he inserted but two short paragraphs and one four and one-half line quotation in chapter VI on this entire topic (pp. 110–12, the 1990 edition).

The first paragraph deals with Wołyń and seems, in part, to lay the blame for the "fratricidal conflict" on the Polish doorstep (i.e., some Poles, responding to Ukrainian hostility, denounced "covert Ukrainian nationalists to the Germans"). It ends abruptly with the statement that "up to the summer of 1943 . . . this spiral of intensifying antagonism had resulted in relatively few killings, at least among civilians." Not another word about Wołyń.

The second paragraph deals with Galicia. Here he states: "By the spring of 1944, the German police reported widespread attacks on Polish villages in Galicia; in April, 1944, alone the UPA killed 645 Poles. Motivating these killings, the report alleged, was a UPA order that all rural Poles were to be driven out of East Galicia—or shot if they remained." The short quote which follows is the remark of a *Waffen-SS* officer (Fritz Arlt) that the Ukrainian national bands did indeed "kill, often in the most brutal manner, Poles, Czechs, and ethnic Germans living in the countryside." (What? No Jews?) *Finis.*

Two footnotes explain the reasons for the unfinished chapter: one on the same page as the section on Galicia, and one in the following chapter (p. 131). Armstrong's first reason for relying "almost entirely" on German reports, which he admits are mostly "short military memoirs of encounters with the UPA," is that "the Ukrainian nationalist postwar sources on the subject are usually reticent." (I wonder why? To me that silence is absolutely deafening! It tells me more than all the Polish, German, and Russian sources put together.) His second reason is that the "abundant" postwar publications in Poland cannot be trusted—as if the Communist regime in Poland had a monopoly on propaganda and as if propaganda and the truth were always mutually exclusive categories. He puts it another way: "I am not competent to assess the degree to which such materials accord with a shifting official line." (Am *I* 100 percent certain that these Polish sources are trustworthy? Of course not. Their consistency, however, with known historical data, oral history accounts abroad, and my family's firsthand experience, leads me to believe that, by and large, they speak the truth. Now that Poland is free once more, I would be surprised indeed if the untrammeled scholarly Polish press were to "reevaluate" its earlier position on this matter.)

Armstrong repeats his brief apologia again in the footnote on p. 131 with a new beginning: "Moreover, neither my grasp of the Polish language nor of the intricacies of changing political restrictions on Polish historiography permits me to treat the Polish sources in detail." I trust he is better versed in Ukrainian, German, and Russian. But were there no translators in 1955, 1965, 1980, or 1990; no Polish sources other than those coming from the Soviet bloc; no Polish émigrés; no Polish displaced persons in the free world? Much of his own work is based on oral history, after all: seventy-three formal interviews as well as numerous informal ones.

It would have been better if he had never begun to write that unfinished chapter, let the classic—so loved by the Ukrainian press—stand, and altogether kept his silence on the matter, a matter which, in any case, he considers "too peripheral" to the theme of his book called *Ukrainian Nationalism.*

Finally, I take strong exception to the following words (present in all editions): "moderate, though somewhat indecisive tactics"—as applied to the *Bulba* "partisans" (a word he uses very often, but without the quotation marks) in contrast to the "more extreme course taken by the Bandera followers." Here is the entire passage (p. 279):

> Evidently the moderate, though somewhat indecisive tactics of the "Bub'ba" partisans were at first preferred by the peasants, who desired a leadership

composed of their own countrymen, yet not highly doctrinaire or radical in its demands. Later, the depredations of the German administration and the general unrest prevailing in Volhynia appear to have led large numbers of the younger peasants to support the more extreme course taken by the Bandera followers.

Although Bandera certainly was an extremist, Borovets was no moderate, and if Armstrong and his family had been in Wołyń at the time, and if his family name had been "Armstrongski," he would have no doubts about that whatsoever.

107. Szcześniak and Szota, *op. cit.*, pp. 202–4. See also Dallin, *op. cit.*, pp. 624–25.

108. For a listing and dates of the more serious terrorist and diversionary activities perpetrated by the UPA from 1945 to 1947, see Szcześniak and Szota, *op. cit.*, pp. 530–36.

109. Kamenetsky, *op. cit.*, p. 70. Needless to say, I question everything in this paragraph from the first semicolon to the beginning of the penultimate sentence. I will shortly comment on the "popular" support for the UPA.

110. A full-page circular entitled "To the People of the Occupied Territories," February 2, 1944. Issued by the Communist Party under the signatures of Hreczucha, Kornijec, and Chruszczow. Archiwum Wojskowego Instytutu Historycznego (Archive of the Military Historical Institute) (hereafter: AWIH), t-202/III/133, in Szcześniak and Szota, *op. cit.*, p. 483. (Translation mine.)

Incidentally, the Ukrainian Nationalists did not like the term "fascist" being applied to them or their movement. I suppose Hitler and Mussolini disliked it as well. According to *Webster's*, fascism is a system of government characterized by rigid one-party dictatorship, forcible suppression of opposition, belligerent nationalism, racism, and militarism. It is also a description of a political movement based on such doctrines and policies. Here is but one transparent apologia from those times as to why Ukrainian nationalism should not be confused with fascism. The author was an editor of the OUN's official organ, *Rozbudova natsii*:

> Fascism is the movement of a *sovereign* people; it is a current that developed out of a *social* environment and fought *for power within its own state.* Ukrainian nationalism is a *national-liberation movement* whose task is the *struggle for statehood*, to which it must lead the *broadest masses* of the Ukrainian people. Accordingly, Ukrainian nationalism not only cannot be identified with Italian fascism, but cannot even be compared too closely with it.

Rozbudova natsii (*The Reconstruction of the Nation*), no. 8–9 (1929), p. 262, as quoted by Yurkevich in Boshyk (ed.), *op. cit.*, p. 69.

Be that as it may, on June 3, 1938, the following words appeared in *Nash Klich*, a Ukrainian Nationalist newspaper: "There is now a sociopolitical system which is developing the world over: in one country it manifests itself as Fascism, in another as Hitlerism, and we name it here Nationalism." In Sabrin (ed.), op. cit., p. 15.

111. Hunczak in Boshyk (ed.), *op. cit.*, p. 45.

112. Armstrong, *op. cit.*, pp. 143–44 (Emphasis mine.)

113. Dmytro Manuïls'kyi, *Ukraïns'ko-nimets'ki natsionalisty na sluzhbi u fashysts'koi Nimechchyny: Dopovid' 6-ho sichnia 1945 roku na naradi uchyteliv zakhadnykh oblastei Ukraïny (The Ukrainian-German Nationalists in the Service of*

Fascist Germany: Report of January 6, 1945, to the Conference of Teachers of the Western Oblasts of the Ukraine) (Kiev: Ukraïns'ke Derzhavne Vydavnytsvo, 1945), p. 21. In Armstrong, *op. cit.*, p. 176.

114. Agencja Informacyjna "*Wieś*" nr. 33 (spec.), Warszawa, IX, September 8, 1943. In Szcześniak and Szota, *op. cit.*, p. 147. (Translation mine.)

115. *Ukrainski Shchodenni Visti,* July 26, 1941, in Sabrin (ed.), *op. cit.,* p. 225.

116. The idea of "nationalism" or "national consciousness" is really a nineteenth-century phenomenon. Its roots, however, lie in centuries-old antagonisms between or among territorial neighbors. I am not about to review the mountains of archeological, historiographical, archival, ecclesiastical, cultural, national, or regional studies pertaining to Western Ukraine or, more specifically, *Halychyna* (Galicia) and *Lodomeria* (the early Latin word for Wołyń). Paul Robert Magocsi's admirable work, *Galicia: A Historical Survey and Bibliographic Guide, op. cit.*, with its 3,000 references and 1,000, notes is enough to keep any interested party busy for a lifetime. See also Peter J. Potichnyj (ed.), *Poland and Ukraine Past and Present* (Edmonton: The Canadian Institute of Ukrainian Studies, 1980)—a collection of papers presented at the Eleventh (1977) Annual McMaster Conference in Canada.

Suffice it to say that the seeds of the Ukrainian-Polish antipathy in this whole area reach back to the Middle Ages when Poland was a free, wealthy, powerful, Catholic, and sprawling nation (the Polish-Lithuanian Commonwealth established in 1569—which never considered Ukraine as an equal partner and which, in addition, persecuted the Orthodox church). As with all European powers in those days, Poland's economy was rooted in the manorial system of agriculture, i.e., serfdom. As elsewhere, this heavy yoke was resented by the peasantry, both the Poles and the many ethnically diverse groups who bore its burdens. Often these discontents manifested themselves in the form of peasant revolts (e.g. the 1490–92 uprising in southeastern Galicia), various brigand and *haydamak* movements (in the seventeenth and eighteenth centuries), and revolutions (e.g. the Cossack revolution of 1648 under Bohdan Khmelnytsky). Sometimes these revolutions proved counter-revolutionary, as in the case of Khmelnytsky's signing of the Treaty of Pereyaslav in 1654 which allied the Ukraine with Russia against mighty Poland to its own undoing. As Taras Shevchenko put it in his famous poem and political testament, entitled "To the Dead, the Living, and to those yet Unborn, My Countrymen all, Who Live in Ukraine, and Outside Ukraine, My Friendly Epistle":

> And yet you boast that with our frown
> We once sent Poland toppling down!...
> You are quite right: for Poland fell;
> And in the wreck crushed us as well.

(In all this, it is clear that the destinies of these two nations were inextricably linked from the very beginning, unfortunately, to the detriment of one another. And one continues to wonder how things would have turned out for both of them had they been able to resolve their differences and enter into an alliance either with or against Mother Russia.)

With the repeal of serfdom by Austria in 1848 and by Russia in 1861, there came into existence a whole class of people (predominantly Ukrainian) whose sociocultural, sociopolitical, and socioeconomic needs had to be taken into account by whoever happened to occupy that particular piece of troublesome real estate called Western Ukraine. However, age-old patterns are hard to change and so, as we have seen, the "old system" continued under many and sundry forms and policies well into the twentieth century, especially in Wołyń. In the nineteenth century, the continued opposition to that exploitative economic system, combined with a rising rate of literacy, the international situation (the various partitions of Poland since the 1770s), and the spirit of the times, took on the guise of "nationalism."

However, from the very beginning (the ninth or tenth centuries, when Europeans began to identify themselves in terms of their ethnolinguistic heritage), whatever the nature of the protest, it was much more than simply a "class struggle" between the rich and the poor. It was much more than a protest over the oppressive conditions of life. It was much more than a struggle for territory, for *Lebensraum*, or freedom, or sovereignty, or independence—unless these concepts also include "culture." That's really what is was and still is all about: the very soul of the people, *ethnic* identity, always a two-edged sword. I may add that, somehow, America has been able to deal with the ethnic issue much better than the rest of the world—although, to be sure, at the expense of the entire native population of this continent and with the exception of that one "peculiar institution" called slavery and its pernicious fallout. God bless America, nonetheless.

Shevchenko's poem can be found in C. H. Andrusyshen and Watson Kirkconnell (translators), *The Poetical Works of Taras Shevchenko: The Kobzar* (Canada: University of Toronto Press, 1964), p. 249. The quoted verse is on p. 255.

117. Szcześniak and Szota, *op. cit.*, p. 156. (Translation mine.)

118. Cybulski, *op. cit.*, p. 17.

119. Dallin, *op. cit.*, p. 108.

120. Józef Sobiesiak and Ryszard Jegorow, *Burzany* (Lublin: Wydaw. Min. Obrony Narodowej, 1974), p. 261. (Translation mine.)

121. Armstrong, *op. cit.*, pp. 279, 289. "Strong" is a very weak adjective to use in the above context. Perhaps my maternal uncle, Paweł, overstated the case somewhat when he said in 1943, "There is not one Ukrainian house without a bandit." But then again, unlike John Armstrong, Paweł Górski had to pay for his bold assertion with his life. (See p. 85).

122. Iaroslav Halan, born on July 27, 1902, in Dynów, the county of Rzeszów, was a journalist and writer who authored numerous plays, novels, short stories and political pamphlets. In such works as *Under the Golden Eagle, Father of Darkness* (*Pod złotym orłem, Ojciec ciemności*) and the play "Love at Dawn" (*Miłość o świcie*), he attempted to expose the cruelty of the Ukrainian Nationalists. As a Ukrainian Communist, he was subsequently jailed by the Piłsudski *sanacja* regime for his political activities. On October 24, 1949, while serving in the cabinet, Halan was axed to death by the *Banderowcy*. The excerpts above appear in his article "*Na dnie*" (On the bottom) in *Wolna Polska* (Moskwa) nr. 11/52, 3-24/1944, as quoted by Szcześniak and Szota, *op. cit.*, p. 170. Also, see n. 84. (Translation mine.)

According to Armstrong (*op. cit.*, p. 222, 1990 edition), Halan was a Communist sympathizer and eventually joined the Communist Party. As an atheist, he "evidently collaborated with defectors to Orthodoxy" and "specialized in anti-clerical propaganda ... which assailed the Ukrainian Catholic Church, including the reverend Metropolitan Sheptyts'kyi, and the nationalist organizations." The UPA "freely accepted [the] responsibility for killing" him.

123. *Historia Wielkiej Wojny Narodowej* ... t. 3 (Warszawa: Wydawn. Ministerstwa Obrony Narodowej, 1963), p. 531. In Szcześniak and Szota, *op. cit.*, p. 157. (Translation mine.)

124. See Zofia Drożdż-Satanowski *et al.* (eds.), *Przez Uroczyska Polesia i Wołynia* (A collection of memoirs of Polish and Russian partisans in Western Ukraine) (Warszawa: Wydawn. Ministerstwa Obrony Narodowej, 1962).

125. See Szcześniak and Szota, *op. cit.*, p. 177.

126. AWIH, t-202/III/131, in Szcześniak and Szota, *op. cit.*, p. 482. (Translation mine.)

127. Szcześniak and Szota, *op. cit.*, p. 150.

128. *Ibid.*, n. 29.

129. *Ibid.*, p. 178.

130. Rosenberg, June 20, 1941, *TMWC*, Vol. XXVI, pp. 618–20 (N.D. 1058-PS). In Dallin, *op. cit.*, pp. 110–11.

131. *TWC*, N.D. 1058-PS.

132. Speech of Governor Frank, January 4, 1944. In John A Lukacs, *The Great Powers and Eastern Europe* (New York: American Book, 1953), p. 570.

133. In Werth, *op. cit.*, p. 945.

134. *Ibid.*

135. Werth, *op. cit.*, p. 945. (Emphasis mine.)

136. Sabrin (ed.), *op. cit.*, p. 5.

Chapter 3: Tales of Terror

1. Shevchenko, *op. cit.*, pp. 66, 68, 83, 88. Taras Shevchenko (1814–1861) is the most famous author in Ukrainian literature. These verses as well as all the rest in this and the next chapter come from his long poem "The Haydamaks," originally published in 1841. The collected poems of Shevchenko appear in *The Kobzar* (The Minstrel), a work which has become a kind of a Ukrainian Bible of inspiration and national pride.

The term *haydamak* (from Turkish for "robber," "pillager") was applied to the Ukrainian rebels who, binding themselves by a holy oath from which no mortal man could release them, proceeded to kill the Polish people and all those of non-Orthodox faith who allied themselves with them. The bloodiest of these peasant uprisings occurred in 1734, 1750, and 1768.

2. Szcześniak and Szota, *op. cit.*, p. 165. (Translation mine.) According to Ukrainian estimates, in 1941 the OUN had about 20,000 members, half of whom were under the age of twenty-one. In 1942, the "Taras Bulba" contingent in Wołyń boasted 15,000 armed men who terrorized an area of some 50,000 sq. km. and two million people. Although in its propaganda leaflets it often claimed, "We are a million," by the fall of 1943, the UPA's total membership was 40,000. For references on OUN/UPA membership see Boshyk (ed.), *op. cit.*, pp. 19, 29–30, and 73.

3. "Death to the Poles, Jews, and Muscovites!" Sometimes an attempt was made to divide and conquer. For example: the residents of Hanaczów (May 1944), Huta Pieniacka (February 1944) and Huta Brodzka (May 1944) were promised to have their lives spared in return for handing over the Jews to the UPA. The letter to the residents of Huta Brodzka stated: "Polish people of Huta (Brodzka). We turn to you to hand over the Jews, since otherwise we will inundate you with fire and iron. Consider your children, women and the aged. The Jews are not worth it. You have one night to make your decision. At dawn we will begin the attack, in which case no one will be spared."

The Jews, that is to say, these people's neighbors were not "handed over." In the attacks which followed, many Jewish and Polish people perished. In Huta Pieniacka alone over 1,000 people died, 600 of whom were burned alive in a church by the combined forces of the UPA and the Ukrainian *SS Galizien*. See *Na Rubieży*, ISNN 1230-4387 (Wrocław: Stowarzyszenie Upamiątnienia Ofiar Zbrodni Ukraińskich Nacjonalistów, Biuletyn nr. 3/1993[4]), p. 7. (Translation mine.)

4. Szcześniak and Szota, *op. cit.*, p. 173. (Translation mine.) Notices hung on Polish homes in the villages in the province of Stanisławów on June 6, 1944.

5. It is noteworthy that, although tens of thousands of Polish people lived in that vicinity as well, they were not subjected to Ukrainian ethnic cleansing. Rather, the Ukrainians and the Poles there joined ranks against their common enemy. See Wroński in Cybulski, *op. cit.*, p. 14.

6. According to Armstrong this is uncertain. See Armstrong, *op. cit.*, pp. 139–40.

7. See Hilberg, *op. cit.*, p. 205.

8. Additional sources on Polish partisans: S. Wroński, "Mało Znana Karta Historii" in *Trybuna Ludu*, 6, Vol. IV (1960), nr. 97; B. Hillebrandt, "Działalność Bojowa Zgrupowania Polskich Oddziałów Partyzanckich na Polesiu, Wołyniu i Lubelszczyznie w Latach 1942–1944" in *Wojskowy Przegląd Historyczny* (1961), nr. 3, p. 40–58. Memoirs: Mikołaj Unicki, *Pamiętnik "Muchy"* (Warszawa: Wydawn. Ministerstwa Obrony Narodowej, 1959); Józef Sobiesiak and Ryszard Jegorow, *Ziemia Płonie* (Lublin: Wydawn. Lubelskie, 1974); Zofia Drożdż-Satanowski *et al.* (eds.), *op. cit.*

9. Hitler. A memorandum (July 16, 1941) dealing with a discussion between Hitler and Rosenberg, Lammers, Keitel, and Göring. *TWC*, N.D. 221-L. In Kamenetsky, *op. cit.*, p. 68.

10. *TMWC*, Vol. IV, p. 26. In Werth, *op. cit.*, p. 724.

11. Werth, *op. cit.*, p. 726.

12. For a comprehensive study of the *AK Wołyń*, see Fijałka, *op. cit.*

13. *Ibid.*, p. 47. For additional sources on civil-defense centers in Wołyń, see E. Łoziński, "Obrona Przebraża 30 Sierpnia 1943 r." in *Wojskowy Przegląd Historyczny* (1964), nr. 2, pp. 293–99; G. Fedorowski, *Leśne Ognie* (Warszawa: Wydawn. Ministerstwa Obrony Narodowej, 1983); M. Juchniewicz, *Polacy w Radzieckim Ruchu Podziemnym i Partyzanckim 1941–1944* (Warszawa: Wydawn. Ministerstwa Obrony Narodowej, 1973), pp. 155–63; Cybulski, *op. cit.*; J. Sobiesiak, *Przebraże* (Lublin: Wydawn. Lubelskie, 1973).

14. Fijałka, *op. cit.*, p. 49. Other authors estimate the number of people in Huta Stepańska to have been between 16,000 and 18,000.

15. Wroński in Cybulski, *op. cit.*, p. 16. Cybulski (p. 203) sets the number at 25,000. According to Szcześniak and Szota, *op. cit.*, p. 120, around 4,000 UPA members together with around 6,000 mobilized local Ukrainian inhabitants participated in these attacks.

16. Shevchenko, *op. cit.*, pp. 90, 98.

17. The eyewitness account of Dr. Otto Korfes, a former general of the *Wehrmacht*, describing one of the many crimes committed against the Polish and Jewish civilian populations by the *Banderowcy* who assisted the SS and the Gestapo. "Mitellungsblatt," 1959, z. 11. In Szcześniak and Szota, *op. cit.*, p. 110 and n. 134. (Translation from the Polish, mine.)

18. For this account see Cybulski, *op. cit.*, pp. 65–67.

19. *Ibid.*, pp. 69–73.

20. This account can be found in Józef Turowski and Władysław Siemaszko, *Zbrodnie Nacjonalistów Ukraińskich Dokonane Na Ludności Polskiej Na Wołyniu 1939–1945* (Warszawa: Główna Komisja Badania Zbrodni Hitlerowskich w Polsce—Instytut Pamięci Narodowej in conjunction with Środowisko Żołnierzy 27 Wołyńskiej Dywizji Armii Krajowej w Warszawie, 1990), p. 22. The second account together with the quoted passage (translation mine) can be found in Sobiesiak and Jegorow, *Burzany, op. cit.*, p. 124ff.

21. This account is based on an interview with Stanisław Domalewski, an acquaintance of my family.

The town of Kazimierzów and its church were founded in 1629 by Prince Albrecht Stanisław Radziwiłł. In 1665, the town was completely destroyed by the Tatars and Cossacks, and on its ruins emerged the village of Kazimirka. The chapel was rebuilt in

1670 by the Rev. Feliks Bachowski. According to tradition, the painting of Our Lady above its altar was executed by Antoni Samołowiec and brought to Poland from the Holy Land by Prince Radziwiłł, the Orphan. As the fame of the chapel and its miraculous painting spread throughout Poland, the Rev. Jan Bielecki enlarged the chapel into a church (1770) in order to accommodate the constant stream of pilgrims. In subsequent years, a gold-leaf altar as well as an ornate pulpit were added. Eventually, the Blessed Mother was robed in a silver cloak, adorned with strings of pearls and coral, and graced with a precious-stone necklace set in gold and silver.

This ornate work of art hung over the main altar in back of another painting, that of St. Kazimierz (Casimir), the church's patron saint. On special occasions (such as weddings) and on all Sundays and holy days, St. Kazimierz would be yanked up into the rafters of the church and the magnificent gold curtain separating the two paintings would be drawn to reveal Our Lady of Kazimirka. It may be added that in Wołyń, as in all of Poland, the veneration of God's Mother equaled in intensity and sometimes even surpassed the worship of God the Father, God the Son, and God the Holy Ghost.

22. Hieronim Zarenbiński, Łucjan Rudnicki, his son Józef, Józef Wajdyk, Jan Burzyński, Feliks Burzyński, and Bronisław Burzyński. The last three were unrelated.

23. During his interview, Stanisław Domalewski said: "We all took an oath of secrecy. Perhaps, after so many years, it would not be a sin to tell this story now."

24. The following narrative is based on an interview with Ewa Kujański (maiden name, Kołosowski), Ewa Holubecki's granddaughter. At the time of my interview, Mrs. Kujański, a dear friend of my family, was dying of cancer in Chicago. Her mind, however, was quite lucid and her deathbed recollections, undimmed by forty-four years of tribulation, gave me the impression of a polished soliloquy which she must have been rehearsing for many, many years—as if in preparation for this one, final rendition. When I would interrupt her from time to time, usually for the purpose of genealogical clarification, she would say: "Oh, I go on blabbering away but, yes, yes, you must get it right. It must be put down correctly." And very patiently she would retrace her steps and explain to me again the things I needed to know. Then, she would resume her life's story at the precise point of the interruption. This particular interview constituted for me one of the highlights of this long journey into the past. Shortly after the interview Mrs. Kujański, to the regret of us all, passed away.

25. In her long narrative, Mrs. Kujański did not distinguish between the Ukrainian Nationalists and the general Ukrainian population. She only used the term *Bulbowcy* once or twice. Although the atrocities of which she spoke fit the general pattern of terrorist activity, in her own mind (as well as in the minds of others with whom I spoke), given the passage of time, the various distinctions within the Ukrainian population blurred and they simply used the word *Ukraincy.* After all, no one wore name tags in those days stating: "I am such and such."

Moreover, I was left with the distinct impression that although the vast majority of these heinous crimes were committed by the semi-organized, roving bands of Ukrainians, some also transpired at the hands of the victims' own neighbors. I was, furthermore, left with the impression that not all the Ukrainians approved of these practices and that many were genuinely sympathetic to the plight of the Polish people in Wołyń to the point of risking their own lives. Understandably, all the people with whom I spoke, including the members of my own family, professed a deep distrust of all Ukrainians from Wołyń—a distrust which is now generalized toward all Ukrainians wherever they may be. The word *Ukraincy* was voiced in such a way that I sometimes felt as if one would jump out from behind the sofa, brandishing an axe or a scythe and screaming: "*Smert Lacham, Zhydam, i Moskvycham! . . . Khay zhyve samostiyna Ukraïna! . . . Khay zhyve Bandera!*" . . . *or "Bulba" . . . or Melnyk.*

Throughout my interviews, always conducted indoors, my tape-recorder was viewed with suspicion and from time to time I would be asked to turn it off for a while. My own sister Anna, said: "All this has passed and perhaps it would be best if you did not write of these things lest some calamity befall us after such a book. Here in America there are many Ukrainians from those parts of Poland. Be careful of what you write. We live here in peace, let it remain that way."

I hope to God that I am not wrong in my contention that such instances of moral degeneracy occur only within specific historical contexts, that only the worst possible political systems bring forth the worst possible array of human emotions, and that America has never been, is not now, and never will be one of those perversely deranged, misanthropic systems!

26. Mrs. Piotrowiak lived in her native village until 1946. She now lives in America. The following account is based on a six-hour interview (with one day's notice) conducted on July 4, 1993. I include it here to show that the whirlwind of destruction which began in Wołyń did not cease at its borders. For a treastise on Galician Ukrainian Nationalists, see Edward Prus, *Kurhany* (Warszawa: Polska Oficyna Wydaw. "BGW," 1993).

The designation "Berezów" applied to a cluster of four villages. There was Berezów Niżny (Lower Berezów), Berezów Średni (Middle Berezów), Berezów Wyżny (Upper Berezów) and Berezów Bani. The term "*bani*" has many meanings from the noun "sphere" to the phrase "*do bani*" which means "rotten," "no good," "good for nothing," and also, "to hell with it." I believe the phrase "*do bani*" describes all the Berezóws of the day most admirably. Villages and towns with similar names were not unusual. In Wołyń, for example, quite near us, there was Niespodzianka I (Surprise I), Niespodzianka II (Surprise II), and Niespodzianka III (Surprise III). In terms of the events herein described, that also was a very apt designation for those villages of those days. We were certainly all surprised!

27. *Kocib, Kossiw, Kosiv* (Kiev: Ministetstvo, 1971), p. 21. A tourist guide and a pictorial essay on regional handicraft written in Ukrainian, German, and English—but not Polish. In the early 1940s, this section of Poland was a part of *Małopolska* and the Polish residents called the town *Kosów*—but that name does not appear in the trilingual title either.

There is a beloved Polish folk song about this area, which begins with the lively verse:

Tam szum Prutu Czeremoszu hucułom przygrywa
A ochocza kołomyjka do tańca porywa
Dla hucuła nie ma życia jak na połoninie
Gdy go losy w doły rzucą wnet z tęsknoty ginie.

There, the murmur of the Prut and Czeremosz plays for
the *Hutsuls.*
And the desire for the *kołomyjek* tugs at one to dance.
For the *Hutsul* there's no life like that in *połonina*
When fate casts him down in valleys, he soon perishes
from longing.

Prut and *Czeremosz* are names of rivers; *Hutsuls*, as in the tourist guide, is a designation for the local inhabitants; *połonina* literally means a field, the same root from which the word *Poland* comes; *kołomyjek* is a folk dance named after the town of Kołomyja. Incidentally, "Kołomyja" literally means "to wash wheels." The name probably originated from the practice of passing merchants' washing cart wheels at the ford of the river. (Translation mine.)

When I recalled the first line of this delightful folk song from my childhood memories, Mrs. Piotrowiak graciously obliged me by singing the entire song.

28. "Death to the Poles, Death to the Moscow-Jewish Commune" (i.e., Communism). Although she did not say and I did not ask, perhaps Helena also remembered that popular Ukrainian song called "The March of the Ukrainian Partisans" which the *Melnykowcy* liked to sing in 1942, which was so popular among some of the detachments of the *SS Galizien*, and which ended with the following refrain:

> *Smert! Smert Lacham! Smert!*
> *Smert moskowsko-żydowskij komuni!*
> *W bij krywawyj OUN nas wede*
> *My bjem komunu i Lachiw. . . .*
>
> Death! Death to the Poles! Death!
> Death to the Moscow-Jewish Commune!
> The OUN will lead us in the bloody combat
> We kill the Commune and the Poles. . . .

These verses can be found in AWIH, t-202/III/129, p. 11 and 44, Akta Delegatury Rządu, in Szcześniak and Szota, *op. cit.*, p. 130. (Translation mine.)

The Jewish-Communist-Polish connection needs a brief explanation. In those dark days many people of many nations, laboring under the conspiratorial theory of history, believed that Communism was a Jewish plot against the world; hence the association with Moscow. ("Wasn't Marx a Jew?" "Wasn't Stalin surrounded by Jewish advisors?" etc., etc.)

In Poland, moreover, and certainly in Wołyń, the Jews were often associated with the ruling class, i.e., the *szlachta*, the *polskie pany*—perhaps because they used to say, "The streets are Polish, but we own the buildings," or so I've been told by a Ukrainian acquaintance who prefers to remain anonymous. In truth, however, the mad reasoning of prejudice and discrimination follows a logic unique unto itself and needs no other rationalization.

29. "Beyond the San [river] is Polish; on this side of the San is ours."

30. "Hey, young men, *yunaky*,
Soon the Poles will be subjected to a pogrom.
We will butcher them with knives, pierce them with a spear.
We will cleanse the Ukraine of trash
Then, in the Ukraine life will be free."
[Translation mine.]

The term *yunaky* (Pol.: *junacy*) in the first line means "dashing, reckless fellows," "young soldiers," but also, in those days, stood for the members of the young men's "labor" brigade. The term "labor" as in the phrase "labor brigade" or "labor school" as well as the term "agricultural" was a code name for training activities connected with nationalistic enterprises, including terrorism. Helena recalls that at the beginning of the overt hostilities, her mother wanted to enroll Michał in the local "labor school" for what she took to be an agricultural curriculum. After a long look of incredulity, she was told by a Ukrainian friend: "Your son wouldn't last one day in that school." That's how she found out just what kind of school it was.

According to Helena, in her village as well as the surrounding villages, *all* young Ukrainian men were, if not in spirit, then at least in name, *Banderowcy*. "Because," she added, "they either had to join or be killed." She tells of a story of Bohdan Steblychyn, a seventeen-year-old Ukrainian lad who returned from Germany after being abducted for forced labor and refused to join the *Banderowcy*:

> They dragged him out of his aunt's home [with whom his ill mother was staying] at night and shot him about 200 meters from the house. When his mother heard the shots ring out, she wrung her hands in sorrow and cried out: "They killed my Bohdanek!"—even before anyone told her. Later she said that it would have been better if he had stayed in Nazi Germany.

This particular family lived about one kilometer from Mrs. Przygrodzki Piotrowiak in Berezów Niżny. She continued:

> I knew nothing about this until the next morning when I went to pasture our two cows. I remember that the old one, who would always take the lead, suddenly jumped over to one side and snorted because there was something in her path. When I went to see what had spooked her, I saw Bohdan's body lying there. Someone had covered it with a blanket.

31. The Ukrainian word for forester is *popereznya.*

32. A colloquialism for Russian-made automatics with large round disks underneath.

33. That year, the "Ukrainian" (Orthodox) Easter came about two weeks after the "Polish" (Catholic) one. "That was the kind of Easter present they gave us that year," said Helena.

34. Michał Przygrodzki (not related to the Przygrodzki family in this account) had two daughters, one married and one single. In the course of that night, the husband of the married daughter was murdered. She was left with two children, a boy and a girl. Later, she became pregnant by a Ukrainian who came to "visit" her. (What's a poor girl to do? By this time all the Polish boys and men were either dead, or in the towns, or in perpetual hiding.) Her sister also became pregnant by another "visiting" Ukrainian. When both were already in advanced stages of their pregnancy, they were taken one night to the oil pits (*studnie ropy naftowej*) just on the outskirts of Berezów Niżny, and drowned. Whether the fathers of the unborn children were involved in this bestial act, no one knows.

Therein, too, perished Mr. Nykola Dmytryszkiw. On the night of the attack, his house was burned and his son was murdered. He escaped and somehow managed to survive for a while. Once, when he emerged from hiding and came to call upon his wife and his ten remaining children—all girls—who now resided in the barn, he was apprehended and drowned in one of the oil wells as well. Helena saw his body in the dark well, face-down and bloated. She knew it was he by the belt in the back of the coat he always wore with the four buttons arranged in a square. She then told his oldest daughter, Julia, of her father's tragic demise. Julia, at that time, worked in Helena's parents' fields in exchange for food which she brought home for her mother and her nine younger sisters.

35. Unrelated to Helena's family.

36. Gienek's sister now resides in Canada.

37. I found it interesting that in all my interviews, it was the women who remembered all the tiniest details of their horrible experiences while the men, often speaking in generalities, focused on the "larger picture"—a gender-related mode of perception and recall, I surmise.

38. Hats with the Hetman's trident in the front. The adjective *mazepenkie* is a colloquialism which refers to that particular style of hat and defies translation. The hats were probably named after the eighteenth-century Ukrainian hero Hetman Ivan Mazepa.

39. This was a very clever lie for a twelve-year-old—a very good example, I suppose, of why Helena managed to survive the war. Those who were not so clever, or so lucky, simply perished. Their stories will never be told.

The word *kutya* deserves a brief explanation. On Christmas Eve, whereas the Polish people shared the *opłatek*, the Ukrainians had their *kutya*—a soup consisting of spring wheat, poppy seeds, walnuts, raisins, sugar, and honey. The *kutya* was served as the first course of Christmas Eve. The traditional ceremony went something like this: A single earthen bowl (*makitra*) would be placed in the middle of the table from which the father would take a spoonful of the *kutya* and, after exchanging wishes with all the members of the family, would throw it up toward the ceiling before partaking of the repast. The mother and finally the children would then have their servings. Much as the children (but certainly not the wife) would have liked to follow the example of the father, the privilege of tossing the *kutya* toward the ceiling was his alone. This was predominantly a village custom, although not unknown or unpracticed among the middle and upper strata of Ukrainian society.

40. Another episode dealing with the practice of nailing people to trees can be found in a London publication: *Kwartalnik Kresowy*, ISSN 0306 1221, Zeszyt No 125–126 (31.12.1988. Dodatek wydany w r. 1993), p. 42. A handwritten note next to a grisly photograph reads: "Kozowa-vicinity, county of Brzezany, district of Tarnopol, Autumn, 1943. In the vicinity of Kozowa, along an avenue of old trees, the *Banderowcy* carried out a massive murder of Polish children—a sinister, barbaric atrocity. Around the trunk of every tree, small children were nailed creating so-called 'wreaths.' They called this avenue 'The road to Independent Ukraine [*samostijnej Ukrainy*].' The photograph attests to the crime: four little children on one side of the tree."

The photograph, which shows three small, limp bodies bound to a tree by two strands of wire, however, does not seem to match the narrative. The same photograph appears in *Na Rubieży, op. cit.*, 3/1993(4), p. 16. The text on the following page of that publication (presumably referring to this particular photograph) states: "An eyewitness, Jan Kłos, reported that in his village the UPA fastened a number [*kilkanaścioro*, i.e., between 10 and 20] of Polish children by their heads 'in wreaths' with barbed wire to a number [*kilkanaście*] of trees lining an avenue to a farmstead. Over them, some ingenious fellows ['*dowcipniś*'] hung a sign across the roadway: 'The road to *samostijnej Ukrainy*.'" (Translations mine.)

The reader may make what she or he will of such discrepancies. The fact remains: someone did indeed execute these three innocents in this barbaric fashion! How I wish Helena would have taken a picture of old Vasyl and Anna! What a fine generational pair these two photographs, placed side by side, would have made: Vasyl and Anna on the weeping willow and the three nameless children on the sturdy oak!

41. Shevchenko, *op. cit.*, pp. 102–4. Maksim Zalizniak and Ivan Gonta were two of the leaders of the third *haydamak* insurrection.

42. The residents of Leonówka, beginning with the entrance nearest Żalanka were, by house numbers: 1. Jan and Teresa Bagiński, nine children; 2. Władysław and Marcelina Piotrowski, seven children; 3. Stanisław and Janina Bagiński, six children; 4. Antoni Babiszkiewicz, his wife, five children; 5. Adam Polekowski, his wife, two children; 6. Antoni and Anna Bagiński, one son; 7. Antoni Reszczyński, his wife, five children; 8. Stanisław and Marynia Piotrowski, four children; 9. Antoni Filiczkowski, his wife, seven children; 10. Antoni Bagiński, his brother and sister; 11. Jan and Kon-

stancja Bronowicki, five children; 12. Bronisław and Bronisława Urbanowicz, five children; 13. Michał and Weronika Urbanowicz, seven children; 14. Bronisław Romanowski, his wife, one child; 15. Mr. and Mrs. Urbanowicz, eight children; 16. Aleksander and Antonina Bagiński, one daughter; 17. Anastasia Bagiński (widow), one son; 18. Felek Łoś; 19. Felek and Anna Domalewski, Felek's mother and sister; 20. Tomasz and Zofia Sigda, one son; 21. Władysław Bagiński, his wife, five children; 22. Wiktor Urbanowicz, his wife, four children; 23. Andrzej Urbanowicz, his wife, three children; 24. Antoni Kownacki, his wife, four children; 25. Piotr Urbanowicz and his brother; 26. Stefan Urbanowicz (widower), three children; 27. Czesław Łoś, his mother and sister. There were perhaps two or three other families not included in this list. Moreover, an additional eight to ten Polish families lived on the outskirts of the village including those of Prokopowiec, Paśnieski, Kościelny, Bednarek, and two more Bagińskis.

I find this list particularly remarkable because it was recited to me spontaneously from memory, a half-century after the events of which I write, by Stanisława (Stasia) Plaza, my first cousin, the oldest daughter of Władysław and Marcelina Piotrowski—the occupants of the second home listed above. (We were seated at the dinner table at the time in Chicago. As usual, I had my tape recorder going and my pen and pad nearby.) This listing of families by house number and name, together with the many intimate details about each one which go beyond the purview of this narrative, is an eloquent tribute not only to Stasia's amazing powers of recall, but also to the tremendous social solidarity and cohesion which characterized the *Gemeinschaft,* prewar, European village life. The tragic story of the Leonówka massacre is the heart-rending account of her own village and family.

43. After the Soviet invasion, Zofia was replaced by a Soviet instructor and all lessons were conducted in Russian.

44. Later destroyed by the Germans; 600 people perished.

45. For Stanisław, however, this was but a temporary reprieve. After his deportation to Germany, he was placed in solitary confinement and cruelly starved to death.

46. Shevchenko, *op. cit.*, pp. 91, 113.

47. Now residing in Chicago.

48. Shevchenko, *op. cit.*, pp. 93–94.

49. This and the accounts which follow are taken from Turowski and Siemaszko, *op. cit., passim.* The entries in this work are chronologically arranged. See also Mikołaj Terleś, *Ethnic Cleansing of Poles in Volhynia and Eastern Galicia 1942–1946* (Toronto: Alliance of the Polish Eastern Provinces, 1993). For personal testimonies regarding Ukrainian Nationalist atrocities against the Polish population of Wołyń and Poland's other eastern provinces, see: Jędrzej Giertych, "O Przeprowadzonej Przez Ukrainców Rzezi Polskiej Ludności" in Jędrzej Giertych (ed.), *Komunikaty Towarzystwa imienia Romana Dmowskiego,* Vol. II (London: Veritas, 1980), pp. 300–52.

50. Aleksander Korman, "Osobowe i materialne straty Polaków wynikłe z działalności terrorystów OUN-UPA." *Semper Fidelis* (1993), nr. 2 (15), p. 20.

51. *Ibid.,* p. 19. See also Szcześniak and Szota, *op. cit.*, p. 170.

52. Szcześniak and Szota, *op. cit.,* p. 174.

53. See Fijałka, *op. cit.*, pp. 45–46. What an interesting number, the number 40,000—and how well it seems to match its historical twin: the 40,000 members of the UPA at the end of 1943. And even if someday the terrible Angel of Death will enumerate for us all the unmarked graves of those who died and those who caused death, and add to the two forty-thousands a thousand forty-thousands more, who will tally up for us all the needless suffering and the guilt of World War II?

54. Szcześniak and Szota, *op. cit.*, p. 170.

55. Iaroslav Dashkevych, *Ukrajinskyj Czas,* Lwów, (Dec. 1991). In Prus, *Banderowcy—Defekt Historii, op. cit.*, pp. 48–49. (Translation mine.)

56. Korman, "Osobowe i materialne straty Polaków...", *op. cit.*, p. 19.

57. *Ibid.*

58. *Ibid.*, p. 18. (Translation mine.) Currently, various Polish and Jewish organizations are attempting to remember and honor the victims of the Ukrainian Nationalists by compiling extensive lists of those killed along with photographs, documents, and personal testimonies of the survivors. Several such chronicles appear in the Wrocław publication *Na Rubieży, op. cit.*, 2/93/(3) and subsequent editions. The 2/93/(3) list (pp. 28–30) contains the family names (arranged by house numbers) of those known to have been murdered by the Ukrainian Nationalists on August 30, 1943, in the following villages of Wołyń: Kąty (138 killed, including 63 children), Jankowce (79, including 18 children), Ostrówki (438, including 146 children), and Wola Ostrowiecka (529, including 220 children). Sometimes a simple note follows the name: parish priest, teacher, pregnant Ukrainian woman, Ukrainian family. In one case, no name was given and the person was simply listed as "a nun." Another such list for the village of Jeziorany Szlacheckie appears in Henryk Komański, "Zagłada polskiej wsi (19–23 czerwca 1943 r.)" *Semper Fidelis* (1993), nr. 3 (16), p. 19. For a summary of over 100 eyewitness accounts of similar atrocities compiled by Archbishop of Lwów, Eugeniusr Baziak, see Wacław Szetelnicki, *Zapomniany Lwowski Gohater ks. St. Frankl* (Rome, 1983), pp. 117–139.

59. Fijałka, *op. cit.*, p. 46. (Translation mine.)

60. Armstrong, *op. cit.*, p.74, hints at this when he refers to Metropolitan Sheptytsky's support for the *SS Galizien* and his concern that, in Armstrong's words, "extreme elements among the Poles ... were killing their opponents among the Ukrainians, just as the OUN-B was slaughtering [a clear and unambiguous designation to be sure] Poles in Volhynia." I interpret this statement as follows: Polish chauvinists were killing Ukrainian chauvinists, while Ukrainian chauvinists were slaughtering all the Poles. With this I agree and will even go a step further.

61. For these sad accounts see Szcześniak and Szota, *op. cit.,* pp. 186–88, and 346.

62. Shevchenko, *op. cit.*, pp. 98–99. In trying to impose Catholicism on the Ukrainians by fire and sword, the Jesuits gave the peasants another reason to revolt. The Polish pogroms of Orthodox Ukrainians in the Kiev region in 1766, for example, did not endear the Ukrainians either to the secular or religious authorities of Poland.

It may come as a surprise to the reader that for all his nationalistic and incendiary writings Shevchenko was not ill-disposed to the Polish people, nor they to him. As a young man, Shevchenko enjoyed a brief romantic liaison with a Polish girl, Dunia Husikovska by name. Later, while in exile in Central Asia, he befriended several Poles in similar straits. He also cultivated a deep friendship with Bronisław Zaleski, to whom he dedicated his conciliatory poem called "To the Poles."

In turn, Lenard Sowiński published a study on Shevchenko and, although revolted by its content, translated "The Haydamaks" anyway into the Polish language. Another Pole, G. Bataglia, published the very first monograph on Shevchenko's life and works. Finally, at his funeral, one of the ten orations was delivered in the Polish language by a student, W. Choroshewski.

True, Shevchenko dealt harshly with the Polish ruling class, but he also dealt just as severely with the Tsarist regime and even more so with the Ukrainian gentry, which he considered to be worse than the other two. This comes out loud and clear in his poem "The Great Mound" and "My Friendly Epistle," where he states (p. 255):

Thus in her struggle, our Ukraine
Reached the last climax of pure pain:
Worse than the Poles, or any other,
The children crucify their mother; . . .

Moreover, Shevchenko longed for peace and brotherhood with the Polish people. The poem "To the Poles" ends with the following lines (p. 330):

Link then your right hand with a Cossack's hand
And offer him your true and candid heart!
And once again, in the dear name of Christ,
We shall renew our gentle paradise.

Finally, in the preface to "The Haydamaks" which, incidentally, follows the long work, Shevchenko states (p. 125):

> "Thank God, all that is past!" The more so if we recall that we are children of the same mother, that we are all Slavs. Even if one's heart aches, the story must be told: let the children and the grandchildren see that their fathers were mistaken, let them again make friends with their enemies, and let the land of the Slavs, covered with wheat and rye as with gold, remain undivided from sea to sea forever!

As we know, these words of wisdom were ignored by our fathers and grandfathers, and so history repeated itself with a vengeance. What about today, now that both nations have cast off their yokes of servitude to both Germany and the Soviet Union?

As one peruses recent Polish and Ukrainian publications and news releases, it becomes evident that a full half-century after the events of which I speak, and many more generations after Shevchenko, the battle between the Polish people and the Ukrainian neo-Nationalists both in Europe and abroad continues unabated—this time, fortunately, only in the press. (I am painfully aware that this publication itself will be perceived by some as a perfect example of this war of words.)

Who are these Ukrainian neo-Nationalists? According to I. Gartner, "Ukrainian Nationalism since W.W. II" in Sabrin (ed.), *op. cit.*, p. 227, (in Sabrin ed.), *op. cit.*, p. 227, in America and Canada:

> The main Ukrainian Nationalist organizations are: UCCA—"Ukrainian Congress Committee of America," UACC—"Ukrainian American Coordinating Council," UCC—"Ukrainian Canadian Committee," and WCFU—"World Congress of Free Ukrainians."
>
> The old Bandera faction of the "Organization of Ukrainian Nationalists"—OUN—maintains its world headquarters in Munich, West Germany, and its U.S. headquarters in New York City.
>
> In the U.S., the *National Tribune* (published in New York) is the mouthpiece of the die-hard, Nationalist OUN "patriots" with European experience. Their counterpart in Canada, is called *Homin Ukrainy* or *Ukrainian Echo.* Both are weeklies. Other publications available are: *America, Svoboda (Liberty), Ukrainian News, Ukrainian Voice, Ukrainian Weekly, Ukrapress,* and *Lemko Voice.*

A similar list could be constructed for European-based Ukrainian neo-Nationalism.

In this battle the Polish side accuses the Ukrainian neo–Nationalists of attempting to rewrite history, of minimizing the extent of the atrocities committed by their fathers, of trying to "rehabilitate" the OUN/UPA, and of a continued policy of ethnic harassment in the former territories of Poland (e.g., Prus, *Bluff XX Wieku, op. cit.*, pp. 237–44). I may add that it is not only the Polish survivors of Ukrainian nationalism who feel this way. The committee, which dedicated its work, *Alliance for Murder*, to the memory of the Jewish victims of the Ukrainian Nationalists, states (p. 241–42):

> Former OUN-UPA leaders (and others), active in Western Ukraine during the Nazi era, are now eulogized by their followers, ideological comrades, and apologists in the U.S. and Canada.
>
> Without any feeling of shame, they are portrayed as "great ideologues" of Ukrainian Nationalism "great strategists" of the past "liberation struggle," and "heroes" raised in the "Christian spirit," for "God and Ukraine". . . .
>
> The naked fact remains that the U.S.-born and Canadian-born Ukrainian Nationalist leadership didn't find the courage (almost five decades later) to come out with the truth, to disassociate themselves from the old "heroes," and the Nationalist "patriots" of the past. The old policy remains: No remorse, no regret, and don't admit anything. . . .
>
> This is precisely the reason why Ukrainian Nationalist (and other) Nazi collaborators deserve another Nuremberg.

On the other hand, while some Ukrainian neo–Nationalists continue to deny their role in the atrocities attributed to them, others simply pass over them in silence or question their extent, point to similar atrocities committed against the Ukrainians, and plead for an understanding of the unique and difficult historical position in which the OUN/UPA found itself during World War II, surrounded as it was by enemies on all sides, having to choose between Hitler and Stalin and remembering both its ancient and interwar suffering at the hands of the Polish government in Western Ukraine.

On the national (or should I say political) level, Lech Wałęsa has agreed to abide by the 1939 Ribbentrop-Molotov line of demarcation, thus, in effect, relinquishing Poland's "historical right" to its former eastern territories. Poland, in fact, was the first nation to recognize Ukraine's independence. For his part Leonid Kravchuk has condemned the Ukrainian Nationalist movement of World War II, has admitted the full extent (by using the highest Polish estimates) of the atrocities committed against the Polish people by the nationalists, and has distanced himself from any attempt to "rehabilitate" the OUN/UPA or to continue its life under any other designation. These attempts at reconciliation have not pleased everyone to be sure, and one can only wonder about the future relations between Poland and Ukraine, two great and now sovereign nations sharing a common border and so bloody a past.

63. All of these instances of terror and degradation (and there were others) were related to me in the course of my interviews. The incident of the cat was said to have occurred in the province of Wołyń; of the sawing in half, in the village of Chlebowice near the small town of Świrz, in the province of Tarnopol; of the son being killed by his father, in Świrz. These three incidents come from Mrs. Piotrowiak. The first is based on hearsay. The second comes from her brother-in-law, Jan Grzeszczyszn (Jan Gres) who lived in Chlebowice and now lives in New Jersey. The last comes from Mrs. Piotrowiak's former neighbor in Poland after the war, Mrs. Anna Lewandowski (maiden name, Matkowski), who lived in Świrz during the war. According to Mrs. Lewandowski, the son, a *Banderowiec*, confided in his Ukrainian father that he had received an order to kill his own mother that night. This act, he was told, would make him a trustworthy

member of the organization. Supposedly, the father answered, "*Trudno, yak mash taky rozkaz, rub yak uwazhash.*" (That's too bad, if you have such an order, do as you see fit.) That night, after all were in bed, the father killed the son.

Were it not for the fact that my family and I lived through all of this, I would be hard pressed to believe any of it, despite all the published testimonies and the evident and unquestionable sincerity of those with whom I spoke. "Old country prejudices, hearsay, and anti–Ukrainian propaganda," I would have thought to myself. However, anyone who, with an open mind, delves into the phantasmagoric history of Western Ukraine, and specifically into the vortex of the Polish Holocaust in Wołyń during the Second World War, *must* walk away convinced that such terrible things did indeed occur.

Unfortunately, very little on this topic can be found in "official" or scholarly works in the English language. I will not go into the various reasons for this lack of information in our national histories of the Second World War. Needless to say and understandably so, in many instances very little or no "hard" evidence exists anywhere regarding these matters. (Shall we call in the forensic specialists to dig up the dead?) In the absence of standard forms of documentation, the only possible approach left to such veiled episodes in our collective history is the "oral history" approach—provided there are survivors. History, after all, is the *remembered* past.

Incidentally, this was the approach that Shevchenko used in 1841 for his masterful "Haydamaks." In his preface he states: "What happened in our Ukraine in 1768 I relate just as I heard it from old people: I have not read anything that is in print about it, nor any criticism concerning it, for, it appears, nothing of the sort is available." He ends: "My grandfather (may he enjoy good health), whenever he begins to relate something that he himself did not see, but only heard, says at the very outset: 'If the older people lie, I lie with them.'" Shevchenko, *op. cit.*, p. 125.

As for the survivors with whom I spoke, they were without exception people of deep religious faith, God-fearing people, and mostly very, very old. Ewa Kujański, as the saying goes, already had one foot in the grave. Did she lie? Did she fabricate? Did she stretch the truth? Did the cancer of her body reach into the inner recesses of her mind? Was that dying old woman vengeful? We must all decide that one for ourselves.

64. Shevchenko, *op. cit.*, pp. 113–21. The explanatory footnote on p. 113 reads:

> Ivan Gonta who was the commander of the "court" Cossacks who from 1757 served the Polish magnate Potocki. The latter trusted him so much that he sent him to the town of Uman to be at the disposition of the Polish Governor Mladanowich there. For his services to the Poles he was given two nearby villages as usufruct. While with the Poles, Gonta married a Polish lady and by her had two sons who were baptized into Roman Catholicism. When the insurrection of the haydamaks under Maksim Zalizniak began, Gonta was ordered to suppress it. However, his patriotic feeling asserted itself, and he joined forces with Zalizniak. Both of them captured Uman by storm. After changing sides, Gonta's ferocity in battle knew no bounds, and he allowed no mercy in his dealings with the Poles and their allies.

Chapter 4: Farewell Forever, Ryświanka

1. Shortly before we were deported to Germany, we heard with heavy hearts that Mr. and Mrs. Filip and Ludwika, their youngest daughter, were slaughtered by the same group of *Bulbowcy* who left us homeless. Their three oldest daughters, Halina, Marysia, Zosia, and their married son, Staszek, survived the war.

2. Recollections of a Soviet eyewitness during Stalin's war against the Ukrainian peasants in the early 1930s. Vasily Grossman, *Forever Flowing*, translated from the Russian by Thomas P. Whitney (New York: Harper and Row, 1972), p. 145.

3. For a personal account of the events transpiring in Tuczyn at this time, including the Ukrainian Nationalist participation in the liquidation of the Tuczyn Jewish Ghetto, see "Relacja Zbigniewa G. Sudułła, zamieszkałego w Australii, O Rzeziach Ukraińskich w Rejonie Tuczyna nad Horyniem w Powiecie Rówieńskim na Wołyniu," in Giertych (ed.), *op. cit.*, pp. 325–32.

4. Mr. Gruntkowski was a skilled carpenter. He was given quarters and forced to work for the SS in Równe.

5. Shevchenko, *op. cit.*, p. 123.

6. Source: Public Archives of Canada, Ottawa, Citizenship and Immigration Branch, RG 26 vol. 147, file 3-43-1. In Boshyk (ed.), *op. cit.*, pp. 233, 235, 238–39.

Chapter 5: In the Eye of Satan

1. *NCA*, Vol. III, p. 144 (N.D. 084-PS).

2. Leon E. Seltzer (ed.), *The Columbia Lippincott Gazetteer of the World* (New York: Columbia University Press, 1962), "Essen," p. 589.

3. *TWC*, Vol. XXXV, pp. 73–75 (N.D. 303-PS).

4. Defense Exhibits (Nuremberg documents in the National Archives Virginia annex and at the International Court of Justice, the Hague) 971, file date 8/14/42, D-348. In William Manchester, *The Arms of Krupp 1587–1968* (New York: Bantam, 1970), p. 544.

5. Himmler explaining the policy change to the SS at Posen in 1943. *NCA*, Vol. IV, p. 558 (N.D. 1919-PS).

6. Nazi industrialist Krupp, N.D. 13173-14204; Nuremberg Transcript of Military Tribunals Case No. 10 (the Krupp Case) pp. 18–113 (12/8/45); *TWC*, Vol. IX, p. 115.

7. Dr. Wilhelm Jaeger: "Only bad meat, such as horsemeat or meat which had been rejected by veterinarians as infected with tuberculosis germs was passed out in these camps." *NCA*, Vol. VII, pp. 2–7 (N.D. D-288).

8. Führer, Testimony in Alfried Krupp case 5/17-18/48. Nuremberg Transcript 8277-8328, *TWC*, Vol. IX, p. 1107.

9. *NCA*, Vol. VII, pp. 2–7 (N.D. D-288).

10. *Ibid.*

11. "No work, no feeding." In German, the verb *essen* means "to eat"; the verb *fressen,* on the other hand, is an impersonal term referring to the "feeding" of animals.

12. Findings of the Nuremberg Tribunal. *TWC*, Vol. IX, p. 116, 1409, Defense Exhibits D-274.

13. Defense Exhibits DE-1363. Adolf Trockel Testimony in Alfried Krupp Case 5/13/48, 5/21/48, Nuremberg Transcript 7715.

14. Defense Exhibits D-310.

15. *Ibid.*, D-297. Testimony of Herman Lux 5/27/48, Nuremberg Transcript 10277, Nazi industrialist Krupp 7014.

16. *Ibid.*, DE-1023. Theodor Rohlfs' testimony in Alfried Krupp Case 5/19/48, Nuremberg Transcript 8551-73. In Manchester, *op. cit.*, p. 573.

17. TWC, Vol. IX, pp. 1062–63. In Manchester, *op. cit.*, pp. 590–91.

As I transcribe these lines on a beautiful summer day in fair New Hampshire, I am disturbed by a little grey mouse that has made her home in the billowing moss at the edge of the tree line. I study that busy little mouse. My throat goes dry. "What would it take," I think, "to make me eat that fat little mouse?"

18. *NCA*, Vol. VII, pp. 2–7 (N.D. D-288).

19. *Ibid.*, pp. 260–64 (N.D. EC-68).

20. *Ibid.*, Vol. V, pp. 744–54 (N.D. 3040-PS).

21. In Lewis L. Snyder, *The War: A Concise History 1939–1945* (New York: Messner, 1960), p. 399.

22. *Ibid.*

23. In Theodore H. White, *Fire in the Ashes: Europe in Mid-Century* (New York: Sloane, 1953), pp. 177–78, 178.

24. In Snyder, *op. cit.*, p. 399.

25. *United States Strategic Bombing Survey* (hereafter: *SB*), Washington, 1947. Quoted in J.C.S. Fuller, *The Second World War, 1939–45: A Strategical and Tactical History* (New York: Meredith, 1948), p. 229.

26. *SB*, p. 93.

27. *SB, Gusstahlfabrik,* p. 20.

28. Winston S. Churchill, *The Hinge of Fate* (New York: Houghton Mifflin, 1950), p. 756.

29. Churchill's statement as reported in *The Times* (London), February 2, 1943.

Supposedly, at the beginning of the war, all sides were bound by the following "Rules of Warfare" set down in Article 22, Part II, of the 1922 Washington Conference on the Limitations of Armaments: "Aerial bombardment for the purpose of terrorizing the civilian population, of destroying or damaging private property not of a military character, or of injuring non-combatants, is prohibited." In Fuller, *op. cit.*, pp. 220–21. On February 15, 1940, when I was five days old, British Prime Minister "Peace in our time" Chamberlain told the House of Commons: "Whatever be the length to which others might go, the Government will never resort to blackguardly attacks on women and children and other civilians for the purpose of mere terrorism." In *ibid.* It is Fuller's contention that Churchill began the war of "devastation and terrorization," not Hitler (p. 222).

30. In *ibid.*, p. 229.

31. *Ibid.*

32. *Ibid.*, p. 405.

33. Chester Wilmot, *The Struggle for Europe* (New York: Harper, 1952), p. 553.

34. Gert von Klass, *Die Drei Ringe* (Tübingen: R. Wunderlich, 1953), p. 436.

35. In Manchester, *op. cit.*, p. 562.

36. Eyewitness account of the attack on Hamburg in the last week of July 1943. *SB*, in Fuller, *op. cit.*, p. 228.

37. Nazi industrialist Krupp 11728. In Manchester, *op. cit.*, pp. 562–63.

38. Fuller, *op. cit.*, p. 228, n. 16.

39. *NCA*, Vol. V, p. 765 (N.D. 3044-B-PS).

40. In Allan Bullock, *Hitler: A Study in Tyranny* (New York: Harper and Row, 1971), p. 463.

41. A summary of the testimony of Fritz Fell in Alfried Krupp Case 2/4/48. Nuremberg Transcript 3108-36. Manchester, *op. cit.*, pp. 648–49.

42. Speer's description of the Bormann decree as quoted in Shirer, *op. cit.*, p. 1433.

43. Manchester, *op. cit.*, p. 626.

Chapter 6: Meiningen, Ach Meiningen

1. World War II death tolls [total (civilian/military)]. Allies: Belgium—200,000 (90,000/110,000), Netherlands—206,000 (200,000/6,000), U.S.—408,000 (0/408,000), Britain—450,000 (100,000/350,000), France—650,000 (450,000/200,000), Yugoslavia—1.4 million (1 million/400,000), China—2.2 million (850,000/1.35 million), Poland—6.6 million (6 million/600,000), Soviet Union—15 million (7.5 million/7.5 million). Axis: Italy—220,000 (70,000/150,000), Japan—2 million (500,000–1.5 million), Germany—6.2 million (1.47 million/4.75 million). Axis controlled: Czechoslovakia—280,000 (250,000/30,000), Austria—405,000 (125,000/280,000), Romania—640,000 (300,000/340,000), Hungary—850,000 (450,000/400,000). Ruth Leger Sivard, *World Military and Social Expenditures 1987–88* (Washington, D.C.: World Priorities, 1987), pp. 29–31.

2. Nuremberg Indictment as quoted by Snyder, *op. cit.*, p. 424.

3. Report of a Congressional Investigating Committee on the conditions at Buchenwald. *Ibid.*, pp. 424–25.

4. Edward R. Murrow of C.B.S. *Ibid.*, p. 425.

5. Patrick Gordon-Walker. *Ibid.*, pp. 425–26.

6. The reaction of the 1,200 German civilians on the forced tour of Buchenwald, according to Gene Currivan of the *New York Times*. *Ibid.*, p. 425.

7. Shirer, *op. cit.*, p. 1483. The *Reichskommissar* of the Ukraine, Erich Koch, "was captured by the Western powers and turned over to Poland in 1950 for prosecution as a war criminal. It took Polish authorities nine years to bring him to trial and then only for crimes committed while *Gauleiter* of East Prussia. In 1959 he was sentenced to death, but the sentence was never carried out. He lives under very favourable conditions in the Polish prison of Barczewo. The USSR has never asked for his extradition. The reasons for this unprecedented 'Humanitarianism' on the part of the Polish and Soviet authorities remain a mystery." Bohdan Krawchenko, "Soviet Ukraine Under Nazi Occupation, 1941–4," in Boshyk (ed.), *op. cit.*, pp. 34–35, n.86.

Chapter 7: Of Displaced Persons

1. Much of this chapter is based on the U.N. proceedings as found in the *Yearbook of the United Nations*, Vols. 1946–47, 1947–48, 1948–49, and 1950 (New York: U.N. Department of Public Information).

2. *Official Documents, Texts of Selected Documents on U.S. Foreign Policy 1918–1952,* (New York: Woodrow Wilson Foundation, 1952), pp. 10–19.

3. In Snyder, *op. cit.*, p. 406.

4. Source: United Nations (UNRRA) Archives, New York. PAG-4/3.0.11.0.1.4:2, "Council Resolution 92 etc." In Boshyk (ed.), *op. cit.*, pp. 211–12.This same report includes an interesting section on Polish-Ukrainians:

> Despite repeated instructions from UNRRA directors, this group insists on describing itself as "Polish-Ukrainian" or "Ukrainian Stateless." The constant dissemination of nationalistic propaganda has completely alienated them from the idea of adherence to either Poland or Russia, and thereby has eliminated all chance for a voluntary repatriation of Ukrainian peoples. Like the Poles, they give mainly political reasons for not wanting to return home but they are generally more violent in their attacks on Russia, and express fear of forced labor conditions, even "deportation to Siberia," should they dare to

return. Some give supposed first hand accounts of previous persecution, such as "I don't wish to be repatriated to the Ukraine because my father was killed by the communists for his political and religious ideas and I was sent to Siberia, and had to stay for five years in a concentration camp." About 10% of the Ukrainians included in their reasons descriptions of the absence of political, cultural, religious and personal freedom at home, while others compared "Bolshevik totalitarianism" with Nazism.

They claim that their country is occupied and since they do *not* wish to become citizens of the USSR, they have in effect no fatherland to which to return. Some stated that they want a free, autonomous Ukrainian state, even within the boundaries of the new Poland. An important factor in this separatists movement has been the activity of the Greek-Orthodox clergy, who constantly use their strong influence against repatriation. As a logical consequence of this clerical influence, and the fact that Ukrainians are predominantly orthodox [sic], they seem to be much more concerned over the lack of religious freedom than do the Poles.

A few of the Ukrainian DPs lost large land holdings in the collectivization of estates by the Soviet government, so that they have a bitter personal enmity toward the new economic system. Others merely stated their dislike for a system where there is no private property.

5. Statistical estimate of Casimir Smogorzewski, cited in Konovalov (ed.), *Russo-Polish Relations* (London: Cresset, 1945), p. 83.

6. Source: United Nations (UNRRA) Archives, New York. PAG-4/3.0.11.3.0.-9, "Confidential Report on the General Situation of the DP's." In Boshyk (ed.), *op. cit.*, pp. 225–232.

7. *Yearbook of the United Nations, op. cit.*, 1946–47, p. 806.

8. *Ibid.*, 1950, p. 570.

9. *Ibid.*, p. 579.

10. *Ibid.*, 1946–47, p. 73.

11. *Ibid.*

12. *Ibid.*, p. 74.

13. *Ibid.*

14. *Ibid.*, 1947–48, p. 957.

15. *Ibid.*, 1946–47, p. 807.

16. *Ibid.*, p. 810.

17. *Ibid.*, 1947–48, p. 959.

18. *Ibid.*

19. *Ibid.*, 1948–49, pp. 585–86.

Chapter 10: The Slings of Fortune

1. I have taken the liberty of translating and editing the following accounts of my three sisters.

2. And thoughts of revolution on their mind, I may add.

3. What an interesting Polish word. One is tempted to translate it into its English phonetic equivalent: "troops." But it really means "corpses" or "cadavers." In a deeper sense, however, it means "troops" as well.

4. The "strategic" bombing of Schweinfurt began in June of 1943. In a series of raids on the German aircraft industry, 12,000 tons of bombs were dropped on Schwein-

furt's ball-bearing plants and on poor Janina's head. These attacks were suspended for a period of four months after the October 14 raid as a result of unusually heavy American losses. Out of 228 U.S. bombers, 62 were lost and 138 damaged, some beyond repair. Fuller, *op. cit.*, p. 224 and n. 12.

5. That particular photograph of me was taken in Essen.
6. See p. 86.
7. Later, this particular baby was taken to the hospital where he also "died."

Index

E

H

M

N

O

T

U

Y

Z

Y

Z